高等学校应用型特色规划教材　经管系列

国际贸易实务与案例分析
(双语版)

马　俊　杨云匀　郑汉金　主编

清华大学出版社
北　京

内 容 简 介

本书涵盖交易前准备、交易磋商、合同订立履行、争议解决等一般贸易进出口业务全过程，还专门增加加工贸易、对销贸易、招投标、包销、代理、寄售、拍卖、商品期货交易等其他贸易方式和2020版《国际贸易术语解释通则》(INCOTERMS 2020)相关知识。特别撰写了流程案例与专题案例及解析，协助读者将外经贸知识转化为实实在在的业务能力，助力国际经贸高素质复合式应用型人才培养。中英双语编写，兼顾不同英语程度的读者，方便对照学习参考。

本书可作为高校国际经济与贸易、国际商务、商务英语、外贸英语等专业的教材，还可供强调案例分析、模拟训练等方法的国际商务硕士培养使用，也可供外经贸企业、跨国公司、三资企业和其他涉外机构业务人员参考。

本书封面贴有清华大学出版社防伪标签，无标签者不得销售。
版权所有，侵权必究。举报：010-62782989，beiqinquan@tup.tsinghua.edu.cn。

图书在版编目(CIP)数据

国际贸易实务与案例分析：双语版/马俊，杨云匀，郑汉金主编. —北京：清华大学出版社，2021.7（2025.1重印）
(高等学校应用型特色规划教材. 经管系列)
ISBN 978-7-302-57628-0

Ⅰ. ①国… Ⅱ. ①马… ②杨… ③郑… Ⅲ. ①国际贸易—贸易实务—高等学校—教材 Ⅳ. ①F740.4

中国版本图书馆 CIP 数据核字(2021)第 037423 号

责任编辑：温 洁
封面设计：杨玉兰
责任校对：周剑云
责任印制：宋 林

出版发行：清华大学出版社
　　网　　址：https://www.tup.com.cn, https://www.wqxuetang.com
　　地　　址：北京清华大学学研大厦 A 座　　邮　　编：100084
　　社 总 机：010-83470000　　邮　　购：010-62786544
　　投稿与读者服务：010-62776969，c-service@tup.tsinghua.edu.cn
　　质量反馈：010-62772015，zhiliang@tup.tsinghua.edu.cn
　　课件下载：https://www.tup.com.cn，010-62791865

印 装 者：三河市君旺印务有限公司
经　　销：全国新华书店
开　　本：185mm×230mm　　印　张：22.25　　字　数：484千字
版　　次：2021年8月第1版　　印　次：2025年1月第4次印刷
定　　价：59.00元

产品编号：086954-01

出版说明

  应用型人才是指能够将专业知识和技能应用于所从事的专业岗位的一种专门人才。应用型人才的本质特征是具有专业基本知识和基本技能，即具有明确的职业性、实用性、实践性和高层次性。进一步加强应用型人才的培养，是"十三五"时期我国经济转型升级、迫切需要教育为社会培养输送各类人才和高素质劳动者的关键时期，也是协调高等教育规模速度与培养各类人才服务国家和区域经济社会发展的重要途径。

  教育部要求今后需要有相当数量的高校致力于培养应用型人才，以满足市场对应用型人才需求量的不断增加。为了培养高素质应用型人才，必须建立完善的教学计划和高水平的课程体系。在教育部有关精神的指导下，我们组织全国高校的专家教授，努力探求更为合理有效的应用型人才培养方案，并结合当前高等教育的实际情况，编写了这套《高等学校应用型特色规划教材》丛书。

  为使教材的编写真正切合应用型人才的培养目标，我社编辑在全国范围内走访了大量高等学校，拜访了众多院校主管教学的领导，以及教学一线的系主任和教师，掌握了各地区各学校所设专业的培养目标和办学特色，并广泛、深入地与用人单位进行交流，明确了用人单位的真正需求。这些工作为本套丛书的准确定位、合理选材、突出特色奠定了坚实的基础。

◆ 教材定位

- 以就业为导向。在应用型人才培养过程中，充分考虑市场需求，因此本套丛书充分体现"就业导向"的基本思路。
- 符合本学科的课程设置要求。以高等教育的培养目标为依据，注重教材的科学性、实用性和通用性。
- 定位明确。准确定位教材在人才培养过程中的地位和作用，正确处理教材的读者层次关系，面向就业，突出应用。
- 合理选材、编排得当。妥善处理传统内容与现代内容的关系，大力补充新知识、新技术、新工艺和新成果。根据本学科的教学基本要求和教学大纲的要求，制订编写大纲(编写原则、编写特色、编写内容、编写体例等)，突出重点、难点。
- 建设"立体化"的精品教材体系。提倡教材与电子教案、学习指导、习题解答、课程设计、毕业设计等辅助教学资料配套出版。

◆ 丛书特色

- 围绕应用讲理论，突出实践教学环节及特点，包含丰富的案例，并对案例作详细解析，强调实用性和可操作性。
- ➢ 涉及最新的理论成果和实务案例，充分反映岗位要求，真正体现以就业为导向的培养目标。
- ➢ 国际化与中国特色相结合，符合高等教育日趋国际化的发展趋势，部分教材采用双语形式。
- ➢ 在结构的布局、内容重点的选取、案例习题的设计等方面符合教改目标和教学大纲的要求，把教师的备课、授课、辅导答疑等教学环节有机地结合起来。

✧ 读者定位

本系列教材主要面向普通高等院校和高等职业技术院校，适合应用型、复合型及技术技能型人才培养的高等院校的教学需要。

✧ 关于作者

丛书编委特聘请执教多年且有较高学术造诣和实践经验的教授参与各册教材的编写，其中有相当一部分教材的主要执笔者是精品课程的负责人，本丛书凝聚了他们多年的教学经验和心血。

✧ 互动交流

本丛书的编写及出版过程，贯穿了清华大学出版社一贯严谨、务实、科学的作风。伴随我国教育改革的不断深入，要编写出满足新形势下教学需求的教材，还需要我们不断地努力、探索和实践。我们真诚希望使用本丛书的教师、学生和其他读者提出宝贵的意见和建议，使之更臻成熟。

清华大学出版社

前　言

　　本书将一般贸易进出口业务环节、交易条款、方式方法和流程案例、专题案例相结合，涵盖进出口交易前准备、交易磋商、合同订立履行、贸易争议解决等国际贸易业务全过程，并专门增加一般贸易之外的其他贸易方式，如加工贸易、对销贸易、招投标、包销、代理、寄售、拍卖、商品期货交易等内容，还特地增加 2020 年 1 月 1 日起正式生效的 2020 版《国际贸易术语解释通则》(INCOTERMS 2020)的相关内容。

　　全书编写思路清晰、内容完整、结构合理。以中英双语编写，兼顾不同英语程度的读者，方便对照学习、参考。

　　编者特别撰写"国际货物贸易流程案例"与"国际货物贸易专题案例及解析"两章，以协助读者将外经贸知识转化为实实在在的业务能力，助力国际经贸高素质复合式应用型人才培养。

　　昆明学院马俊主持本书编写，负责全书构思、方案、框架和校对工作，全书共 11 章，马俊负责第 9 章、第 10 章、第 11 章的编写，杨云匀负责第 3～6 章的编写，郑汉金负责第 1 章、第 2 章、第 7 章、第 8 章的编写。

　　本书可作为高等学校国际经济与贸易、国际贸易、国际商务、商务英语、外贸英语等专业的国际贸易实务、进出口实务、国际贸易实务案例分析、外贸英语等课程的教材，也可供外经贸企业、跨国公司、三资企业和其他涉外机构业务人员学习参考。

　　国际商务硕士(MIB，Master of International Business)教育作为专业学位硕士研究生(专硕)培养项目，强调运用案例分析、模拟训练等方法。本书契合国际商务硕士培养思路，理论联系实际，提供丰富的案例和准确到位的解析，因此，本书还可供国际商务硕士教学使用。

　　本书有丰富的配套教学资源，下载地址：www.tup.tsinghua.edu.cn。

　　在编写过程中，编者参阅了大量专家学者的著述，参考了不少国际贸易实务行家的宝贵经验，在此表示诚挚的感谢！由于编者理论和经验不足、水平有限，书中难免存在错漏和不尽如人意之处，敬请广大业界、学界专家和读者批评指正！

编　者

目　　录

Chapter 1　General Procedures of International Cargo Import and Export 1

第 1 章　国际货物贸易的一般程序 1

    Section 1　Preparation for Import and Export 1
    第 1 节　交易前准备 1

    Section 2　Business Negotiation 2
    第 2 节　交易磋商 2

    Section 3　Contract Conclusion 12
    第 3 节　合同订立 12

    Section 4　Contract Performance 26
    第 4 节　合同履行 26

    Terminology 本章术语 32
    Exercises 本章练习 32
    Answers for Reference 参考答案 32

Chapter 2　Subjects of Contract 35

第 2 章　国际货物贸易交易标的 35

    Section 1　Quality of Commodity 35
    第 1 节　商品品质 35

    Section 2　Quantity of Goods 44
    第 2 节　商品数量 44

    Section 3　Packing and Marks of Goods 49
    第 3 节　商品包装与标志 49

    Terminology 本章术语 55
    Exercises 本章练习 56
    Answers for Reference 参考答案 56

Chapter 3　Pricing of Goods 58

第 3 章　国际货物贸易商品定价 58

    Section 1　Components of Price Term and Trade Terms 58

第1节 价格构成与贸易术语 58

Section 2　Influencing Factors on Pricing 86

第2节 影响定价的因素 86

Section 3　Money of Account, Money of Payment and Value Keeping Clause 88

第3节 计价货币、支付货币与保值条款 88

Section 4　Pricing Methods 90

第4节 定价方法 90

Section 5　Commission and Discount 91

第5节 佣金与折扣 91

Terminology　本章术语 94

Exercises　本章练习 95

Answers for Reference　参考答案 96

Chapter 4　Payment of Goods 101

第4章　国际货物贸易货款支付 101

Section 1　Instruments of Payment 102

第1节 支付工具 102

Section 2　Modes of Payment 115

第2节 支付方式 115

Section 3　Payment Terms in The Contract 154

第3节 合同中的支付条款 154

Terminology　本章术语 159

Exercises　本章练习 160

Answers for Reference　参考答案 162

Chapter 5　Delivery of Goods 164

第5章　国际货物贸易运输 164

Section 1　Modes of Transport 165

第1节 运输方式 165

Section 2　Transport Documents 182

第2节 运输单据 182

Section 3　Clauses of Shipment 193

第3节 装运条款 193

Terminology　本章术语 198

　　　　Exercises 本章练习 199

　　　　Answers for Reference 参考答案 200

Chapter 6　Cargo Transport Insurance 201

第 6 章　国际货物贸易运输保险 201

　　　　Section 1　Ocean Marine Cargo Transport Insurance 202

　　　　第 1 节　海运货物保险 202

　　　　Section 2　Cargo Transport Insurance of Other Transport Modes 221

　　　　第 2 节　其他运输方式货物保险 221

　　　　Terminology 本章术语 224

　　　　Exercises 本章练习 225

　　　　Answers for Reference 参考答案 227

Chapter 7　Inspection of Commodity 229

第 7 章　国际货物贸易商品检验 229

　　　　Section 1　Functions and Classifications of Inspection 229

　　　　第 1 节　商品检验的作用与分类 229

　　　　Section 2　Inspection Clause in Contract 231

　　　　第 2 节　合同中的商检条款 231

　　　　Terminology 本章术语 237

　　　　Exercises 本章练习 237

　　　　Answers for Reference 参考答案 238

Chapter 8　Settlement of Trade Disputes 240

第 8 章　贸易争议的解决 240

　　　　Section 1　Dispute and Claim 240

　　　　第 1 节　争议与索赔 240

　　　　Section 2　Disputes Settlement 245

　　　　第 2 节　纠纷解决 245

　　　　Section 3　Force Majeure 251

　　　　第 3 节　不可抗力 251

　　　　Terminology 本章术语 255

　　　　Exercises 本章练习 255

Answers for Reference 参考答案 257

Chapter 9　Other Modes of International Business 259
第 9 章　一般贸易外的其他贸易方式 259

Section 1　Exclusive Sales 259
第 1 节　包销 259

Section 2　Agency 262
第 2 节　代理 262

Section 3　Consignment 267
第 3 节　寄售 267

Section 4　Auction 271
第 4 节　拍卖 271

Section 5　Tendering/ Bidding 273
第 5 节　招标投标 273

Section 6　Counter Trade 276
第 6 节　对销贸易 276

Section 7　Processing Trade 279
第 7 节　加工贸易 279

Section 8　Futures 280
第 8 节　商品期货交易 280

Terminology 本章术语 283

Exercises 本章练习 284

Answers for Reference 参考答案 284

Chapter 10　Case on Procedures of International Business 286
第 10 章　国际货物贸易流程案例 286

Procedure 1　Establishment of Business Relation 286
流程 1　建立业务关系 286

Procedure 2　Inquiry 287
流程 2　询盘 287

Procedure 3　Offer 288
流程 3　发盘 288

Procedure 4　Counter Offer 289
流程 4　还盘 289

Procedure 5　Acceptance 290
流程 5　接受 290

Procedure 6　Contracting 292
流程 6　签约 292

Procedure 7　L/C Notifying, Examination and Amendment 296
流程 7　信用证通知、审核和修改 296

Procedure 8　Shipping Space Booking 303
流程 8　订舱托运 303

Procedure 9　Inspection and Customs Clearance 307
流程 9　商检和通关 307

Procedure 10　Insurance 313
流程 10　保险 313

Procedure 11　Delivery 315
流程 11　装运 315

Procedure 12　Documents Preparation for Bank Negotiation 316
流程 12　制单议付 316

Chapter 11　Cases on Different Subjects of International Business 318
第 11 章　国际货物贸易专题案例及解析 318

Section 1　Cases on Trade Terms 318
第 1 节　贸易术语案例 318

Section 2　Cases on Quality 321
第 2 节　货物质量案例 321

Section 3　Cases on Quantity 323
第 3 节　货物数量案例 323

Section 4　Cases on Packing and Marks 326
第 4 节　货物包装与标志案例 326

Section 5　Cases on Pricing 328
第 5 节　定价案例 328

Section 6　Cases on Delivery 331
第 6 节　货物装运案例 331

Section 7　Cases on Insurance 334
第 7 节　货物运输保险案例 334

Section 8　Cases on Payment 336

第 8 节　支付案例 336

Section 9　Cases on Disputes Settlement 340

第 9 节　纠纷解决案例 340

参考文献 344

Chapter 1　General Procedures of International Cargo Import and Export

第 1 章　国际货物贸易的一般程序

Section 1　Preparation for Import and Export

第 1 节　交易前准备

The basic procedures of export and import may be summed up in following three stages, namely, preparation for export and import, business negotiation and contract conclusion, contract performance. In a sense, as the first step of an international trade, the preparation for export and import lays a good foundation for the next stages.

国际贸易一般经历三个阶段，即交易前准备、交易磋商与合同订立、合同履行。交易前准备阶段是国际贸易的开端，是国际贸易后续阶段的基础。

1. Preparation for Export　出口交易前准备

Preparation for export generally involves market research, pricing, preparing goods, advertising, establishment of business relations, etc.

一般而言，出口交易前准备工作主要包括：海外市场调研、定价、出口货源落实、广告宣传、建立业务关系等。

(1) Market Research　市场调研

In international trade business, the market research usually focuses on specific importing country with regard to its political and economic conditions, its foreign policy and trade policy, its principal trading countries, its usual exporting and importing commodities, etc. The market research also aims at the target market conditions of the importing country in general, the related products in particular, especially the varieties, styles, qualities, packing, etc. of the products and their sale, cost, consumption, prices, principal suppliers, etc. Meanwhile, the market research should try to discover the prospective clients.

国际贸易市场调研主要包括：国别调研，即特定进口国的政治、经济状况，外贸政策，主要贸易伙伴，主要进出口产品等；目标市场调研，尤其是相关产品调研，具体包括产品品种、规格、性能、包装及其销售情况、成本、消费、价格、主要供应商等；潜在客户挖掘。

(2) Establishment of Business Relations 建立业务关系

When contacting a client for business for the first time, however, it is always advisable to take a policy of caution. The exporter needs to get much necessary information about the client as reputation, credit, financial status and business mode, etc. before concluding a transaction, especially one that requires a large sum of money.

交易前，尤其是金额较大的交易，建议出口商持谨慎态度，充分了解客户的信誉、资金状况和业务模式等详细情况。

2. Preparation for Import 进口交易前准备

Market research still plays an important role in the import business. Market research helps collect information necessary for importer's analytical study of the capability, reputation, credit standing and business mode of both the producers and suppliers, and comparison of prices, qualities, specifications and technology of similar products so as to select reliable clients, and minimize importing cost.

进口交易前的市场调研同样十分重要。通过市场调研，进口商可以分析研究生产供应商的能力、资信、业务模式，比较同类产品的价格、质量、规格和技术，从而选择可靠的客户，降低进口成本。

Section 2　Business Negotiation

第 2 节　交 易 磋 商

Business negotiation is a bargain process involving potential parties (buyer and seller) to a contract with the aim of coming into an agreement.

交易磋商是买卖双方就买卖商品的有关交易条件进行协商，以期达成交易的过程。

International business negotiation usually falls into verbal and written forms. Negotiation, such as China Export Commodities Fair, small exchange meeting, personal or delegation dispatched abroad, reception of foreign trade groups and even by telephone, takes verbal (or oral) form. Written form involves negotiation through letters, telexes, faxes and even electronic mails.

交易磋商的形式可分为口头磋商和书面磋商两种。口头磋商包括参加广交会、小交会、派遣出国推销人员、贸易代表团、接待国外贸易团以及电话洽谈。书面磋商是指通过信件、电传、传真及电子邮件方式进行磋商。

pThe process of international trade negotiation commonly contains inquiry, offer, counter offer and acceptance, in which, offer and acceptance are not only indispensable process, but the base of a contract.

一般而言，交易磋商包括四个环节：询盘、发盘、还盘和接受。其中，发盘和接受是每笔交易必经的两个基本环节，是交易成立的两要素。

1. Inquiry 询盘

Inquiry refers to intention made by a party interested in the purchase or sale of goods specified therein, indicating particular, desirable conditions regarding price and delivery terms, etc. addressed to a prospective supplier or buyer with a view to obtaining an offer or bid. Inquiry usually serves as the starting point of trade negotiation, without legally binding force upon the party made it.

询盘，又称询价，是指买方为了购买或卖方为了出售商品，向对方提出的一些有关价格和运输等交易条件的询问。询盘往往是交易磋商的起点，在法律上对双方并无法律约束力。

Both the buyer and the seller can make an inquiry. The inquiry made by the buyer is usually called "invitation to offer", and the inquiry made by the seller is usually called "invitation to bid".

询盘可由买方发出，也可由卖方发出。前者习惯被称为"邀请发盘"，后者习惯被称为"邀请递盘"。

2. Offer 发盘

(1) Definition of Offer 发盘的含义

According to the United Nations Convention on Contracts for the International Sale of Goods (CISG), article 14 (1), "A proposal for concluding a contract addressed to one or more specific persons constitutes an offer if it is sufficiently definite and indicates the intention of the offeror to be bound in case of acceptance. A proposal is sufficiently definite if it indicates the goods and expressly or implicitly fixes or makes provision for determining the quantity and the price."

《联合国国际货物销售合同公约》(以下简称《公约》)第14条第1款规定："向一个或一个以上特定的人提出的订立合同的建议，如果十分明确并且表明发盘人在得到接受时承受约束的意旨，即构成发盘。一个建议如果写明货物并且明示或暗示规定数量和价格或规定如何确定数量和价格，即为十分确定"。

An offer can be made by the seller or the buyer. The former is usually called "offer", and the latter is usually called "bid". The party who makes the offer is referred as "offeror", while the opposite party as "offeree".

发盘可由卖方发出，也可由买方发出。前者习惯被称为"发盘"，后者习惯被称为"递盘"。业务中将提出建议方称为发盘人，接受方称为受盘人。

(2) Necessary Conditions for an Offer 构成发盘的有效条件

① Address to one or more specific persons 向一个或一个以上特定的人提出

The CISG article 14 (2) stipulates, "A proposal other than one addressed to one or more specific persons is to be considered merely as an invitation to make offers, unless the contrary is clearly indicated by the person making the proposal." The common commercial advertisement, the catalogues and a price list sent to clients are merely deemed as invitations to make offers.

《公约》第14条第2款规定："非向一个或一个以上特定的人提出的建议，仅应视为邀请做出发盘，除非提出建议的人明确地表示相反的意见。"普通商业广告及向国外客商寄发的商品目录、价目单等行为通常只能视为邀请发盘。

② Indicate contractual intent 表明订约意旨

Offer should indicate the intention of the offeror to be bound in case of acceptance. Indication of contractual intent can be made either expressly by state "offer" "bid" or by stipulating the time of validity of the offer, or implicitly with a customary way to both parties.

发盘应表明发盘得到接受时，将按发盘的条件承担与受盘人订立合同的法律责任。表明订约意旨可以是明示的，或是暗示的。前者如写明"发盘""递盘"或明确规定发盘有效期等，后者如按双方业已形成的习惯做法来确定。

The proposal with any restrictive conditions, such as "subject to confirmation" "subject to prior sale" "subject to our approval of sample" "subject to licence obtainable", is regarded as an invitation to make an offer.

如果建议中附有保留或限制性条件，例如："经确认为准""以未售出为准""以我方认可样品为准""以领取许可证为准"，则该项建议就不能构成发盘，而仅应被视为邀请发盘。

③ Definite in contents 内容十分确定

According to the CISG, article 14 (1), "A proposal is sufficiently definite if it indicates the goods and expressly or implicitly fixes or makes provision for determining the quantity and the price." It means that a sufficiently definite offer should include three basic elements: name and quality of the commodity, quantity, price. In order to avoid misunderstandings and possible disputes, in our practice, an effective offer shall include the name and quality, quantity, packing, price, terms of delivery of the goods and terms of payment.

《公约》第14条第1款规定："一个建议如果写明货物并且明示或暗示地规定数量和价格或规定如何确定数量和价格，即为十分确定。"可见，一项有效的发盘要包括三个基本要素：品名品质、数量、价格。为防止误解和可能发生的争议，我国对外贸易实践中，一项完整的发盘要包括品名、品质、数量、包装、价格、交货和支付条件。

Sometimes an offer seems to be short of some main terms, but actually complete. For example, both parties concerned have concluded a general agreement in advance, or quote the correspondences to each other, the precedent contracts, and the usual practice formed in the precedent business between both parties.

有时，一项发盘的交易条件表面上不完整，而实际上是完整的。例如，交易双方事先已订立"一般交易条件"；援引来往的函电或以前成交的合同；交易双方在先前的业务中已形成的习惯做法。

④ Be communicated to the offeree 传达到受盘人

According to the CISG, article 15 (1), "An offer becomes effective when it reaches the offeree." The offeree cannot make acceptance initiatively before receiving the offer even though he has been informed of the contents of the offer in other ways.

《公约》第 15 条第(1)款规定："发盘于送达被发价人时生效"。即使受盘人在此之前已通过其他途径得知了发盘的内容，也不能在收到发盘前主动对该发盘表示接受。

(3) Time of Validity or Duration of an Offer 发盘的有效期

The time of validity or duration of an offer refers to the binding time of the offeror over the offeree and the time limit for the offeree to accept. The acceptance made by an offeree is effective merely within the validity date and the offeror is bound to the obligation to conclude the contract with the offeree upon the offer terms within the validity date.

发盘的有效期是指发盘对发盘人约束的期限，也是受盘人接受发盘的期限。只有在有效期内，受盘人对发盘的接受才有效，发盘人也才承担按发盘条件与受盘人成交的责任。

The validity time of an offer is usually stipulated in the following ways:
对发盘有效期的规定有以下几种情况：

① Stipulating the last accepting time 规定最迟接受期限

Such as, "subject reply reaching here 15th" "offer valid until Friday our time" "offer subject reply 15th our time".

如"发盘限 15 日复到""发盘有效至我方时间星期五""发盘限我方时间 15 日复"。

Because of the time differences in the world, there should be a very clear stipulation for the time limitation which time is the stated time. In practice, the offeror prefers to adop his end.

由于不同国家之间往往存在时差，因此发盘中应明确以哪方时间为准。实际业务中，发盘人大多规定以其所在地时间为准。

② Stipulating a period of accepting time 规定一段接受时间

Such as, "the offer is valid/ open/ effective for 10 days".

如"发盘有效期 10 天"。

According to the CISG, article 20, "(1) A period of time for acceptance fixed by the offeror in a telegram or a letter begins to run from the moment the telegram is handed in for dispatch or from the date shown on the letter or, if no such date is shown, from the date shown on the envelope. A period of time for acceptance fixed by the offeror by telephone, telex or other means of instantaneous communication begins to run from the moment that the offer reaches the offeree. (2) Official holidays or non-business days occurring during the period for acceptance are included in calculating the period. However, if a notice of acceptance cannot be delivered at the address of the offeror on the last day of the period because that day falls on an official holiday or a non-business day at the place of business of the offeror, the period is extended until the first business day which follows."

《公约》第 20 条规定:"(1)发盘人在电报或信件内规定的接受期间,从电报交发时刻或信上载明的发信日期起算,如信上未载明发信日期,则从信封上所载日期起算。发盘人以电话、电传或其他快速通信方法规定的接受期间,从发盘送达被发盘人时起算。(2)在计算接受期间时,接受期间内的正式假日或非营业日应计算在内。但是,如果接受通知在接受期间的最后 1 天未能送到发盘人地址,因为那天在发盘人营业地是正式假日或非营业日,则接受期间应顺延至下一个营业日。"

③ The validity time is not stipulated definitely 不明确规定有效期

When the validity time is not specified in the offer, the offeree's acceptance shall be made within a reasonable time. There is no internationally unified stipulation of the "reasonable time". Generally it is decided according to the characteristics of the commodity and the industrial usual practice. For the commodity with a stable market, the offer's validity time will be longer and it's shorter on the contrary. Due to the uncertainty of the stipulation, it will bring about disputes, therefore, the offer is seldom sent in this way.

当发盘未具体列明有效期时,受盘人应在合理时间内接受才能有效。对"合理时间",国际上并没有统一规定,一般由商品的特点和行业习惯决定。对于市场行情稳定的商品,有效期通常较长,反之则较短。由于这种规定具有很大的不确定性,容易产生纠纷,在进出口业务中一般较少采用。

④ Duration of an oral offer 口头方式发盘的有效期

According the CISG, an oral offer is valid only when the offeree accepts the offer on the spot unless the offeror has the extra declaration in the offer.

根据《公约》规定,采用口头方式发盘时,除发盘人发盘时另有声明外,受盘人只能当场表示接受,方为有效。

(4) Termination of an Offer 发盘的终止

Termination of an offer means the offer is no longer valid. An offer may be terminated in any one of the following ways:

发盘的终止即发盘的失效。发盘在下列情况下失效:

① The offer is not accepted within the validity 在有效期内未被接受

② The offeree rejects the offer or makes a counter offer 受盘人拒绝或还盘

③ There appears force majeure, namely war, government prohibition, the party in question is incapacity, bankruptcy or death. 出现不可抗力，如战争、政府禁令、当事人丧失行为能力或破产、死亡等。

④ The offer has been lawfully withdrawn or revoked by the offeror 发盘人依法撤回或撤销发盘

"Withdrawal" happens before the offer comes into force, in which the offeror takes actions to prevent it from becoming valid. As stipulated in the CISG, article 15 (2), "An offer, even if it is irrevocable, may be withdrawn if the withdrawal reaches the offeree before or at the same time as the arrival of the offer."

"撤回"是指在发盘尚未生效时，发盘人采取行动阻止它的生效。《公约》第 15 条第 2 款规定："一项发盘，即使是不可撤销的，也可以撤回，如果撤回通知在发盘到达受盘人之前或同时到达受盘人。"

"Revocation" happens after the offer becomes valid in which the offeror terminates the effect of the offer by taking some measures. As to the revocation of an offer, each country has different expressions in law. Splitting the difference, it is stipulated in article 16 of the CISG, "(1) Until a contract is concluded an offer may be revoked if the revocation reaches the offeree before he has dispatched an acceptance. (2) However, an offer cannot be revoked: (a) if it indicates, whether by stating a fixed time for acceptance or otherwise, that it is irrevocable; or (b) if it was reasonable for the offeree to reply on the offer as being irrevocable and the offeree has acted in reliance on the offer."

"撤销"是指发盘生效后，发盘人以一定方式解除发盘的效力。关于发盘的撤销，各国的法律规定存在较大差异。《公约》采取了折中的办法，第 16 条规定，"(1)在未订立合同之前，发盘得以撤销，如果撤销通知于受盘人发出接受通知之前送达受盘人；(2)但在下列情况下，发盘不得撤销：(a)发盘写明接受发盘的期限或以其他方式表示发盘是不可撤销的；或(b)受盘人有理由信赖该项发盘是不可撤销的，而且受盘人已本着对该项发盘的信赖行事。"

It shall be noted that it is usually too late to withdraw an offer when it has been dispatched for the moment that the developed and modern communication means such as E-mail are adopted across the world. So, to prevent the error in the contract and avoid unnecessary loss, we shall work more carefully in the actual operation.

需要注意的是，在当前通信设施非常发达和各国普遍采用现代化通信(如电子邮件)的条件下，当发现发盘中存在问题而想撤回时，往往已经来不及了。为了防止出现差错和避免发生不必要的损失，在实际业务中应当审慎行事。

3. Counter Offer 还盘

Counter offer means a reply made by the offeree to the offer, not accepting the terms of the offer completely and with the proposal to modify or change it. A counter offer terminates the validity of the original offer, which cannot thereafter be accepted unless the offeror agree to reinstate it.

"还盘"是指受盘人不同意或不完全同意发盘人提出的各项条件，并提出了修改或变更的表示。一经还盘，原发盘即失效，除非得到原发盘人同意，受盘人不得在还盘后反悔再接受原发盘。

It is stipulated in the CISG, article 19, that "(1) A reply to an offer which purports to be an acceptance but contains additions, limitations or other modifications is a rejection of the offer and constitutes a counter-offer. (2) However, a reply to an offer which purports to be an acceptance but contains additional or different terms which do not materially alter the terms of the offer constitutes an acceptance, unless the offeror, without undue delay, objects orally to the discrepancy or dispatches a notice to that effect. If he does not so object, the terms of the contract are the terms of the offer with the modifications contained in the acceptance. (3) Additional or different terms relating, among other things, to the price, payment, quality and quantity of the goods, place and time of delivery, extent of one party's liability to the other or the settlement of disputes are considered to alter the terms of the offer materially."

《公约》第 19 条对还盘的规定如下："(1)对发价表示接受但载有添加、限制或其他更改的答复，即为拒绝该项发价，并构成还价。(2)但是，对发价表示接受但载有添加或不同条件的答复，如所载的添加或不同条件在实质上并不变更该项发价的条件，除发价人在不过分迟延的期间内以口头或书面通知反对其间的差异外，仍构成接受。如果发价人不做出这种反对，合同的条件就以该项发价的条件以及接受通知内所载的更改为准。(3)有关货物价格、付款、货物质量和数量、交货地点和时间、一方当事人对另一方当事人的赔偿责任范围或解决争端等的添加或不同条件，均视为在实质上变更发价的条件。"

A counter offer without the offer's terms is regarded as an invitation of an offer. Whereas, a counter offer containing an offer's terms is taken as a new offer with the counter offeror as the new offeror and the original offeror as a new offeree. The new offeree is granted with the right to accept, refuse or make a counter offer again.

还盘的内容，凡不具备发盘条件的即为邀请发盘。凡具备发盘条件的，就构成一个新的发盘，还盘人称为新发盘人，原发盘人称为新受盘人，他有对新发盘做出接受、拒绝或再还盘的权利。

4. Acceptance 接受

(1) Definition of Acceptance 接受的含义

It is stipulated in the CISG, article 18 (1), that "A statement made by or other conduct of the offeree indicating assent to an offer is an acceptance. Silence or inactivity does not in itself amount to acceptance." The contract is established once the offer is accepted. The both parties concerned shall perform the obligation stipulated in the contract and own the relevant rights.

《公约》第18条第1款对接受做了如下定义："受盘人声明或作出其他行为表示同意一项发价，即是接受。缄默或不行动本身不等于接受。"发盘一经接受，合同即告成立。双方均应履行合同所规定的义务并拥有相应的权利。

(2) Necessary Conditions for Acceptance 构成接受的要件

① The acceptance must be made by the specific offeree 接受必须由特定的受盘人作出

As the offer should be addressed to one or more specific persons, acceptance should be made by that person. Acceptance made by the person other than those addressed in the offer would result in an ineffective acceptance.

一项有效的发盘必须是向一个或一个以上特定的人作出的。因此，对发盘表示接受，也必须是发盘中所指明的特定的受盘人。任何第三者针对该发盘作出的接受都是无效的。

② An acceptance must be indicated 接受必须表示出来

The offeree may indicates an acceptance in two ways: by statement, that is to say, the offeree indicates an assent to an offer orally or in writing, and by performing an act such as delivery by seller or making payment by buyer. In any case, silence or inactivity does not in itself amount to acceptance.

受盘人表达接受的方式有两种：用声明或行为来表示。前者指受盘人用口头或书面形式向发盘人表示同意发盘；后者如卖方发运货物或买方支付价款来表示接受。任何情况下，缄默或不行动本身不等于接受。

③ The acceptance must be unconditional 接受必须是无条件的

Unconditional means that the contents of the acceptance must be in compliance with the offer. In principle, modifications to the condition of the offer is regarded as a counter offer.

所谓无条件接受，即接受的内容必须与发盘相符。修改发盘通常被认为是还盘。

According to the CISG, article 19, a reply to an offer, which purports to be an acceptance but contains additional or different terms, is divided into two types: a reply altering the offer substantially or not altering the offer substantially. The former is regarded as a counter offer, which is an invalid acceptance, and the latter is still taken as an effective acceptance "unless the offeror, without undue delay, objects orally to the discrepancy or dispatches a notice to that effect".

依据《公约》第19条,对发盘表示接受但载有添加或不同条件的答复分为实质性变更发盘条件的接受和非实质性变更发盘条件的接受两种。前者视为还盘,是一项无效的接受,合同不能成立;后者仍然是一项有效的接受,只要发盘人不表示反对,合同仍然成立。"如果发盘人不过分迟延的时间内以口头或书面通知,反对其间的差异",则这项接受就是无效接受,合同不成立。

The CISG distinguishes the substantial acceptance and the unsubstantial acceptance according to the alteration of six elements as follows: "Additional or different terms relating, among other things, to the price, payment, quality and quantity of the goods, place and time of delivery, extent of one party's liability to the other or the settlement of disputes are considered to alter the terms of the offer materially."

《公约》把下列六个条件作为区分实质性和非实质性变更发盘条件的接受:"有关货物价格、付款、货物质量和数量、交货地点和时间、一方当事人对另一方当事人的赔偿责任范围或解决争端等的添加或不同条件,均视为在实质上变更发价的条件。"

④ The acceptance must reach the offeror within the validity of the offer 接受必须在发盘有效期内传达到发盘人

According to the CISG, article 18 (2), "An acceptance of an offer becomes effective at the moment the indication of assent reaches the offer." In case that the offer is made orally, the offeree shall make a reply to accept or not immediately unless the offeror and the offeree have agreed otherwise on the period for the acceptance. In case that the offer is made in writing (such as telegram, fax, letter etc.), the acceptance shall reach the offeror within the fixed effective period or a reasonable time if not fixed.

《公约》第18条第2款规定:"接受于到达发盘人时生效。"如果以口头方式作出发盘,除非发盘人与受盘人另有约定接受的具体期限,否则,受盘人应立即作出接受与否的意思表示。如果以书面(电报、传真、信函等)方式作出发盘,接受应当在规定的有效期内或合理的期限内到达发盘人。

(3) Late Acceptance 逾期接受

A late acceptance means the notice of an acceptance reaches the offeror after the effective time or a reasonable time if the effective time is not fixed. A late acceptance is not effective commonly, however, according to the CISG, article 21, the late acceptance is still effective in the following cases.

逾期接受又称推迟或迟到接受,是指接受通知到达发盘人的时间已经超过了发盘规定的有效期,或者在发盘未规定有效期时,已超过了合理的时间。逾期接受在一般情况下无效,但《公约》第21条规定,下列情况下,逾期接受仍然有效。

"(1) A late acceptance is nevertheless effective as an acceptance if without delay the offeror orally so informs the offeree or dispatches a notice to that effect. (2) If a letter or other writing containing a late acceptance shows that it has been sent in such circumstances that if its transmission had been normal it would have reached the offeror in due time, the late acceptance is effective as an acceptance unless, without delay, the offeror orally informs the offeree that he considers his offer as having lapsed or dispatches a notice to that effect."

"(1)逾期接受仍有接受的效力,如果发价人毫不迟延地用口头或书面将此种意见通知被发价人。(2)如果载有逾期接受的信件或其他书面文件表明,它是在传递正常、能及时送达发价人的情况下寄发的,则该项逾期接受具有接受的效力,除非发价人毫不迟延地用口头或书面通知被发价人:他认为他的发价已经失效。"

(4) The Withdrawal of an Acceptance 接受的撤回

The withdrawal of an acceptance means that the offeree takes some measures to prevent the acceptance from coming into effect when he has made acceptance to the offeror.

接受的撤回指的是受盘人在对发盘人发出接受通知后,采取某种方式阻止该接受生效的行为。

It is stipulated in the CISG article 22, that "An acceptance may be withdrawn if the withdrawal reaches the offeror before or at the same time as the acceptance would have become effective." When an acceptance has reached the offeror, namely the acceptance has come into effect, the contract is established, which cannot be withdrawn or amended as the withdrawal or amendment for the moment equals to the revocation or the amendment of the contract.

《公约》第22条规定:"接受得以撤回,如果撤回通知于接受原应生效之前或同时送达发价人。"如接受已送达发盘人,即接受一旦生效,合同即告成立,就不得撤回接受或修改其内容,因为这样做无异于撤销或修改合同。

It shall be noted that it is usually too late to withdraw an acceptance when it has been dispatched for the moment that the developed and modern communication means such as E-mail are adopted across the world. So, to prevent the error in the contract and avoid unnecessary loss, we shall work more carefully in the actual operation.

需要注意的是,在当前通信设施非常发达和各国普遍采用现代化通信(如电子邮件)的条件下,当发现接受中存在问题而想撤回时,往往已经来不及了。为了防止出现差错和避免发生不必要的损失,在实际业务中应当审慎行事。

5. Example of Business Negotiation 交易磋商用语举例

(1) Inquiry 询盘

We're interested in Color TV Shanghai Brand Model 345. Please send us an offer at a favorable price.

(2) Offer 发盘

Your E-mail of Oct. 8th was received. We offer subject to your reply reaching us 15th as follows:

Color TV Shanghai Brand, Model 345

1000 sets, packed in export cantons of one set each (to be transported in 20' container of 500 cartons each)

USD 150 per set CFR Karachi

Shipment by Irrevocable Sight Credit

(3) Counter Offer 还盘

① Referring to your E-mail of Oct. 10th, we regret to note that the price you offered is too high. We counter offer USD 130 per set CFR Karachi.

② Your E-mail of 12th to hand. The best we can do is USD 140 subject to your reply to reach us Oct. 18th.

(4) Acceptance 接受

With reference to your E-mail of Oct. 14th, we accept.

Section 3 Contract Conclusion

第3节 合同订立

1. Definition of Contract 合同的含义

International trade contract, also called "international purchase and sales contract" is the agreement reached by the parties from different countries or regions for a deal of certain merchandise, thus serving as a basis for the implementation of obligations for contracting parties. The kind of contract is a legal document protected and governed by the law of a certain country, binding each side with equal legal effect, thus providing a basis of the solution of disputes in international trade by mediation, arbitration and lawsuit.

外贸合同，又称国际货物购销合同，是地处不同国家或地区的当事人双方买卖一定货物达成的协议，是当事人各自履行约定义务的依据。外贸合同受国家法律保护和管辖，是对签约各方都具有同等约束力的法律性文件，是解决贸易纠纷，进行调解、仲裁与诉讼的法律依据。

2. Significance of Contract Signing 签订书面合同的意义

It's not necessary for an effective contract to sign a contract in written form. In business negotiation, a deal is concluded after an offer is accepted, then a contract relationship is established by the buyer and the seller. It is stated in the CISG, article 11, that "A contract of sale need not be concluded in or evidenced by writing and is not subject to any other requirement as to form. It may be proved by any means, including witnesses." However, in the international business practice, the parties concerned will usually sign a contract in written form after reaching an agreement through negotiation as there are three aspects of significance to sign a contract in written form.

签订书面合同不是合同有效成立的必要条件。在交易磋商过程中,一方发盘经另一方接受后,交易即告成立,买卖双方就构成了合同关系。《公约》第11条规定,"销售合同无须以书面订立或书面证明,在形式方面也不受任何其他条件的限制。销售合同可以用包括人证在内的任何方法证明。"但是,在国际贸易实践中,在当事人双方经过磋商一致,达成交易后,一般均须另行签订一份书面合同。签订书面合同有以下三方面的意义。

(1) The Evidence to Prove a Contract is Established 合同成立的证据

According to the relevant law and rules, a contract must be certified with proof including witness testimony and material evidence. For a contract concluded by the negotiation with letter, email or fax, it is no problem to provide the proof in writing. However, for a contract established through the oral negotiation, it is hard to prove it. Therefore, a contract established by an oral negotiation will probably not be protected by law due to the failure of being verified if the contract is not confirmed in written form, even the contract will be invalid. So, for an agreement reached through oral negotiation in particular, it is necessary to sign a contract in written.

根据法律要求,凡是合同必须能得到证明,提供证据,包括人证和物证。在用信件、电子邮件或传真磋商时,书面证明不成问题。但是,通过口头磋商成立的合同,举证就难以做到。因此,口头磋商成立的合同,如不用一定的书面形式加以确定,就将由于无法证明而不能得到法律的保障,甚至在法律上无效。签订一份书面合同对于口头磋商达成的协议尤其重要。

(2) The Term with which a Contract Comes into Effect 合同生效的条件

If one party claims that it is subject to the contract in written form during the negotiation, then the contract is not established until a formal contract in written form is signed even though both parties concerned have reached an agreement on all trade terms. In this case, signing a written contract is the term for the contract coming into effect.

如果在买卖双方磋商时,一方曾声明以签订书面合同为准,即使双方已对交易条件全部协商一致,也必须在正式签订合同后,合同才能成立。在这种情况下,签订书面合同就成了合同生效的条件。

(3) The Basis on which a Contract is Fulfilled 履行合同的依据

Whether the deal is reached through oral negotiation or in written form, the trade terms agreed shall be combined clearly and completely and listed in a contract with a certain format. It is very important for both parties to further make clear of the rights and obligations of them, and with definite basis to fulfill the contract better.

不论通过口头还是书面形式磋商达成交易，均须把协商一致的交易条件综合起来，全面、清楚地列明在一份有一定格式的书面合同上，有助于进一步明确双方的权利和义务，以及为合同的履行提供更好的依据。

3. Forms of Written Contract 书面合同的形式

There is no specific limit on the form of a written contract. The both parties concerned may adopt any one of these forms including Contract, Confirmation, Agreement or Memorandum. In addition, there are letter of intent, purchase order, authorization order sheet and the like to be taken as the form of a contract. Although the format and contents of these forms of written contract are different, the legal effectiveness of them is the same.

关于书面合同的形式，并无特别限制，买卖双方可采用正式合同、确认书、协议，也可采用备忘录等形式。此外，还有意向书、订单和委托订购单等。这些形式的书面合同格式和内容的繁简有所不同，但法律效力是一样的。

In our foreign trade business, contracts and confirmations are mainly adopted. The contract may be classified into Sales Contract and Purchase Contract. The former is drawn up by the seller while the latter is made by the buyer. A confirmation is a simplified form of a contract, which may be classified into Sales Confirmation and Purchase Confirmation. A Sales Confirmation is issued by the seller while a Purchase Confirmation is issued by the buyer.

我国外贸实践中，采用合同和确认书两种形式的居多。合同可分为销售合同和购货合同。前者是卖方草拟的合同，后者是买方草拟的合同。确认书是合同的简化形式，可分为销售确认书和购货确认书。前者是卖方出具的确认书，后者是买方出具的确认书。

4. Contents of Written Contract 书面合同的内容

A written contract is usually composed of three parts which are head, body and ending.
书面合同一般包括三个部分：约首、本文、约尾。

(1) Head 约首

Head of a contract is the first part of a contract including the name of contract, number of contract, signing date and signing place, information of parties involved.

约首，即合同的首部，一般包括合同名称、合同编号、签约时间和地点、合同当事人信息。

(2) Body 本文

Body of a contract is the main part of a contract specifying the trade terms in details such as commodity, quality, specification, quantity or weight, package, price, delivery terms, transportation, insurance, payment, inspection, claims and compensation, force majeure and arbitration etc.

本文是合同的主要组成部分,是对各项交易条件的具体规定,包括品名、品质、规格、数量或重量、包装、价格、交货条件、运输、保险、支付、检验、索赔、不可抗力和仲裁等内容。

(3) Ending 约尾

The last part of a contract is usually covering the following points: copies of contract, the date and place of contract establishment the signatures and stamps of both parties and so on.

约尾,即合同的尾部,一般包括合同的份数、订约日期、订约地点和双方当事人签字盖章等内容。

5. Sample of Written Contract 书面合同样本

外贸合同
Sales Contract

日期 Date:	合同号 Contract No.:
卖方 **Seller**:	买方 **Buyer**:
地址 Address:	地址 Address:
电话 Tel:	电话 Tel:
传真 Fax:	传真 Fax:
Email:	Email:
联系人 Contact Person:	联系人 Contact Person:

最终用户:

本合同由买卖双方订立。根据本合同规定的条款,买方同意购买且卖方同意出售下述货物:

This Contract is made by and between the Buyer and the Seller, whereby the Seller agrees to sell and the Buyer agrees to buy the below-mentioned goods on the terms and conditions stipulated hereunder:

1	货物详情 Particulars of the Goods			
	货名及规格 Goods and Specifications	数量 Quantity	单价 Unite Price	总价 Total Amount
	生产国别和制造厂商:			
	SAY USD			

续表

2	贸易条款 Delivery Terms	2.1	交付条件 Delivery Terms: FCA Beijing
		2.2	在本合同中，描述双方权利义务的贸易术语如FCA，应按照位于巴黎的国际商会最新出版的《国际贸易术语解释通则》("Incoterms")解释。 For purposes of this Contract, trade terms (e.g., FCA) used to describe the rights and obligations of the parties shall have the meanings assigned to them by the latest Incoterms published by the International Chamber of Commerce, Paris.
3	装运条款 Shipping Terms	3.1	交货时间 Time of Delivery: 收到预付款后60个工作日内，并且在免税办理完成后 Within 60 working days after signing the contract and Tax-Free procedure completed.
		3.2	装运口岸 Port of Shipment: MAIN AIRPORT
		3.3	到货口岸 Port of Destination: AIRPORT
		3.4	每批货物装运起航后，卖方即以传真通知买方合同、货名、数量、重量、总值、开航日期和目的口岸。 Immediately after the goods have been shipped and departed, the Seller shall notify the Buyer by fax the contract number, name of goods, quantity, weight, total value, Flight No., shipping date and the port of destination. 货物允许转运，但不可分批运输。 Trans-shipment is acceptable, but partial shipment is not allowed.
4	付款条件 Payment		100%信用证付款，90%即期信用证，10%根据最终用户签字盖章的验收报告付款。 L/C 100%, 90% will be paid at sight, 10% will be paid against final acceptance signed and sealed by buyer and End user.
5	包装及标准 Packing & Standards		货物应具有防潮、防锈蚀、防震并适合远洋运输的包装。由于货物包装不充分或不适当而造成的货物残损、灭失应由卖方负责。卖方应在每个包装箱上用不褪色的颜色标明尺码、包装箱号码、毛重、净重及"此端向上""防潮""小心轻放"等标记，并刷唛头。 唛头：××× The packing of the Goods shall be preventive from dampness, rust, moisture, erosion and shock, and shall be suitable for ocean transportation. The Seller shall be liable for any damage and loss of the Goods attributable to the inadequate or improper packing. The measurement, number of package, gross weight, net weight, and the cautions such as "DO NOT STACK UP SIDE DOWN", "KEEP AWAY FROM MOISTURE" "HANDLE WITH CARE" shall be stencilled on the surface of each package with fadeless marks, and the shipping mark shall be stencilled:. Shipping Mark: ×××

续表

6	Insurance 保险		合同下提供的货物在制造、购置、运输、存放及交货过程中的丢失或损坏,应该按照发票金额的110%投保一切险。The Goods supplied under the Contract shall be insured with All Risks at 110% of the invoice value against loss or damage incidental to manufacture, acquisition, transportation, storage, and delivery.
7	检验与验收 Inspection & Testing and Acceptance	7.1	发货前,卖方制造厂应对货物的符合合同标准进行检验,出具检验证明书或出厂合格证书。Prior to shipment, the Seller manufacturer shall conduct inspection/test on the Goods' conformity to the Contract Specifications, and issue an inspection certificate or conformity certificate.
		7.2	货物交付后,买方应在十五(15)天内对货物的数量、规格及表面状况进行开箱检验。买方应提前通知卖方检验时间和地点,卖方有权委派代表参加检验。如果出现短缺、破损或错发等,买方应立即通知卖方任何不符情况;如果出现短缺、破损或错发的,由卖方补足、替换或重发并承担相关的费用。若在上述期限内买方未通知卖方任何不符情况,则视为所交付货物的数量、规格及表面状况均符合双方约定。Within fifteen (15) days after delivery of the Goods, the Buyer shall conduct an "open box" inspection of the Goods in respect of their quantity, specifications and apparent order and condition. The Buyer shall inform the Seller in advance and the Seller has the right to send its representative to join the inspection. In case of shortage, damage or wrong delivery, the Buyer shall promptly notify the Seller of the discrepancies, and the Seller will make up the shortage, replace the damaged Goods or send the correct Goods, and bear the related costs. If the Buyer does not notify the Seller of any such discrepancies within the prescribed period, the quantity, specifications and apparent order and condition of the delivered Goods shall be deemed in compliance with this Contract.
		7.3	在货物到达目的地口岸90天内,如发现货物的质量与本合同规定不符或发现货物无论任何原因引起的缺陷包括内在缺陷或使用不良的原料,除属于保险公司或承运方责任之外,买方应申请中国进出口商业检验局对有关的货物进行检验,买方有权根据商检证书向卖方索赔。If within 90 days after arrival of the Goods at the destination, should the quality of the Goods be found not in conformity with the contracted stipulations, or should the Goods prove defective for any reasons, including latent defect or the use of unsuitable materials, the Buyer shall arrange for an inspection to be carried out by the China Commodity Inspection Bureau and have the right to claim against the Seller on the strength of the inspection certificate issued by the Inspection Bureau, with the exception to those claims for which the insurance company or the freight forwarder are liable.

续表

8	质量保证 Warranty	8.1	卖方保证合同下所提供的货物是全新的、未使用过的、最新的或最现代型号的，没有设计、材料或工艺上的缺陷(买方要求的设计或材料除外)。卖方同时保证所提供的货物质量符合其发布的技术规格或双方另行书面约定的标准。 The Seller warrants that the Goods supplied under the Contract are new, unused, of the most recent or current models and they incorporate all recent improvements in design and materials unless provided otherwise in the Contract. The Seller further warrants that all Goods supplied under the Contract shall have no defect, arising from design, materials, or workmanship (except when the design and/or material is required by the Buyer). The Seller also warrants that the Goods supplied conform to its published specifications or the specifications agreed upon in writing by the Parties.
		8.2	除非本合同另有规定，质量保证期限为自货物验收后十二(12)个月，或自货物交运之日起十四(14)个月，以先到日期为准。 Unless otherwise specified in the Contract, such warranty shall be valid for one (1) year from the date of acceptance of the Goods, or fourteen (14) months from the date of shipment, whichever is earlier.
		8.3	上述质量保证责任不涵盖由于由货物以外的原因(比如意外事件/自然灾害，断电或电涌，货物储存不当或不按照使用指南操作等)造成的质量问题。 The above quality warranty does not cover problems caused by factors external to the Goods such as accident or disaster, power failure or electrical power surge, improper storage of the Goods or use of the Goods not following the use instructions.
		8.4	如卖方出售的任何货物或者其部分采购自第三方供应商，则卖方的货物质量保证限于第三方供应商提供的货物质量保证。 The Seller's warranty with respect to any goods or any components thereof furnished to the Seller by any third party suppliers and sold by the Seller to the Buyer shall be limited to the warranty provided by such third party suppliers therefore.
9	付款条件 Payment Term	9.1	买卖合同价格以下列方式支付： 合同签订后电汇30%预付款，发货前2周电汇付清70%余款。 30% contract value will be pre-paid by T.T.; the rest 70% of contract value will be paid within two weeks before shipment.
		9.2	买方如有款项到期未付，应向卖方支付该款项自到期日至付款日的利息，利率按每天 0.05%计算。如到期未付款项为外币，买方也应承担卖方因其延迟付款而遭受的汇率损失。如买方未按时支付任何价款或未依约按时开立信用证超过60天的，卖方可以解除合同并要求买方赔偿损失。

续表

			Any default in payment by the Buyer will entitle the Seller to the interest on that outstanding amount at the rate of point zero 5 percent (0.05 %) per day from the due date thereof through the date of the completion of such payment. In the event the overdue payment is in foreign currency, the Buyer shall also compensate the Seller for the currency fluctuation losses (if any) caused by the default in payment by the Buyer. In the event the Buyer is in default of any payment due or fails to open a letter of credit in time and as agreed, and the default is more than 60 days, the Seller is entitled to terminate the Contract and claim compensation against the Buyer.
10	延迟交货及违约责任 Late Delivery & Liability for Breach	10.1	除合同第 11 条不可抗力原因外，如卖方不能按合同规定的时间交货，买方同意在卖方支付违约金的条件下延期交货。罚款可由议付银行在议付货款时扣除，违约金按每 7 天收延迟货物价值的 0.5%计算，不足 7 天按 7 天计，但最高罚款总额不超过迟交货物总价的 5%。如卖方延期交货超过合同规定 90 天时，买方有权撤销合同，此时，卖方仍应毫不迟延地按上述规定向买方支付违约金。 Except for force majeure causes under Clause 11 hereunder, if the Seller cannot make delivery on time as stipulated in the Contract, the Buyer shall agree to take the postponed delivery on the condition that the Seller agrees to pay liquidated damages. The rate of such liquidated damages shall be 0.5% of value of the delayed Goods per 7 days, and if less than 7 days shall be countered as 7 days. The liquidated damages shall not exceed 5% of the total value of the goods. If the delivery delay is more than 90 days than the stipulated date of delivery, the Buyer has the right to terminate the Contract, and the Seller, in spite of the termination, shall nevertheless pay the aforesaid liquidated damages to the Buyer without delay.
		10.2	如买方要求卖方延迟或者中止履行合同，卖方书面同意的，如所要求的中止或者延迟时间超过 30 天，买方应向卖方支付所涉产品价款的 20%作为中止/延迟履行费。 If the Buyer requests the Seller to delay or suspend its performance of this Contract, which the Seller agrees in writing, and if period of delay or suspension as requested is longer than 30 days, the Buyer shall be required to pay the Seller a suspension/delay fee, equal to 20% of the total value of the goods concerned.
		10.3	除法律另有规定外，任何一方均不对另一方因本合同而产生的间接损失（如收入或利润损失、商誉损失、数据损失等）承担责任。买卖双方在合同项下违约向对方承担的责任限于合同的总价。 Unless the law provides otherwise, neither party shall be liable to the other party for indirect losses (e.g., loss of revenue or profit, loss of goodwill, loss of data) in connection to or arising out of this Contract. The aggregate liability of a party to the other party shall not exceed the total Contract price.

续表

		10.4	上述 10.3 条不适用于(1)造成对方人身伤害的；(2)因故意或重大过失造成对方财产损失的。 The foregoing Section 10.3 shall not apply to (1) bodily injury; (2) property damages caused by wilful misconduct or gross negligence.
11	出口限制 Export Control		买方承认，每件产品以及任何相关软件和技术，包括卖方所提供的或文件中包含的技术信息(合称"物品")，可能受美国政府出口管制的约束。买方在取得相关的政府机构许可(如美国政府有此要求)之前，不得：(1) 出口或再出口任何物品；或者(2)将任何物品出口、再出口、分销或供应到被美国政府实施限制或禁运政策的任何国家(包括但不限于古巴、朝鲜、苏丹、叙利亚和伊朗)，或出口、再出口、分销或供应给已遭美国政府拒绝或限制其参与出口活动的任何个人或实体。买方保证所有从卖方获得的物品都将用作商业用途，不会用于任何军事，核扩散，生化武器以及导弹技术领域。如卖方要求，买方应向卖方提供关于买方已出口或将要出口的任何物品的最终用户和最终用途的信息。买方应就与进出口管制法律法规有关的任何官方或非官方的审核或检查，与卖方充分合作；并就买方或其雇员、顾问或代理人违反本条规定的任何行为，向卖方赔偿并使卖方免受该等违反所造成的或与之相关的损害。 Buyer acknowledges that the Product and any related software and technology, including technical information supplied by the Seller or contained in documents (collectively "Items"), may be subject to export controls of the U.S. government. Buyer may not, without first obtaining the required license to do so from the appropriate U.S. government agency if so required: (i) export or re-export any Item, or (ii) export, re-export, distribute or supply any Item to any restricted or embargoed country (including but not limited to Cuba, North Korea, Sudan, Syria and Iran) or to a person or entity whose privilege to participate in exports has been denied or restricted by the U.S. government. Buyer certify that all the products received from Seller are intended for use in commercial applications only and are not intended for use in any military or nuclear, chemical or biological proliferation end applications or missile technology. Buyer shall, if requested by Seller, provide information on the end user and end use of any Item exported or to be exported by Buyer. Buyer shall cooperate fully with Seller in any official or unofficial audit or inspection related to applicable export or import control laws or regulations, and shall indemnify and hold Seller harmless from, or in connection with, any violation of this Section by Buyer or its employees, consultants, or agents.

续表

12	不可抗力 Force Majeure	12.1	由于不可抗力的原因，而不能履行合同或延迟履行合同的一方无须为此承担违约责任，但应立即以书面形式通知对方并提供不可抗力发生以及持续期间的充分证据。如果不可抗力发生超过6个月以上，任何一方都有权终止合同。
			The party shall not be responsible for delay or non-performance of the Contract which are affected by a force majeure event, but shall promptly notify the other party in writing and furnish sufficient proof of the occurrence and duration of such force majeure event. If the force majeure event lasts for more than six (6) months, either Party has the right to terminate the Contract.
		12.2	"不可抗力"是指那些合同一方无法控制、无法预见、无法避免的事件和情况，其发生也不是卖方的违约或疏忽而造成的。这些事件包括但不限于战争或革命、火灾、洪水、流行病、防疫限制和禁运。
			"Force Majeure" means an event which is beyond the control of the Parties, not foreseeable and unavoidable. Such events may include but not restricted to, war or revolution, fires, floods, epidemics, quarantine restrictions, and freight embargoes.
13	适用法律 Governing Law		合同应适用中华人民共和国法律。如合同使用国际贸易术语，则该术语应按照最新出版的《国际贸易术语解释通则》予以解释，但是合同的约定优先于该通则的规定。
			The Contract shall be governed by the laws of the People's Republic of China. Any international trade terms, if used in this Contract, shall be construed in accordance with the latest International Rules for the Interpretation of Trade Terms (INCOTERMS), unless otherwise provided in this Contract.
14	争议解决 Dispute Resolution		因合同而产生的或与合同有关的任何争议应通过友好协商解决，如无法协商解决，争议应提交中国国际经济贸易仲裁委员会依据申请仲裁时该会有效的仲裁规则进行仲裁。仲裁应在[上海]进行。仲裁裁决是终局的，对双方具有约束力。
			Any dispute arising from or in connection with this Contract shall be settled through friendly negotiation. In case that no such settlement is reached, the dispute shall be submitted to the China International Economic and Trade Arbitration Commission ("CIETAC") for arbitration in accordance with its rules in effect at the time of applying for arbitration. The venue of arbitration shall be in [Shanghai]. The arbitral award is final and shall bind upon both parties.

续表

15	杂项条款 Mis. Provisions	15.1	除非合同明确提及，卖方所提供的商品目录、说明书、传单、广告、价目表中包含的任何有关货物及其用途的信息，如重量、大小、容量、颜色以及其他数据仅作参考指示之用，不作为合同的条款而生效。 Any information relating to the Goods and their use, such as weight, dimensions, capacities, prices, colours and other data contained in catalogues, prospectuses, circulars, advertisements, illustrations, price-lists of the Seller, shall not take effect as terms of the Contract unless expressly referred to in the Contract.
		15.2	除非另有约定，尽管买方有可能得到软件、图纸等，但买方并不因此而获得它们的产权。卖方仍是与货物有关的知识产权或工业产权的唯一所有者。 Unless otherwise agreed, the Buyer does not acquire any property rights in software, drawings, etc., which may have been made available to the Buyer. The Seller also remains the exclusive owner of any intellectual or industrial property rights related to the Goods.
		15.3	卖方提供给买方的所有相关资料(包括但不限于所有定价、折扣及技术信息)为卖方的商业秘密。买方同意(a)为该等信息保密不向任何第三方披露；及(b)只为与货物有关的用途使用该等信息。 All relevant material provided to the Buyer by the Seller, including but not limited to all pricing, discounts and technical information, are trade secrets of the Seller. The Buyer agrees to (a) keep such information confidential and not disclose to any third party; (b) only use the information for purposes related to the Goods.
		15.4	根据合同要求向对方发出的任何书面通知或通信往来在专人递送至时或以邮政特快专递寄出到对方的营业地址后三(3)个工作日视为送达。 Any written notice or communication shall be deemed delivered (1) at the same time by hand delivery; (2) three (3) dates later if by courier to the other party's business address.
		15.5	合同及所有附件自双方正式签字或盖章后即生效。 The Contract and all annexes shall come into effect after the Parties have duly signed or stamped.
		15.6	本合同以中英文签署。若中英文存在不一致的，以中文为准。 The Contract is entered into in both Chinese and English. In case of any discrepancy between the Chinese and English versions, Chinese version shall prevail.
		15.7	本合同及其附录组成完整的协议，并取代双方之间与本合同标的有关的所有口头或书面协议或理解。本合同仅在双方达成一致并书面签署时方能进行修改。

		This Contract and its Appendices attached hereto constitute an integral agreement, which replacing, whether in oral or in written, all agreements or understandings between the two parties in relation to the subject matter under this Contract. This Contract can only be amended by means of mutual agreement in a written form and executed by both parties hereto.
买方 Buyer:		卖方 Seller:

Sales Confirmation
成交确认书

No.:

Date:

Signed at:

The Buyer 买方:	The Seller 卖方:
Add 地址:	Add 地址:
Tel 电话:	Tel 电话:
Fax 传真:	Fax 传真:

This contract is negotiated and executed by and between the buyer and seller, which means the buyer agrees to buy and the seller agrees to sell the product according to the terms and conditions stipulated below:

买方与卖方就以下条款达成协议:

1. COMMODITY(商品): Please refer to the detailed breakdown as attached.(as in the appendix)

详见清单.(附页)

名称及规格 Description	单位 Unit	平均单价 Average unit price (JPY)	数量 Qty	总价 Amount
				FOB PORT
TOTAL VALUE FOB OSAKA PORT OR KOBE PORT				

2. PACKING(包装):

The commodity is supposed to be packed with infrangible Export standard packaging that suitable for long distance ocean and land transportation and well protected against dampness, moisture, shock, rust and rough handling. The Sellers shall be liable for any damage or rust damage to the goods that caused by improper packing, and pay for all cost and loss caused by the damage.

包装：必须采用坚固的出口标准包装，适合于长途海运和陆运，防潮、防震、防锈、耐粗暴搬运。由于包装不良所发生的损失，由于未采用充分或不妥善的防护措施而造成的任何锈损，卖方应负担由此而产生的一切费用和/或损失。

　　3. SHIPPING MARK(唛头)：

　　The Sellers shall mark on each package with fadeless paint the package number, gross weight, net weight, measurement and the wordings: "KEEP AWAY FROM MOISTURE" "HANDLE WITH CARE" "THIS SIDE UP" etc. and the shipping mark: ×××

　　卖方应用不褪色的颜料在每个箱子外部刷上箱号、毛重、净重、尺寸，并注明"防潮""小心轻放""此面向上"等，唛头为：×××

　　4. TIME OF SHIPMENT(装运期)：After 80% T/T Payment

　　5. PORT OF SHIPMENT(装运港)：OSAKA PORT OR KOBE PORT

　　6. PORT OF DESTINATION(目的港)：TIANJIN XINGANG , CHINA

　　7.Price Term(价格条款)：FOB Japanese main port

　　8. Telex Release(电放条款): telex release within 48 hours to the people or the shipping company which are entrusted by consignee.(Include the document that is mentioned in the 11th item)

　　9. More or less clause(溢短装): 5% more or less

　　10. PAYMENT(付款方式):T/T Payment

　　The Buyer shall pay the seller 80% of the sales price by T/T in advance, and the balance should be paid to the Seller after loading.

　　电汇。买方将买卖金额的80%货款预付给卖方，剩余货款在商品装船后支付给卖方。

　　Bank's Name(银行名称)：

　　Bank's Address(地址)：

　　SWIFT Code(SWIFT 代码)：

　　Account No.(账号)：

　　Account(账户名称)：

　　11. DOCUMENTS(单证)：

　　(1) Full set of clean shipping bills of lading　清洁海运提单一套

　　(2) Invoice in three copies　发票一式叁份

　　(3) Packing list in three copies issued by the Sellers　装箱单一式叁份

　　(4) Certificate of Quality issued by the Sellers　制造厂家出具的质量证明书

　　(5) Certificate of Origin　原产地证书

　　(6) Sanitary Certificate　卫生证书

　　(7) Certificate of Non Wooden Packing or Certificate of Fumigation　非木包装声明或熏蒸证

　　In addition the Seller should send an extra set of the document by express airmail that mentioned above directly to the Buyer within 48 hours after shipment.

　　另外，卖方应于货物发运后48小时内，用特快专递寄送一套上述的单据给买方。

　　12. SHIPMENT(运输)：

　　The Sellers shall ship the goods within the shipment time to the loading port. Trans-shipment is not allowed. Partial shipment is not allowed.

　　卖方应于交货期内将合同货物送至装运港，不许分批，不许转运。

13. SHIPPING ADVICE(装运通知):

The Seller should advise the Buyer immediately about the CONTRAT NO. , commodity, quantity, invoiced value, gross weight, name of vessel and delivery date etc. either by fax of E-mail upon the completion of loading goods. Sellers will take all the responsibilities of total loss due to not letting buyers know in time.

卖方应于装货后，立即用传真或邮件将有关合同号、货物、数量、发票价值、毛重、运输工具名称、交货日期、货物预计抵达日等资料通知买方。如果由于卖方未能通知买方而造成的所有损失均由卖方承担。

14. CHECK UPON DELIVER(验收):

The Buyer should finish checking all arriving goods arrived in buyer's warehouse within 20 days.

买方必须在订货的本件商品到达仓库后 20 日内验收完毕。

15. FORCE MAJEURE(不可抗力):

The Sellers shall not be held responsible for the delay in shipment or non-delivery of the goods due to Force Majeure, which might occur during the process of manufacturing or in the course of loading or transit. The Sellers shall advise the Buyers immediately of the occurrence mentioned above and within fourteen days thereafter, the Sellers shall send by airmail to the Buyers for their acceptance a certificate of the accident issued by the Competent Government Authorities where the accident occurs as evidence thereof. Under such circumstances the Sellers, however, are still under the obligation to take all necessary measures to hasten the delivery of the goods. In case the accident lasts for more than 10 weeks, the Buyers shall have the right to cancel the Contract.

对于制造或装船运输过程中可能产生的不可抗力而造成的迟交货或不能交货，卖方可以不承担责任。卖方应立即在不可抗力产生的 14 日内将有关情况通知买方，并且卖方应用航空邮件将有关政府当局部门出具的证明不可抗力产生的文件寄送给买方。在此情况下，卖方仍应尽最大努力采取各种措施促使货物的发运。如果事故持续 10 周，买方有权取消该合同。

16. ARBITRATION(仲裁):

Any distributes arising or in connection with this Contract shall be submitted for first arbitration in Osaka Court and the local court in the shop's area.

发生本合同及与此关联的一切纠纷时，大阪地方法院及买方所在地所辖法院为一审专属管辖法院。

17. BANK CHARGES(银行费用): All bank charges outside China will be on the account of the Sellers.

所有中国之外的银行费用均由卖方承担。

18. OTHERS(其他): This contract signed in two copies, the seller holds one copy and the buyer holds the other one.

本合同一式贰份，卖方执壹份，买方执壹份。

THE BUYERS 买方：　　　　　　　　　　　　　THE SELLERS 卖方：

Date 日期：　　　　　　　　　　　　　　　　　Date 日期：

Section 4　Contract Performance

第4节　合 同 履 行

1. Performance of Export Contract　出口合同的履行

In case of CIF term and L/C payment, the general procedures to fulfill an export contract are follows: preparation of goods, urging the importer to apply for L/C, examination of L/C, amendment of L/C, booking vessel, going through the export inspection and making customs declaration, making insurance, loading goods, the arrangement of shipping documents and the settlement of payment.

CIF 术语，L/C 支付的合同，出口履约程序一般包括：备货、催证、审证、改证、租船订舱、报验、报关、投保、装船和制单结汇等环节。

(1) Preparation of Goods　备货

After a contract is made, it is the main task for the exporter to prepare the goods for shipment and check them against the terms stipulated in the contract. The quality, specification, quantity, marking and packing should be in line with the contract or the L/C, the date for the preparation should agree with the sipping schedule.

合同签订后，出口商的主要任务就是为装船而准备货物，并按合同条款对货物进行检查。货物的品质、规格、数量、唛头和包装必须与合同或信用证一致。备货时间应结合船期安排。

(2) Ensure the Issuance of L/C　落实信用证

① Urging L/C　催证

For the business with L/C payment, especially the business in large amount or the business of commodities made to order, the timely issuance of L/C upon the agreement is the basis of the seller's fulfillment of contract. It is very important for the buyer to issue the L/C timely, otherwise the seller has not enough time to arrange for the production or get supply of goods. In the business practice, some importers may delay or not open the L/C for various reasons. Therefore, the seller shall remind the buyer to open the L/C in time to ensure the smooth fulfillment of the contract.

按信用证付款方式成交，尤其是大宗交易或按买方要求而特制的商品交易，买方按约定的时间开证是卖方履行合同的前提，否则买方无法安排生产或组织货源。但在实际业务中，有些进口商会由于各种原因迟开或不开信用证。因此，卖方应结合备货情况，及时提醒买方开立信用证，以保证合同的顺利执行。

② Examination of L/C 审证

In practice, the L/C issued may be different from the contract clauses due to various reasons such as the work neglect, the mistakes of telegram transfer, the different usual practices in trade, or the importer's deliberate addition of the beneficial clauses to him; or there are some soft clauses in the L/C which cannot be met by the seller. As a result, the seller cannot settle the payment according to the L/C. For the safe collection of payment, upon receipt of the L/C, the seller shall examine it very carefully to make sure that all terms and conditions are stipulated in accordance with the contract.

实际业务中，由于种种原因，如工作疏忽、电文传递错误、贸易习惯不同或买方有意利用开证的主动权加列对其有利的条款，往往会出现开立的信用证条款与合同规定不符，或者在信用证中加列一些无法满足的信用证付款条件，使得卖方无法按信用证收款。为了其安全收汇，卖方收到信用证后应对照合同逐条进行严格审核。

③ Amendment of L/C 改证

If any discrepancies exist, the seller should contact the buyer immediately for necessary amendments so as to guarantee the smooth execution of the contract.

审核时发现的任何不符点，应该立即联系买方尽快修改，以保证合同的顺利进行。

(3) Inspection and Customs Clearance 报检报关

From August 1st, 2018 on, China Customs is in charge of the inspection and quarantine of import and export commodities throughout our country.

从 2018 年 8 月 1 日开始，我国出入境产品的检验检疫工作由中国海关负责。

Before the goods are loaded, the exporter shall fill in the Export Customs Declaration Form, then makes application to custom together with the commercial invoice, packing list, weight memo and other relevant documents. The commodities which are required by the government to go through the inspection of China Customs are not permitted to be exported if they fail to pass the inspection. After the customs check and verify the goods and documents with stamping "RELEASE" on the shipping order, the goods may be shipped on board with it.

在货物装运前，出口商须填写出口报关单，连同商业发票、装箱单、重量单和其他相关单证向海关申请报检报关。凡属国家规定须法检的商品，经检验不合格的一般不得出口。海关对货、证核查无误后，在装货单上加盖"放行"章，即可凭以装船。

(4) Chartering and Booking Shipping Space 租船订舱

The exporter shall arrange for the shipment when preparing the goods. For the goods in large quantity which need to be transported by a whole ship, the exporter shall charter the vessel. For the goods in small quantity which do not need a whole ship, the exporter may book the liner space through forwarder or shipping company. After the goods are shipped, the captain or the chief mate will issue Mate's Receipt. The shipper exchanges the Bill of Lading with Mate's

Receipt from the shipping company.

出口企业在备货的同时，还需及时办理运输。货物数量大，需要整船载运的，需要办理租船手续；货物数量不大，不需要整船载运的，可由外运公司代为洽订班轮舱位。货物装船后，由船长或大副签发收货单，托运人凭收货单到船公司换取正式提单。

(5) Insurance 投保

The export trade is subject to many risks. For example, ships may sink or consignments may be damaged in transit, etc.. It is customary to insure goods for export against the perils of the journey. Under CIF term, the exporter covers insurance at his own expense as agreed in the contract. Therefore, the export shall arrange for insurance before the shipment. The cover paid for will vary according to the type of goods and the circumstances.

出口贸易要面临很多风险，如船舶可能沉没、货物可能在运输途中受损等。为避免风险，通常要为出口货物投保。CIF 术语成交，按合同规定，卖方负责投保并支付保费。因此，出口商应在货物装运前，及时向保险公司办理投保手续。所购的险种应根据货物的种类和环境的不同而不同。

(6) Documents Preparation for Bank Negotiation 制单收汇结汇

After the goods have been exported, the exporter shall prepare the full set of documents upon the request of credit. Within the validity of credit, the exporter shall present the documents to the bank for negotiation and payment. Documents should be correct, complete, concise and clean. Only after the documents are checked to be fully in conformity with the L/C, the opening bank makes the payment. Payment shall be disregarded by the bank for any discrepancies in the document.

出口货物在装运之后，出口商应按照信用证要求正确缮制各种单据，在信用证规定的交单有效期内，递交银行办理议付结汇手续。缮制的单据必须正确、完整、简明、整洁。开证行只有在审核单证和信用证完全相符后才付款。单证中任何不符点都会遭到银行的拒付。

(7) Tax Refund 出口退税

To encourage exporting, indirect taxes such as value-added tax (VAT) and consumption tax will be returned or rebated to the exporter after the conclusion of export business. To complete tax refund, the exporter should fill in Export Tax Refund Application Form and submit related documents to the local branch of SAT (State Administration of Taxation).

为了鼓励出口，出口国政府对出口货物退回其按本国税法规定已经缴纳的间接税，如增值税、消费税。申请出口退税出口商须填写出口退税申请表并向国家税务总局地方分局提交相关单证。

2. Performance of Import Contract 进口合同的履行

In case of FOB term and L/C payment, the general procedures to fulfill an import contract are follows: opening L/C, preparing for shipment, insurance, checking documents and making payment, inspection and custom clearance, taking delivery and reinspection, disputes settlement.

FOB 术语，L/C 支付的合同，进口履约程序一般包括开立信用证、运输、保险、审单付款、报检报关、提货复验、争议解决等环节。

(1) Opening L/C 开立信用证

It is one of the most important obligations for the importer to open L/C within the deadline required in the contract to the exporter. The importer should also make sure that terms of the L/C are in strict conformity with the contract. If any discrepancies found in the L/C, the exporter will ask for amendments and the importer needs to request the issuing bank to make appropriate amendments according to the contract agreed by both parties.

进口商应在合同规定的期限内向开证行办理开证申请手续，而且信用证内容应该与合同一致，否则应向开证行提出修改申请。

(2) Preparing for Shipment 运输

Under FOB term, the importer is responsible for the delivery of cargo in the nominated port of the shipment. The exporter shall inform the importer of the predict shipment date after receiving L/C. Then, on receipt of the above advice, the importer shall contact the forwarder to arrange for charter or booking vessel. Following it, the importer shall inform the exporter of the vessel name, shipment date within the specified time so that the exporter can arrange for the cargo for shipment.

在 FOB 合同下，应有进口方负责派船到指定装运港接运货物。出口方收到信用证后应将预计装船日期通知进口方。进口方接到上述通知后，应及时向货运代理公司办理租船订舱手续。在运输手续办妥后，进口方应按规定的期限将船名即船期及时通知出口方以便其备货装船。

To avoid the disjoint of goods preparation and shipment, the importer shall remind the exporter to send shipping advice as soon as the goods are shipped so that the importer may have enough time to effect insurance and prepare for the receipt of the goods.

为了防止船货脱节，进口商还应提醒出口商在货物装船后立即发出装船通知，以便进口商及时办理保险和做好接货等工作。

(3) Insurance 保险

In China, there are two ways to cover the insurance for the imported cargo in transportation, which are the insurance for each shipmen and open cover for future shipments.

我国对进口货物运输投保一般采取逐笔投保和预约投保两种方式。

Importer or consignee signs an insurance contract called Open Cover with the insurance company, specifying different coverage for different cargo, so the insurance procedures are simpler. On the receipt of the shipping advice, the importer only needs to send the cargo import advice to the insurance company (listing contract number, loading port, vessel name, shipment date, voyage No., cargo name, quantity, and amount etc.). After checked and stamped by the insurance company, the insurance procedures are finished, and the insurance company takes responsibility for the cargo.

预约投保方式是进口商或收货人同保险公司签订预约保险合同,其中对各种货物应投保的险别做了具体规定,故投保手续比较简单。进口商收到装船通知后,只要填制进口货物通知送保险公司(该通知上列明合同号、起运口岸、船名、起运日期、航线、货物名称、数量、金额等内容),经保险公司审核签章,就办妥了保险手续,保险公司则对该批货物负自动承保责任。

(4) Checking Documents and Making Payment 审单付款

After receiving the draft and the shipment documents, the payment bank (usually the issuing bank) will check and examine them in accordance with the clause of credit.

付款银行(通常是开证行)收到国外寄来的汇票及单据后,对照信用证的规定进行审核。

The issuing bank shall give the documents to the importer for recheck before making payment even though the bank has confirmed the documents are in compliance with the credit. According to the usual practice of Chinese bank, the issuing bank will fulfill payment at the request of the credit unless the importer doesn't agree within 3 work days. At the same time, the importer makes payment in RMB according to the listed Forex rate quotation to the issuing bank for the shipment documents.

如果开证行认为单据与信用证规定相符,在向外付款前也要交进口商复审。按照我国习惯,如果进口商在三个工作日内没有提出异议,开证行即按信用证规定履行付款义务。同时进口商用人民币按照国家规定的有关外汇牌价向银行买汇赎单。

In case that the documents are found not complying to the credit, it shall be settled properly depending on the specific situation, including refusal to payment, pay on receipt of cargo and inspection approval, requiring the amendment of documents, and holding the right of recourse for payment and so on.

如果审核单据发现单、证不符,可根据具体情况作出适当处理。例如,拒付;货到检验合格后付款;凭卖方或议付行出具担保付款;要求进口商修改单证;在付款的同时提出保留索赔权等。

(5) Inspection and Customs Clearance 报检报关

From August 1st, 2018 on, China Customs is in charge of the inspection and quarantine of import and export commodities throughout our country.

从2018年8月1日开始，我国出入境产品的检验检疫工作由中国海关负责。

After the arrival of the goods, the importer shall fill in the Import Customs Declaration Form, then makes application to custom together with the commercial invoice, bill of lading, packing list, weight memo and other relevant documents. The commodities which are required by the government to go through the inspection of China Customs are not allowed to be put into production, sold or used if they fail to pass the inspection. After the customs examination and the importer's payment of duty, the customs declaration form and B/L are signed and stamped, upon which the importer gets the cargo.

在货物抵达后，进口商须填写出口报关单，连同商业发票、提单、装箱单、重量单和其他相关单证向海关申请报检报关。凡属国家规定法检的商品，经检验不合格的一律不准投产、销售和使用。进口货物经海关查验并纳税后，由海关在报关单和提单上签字和加盖"验讫"章，进口商凭海关签字、盖章的提单提取进口货物。

(6) Taking Delivery and Reinspection 提货复验

After taking delivery of the goods from the carrier, the importer should inspect the goods to ensure that the goods delivered conform to the description of the goods in the contract. If the quality, quantity or packing of the goods is found not in conformity with the stipulation in the contract, the importer has the right for compensation, or even to reject the goods. If some damaged of the goods are found, the importer should bring forward the related inspection certificates issued by independent public inspection authority accepted by both parties.

提货后，进口商应检查所交货物是否与合同规定相符。若发现品质、数量或包装与合同规定不符，进口商有权提出索赔，甚至拒收货物。若发现货损，进口方须取得经双方认可的第三方检验机构出具的检验证书。

(7) Disputes Settlement 争议解决

Sometimes complains or claim inevitably arise in spite of the careful performance of a contract by the exporter and importer. They are likely to be caused by various reasons such as more or less quantity delivered, wrong goods delivered, poor packing, inferior quality, discrepancy between the samples and the goods which actually arrived, delay in shipment, etc.. In accordance with specific conditions, complains and claims may be made to the exporter importer, insurance company or shipping company. Once dispute arise, it is advised that arbitration is better than litigation, and conciliation is better than arbitration.

有时尽管进出口双方小心谨慎地履行合同，但抱怨和索赔可能由于各种原因引起，如交货数量或多或少、发错货、粗劣的包装、质量低劣、样品和实际到货之间存在差异、发运的迟误等。根据具体情况，抱怨和索赔可以向出口商、进口商、保险公司和运输公司提出。一旦发生争议，明智的选择是仲裁优于诉讼，调解优于仲裁。

Terminology 本章术语

1. business negotiation 交易磋商
2. inquiry, enquiry 询盘、询价
3. offer 发盘、发价
4. firm offer 实盘
5. non-firm offer 虚盘
6. counter offer 还盘
7. acceptance 接受
8. the United Nations Convention on Contracts for the International Sale of Goods (CISG) 《联合国国际货物销售合同公约》(简称《公约》)

Exercises 本章练习

1. What is offer? What are the necessary conditions for a valid offer?
   什么是发盘？构成一项有效发盘的条件是什么？
2. What are the provisions in the CISG for the offer's withdrawal and revocation?
   《公约》关于发盘能否撤回和撤销是怎样规定的？
3. What is the acceptance? What are the conditions for a valid acceptance?
   什么是接受？构成一项有效接受的条件是什么？
4. Can the acceptance be withdrawn?
   接受能否撤回？

Answers for Reference 参考答案

1. Offer means that one party proposed the all trade conditions to the other definitely aimed to conclude the contract. Once the other side accepts, the contract is concluded.

   发盘是指一方当事人以缔结合同为目的，将交易的全部条件十分明确肯定地向另一方所做的一种意思表示。

   According to CISG, a firm offer should conclude the following parts.
   根据《公约》的规定，一个有效的实盘应包括以下内容。
   (1) Address to one or more specific persons 向一个或一个以上特定的人提出
   (2) Indicate contractual intent 表明订约意旨

(3) Definite in contents 内容十分确定

(4) Be communicated to the offeree 传达到受盘人

2. (1) Withdrawal of an offer 发盘的撤回

According to the CISG, Art.15, "(1) An offer becomes effective when it reaches the offeree." "(2)An offer, even if it is irrevocable, may be withdrawn if the withdrawal reaches the offeree before or at the same time as the offer."

《公约》第 15 条规定："(1)发盘于送达受盘人时生效。(2)一项发盘，即使是不可撤销的，得以撤回，如果撤回通知于发盘送达受盘人之前或同时送达受盘人。"

(2) Revocation of an offer 发盘的撤销

It is stipulated in Article 16 of the CISG, "(1) Until a contract is concluded an offer may be revoked if the revocation reaches the offeree before he has dispatched an acceptance. (2)However, an offer cannot be revoked: (a) if it indicates, whether by stating a fixed time for acceptance or otherwise, that it is irrevocable; or (b) if it was reasonable for the offeree to rely on the offer as being irrevocable and the offeree has acted in reliance on the offer."

《公约》第 16 条规定，"(1)在未订立合同之前，发盘得以撤销，如果撤销通知于受盘人发出接受通知之前到达受盘人；(2)但在下列情况下，发盘不得撤销：(a)发盘写明接受发盘的期限或以其他方式表示发盘是不可撤销的；或(b)受盘人有理由信赖该项发盘是不可撤销的，而且受盘人已本着对该项发盘的信赖行事。"

3. Acceptance means that the offeree agrees with the trade terms of the offer unconditionally within the validity period of the offer, and is willing to conclude the contract with the offeror based on these terms.

接受，法律上称为"承诺"，是指受盘人在发盘的有效期内，无条件地同意发盘中提出的各项交易条件，愿意按这些条件和对方达成交易、订立合同的一种意思表示。

(1) An acceptance must be made by the specific offeree 接受必须由特定的受盘人作出

(2) An acceptance must be indicated by statement or by performing an act 接受必须通过申明或行动表示出来

(3) The contents of the acceptance must be in compliance with the offer 接受的内容必须与发盘相符

(4) An acceptance must be delivered to the offeror within the validity of the offer 接受必须在发盘有效期内传达到发盘人

4. It is stipulated in Art. 22 of the CISG, that "An acceptance may be withdrawn if the withdrawal reaches the offeror before or at the same time as the acceptance would have become effective". An acceptance will become effective when it reaches the offeror, so it can be withdrawn or amended so long as the notice of withdrawal or amendment can reach the offeror no later than the notice of the acceptance. When an acceptance has reached the offeror, namely

the acceptance has come into effect, the contract is established, which cannot be withdrawn or amended as the withdrawal or amendment for the moment equals to the revocation or the amendment of the contract.

《公约》第 22 条规定:"如果撤回通知于接受原应生效之前或同时送达发盘人,接受得以撤回。"由于接受在送达发盘人时才产生法律效力,故撤回或修改接受的通知,只要先于接受通知或与接受通知同时送达发盘人,则接受可以撤回或修改。如接受已送达发盘人,即接受一旦生效,合同即告成立,就不得撤回接受或修改其内容,因为这样做无异于撤销或修改合同。

Chapter 2　Subjects of Contract

第 2 章　国际货物贸易交易标的

Section 1　Quality of Commodity

第 1 节　商 品 品 质

1. Name of Commodity　品名

(1) Significance of Stipulating the Name of Commodity　列明品名的重要性

Name of commodity is a concept that can distinguish one goods from others. To some degree, it can reflect natural attributes or performance characteristics of a product. That is to say, products with low processing level usually reflect more natural attributes, while products with high processing level more performance characteristics.

品名，或称商品名称，是指能使某种商品区别于其他商品的一种称呼或概念。商品名称在一定程度上体现了商品的自然属性、用途以及主要的性能特征。加工程度低的商品，其名称一般较多地反映该商品所具有的自然属性，加工程度越高，商品的名称也越多地体现出该商品的性能特征。

According to the precedents over the years, terms of quality, quantity and the delivery time are defined as the terms and conditions in Anglo-American Contract Law. The consequence of breach of the terms and conditions would be very serious. The name of commodity is included in terms of quality, which is part of the quality clause. It is the basis for the buyers and sellers to deliver and receive goods, which also relates to the rights and obligations of both parties. If the goods delivered by the seller do not conform to the agreed name of commodity in the contract, the buyer will be entitled to lodge a claim, reject the goods or even terminate the contract.

根据历年的判例，英美法把合同中的品质条款、数量条款、交货期作为条件条款，如违反条件，后果十分严重。而品名是包括在品质条款中，是品质条款的一部分。品名涉及对商品的描述，是构成商品说明的一个重要组成部分，是买卖双方交接货物的一项基本依据，还关系到买卖双方的权利和义务。如果卖方交付的货物不符合合同规定的品名，买方有权提出损害赔偿、拒收货物甚至撤销合同。

(2) Points for Attention in Stipulating Name of Commodity Clause 品名条款要点

Name of commodity clause is relatively simple. Usually, it is specified in the contract under the subject "name of commodity", or listed under the subject "description of commodity" together with the quality clause. Sometimes it is just described in the beginning of the contract, such as "The seller agrees to sell and the buyer agrees to buy … on the terms and conditions stated below".

品名条款相对比较简单，通常都是在"品名"标题下，或与品质条款一起列在"商品描述"项下。有时直接列在合同的开头部分，如"双方同意按以下交易条件买入/卖出××"。

To avoid possible conflicts, the name of commodity clause should be clearly stipulated. The following points are to be noted in naming the commodity.

为了避免不必要的纠纷，规定品名条款须注意以下几点：

① The name of commodity must be clear and specific, not too vague or general in stipulation. For instance, "Chines Tea" is too general for the buyer and the seller to reach an agreement on name. In contrast, "West Lake Longjing Tea" by adding its type and place of origin, is a more concrete name for two parties to clearly understand each other.

品名规定需明确、具体，切忌空泛、笼统。如"中国茶叶"就过于笼统，买卖双方难以达成共识。而"西湖龙井茶"加上了品种和产地，表达更准确，双方的理解不易出现偏差。

② The name of commodity must be practical, not too belittled or exaggerated in expression. It should express real condition of the goods. For example, "defectless" in "Defecless Cotton Fabric" is an unnecessary modifier, because it is extremely difficult for the seller to fulfill the obligation of producing completely flawless cotton fabric.

品名规定须实事求是，切实反映商品的实际情况，不夸大也不缩小。如"无缺陷的棉布"中"无缺陷的"就是一个不必要的修饰，因卖方很难生产完全没有缺陷的棉布。

③ The name of commodity should be international standardized. A product may have different names in different counties and regions. Take "pineapple" as an example. It is known as "nanas" in Malaysia, "abacaxi" in Brazil and "nanasi" in East Africa. Possibly "pineapple" for it is internationally accepted.

品名规定须使用国际通用名称。有些商品在各地有不同的叫法。以"菠萝"为例，马来西亚称其为"nanas"，巴西叫"abacaxi"，东非叫"nanasi"，交易时尽可能使用国际通用名称"pineapple"。

④ The name of commodity should be properly chosen, if more than one is available. If the stipulation of the name of commodity has little influence on the properties of the subject matter, we should choose and utilize appropriate commodity names to lower costs and reducing tariffs.

同一商品有多个品名可选时,如果对于品名的规定对标的物的性质没有太大影响,那么注意选择和利用可以降低成本、适用较低关税的商品名称。

2. Definition of Quality of Commodity 品质的定义

Quality of commodity refers to the intrinsic attributes and the outer form or shape of the goods. The former includes the physical and mechanical properties, biological features and chemical compositions of the goods, while the latter includes shape, color, transparency, or style of the goods.

品质,又称商品质量,指的是商品本身所具有的内在特征和外观形态。前者包括商品的物理和机械性能、生物特性和化学成分,后者包括商品的外形、色泽、透明度或款式。

3. Methods of Stipulating Quality of Commodity 品质的表示方法

The qualities of commodities can be expressed in different ways. The methods of stipulating quality of commodity depend on the quality, character and the customary usage in practice. In general, there are two ways to indicate the quality of the goods either by actual goods or by description.

不同种类的商品,可以用不同的方法表示品质。表示商品品质的方法主要取决于商品的性质、特点及其在国际贸易中长期以来形成的习惯做法。归纳起来可分为凭实物和凭文字说明表示两大类。

It is worthy to note that one method is better than more to stipulate the quality of goods.

值得注意的是,能用一种方法表示商品品质则不必用两种方法。

(1) Sale by Actual Commodity 凭实物表示品质

① Sale by Inspection 看货买卖

Sale by inspection is a sale made on the basis of the actual quality of the goods that already exist at the time of contracting. Under this term, the buyer or his agent usually examines the goods at the seller's place, and the seller should deliver the examined goods by the buyer after the conclusion of the transaction. The buyer should not raise an objection as long as the seller delivers such goods. This way of sale is usually applied in consignments, auctions and fairs.

看货买卖,是指买卖双方根据成交商品的实际品质进行交易。通常是先由买方或其代理人在卖方所在地验看货物,达成交易后,卖方即按验看过的商品交付货物。只要卖方交付的是验看过的商品,买方一般就不得对品质提出异议。此类方式多用于寄售、拍卖和展卖业务。

② Sale by Sample 凭样品买卖

Sample is a small quantity of a product drawn from a whole lot, shown as evidence of the quality of the whole, or specially designed and processed by the production or user department.

The transaction that is concluded on the basis of the sample representing the quality of the whole lot can be called sale by sample.

所谓样品，是指从一批商品中抽样出来的或由生产和使用部门设计加工出来的能够代表整批商品品质的少量实物。凡以样品表示商品品质并以此作为交货依据的，称为凭样品买卖。

Sale by sample can be further divided into three kinds, i.e., sale by seller's sample, sale by buyer's sample and sale by counter sample.

凭样品买卖可分为凭卖方样品买卖、凭买方样品买卖和凭对等样品买卖三种。

In order to avoid risks, generally the seller would like to adopt sale by seller's sample rather than sale by buyer's sample. If the buyer insists on sale by buyer's sample or can only provide buyer's sample, the seller can make and send a duplicate to the buyer according to the buyer's sample. After the confirmation of the buyer, the sample will serve as the basis of the transaction and delivery. This confirmed duplicate is called counter sample or return sample. Actually, sale by counter sample is a transfer from sale by buyer's sample to sale by seller's sample.

为了规避风险，卖方一般会选择凭卖方样品成交而不是凭买方样品成交。若买方坚持用买方样品或仅能提供买方样品时，卖方可根据买方提供的样品，加工自制一个类似的样品交买方确认，在买方确认后，这一样品就作为成交或交货的依据，该样品称为对等样品，也称回样。凭对等样品买卖实际上是把凭买方样品买卖转化为凭卖方样品买卖。

Example: Sample BN001 Plush Toy Bear Size 20″

例：样品号 BN001 长毛绒玩具熊 尺码 20 英寸

③ Points for Attention in Sale by Sample 凭样品买卖应注意的事项

A. Not all the commodity can be transacted using sale by sample. It is inadvisable to adopt sale by sample when it is difficult to keep the goods in strict accordance with the sample, such as bulk agricultural products, mining products, some of the crafts, etc.. When the quality of goods can be described by the scientific indicators, sale by sample is not suitable.

并不是所有的商品都可以采用凭样品买卖。凡大货不易做到与样品完全一致时，不宜采用凭样品买卖，如大宗农副产品、工矿产品、某些工艺品等。凡能用科学的指标表示商品品质时，不宜采用凭样品买卖。

B. Samples selected should be neither the best nor the worst but the moderate one from the bulk production so as to avoid the possible financial loss due to the disputes arising from the quality inconsistency of samples with that of actual commodity delivered.

样品既不能选最好的，也不能选最差的而应在大批货物中选择中等的实物作为样品，避免由于样品与日后所交货物品质不一致引起纠纷，造成经济损失。

C. When the seller sends out the sample, it is better that the seller will keep the duplicate sample and hand it to an independent third party, such as surveyor, commodity inspection department to be sealed for further check in case of dispute.

寄样时要留有复样，交由独立的第三方，如公证行、商检部门封存，以便日后备查，一旦发生纠纷，以第三方手中的样品作为法律依据。

D. Leave some space for the seller himself for later delivery by adding such clauses in contract as "Quality shall be roughly equal to the sample" or "Quality is nearly the same as the sample". The absolute stipulation like "The whole consignment must be in complete accordance with the sample" should be avoided.

签约时留有余地，加列"品质与样品大致相同"或"品质与样品相似"等条款，以利于卖方日后交货。避免使用"大货与样品完全一致"的绝对表述。

E. For the sake of caution, such clause should be stipulated in the contract "In case the buyer's sample results in any dispute arising from infringement upon the third party's industrial property right, the seller will have nothing to do with it, and it is the buyer to be held responsibility for it."

慎重起见，合同中须订立条款"如发生由于买方样品引起工业产权等第三者权利问题，与卖方无关，概由买方负责"。

F. In order to avoid future disputes, a reference sample should carry the mark clearly showing "For Reference Only". It is not considered as the basis of delivery.

如是参考样品，要在寄样时明确表明是参考样品，不作为交货的依据，以免日后发生纠纷。

(2) Sale by Description 凭文字说明表示品质

① Sale by Specification 凭规格买卖

Specification of goods refers to some major indexes sufficiently indicating the product quality, such as chemical components, content, purity, volume, length, thickness, etc.. The approach of representation by using the specification to indicate the quality is called sale by specification. It is simple and accurate in quality stipulation, and thus becomes the most frequently used method in international trade.

规格是指一些足以反映商品质量的主要指标，如化学成分、含量、纯度、性能、容量、长短、粗细等。用商品规格确定商品品质的方法称为凭规格买卖。这种表示质量的方法简单方便、准确具体，在国际贸易中使用最为广泛。

For example, the specifications of China Northeast Soybean can be expressed as follows: moisture (max.) 15%, oil content (min.) 17%, admixture (max.) 1%, and imperfect grains (max.) 7%.

例如，我国东北豆的规格：水分(最高)15%，含油量(最低)17%，杂质(最高)1%，不完善粒(最高)7%。

② Sale by Grade 凭等级买卖

The grade of the goods refers to the classifications of the commodity of one kind which is indicated by words, numbers or symbols. When the method of "sale by grade" is used, the quality clause is simplified. The quality of the goods can be known by simply stating its grade. However, different countries have their own different grades to illustrate the goods, if the seller and the buyer cannot reach a consensus on the "grades", it's better to stipulate the specifications of each grade as well to avoid controversy.

等级是指对同类商品按照规格中若干主要指标的差异，用文字、数字或符号所作的分类。凭等级买卖简化了品质条款，只要说明等级，就可了解商品的品质。但是，不同国家等级的划分原则各不同，如果双方对等级没有共识，最好在列明等级的同时，一并规定每一等级的具体规格，以避免发生争议。

Example: Fresh Hen Eggs, shell light brown and clean, even in size

    Grade AA: 60-65 gm. per egg
    Grade A: 55-60 gm. per egg
    Grade B: 50-55 gm. per egg
    Grade C: 45-50 gm. per egg
    Grade D: 40-45 gm. per egg
    Grade E: 35-40 gm. per egg

例：鲜鸡蛋　蛋壳呈浅棕色、清洁，品质新鲜，大小均匀

    特级： 每枚蛋净重60～65克
    超级： 每枚蛋净重55～60克
    大级： 每枚蛋净重50～55克
    一级： 每枚蛋净重45～50克
    二级： 每枚蛋净重40～45克
    三级： 每枚蛋净重35～40克

③ Sale by Standard 凭标准买卖

The standard refers to the specifications or grades which are stipulated and announced (laid down and proclaimed) in a unified way by the government department or commercial organization of a country such as the chamber of commerce, etc..

标准是指政府机关或商业团体，如商业协会等统一指定和公布的规格或等级。

The standard of a commodity is subject to change or amendment and a new standard often takes place of the old one. So in case of sales by standard, it is important and necessary to mention in the terms also the name of the publication, in which the standard of the commodity appears, such as "Tetracycline HCL Tablets (Sugar Coated) 250mg. B.P. 2013".

某种商品的标准或等级经常会进行变动和修改，新的标准常常代替旧的标准。因此，

如果按标准买卖,就必须注明是按哪个版本标准,并标明援用标准的版本年份。如"四环素糖衣片,250毫克,2013年英国药典"。

As to agricultural by-products whose quality usually changes greatly, and is difficult to set a fixed standard, the term "F.A.Q" (Fair Average Quality) or "G.M.Q." (Good Merchantable Quality) is often employed to indicate the quality of the products.

对于品质变化较大难以规定统一标准的农副产品,通常采用"良好平均品质"和"上好可销品质"来表示品质。

F.A.Q., also called popular goods, refers to the average quality level of agricultural byproducts within a certain period of time according to the explanation of some countries. This kind of standard is quite ambiguous. In fact, it does not represent any fixed, accurate specification. So, F.A.Q. is generally accompanied with detailed specification.

良好平均品质,俗称大路货。据有些国家解释,指的是农副产品在某一特定的时期内所具有的中等平均水平。这种解释非常含糊不清、模棱两可,事实上它不代表任何固定的、准确的规格。因此,用F.A.Q.表示品质一般会加上具体规格。

Example: Chinese Groundnut, 2019 crop, F.A.Q.
  Moisture: (max.) 13%
  Admixture: (max.) 5%
  Oil content: (min.) 44%

例:中国花生仁,2019年产,大路货
 水分:(最高)13%
 杂质:(最高)5%
 含油量:(最低)44%

G.M.Q. requires the quality of commodity delivered by the seller to be the first-class and suitable for sale. Since such standard is not clear, it is rarely adopted and is generally applied to products such as woods and frozen fish.

上好可销品质是指卖方交货品质只需保证为上好、适合销售即可。这种标准含义不清,在国际贸易中很少使用,一般只适用于木材或冷冻鱼类等物品。

④ Sale by Brand Name or Trade Mark 凭牌名或商标买卖

Brand and trade mark are used to identify the commercial names and marks of different kinds and different quality products of different producers or marketers. As to the goods whose quality is stable, reputation is sound and with which the customers are quite familiar, we may sell it by brand name or trade.

品牌与商标都是用以识别不同生产经营者的不同种类、不同品质产品的商业名称及其标志。用牌名或商标表示品质,一般都是在国际市场上有良好信誉、品质稳定的商品,其品牌名或商标也往往为买方或消费者所熟悉喜爱。

Example: Maling Brand Worcestershire Sauce
例：梅林牌辣酱油

⑤ Sale by Name of Origin 凭产地买卖

Some commodities are more distinctive due to the unique natural condition of place of origin. Exporting companies may take the place of origin into consideration when determine the quality, such as "Fuling Zhacai" and "Guizhou Maotai", by which the products can be more distinctive and hence competitive.

某些商品由于产地的自然条件特殊等原因，制造出来的产品比同类产品更具特色，出口企业在规定品质时，可以考虑将商品的产地作为品名包含内容之一，如"涪陵榨菜""贵州茅台"等，这也可以使自己的产品更具特色，从而增强其竞争力。

⑥ Sale by Description and Illustration 凭说明书和图样买卖

The quality of come commodities, such as large-sized machines, technological instruments, electric machines, etc. cannot be simply indicated by quality indexes, instead it is quite necessary to explain in detail the structure, material, performance as well as method of operation. If necessary, pictures, photos, etc. must be provided also. The contract may stipulate: "Quality and technical data to be strictly in conformity with the description submitted by the seller."

有些商品，如大型机电、仪器产品，无法用几个简单的指标来表示其品质，必须用说明书详细地说明其结构、用材、运转性能及操作方法。如有必要，还要提供图片和照片等。可在合同中规定："品质和技术数据必须与卖方所提供的产品说明书严格相符。"

4. Quality Latitude and Quality Tolerance 品质机动幅度和品质公差

The quality delivered by the seller should be in strict conformity with the terms and conditions in the contract. But due to natural consumption during productions, production craft influence and the goods own characteristics, it is very hard to deliver the goods as per the terms and conditions stated in the contract. For such goods, more or less clause may be adopted in the contract. If the quality delivered by the seller is within the limitation of contract, this delivery can be considered to be in compliance with the contract and the buyer cannot refuse to take the delivery. Quality Latitude/Quality Flexible Allowance and Quality Tolerance are often used in practice.

卖方交货品质必须严格与合同规定的品质条款相符。但是，某些商品由于生产过程中存在自然损耗，以及受生产工艺、商品自身特点等诸多方面原因的影响，难以保证交货品质与合同规定的内容一致。对于这些商品，可以在合同中规定一些灵活条款，卖方所交商品品质只要在规定的灵活范围内，即可认为交货质量与合同相符，卖方无权拒收。常见的规定有品质机动幅度条款和品质公差条款。

(1) Quality Latitude/Quality Flexible Allowance 品质机动幅度

Quality latitude refers to the flexibility for those specific quality indications in a certain range. The following three ways are commonly used to express quality latitude.

品质机动幅度是指对特定品质指标在一定幅度内有灵活性。具体有以下三种规定方法。

① Allowed range: to allow the quality to punctuate within a range.

规定范围：允许卖方交货的品质有上下波动的范围。

Example: Yarn-dyed Gingham   Width 41/42″

例：色织条格布   宽度 41/42″

② The extremes: to require the upper limit and lower limit for the specification of quality.

规定极限：对货物的品质指标规格规定上下限。

Example: Soybean   moisture: 14% max; starch: 18% min

例：大豆   水分最高 14%；淀粉含量最低 18%

③ The variety: to allow the quality fluctuating around a certain index.

规定上下差异：允许卖方交货的品质在某一指标的上下一定范围内浮动。

Example: Down garment   down content 16%   allowing 1% more or less

例：羽绒服   含绒量 16%   允许上下浮动 1%

(2) Quality Tolerance 品质公差

Quality tolerance refers to the mean errors internationally acknowledged about quality of product. Such errors occur unavoidably during the process of manufacturing. As long as the errors of commodities are within the range of quality tolerance, the buyers are not entitled to reject the goods his way is majorly applied to manufacturing products.

品质公差是指国际上公认的产品品质的误差。这一方法主要用于工业制成品。

Example: Exported watch, the error of 0.1 second per 48 hours is acceptable

例：出口手表，允许每 48 小时误差 0.1 秒

As long as it is within the range of quality latitude or quality tolerance, payment is calculated according to price in the contract, instead of reevaluation of the price. For some goods, it can be stipulated in the contract that the price is determined by actual quality of goods delivered based on the mutual negotiation and agreement of both parties. In this case, the price can be re-evaluated according to the actual quality delivered. This is what about Price Adjusting Clause of Quality.

在品质机动幅度或品质公差内，一般不另行计算增减价，即按照合同价计收价款。但有些货物，如果经买卖双方协商同意，也可在合同中规定按交货的品质情况加价或减价，这就是品质增减价条款。

Example: China Sesame seed, Moisture (max.) 8%, Admixture (max.) 2%, Oil Content (wet basis ethyl ether extract) 52% basis. Should the oil content of the goods actually shipped be 1% higher or lower, the price will be accordingly increased or decreased by 1%, and any fraction will be proportionally calculated.

例：中国芝麻，水分(最高)8%，杂质(最高)2%，含油量(湿态、乙醚浸出物)以 52%为基础。如实际装运货物的含油量高或低 1%，价格相应增减 1%，不足整数部分，按比例计算。

Section 2 Quantity of Goods

第 2 节 商 品 数 量

Quantity clause is one of the essential terms and conditions in a contract. It is required that the seller's delivery quantity must be identical to that stipulated in the contract. The CISG stipulates that if the delivery quality is more than quantity agreed upon, the buyer may reject delivery of the excess quantity, or he may take delivery of all or part of the excess quantity, but he must pay for it at the contract rate. If the delivery is less than the agreed quantity, the seller should make up for the shortage within the deadline of delivery date without bringing any unreasonable inconvenience or expense to the buyer. However, the buyer still has the right to claim for compensation.

商品数量是国际贸易货物买卖合同的要件之一，卖方交货数量必须与合同规定的相符。《公约》规定，如卖方交货数量大于约定数量，买方可以拒收多交的部分，也可以收取多交部分中的一部分或全部，但应按合同价格付款；如卖方交货数量少于约定数量，卖方应在规定的交货期届满前补交，但不得使买方遭受不合理的不便或承担不合理的开支，即便如此，买方有保留要求赔偿的权利。

Quantity clause includes quantity and measurement unit of the traded commodities. If the quantity is calculated by weight, the clause should also contain the method of calculating weight such as gross weight, net weight, conditioned weight, etc..

数量条款包括成交商品的数量和计量单位。如果按重量计量，还包括计算重量的方法，如毛重、净重、公量等。

1. Measurement Units 计量单位

In international trade, calculation of quantity is often made in six ways. They are: by weight, by capacity, by numbers, by length, by area and by volume. As to a specific deal, its way of calculation depends on the nature, packing, means of transport and customary practice of the commodity concerned.

在国际贸易中，使用的数量计算方法通常有六种：按重量计量、按容积计量、按个数计量、按长度计量、按面积计量、按体积计量。具体交易时采用何种计量方法，要视商品的性质、包装种类、运输方法、市场习惯等决定。

The measurement units generally used in international trade are listed in the following table

(see Table 2-1 Measurement Units)

国际贸易中常用的计量单位如表 2-1 所示。

Table 2-1 Measurement Units

	Measurement Units
Weight	gram (g), kilogram (kg), ounce (oz), pound (lb), metric ton (M/T), long ton (L/T), short ton (S/T), etc.
Capacity	liter (L), gallon (gal), pint (pt), bushel (bu), etc.
Number	piece (pc), package (pkg), pair, set, dozen(doz), gross (gr), ream (rm), etc.
Length	meter (m), centimeter (cm), foot (ft), yard (yd), etc.
Area	square meter (sq m), square foot (sq ft), square yard (sq yd), etc.
Volume	cubic- meter (cu m), cubic- centimeter (cu cm), cubic- foot (cu ft), cubic- yard (cu yd), etc.

表 2-1 常用计量单位

	常用计量单位
重量	克、千克、盎司、磅、公吨、长吨、短吨等
容积	公升、加仑、品脱、蒲式耳等
个数	只、件、双、套、打、罗、令等
长度	米、厘米、英尺、码等
面积	平方米、平方英尺、平方码等
体积	立方米、立方厘米、立方英尺、立方码等

In international trade, different countries adopt different metrology apart from their different means of calculation and unit of measurement. So, the same measurement unit may indicate different quantity. For example, (UK) long ton = 1016.04690633378 kg, (US) short ton = 907.184748990598 kg.

在国际货物买卖中，除了使用的计量方法、计量单位不同以外，各国使用的度量衡制度也不相同。因此，同一计量单位表示的实际数量有时会有很大不同。如，(英制)1 长吨=1016.04690633378 千克，(美制)1 短吨=907.184748990598 千克。

At present, there are four metrologies commonly used in international trade: the metric System, the British System, the U.S. System and the International System of Units (SI). However, the metric system of S.I. units, the modern system of weights and measures that replaced the older metric system, has been universally accepted and is being adopted in all countries.

目前，国际贸易中通常使用的度量衡制度有四种：公制、英制、美制和国际单位制(简称 SI)。在公制基础上发展起来的国际单位制，已为越来越多的国家所采用。

2. Methods of Calculating Weight 计算重量的方法

In international trade, products are usually measured by weight, which is calculated as follows. It is customary to calculate the weight by net weight if the contract does not stipulate definitely.

国际贸易中，多数商品是按重量计算的，重量计算方法有以下几种。如果合同中没有明确规定，按惯例应按净重计算。

(1) Gross Weight 毛重

Gross weight is the sum of total weight of the commodity itself and the tare (the package weight), which is usually applied to commodity with low value. It is usually stipulated "gross for net" in the contract when calculate weight by gross weight.

毛重是指商品本身重量加上皮重(包装的重量)。这种计重方法一般适用于低值商品，须在合同中注明"以毛作净"。

For example, Northeast China red beans, 100 metric tons in single new gunny bags of about 100 kg each, gross for net.

如，东北小红豆，100 公吨，单层新麻袋装，每袋约 100 千克，以毛作净。

(2) Net Weight 净重

Net weight is the actual weight of commodity without the addition of the tare. In international trade, if the goods are sold by weight, the net weight is often used.

净重即货物自身的实际重量，不包括皮重。国际贸易中，以重量计算的商品，大部分是以净重计价。

There are four ways to calculate tare weight.

国际贸易中，去除皮重的方法有四种。

① Actual tare 实际皮重

It is the actual weight of packages of the whole commodities.

整批商品包装的实际重量。

② Average tare 平均皮重

In this way, the weight of packages is calculated on the basis of the average of a part of the packages.

按部分商品的实际皮重，取其平均值，然后计算出全部皮重。

③ Customary tare 习惯皮重

The weight of standardized package has a generally recognized weight which can be used to represent the weight of such packages.

有些商品的包装比较规格化，并为市场所公认，可以代表这种包装的重量。

④ Computed tare 约定皮重

The weight of packages is calculated according to the tare previously agreed upon by the seller and the buyer instead of actual weight.

无须实际衡量，以买卖双方事先协商约定的皮重为准。

(3) Conditioned Weight 公量

Conditioned weight is the weight derived from the process, with which the moisture content of the commodity is removed and standardized moisture added both by scientific methods. This kind of calculating method is suitable to those cargoes, which are of high economic value and with unsteady moisture content (whose water contents are not stable), such as wool, raw silk, etc..

在计算货物重量时，使用科学方法，抽去商品中所含水分，再加标准水分重量，求得的重量称为公量。这种计重方法主要使用于少数经济价值较高而水分含量极不稳定的商品，如羊毛、生丝等。

(4) Theoretical Weight 理论重量

This method is applicable to commodities with regular specifications and regular sizes, such as galvanized iron and steel plate. Theoretical weight is calculated by multiplying the total number and the weight of each unit.

理论重量适用于有固定规格形状和尺寸的商品，如马口铁、钢板等。每件重量乘以总件数即为理论重量。

(5) Legal Weight and Net Net Weight 法定重量和净净重

According to laws of customs in some countries, specific duty should be levied according to the legal weight of the goods involved. Legal weight equals to the weight of the commodity plus the weight of the package directly touching the goods, such as sales package.

按照一些国家海关法规定，在征收从量税时，商品的重量是以法定重量计算的。法定重量是纯商品的重量加上直接接触商品的包装物料，如销售包装的重量。

Subtracting outer packaging weight from the gross weight is net weight, and then subtracting inner packaging in direct contact with the commodity is "net net weight". It's also mainly used for tax calculating.

从毛重中减去外包装的重量为净重，再从净重中减去直接接触商品的包装重量即为净净重。净净重的计量方法主要也为海关征税时使用。

3. More or Less Clause 数量的机动幅度(溢短装条款)

To successfully fulfill the contract and avoid the disputes, the quantity clause in the contracts should be specific and clear enough without expressions like "about" "approximate" and "or so".

为了便于履行合同和避免引起争议，进出口合同中的数量条款应当明确具体，避免使用"大约""相似""左右"等表达。

However，it is very difficult to measure accurately those bulk goods of agricultural and mineral products like corn, soybean, wheat, coal, etc., in some cases, because of the change of goods resources or the limitation of processing, the quantity of the goods last delivered may be not in accordance with the stipulations in the contract. What's more, influenced by natural conditions, packing patterns, loading and unloading methods, the quantity of goods delivered by the seller usually doesn't conform to the quantity definitely stipulated in the contract. In order to facilitate the processing of the contract, the seller and the buyer will generally use "more or less clause" when stipulating the quantity clause. It means that the buyer and the seller stipulate in a contract that the seller is allowed to deliver the goods within a certain percentage of more or less than the contracted quantity.

但是，有些大宗散装农产品和工矿业产品，如玉米、大豆、小麦、煤等很难计算其准确数量，此外，某些商品由于货源变化、加工条件限制等，往往在最后出货时实际数量与合同规定数量有所出入。并且，受自然条件、包装方式、装卸货方法等因素的影响，卖方所交货物往往很难与合同中规定的数量一致。为了便于顺利履行合同，买卖双方在规定数量条款时通常还会规定"溢短装条款"。买卖双方在合同中规定卖方的实际交货数量可以比合同规定的数量多交或少交百分之几，但不超过一定的范围。

Example: Zinc ingot, 10000 metric tons, with 5% more or less at seller's option.

例：锌锭，10000公吨，卖方可溢短装5%。

A complete more or less clause should include three parts, namely the range of flexibility of quantity, the option of "more or less", and the pricing of the "more or less" part of the goods.

一个完整的溢短装条款包括三部分，即数量机动幅度的范围、溢短装的选择权和溢短装部分的作价方法。

Generally speaking, the seller is to decide the quantity difference when the goods are delivered. As stipulated in a contract, it is also practical to allow the shipper or the party in charge of shipment to decide the quantity according to the capacity of cabin. For example, under the FOB terms, it is the buyer to charter a liner to carry the goods, so in the contract we can stipulate that the shipper or the buyer determines the quantity difference.

按照惯例，实际交货时一般由卖方决定溢短装，也可按合同的规定，根据仓容的大小有船方或负责安排运输的一方来决定。如FOB术语下由买方负责派船，也可在合同中规定由买方或船方来决定机动幅度的大小。

As for the pricing of the "more or less" part of the goods, the price in the contract is taken for granted if there is no other agreement. However, some contracts may stipulate that the price of the "more or less" part of the goods should be determined according to market price at the time of shipment or arrival so that the seller cannot take advantage of the more or less clause to load more or less on purpose and harm the interests of the buyer when international market price fluctuates.

溢短装部分作价办法，如果合同中没做另外规定，一般按合同价格计算。但也有的合同规定按装船日或卸货日的市场价格计算，以免卖方利用溢短装条款在国际市场价格波动时有意多装或少装，给买方带来不利。

According to the convention, when the numbers or items of some commodities (such as automobiles, color televisions and other manufactured goods) can be accurately calculated, it is not suitable to adopt more or less clause. (UCP 600 Article 30)

按惯例，某些个数、件数可以精确计数的商品(如汽车、彩电等工业制成品)不适用溢短装条款。

Section 3　Packing and Marks of Goods

第3节　商品包装与标志

Packing clause is an essential term of an international trade contract. According to the CISG, the buyer is entitled to reject the goods if the seller's delivered goods fail to be packaged in accordance with the agreed terms.

包装条款是国际货物买卖合同的一项主要条款。《公约》规定，如卖方所交的货物未按约定的条件包装，买方有权拒收货物。

In the international trade, while cargoes are transported, they fall into three groups based on whether they need packing or not: nude cargo, bulk cargo and packed cargo. Nude cargo refers to cargoes with stable qualities and to be shipped without any packages or in simple bundles, such as steel products, lead ingot, timber, rubber, automobile, etc.. Bulk cargo refers to goods which are shipped or even sold without packages on the conveyance in bulk, such as oil, ore, grain, coal, etc.. Packed cargo refers to commodities which need packing during the shipping, storing and sales process.

进出口货物根据是否加以包装可分为三大类：裸装货、散装货和包装货。裸装货是指品质稳定、无须包装或只需略加捆扎的货物，如钢材、铅锭、木材、橡胶、车辆等。散装货是只未加任何包装直接付运甚至销售的货物，如石油、矿砂、粮食、煤炭等。包装货指的是在运输、仓储和销售过程中需要包装的货物。

Most of commodities in international trade need certain degree of packing. According to the functions of the package in the process of circulating, packing can be divided into sales packing (also called inner packing) and transport packing (also called outer packing). A third kind of packing, neutral packing is also often used in international trade.

大多数国际贸易货物都属于包装货。根据包装在商品流通过程中的作用，包装可分为销售包装(也称内包装)和运输包装(也称外包装)。另一种包装——中性包装，也经常在国际贸易中使用。

1. Sales Packing (Inner Packing) 销售包装

Sales packing, also called inner packing or small packing, is in direct contact with the commodity and will get into sales outlets with the product to meet the consumer. It is not only adopted as a form of protection to reduce the risks of goods being damaged in transit, but mainly with the purpose of promoting sales.

销售包装又称内包装、小包装，是指直接接触商品并随商品进入销售网点和消费者直接见面的包装。它除了保护商品免受损坏以外，主要起促销作用。

(1) Types of Sales Packing 销售包装的种类

Sales packing can be designed with various packing materials, different structures and styles, based on different characteristics and shape of the goods. Sales packing can be divided into hanging packing, stacked packing, portable packing, easy-open packing, spray packing, set packing, gift packing and reusable packing.

根据商品的特征和形状，销售包装可采用不同的包装材料和不同的造型结构与式样。销售包装可分为挂式包装、堆叠式包装、携带式包装、易开包装、喷雾包装、配套包装、礼品包装以及复用包装。

(2) Instructions and Signs on Sales Packing 销售包装上的标志和说明

① Pictures on the package 包装的图案

Pictures for the sales packing should be pleasing and artistically attractive to reflect the features of goods. The patterns and colors adopted should cater to the national customs and favors of the target countries.

销售包装的图案要美观大方，富有艺术上的吸引力，以突出商品特点。图案和色彩应与有关国家的民族习惯和爱好相适应。

② Verbal instructions 文字说明

There should be necessary verbal instructions on the sales packing, such as k trademark, brand name, commodity name, name of origin, quantity, specification, composition, purpose and usage. The verbal instructions and the pictures on the package should be closely coordinated and set off and complement each other, with the purpose of publicity and promotion. The words used must be concise and understandable to the consumers in the sales market and multiple languages can be used if needed. When verbal instructions and labels are used on the sales packing, the rules about label management in the target countries should also be taken into consideration as well.

销售包装上应有必要的文字说明，如商标、品牌、品名、产地、数量、规格、成分、用途和使用方法等。文字说明应同图案紧密配合、互相衬托、彼此补充，以达到宣传和促销的目的，使用的文字还需简明扼要，并能让销售市场的顾客看懂，必要时也可以同时使用多种语言。在销售包装上使用文字说明或制作标签时，还应注意有关国家标签管理的规定。

③ Bar code 条形码

Bar code, consisted of a group of numbers and black and white parallel lines in different widths and intervals, is a special code language used to input data through computers with photoelectric scanning devices for reading. When the bar code is pointed to the position of the photoelectric scanning device, the information carried by the bar code can be automatically read by the computer, such as the name, category, quantity, production date, manufacturer and place of origin. Commodity without bar codes cannot enter into supermarket. Some countries prohibit importing products without bar codes.

商品包装上的条形码由一组带有数字的黑白及粗细间隔不等的平行条纹所组成，这时利用光电扫描阅读设备为计算机输入数据的特殊的代码语言。只要将条形码对准光电扫描器，计算机就能自动识别条形码的信息，确定品名、品种、数量、生产日期、制造厂商和产地等。没有条形码的商品不能进入超市。有些国家规定没有条形码的商品，不予进口。

2. Transport Packing (Outer Packing) 运输包装

Transport packing, also called outer packing. The major function of transport packing is to protect the goods from the damage and losses during the storage and transportation process, and avoid at utmost the possible influences exerted by the outside circumstance on the way of the transportation. It facilitates the examination, numbering and division.

运输包装，又称外包装，其主要作用在于保护商品，防止在储运过程中发生货损货差，并最大限度地避免运输途中各种外界条件对商品可能产生的影响，方便检验、计数和分拨等。

(1) Types of Transport Packing 运输包装的种类

① Single-piece transport packing 单件运输包装

Single-piece transport packing means that the cargoes are packed as a single unit, i.e., a measuring unit, in the transportation process. It can be sub-divided into case, including wooden case, crate, carton, corrugated carton and skeleton case, etc., drum or cask, including wooden drum, iron drum and plastic cask, etc., bag, including gunny bag, cloth bag, paper bag and plastic bag, etc., bundle or bale, which is suitable for wool, cotton, feather, grege silk and piece goods, etc. which are to be compressed into bales for first and then packed with cotton cloth and gunny cloth strengthened by metal or plastic straps outside.

单件运输包装指的是货物在运输过程中作为一个计件单位的包装，可细分为如下四种：箱，包括木箱、板条箱、纸箱、瓦楞纸箱、漏孔箱等；桶，包括木桶、铁桶、塑料桶等；

袋，包括麻袋、布袋、纸袋、塑料袋等；包，羽毛、羊毛、棉花、生丝、布匹等可紧压的商品可以先经机压打包，压缩体积后，再以棉布、麻布包裹，外加箍铁和塑料带，捆包成件。

② Collective transport packing 集合运输包装

Collective transport packing is also called group shipping packing by which a certain number of single pieces are grouped together to form a big packing or are packed in a big container. Collective transport packing usually includes container, pallet and flexible container.

集合运输包装是指在单件运输包装的基础上，将若干单件包装组合成一件大包装。常见的集合运输包装有集装箱、托盘和集装袋。

(2) Marks of Transport Packing 运输包装的标志

According to its function, marks of transport packing can be classified into the following types: shipping marks, indicative marks, warning marks, weight and volume marks, marks of origin.

运输包装的标志，依据其用途，可分为运输标志、指示性标志、警告性标志、重量体积标志和产地标志等。

① Shipping marks 运输标志

The function of a shipping mark is to identify the goods in the process of transporting, loading and unloading, storage, customs clearance and handover in international. As one of the most important elements agreed on by parties concerned, shipping marks are stenciled not only on the transport parking of cargoes, but also on the invoice, bill of lading, packing lists and some other documents.

运输标志又称唛头，其作用在于使货物在国际贸易运输、装卸、储存、清关交接过程中便于识别。唛头是买卖双方必须达成一致的重要事项之一，不仅须印刷在运输包装之上，还须在发票、提单、装箱单等单据上标出。

Usually four types of information are included in shipping marks as per the ISO standard:
国际标准化组织(ISO)建议的唛头通常包括以下四项信息。

A. Initial letters or abbreviation of a consignee or buyer
收货人或买方名称字首或简写

B. Reference number (contract number, order number，invoice number or credit number)
参考号(合同号、订单号、发票号或信用证号)

C. Destination
目的港(地)

D. Number of package (including the consecutive number of each package and the total number of the shipment)
件数号码(包括每一件货物的顺序号和包装货物的总数)

Example: 例：
　　SMCO……………………….Abbreviation of consignee　收货人简称
2018/C NO.123456………………….Reference No.　参考号
　　NEW YORK ……………………Destination　目的港(地)
　　NO. 1-20………………………..Package No.　件数

② Indicative marks　指示性标志

Indicative marks, shown by graphs or words, are requirements or notes for the carriage, loading, unloading or storage of those goods that are prone to be fragile, damaged and deteriorated. "KEEP DRY" "UPWARD" "FRAGILE" and "NO HOOK" are typical examples.

指示性标志，是根据商品的特性，对一些容易破碎、残损、变质的商品，在搬运装卸和存放保管等方面所提出的要求和注意事项，用图形或文字表示。例如，典型的标志有"怕湿""向上""小心轻放""禁用手钩"等。

③ Warning marks　警告性标志

In warning marks, graphs or words are used to show all kinds of dangerous cargoes such as explosive, inflammable, corrosive, oxidant and radioactive substance. The function of such marks is to warn the persons of handling, transporting and storing to take relevant measures according to the information of such marks so as to ensure the personal and goods safety.

警告性标志，是指在装有爆炸品、易燃物品、腐蚀物品、氧化剂和放射物质等危险货物的运输包装上用图形或文字表示各种危险品的标志。其作用是警告有关装卸、运输和保管人员按货物特性采取相应的措施，以保障人身和物资的安全。

④ Weight and volume marks　重量体积标志

Weight and volume marks indicate the volume or gross/net weight of the package to facilitate loading and unloading, or booking shipping space.

重量体积标志是指在运输包装上标明包装的体积和毛重，以方便储运过程中安排装卸作业和舱位。

Example:

Gross weight 54kgs

Net weight 52kgs

Measurement 42 cm × 28 cm × 18cm

⑤ Marks of origin　产地标志

Some countries view marks of origin as an indispensable part of goods description, and require the name of origin to be marked on both transport packing and inner packing. For instance, Chinese export commodities are always printed with "Made in China".

一些国家要求商品的内外包装上均须注明产地，作为商品说明的一种重要内容。例如，我国出口商品包装上均注明"中国制造"。

3. Neutral Packing and Brand Designated by the Buyer 中性包装和定牌

(1) Neutral Packing 中性包装

Neutral packing is a special type of packing, which makes no mention of the country of origin, the name and address of the manufacture on the product and inner and outer packing. It can be divided into neutral packing with designated brand name and neutral packing without designated brand name. The former means the brand and trade mark designed by the buyer are marked out on the product and package, but with no indication of the country of origin. The latter means neither brand and trade mark nor the country of origin are marked out on the product or package.

中性包装是指在商品和内外包装上不注明生产国别和生产厂商的包装。中性包装又分定牌中性包装和无牌中性包装。定牌中性是指在商品和包装上使用买方指定的商标/牌名，但不注明生产国别。无牌中性指的是在商品和包装上均不使用任何商标/牌名，也不注明生产国别。

The purpose of using neutral packing is to break down the discriminatory tariffs and restrictions of some importing countries. It is also a flexible method adopted by some exporting countries to expand export.

中性包装是为了打破某些进口国关税歧视和限制，也是某些出口商为了扩大出口采用的一些灵活做法。

(2) Brand Designated by the Buyer 定牌

Brand designated by the buyer means that the seller marks trade mark or brand name on the package of the commodity or the commodity itself at the buyer's request.

定牌是指按买方要求在出口国商品和包装上使用买方指定的商标或牌名的做法。

At present, in many countries, commodities sold by supermarkets, large department stores, specialized stores, chain stores are usually marked with their own trademarks or brand names on the package, in order to raise name recognition and promote the worth of goods. Exporters would like to accept brand designated by the buyer with the purpose of taking advantage of the operation abilities and the business and brand reputation of the buyer, so as to raise sales price and expand production. For example, manufacturers of sports shoes' production who have world famous trademarks like NIKE and RECBOK have based their main production in China.

当前，许多国家的超市、大百货公司和专营店、连锁店出售的商品都要在商品或包装上标有本店使用的商标或品牌，以扩大本店的知名度和显示该商品的价值。许多出口商为了利用买主的经营能力及其商业信誉和品牌声誉，提高售价和扩大销路，也愿意接受定牌生产。如生产运动鞋的世界著名商标NIKE、RECBOK，它们的主要生产基地都在中国。

It's important to stipulate explicitly in the contract that if the trademarks or brand provided by the buyer result in any disputes with a third party, it is the provider to assume all the responsibility, in case that the manufacturer infringe the rights of the third party without knowledge, which results in losses.

应在合同中明确规定，客户提供的品牌商标如果和第三方发生纠纷，一切责任由提供方成承担。以免生产商在不知情的情况下侵犯了第三方的权利，造成损失。

4. Clause of Packing 包装条款

The packing clause usually includes packing material, packing method and quantity of the goods. Examples are to be shown as follows.

包装条款通常包括包装材料、包装方式和每件包装的商品数量等。示例如下：

In wooden cases containing 50 paper boxes of one dozen each
木箱装，每箱 50 纸盒，每盒一打

Each set packed in one export carton, each 810 cartons transported in one 40ft container
每台装一个出口纸箱，810 纸箱装 1 只 40 英尺集装箱运送

In cloth bales each containing 20 pcs. of 42 yds
布包，每包 80 套，每套塑料袋装

Terminology 本章术语

1. name of commodity 商品名称，品名
2. description of goods 商品描述
3. original sample/ representative sample 原样/代表样品
4. duplicate/ keep sample 留样
5. counter sample 对等样品
6. sealed sample 封样
7. reference sample 参考样品
8. fair average quality (F. A. Q.) 良好平均品质
9. good merchantable quality (G. M. Q.) 上等可销品质
10. quality latitude 品质机动幅度
11. quality tolerance 品质公差
12. more or less clause 溢短装条款
13. cargo in bulk 散装货
14. nude cargo 裸装货
15. sales packing 销售包装
16. transport packing 运输包装
17. shipping mark 运输标志，唛头

18. neutral packing with designated brand 定牌中性包装
19. neutral packing without designated brand 无牌中性包装

Exercises 本章练习

1. What is more or less clause?
   什么溢短装条款?

2. What is neutral packing with designated brand name?
   什么是定牌中性包装?

3. What are the elements of a standard shipping mark?
   标准的唛头由哪些要素组成?

4. When a sale is made by buyer's sample, how should the seller avoid risks?
   凭买方样品买卖,卖方如何避免风险?

5. What is the quality tolerance? What is quality latitude?
   什么是品质公差? 什么是品质机动幅度?

Answers for Reference 参考答案

1. "more or less clause" means that the buyer and the seller stipulate in a contract that the seller is allowed to deliver the goods within a certain percentage of more or less than the contracted quantity.

"溢短装条款"指的是买卖双方在合同中规定卖方的实际交货数量可以比合同规定的数量多交或少交百分之几,但不超过一定的范围。

2. Neutral packing with designated brand name means the brand and trade mark designed by the buyer are marked out on the product and package, but with no indication of the country of origin.

定牌中性是指在商品和包装上使用买方指定的商标/牌名,但不注明生产国别。

3. Usually four types of information are included in shipping marks as per the ISO standard:

A. Initial letters or abbreviation of a consignee or buyer

B. Reference number (contract number, order number, invoice number or credit number)

C. Destination

D. Number of package (including the consecutive number of each package and the total number of the shipment)

国际标准化组织(ISO)建议的唛头通常包括:收货人或买方名称字首或简写;参考号(合

同号、订单号、发票号或信用证号)；目的港(地)；件数号码(包括每一件货物的顺序号和包装货物的总数)。

4. For the sake of caution, such clause should be stipulated in the contract "In case the buyer's sample results in any dispute arising from infringement upon the third party's industrial property right, the seller will have nothing to do with it, and it is the buyer to be held responsibility for it".

慎重起见，合同中须订立条款"如发生由于买方样品引起工业产权等第三者权利问题，与卖方无关，概由买方负责"。

5. Quality tolerance refers to the mean errors internationally acknowledged about quality of product. Such errors occur unavoidably during the process of manufacturing. Quality latitude refers to the flexibility for those specific quality indications in a certain range.

品质公差是指国际上公认的产品品质的误差。品质机动幅度是指对特定品质指标在一定幅度内有灵活性。

Chapter 3　Pricing of Goods

第 3 章　国际货物贸易商品定价

Terms of price are the core terms in a contract. The content, which is related to buyers and sellers' mutual vital interests and the feasibility of a transaction, is playing an important role in constituting other terms in the contract. Legitimately grasping the methods of pricing and reasonably establishing the terms of price have significance on fulfilling missions of importing and exporting and improving economic benefits.

买卖合同中的价格条款是合同中的核心条款。其内容直接对合同中的其他条款产生重大影响，涉及买卖双方切身利益、涉及双方能否成交的实质问题。正确掌握成交价格，合理采用各种作价方法、订好合同中的价格条款，对贯彻外贸政策，完成进出口任务，提高外贸经济效益意义重大。

Section 1　Components of Price Term and Trade Terms

第 1 节　价格构成与贸易术语

1. Components of Price Term 价格构成

Terms of price are the terms in the contract which stipulate the unit price, total amount, money of account, money of payment, method of pricing and so on. A unit price of commodity is composed of four indispensable parts: Money of Account, Unit Price Figure, Unit of Measurement and Trade Terms. The terms of price in the contract shall truly reflect the result of price negotiation between the buyer and the seller. Therefore, the contents of price terms shall be complete, clear, specific and accurate.

For instance, Unit price: USD 0.7 per box CIF HAMBURG. Total value: USD 14,580 (Say U.S. Dollars Fourteen Thousand Five Hundred and Eighty Only).

价格条款是规定商品单价、总金额、计价货币、支付货币、作价方法等内容的合同条款。商品的单价由四个部分组成，缺一不可：计价货币、单位价格金额、计量单位、贸易术语。合同中的价格条款应真实反映买卖双方价格磋商的结果，因此，条款内容应完整、明确、具体、准确。

例如，单价：每盒 0.7 美元 CIF 汉堡。总金额：14580 美元(壹万肆仟伍佰捌拾美元)。

2. Trade Terms 贸易术语

International commodity prices are consisted of not only unit price and total amount but also related trade terms which indicate liabilities, costs and risks between the seller and buyer.

国际贸易商品价格构成中，除了要规定单价、总额外，还要规定贸易术语，以表明买卖双方在货物交接过程中有关责任、费用、风险的划分问题。

(1) Definitions and Functions of International Trade Terms 国际贸易术语的定义及作用

International trade terms, also referred to as price terms or price conditions, are abbreviations of letters or words specifying specific price composition and liabilities, cost and risk in the delivery of goods between the seller and buyer.

国际贸易术语(International trade Terms)也称为价格术语、价格条件，是指用短语或英文缩写来说明商品的价格构成及买卖双方在货物的交接过程中有关的风险、责任和费用划分问题的专门用语。

Trade terms, which are used as unified and specific language for worldwide merchants, take shape gradually in international practice and greatly simplify dealing procedures, improve efficiency, promote the development of international trade and play significant roles in international trade.

贸易术语是在长期的国际贸易实践中逐渐发展形成的，作为全世界国际贸易行业的统一专门用语，大大简化了交易程序，提高了交易效率，有力地促进了国际贸易的发展，在国际贸易中具有重要作用。

(2) International Trade Customs Relating to Trade Terms 有关贸易术语的国际贸易惯例

International trade customs are universally recognized customary ways of doing business and explanation evolving in the long process of trade development and has been compiled by relative international organizations into rules and regulations which are acquainted, recognized and adopted by many trading organizations in most countries.

国际贸易惯例是在国际贸易的长期实践中逐步发展、形成的具有普遍意义的一些习惯做法和解释，经过有关国际组织的编纂与解释成为规则、条文，并为较多的国家或贸易团体所熟悉、承认和采用。

① Nature of International Trade Customs 国际贸易惯例的性质

A. International trade customs are not compulsory since they are not legislations or laws for all countries, neither legislations or laws of a certain country.

它不是各国的共同立法，也不是某一国的法律，不具有法律的强制性。

B. When both parties cite one international custom, it becomes legally valid and both parties are subject to it.

当买卖双方在合同中援引某项惯例时，则该惯例即具有法律效力，对双方均有约束力，有法律强制性。

C. Even if the contract does not indicate which custom the contract is subject to, the custom still has binding force.

合同中未引入某项惯例，惯例仍有约束力。

When disputes arise during the contract execution, court of justice or arbitration agencies usually makes ruling according to the customs, thus the customs are influential to some extent. Especially lately, some international conventions and laws endow the customs legality. China's laws indicate what the law fails to cover is subject to international trade customs. CISG stipulates that the commonly used and universally known customs which are not excluded from the contract are binding to both parties.

Therefore, it is of great significance to get familiar with the customs and carry out trade practices.

在执行合同中发生争议时，法院判决、仲裁机构仲裁往往以惯例作为准则进行裁决，因此这些惯例实际上有一定的影响力，特别是目前新的趋势，某些国际公约或某些国家以立法的形式直接赋予惯例法律效力。如我国的法律规定：凡是中国法律没有规定的适用国际贸易惯例。《公约》规定：合同没有排除的惯例，已经知道或应当知道的惯例和经常使用反复遵守的惯例对双方当事人均有约束力。

因此熟悉并掌握有关的国际贸易惯例并按照惯例来进行国际贸易业务的操作，具有非常重要的意义。

D. If the contract clauses conflict with customs, the contract to be followed is considered as a basic principle.

如果合同的条款与惯例有冲突，将遵循合同优先惯例的原则。

E. Both parties could make out some clause different from customs when signing a contract on the principle of contract first and contract freedom.

遵循契约至上、契约自由的原则，合同双方当事人在签订合同时也可以做出与惯例不同的规定。

② Three Main International Rules on Trade Terms 三个主要国际贸易惯例

A. "WARSAW-OXFORD RULES 1932"《1932 年华沙—牛津规则》

They are rules for CIF contracts drafted at a conference of the international law association in Warsaw. In the mid 19th century, CIF is widely applied in international trade, however, there are no unified explanations or rules on each party's obligations, misunderstandings and disputes frequently arise. International law association drafted and adopted rules for CIF contracts in the capital of Poland, Warsaw in 1928. After that, this rule was combined into 21 provisions in Oxford conference in 1932 and renamed as Warsaw-Oxford rules 1932 used till now.

Warsaw-Oxford rules state that these rules are not legally binding and are to both parties, option; once the rules are explicitly adopted, both parties shall be subject to them. In sales contract, the clauses could be different from the rules and each rule could be altered or added according to both parities' agreement. If conflicts arise between the clauses and the rules, refer to the clauses. If the contract contains no relating clauses, refer to the rules.

《1932 年华沙—牛津规则》由国际法协会制定，专门解释 CIF 这一贸易术语。19 世纪中叶起，CIF 贸易术语在国际贸易中得到了广泛应用，由于这一贸易术语中买卖双方各自承担的义务没有统一的规定和解释，在交易中经常发生争议和纠纷。国际法协会于 1928 年在波兰首都华沙起草并制定 CIF 统一规则。其后，于 1932 年牛津会议上，将此规则定为 21 条，更名为《1932 年华沙—牛津规则》，沿用至今。

《1932 年华沙—牛津规则》在总则中说明，这一规则并无法律约束力，仅供双方自愿使用，凡明示采用本规则的，合同当事人应按照本规则的规定办理。在买卖合同中，经双方当事人协议，也可以做出与该规则不同的规定，也可以对本规则的任何一条进行变更、修改或增添。如本规则与合同发生冲突，以合同为准。但合同中没有规定的事项，应按本规则办理。

B. Revised American Foreign Trade Definition 1941《1941 年美国对外贸易定义修订本》

Revised American Foreign Trade Definition was developed by nine American business groups in 1919 and was originally called as U.S. Regulations of Export Quotations and Abbreviations. It was later amended at the 27th national foreign trade conference of USA in 1941 and renamed as Revised American Foreign Trade Definition 1941. This revision is approved by a joint committee of Chamber of Commerce of the United States of America, American Importers Association (AIA) and National Foreign Trade Council, etc., and is published by National Foreign Trade Council.

It includes 6 terms, namely, EX (Point of Origin), FOB (Free on Board), FAS, C&F, CIF and EX DOCK and is used in some North American and Latin American countries.

美国对外贸易定义是由美国 9 大商业团体于 1919 年制定，原称为《美国出口报价及其缩写条例》。后来又于 1941 年在美国第 27 届全国对外贸易会议上对该条例进行了修订，定名为《1941 年美国对外贸易定义修订本》。这一修订本经美国商会、美国进口商协会、全国对外贸易协会等所组成的联合委员会通过，由全国对外贸易协会予以公布。

内容包括六种术语：EX (Point of Origin) 产地交货；FOB (Free on Board) 在运输工具上交货；FAS (Free Alongside) 在运输工具旁边交货；C&F (Cost and Freight) 成本加运费；CIF (Cost, Insurance and Freight) 成本加保险费、运费； EX DOCK (Named Port of Importation) 目的港码头交货。术语适用地区：北美、一些拉丁美洲国家。

C. International Rules for The Interpretation of Trade Terms《国际贸易术语解释通则》

International Rules for The Interpretation of Trade Terms (abbreviated as INCOTERMS) are the most widely used, most influential and most important international practices published by ICC and all trade terms in this textbook are subject to it. INCOTERMS was first created in 1936 and has been regularly updated to keep pace of the development of the international trade. The latest version, INCOTERMS 2020 came into force on 1st January, 2020.

INCOTERMS 1990 consists of 13 trade rules. INCOTERMS 2000 groups the 13 rules into 4 categories (See Table 3-1). INCOTERMS 2010 updates and consolidates the "delivered", rules, reducing the total number of rules from 13 to 11. In the INCOTERMS 2010 rules, DAF, DES, DEQ and DDU are replaced by two new INCOTERMS rules DAT and DAP. INCOTERMS 2010 presents 11 rules in two distinct classes: Rules for any mode or modes of transportation, EXW, FCA, CPT, CIP, DAT, DAP and DDP; Rules for sea and inland waterway transportation, FAS, FOB, CFR and CIF (See Table 3-2).In the INCOTERMS 2020 rules, DAT (Delivered at Terminal) has been renamed DPU (Delivered at Place Unloaded) (See Table 3-3).

Table 3-1　Main Trade Terms of INCOTERMS 2000

Group E Departure	EXW		Ex Works
Group F Delivery (Main Carriage Unpaid)	FCA	Shipment Contract	Free Carrier
	FAS		Free Alongside Ship
	FOB		Free On Board
Group C Delivery (Main Carriage Paid)	CFR		Cost And Freight
	CIF		Cost, Insurance and Freight
	CPT		Carriage Paid To
	CIP		Carriage and Insurance Paid To
Group D Arrival	DAF	Arrival Contract	Delivered At Frontier
	DES		Delivered Ex Ship
	DEQ		Delivered Ex Quay
	DDU		Delivered Duty Unpaid
	DDP		Delivered Duty Paid

《国际贸易术语解释通则》(简称《通则》，INCOTERMS)，是目前使用最广泛、影响最大、最重要的一个国际贸易惯例，本书所提到的贸易术语的解释都以该通则为准。《国际贸易术语解释通则》最早发布于1936年，后经多次修订。最新的一次修订就是2020年1月1日生效的《2020通则》。

1990年修订时主要内容包含13个贸易术语。《2000通则》保留了这13个贸易术语，并把贸易术语分成4组(见表3-1)。《2010通则》改为11个贸易术语，删去了原来D组的DAF、DES、DEQ和DDU，新增加了DAT和DAP。《2010通则》把这11个贸易术语分成两组。一组是可以适用于任何运输方式或多种运输方式的术语：EXW、FCA、CPT、CIP、

DAT、DAP 与 DDP；另一组为适用于海运及内河水运的术语：FAS、FOB、CFR 与 CIF(见表 3-2)。《2020 通则》将 DAT(运输终端交货)重命名为 DPU(卸货地交货)(见表 3-3)。

表 3-1 《2000 通则》主要贸易术语

E 组 启运	EXW		工厂交货
F 组 装运(主运费未付)	FCA FAS FOB	出口地交货贸易术语， 装运合同	货交承运人 船边交货 船上交货
C 组 装运(主运费已付)	CFR CIF CPT CIP		成本加运费 成本、保险费加运费 运费付至 运费、保险费付至
D 组 到达	DAF DES DEQ DDU DDP	到达合同	边境交货 目的港船上交货 目的港码头交货 未完税交货 完税后交货

Table 3-2 Main Trade Terms of INCOTERMS 2010

表 3-2 《2010 通则》主要贸易术语

\multicolumn{3}{c}{Group1 Incoterms that apply to any mode of transport are: 第一组：适用于任何运输方式的术语}
EXW	Ex Works	工厂交货
FCA	Free Carrier	货交承运人
CPT	Carriage Paid To	运费付至
CIP	Carriage and Insurance Paid To	运费、保险费付至
DAT	Delivered At Terminal	运输终端交货
DAP	Delivered At Place	目的地交货
DDP	Delivered Duty Paid	完税后交货
\multicolumn{3}{c}{Group2 Incoterms that apply to sea and inland waterway transport only: 第二组：适用于海上和内陆水上运输方式的术语}
FAS	Free Alongside Ship	船边交货
FOB	Free On Board	船上交货
CFR	Cost And Freight	成本加运费
CIF	Cost, Insurance and Freight	成本、保险费加运费

Table 3-3 Main Trade Terms of INCOTERMS 2020

表 3-3 《2020 通则》主要贸易术语

	Group1 Incoterms that apply to any mode of transport are: 第一组：适用于任何运输方式的术语
EXW	Ex Works	工厂交货
FCA	Free Carrier	货交承运人
CPT	Carriage Paid To	运费付至
CIP	Carriage and Insurance Paid To	运费、保险费付至
DPU	Delivered at Place Unloaded	卸货地交货
DAP	Delivered At Place	目的地交货
DDP	Delivered Duty Paid	完税后交货
	Group2 Incoterms that apply to sea and inland waterway transport only: 第二组：适用于海上和内陆水上运输方式的术语
FAS	Free Alongside Ship	船边交货
FOB	Free On Board	船上交货
CFR	Cost And Freight	成本加运费
CIF	Cost, Insurance and Freight	成本、保险费加运费

Incoterms 2020《2020 年通则》

The International Chamber of Commerce (ICC) has announced the publication of Incoterms 2020 in September 2019. This is the first update to Incoterms since they were last revised in 2010. The new rules become effective from 1 January 2020.

Incoterms detail the obligations of the parties as well as the allocation of risk and cost in a trade contracted on three-letter trade terms (such as CIF and FOB). Incoterms are distinct from the meaning of the same three-letter trade terms at common law, and Incoterms will only apply if they are incorporated into the contract (usually by reference).

The newest revisions to the rules have been produced by the ICC Drafting Group, which was made up of eight members from Australia, China, EU member states, Turkey, and the USA. Incoterms 2020 contain six significant changes from Incoterms 2010:

国际商会("ICC")2019 年 9 月正式公布了 2020 年版本的《国际贸易术语解释通则》。这是现行《国际贸易术语解释通则》自 2010 年生效以来进行的第一次修订。新修订的《国际贸易术语解释通则》自 2020 年 1 月 1 日起生效。

《国际贸易术语解释通则》对采用国际贸易术语(如"CIF"和"FOB")订立的合同中各方主体的义务、风险和费用成本的承担进行了详细地解释。值得注意的是《国际贸易术语解释通则》中对国际贸易术语的解释和普通法下的解释有所不同，只有明确约定适用《国际贸易术语解释通则》的情况下，《国际贸易术语解释通则》中的贸易术语才会适用。

最新公布的《国际贸易术语解释通则》由 ICC 起草小组进行修订，该起草小组的八名成员分别来自中国、美国、欧盟成员国、澳大利亚和土耳其。与 2010 版的《国际贸易术语解释通则》相比，新修订的 2020 版主要在以下六个方面进行了改动，具体而言：

a. The FCA rule now contains an additional element relating to bills of lading. Under this option, the buyer and seller agree that the buyer's carrier will issue an on-board bill of lading to the seller after loading, which the seller will then tender to the buyer (likely through the banking chain). A problem with the old FCA rule was that it ended before the loading of the goods, which prevented the seller from obtaining an on-board bill of lading. However, bills of lading are generally required by banks under letters of credit and therefore the FCA rule was revised to take account of this market reality.

修订后的《国际贸易术语解释通则》中 FCA 术语下就提单问题引入了新的附加机制。根据该新引入的附加选项，买方和卖方同意买方指定的承运人在装货后将向卖方签发已装船提单，然后再由卖方向买方做出交单(可能通过银行链)。现行的 FCA 术语中存在的一个主要问题是该术语的效力在货物装船前就已经随货交承运人而截止，这就导致卖方无法获得已装船提单。但是在一般情况下，已装船提单是银行在信用证项下的常见单据要求，因此对 FCA 规则的修订充分考虑到这一市场上的实际情况。

b. Costs are now consistently listed in A9 (seller's obligations) and B9 (buyer's obligations), providing a "one-stop list of costs" for each rule. This new consolidated costs section appears in addition to the allocation of cost under the relevant obligation. For example, in an FOB sale, the costs involved in obtaining the delivery/transport document appear in both A6/B6 and A9/B9.

各个贸易术语项下买卖双方的费用承担在 A9(卖方承担)和 B9(买方承担)中详细载明，该部分为每一个贸易术语都提供了"一站式费用清单"。也就是说除了在具体规定有关义务的条款中对承担该义务产生的费用成本进行分配以外，还新加入将买方卖方各自承担的费用成本一并汇总的部分。例如，在 FOB 贸易术语项下，取得交付或运输相关单据产生的成本除在说明该项义务的 A6/B6 部分载明外，在汇总费用承担的 A9/B9 部分也有载明。

c. The level of minimum insurance in CIF and CIP terms has diverged. CIF terms continue to require the seller to obtain cargo insurance complying with Clauses (C) of the LMA/IUA Institute Cargo Clauses. However, in CIP trades the level of minimum insurance has been increased to that complying with Clauses (A) of the Institute Cargo Clauses (meaning "all risks" cover, subject to exclusions).

CIF 和 CIP 术语中的最低保险范围的规定也有所不同。CIF 术语继续要求卖方购买符合 LMA/IUA《协会货物保险条款》(C)条款要求的货物保险。但是，在适用 CIP 术语的贸易中，最低保险范围已经提高到《协会货物保险条款》(A)条款的要求(即"一切险"，不包括除外责任)。

d. Provision has been made for the seller or buyer to employ their own means of transportation rather than employing a third party carrier, as was assumed in the Incoterms 2010. The changes are reflected in the FCA, DAP, DPU and DDP rules.

当采用 FCA、DAP、DPU 和 DPP 术语进行贸易时，买卖双方可以使用自有运输工具，而不再像 2010 版那样推定使用第三方承运人进行运输。

e. The DAT (Delivered at Terminal) rule has been renamed DPU (Delivered at Place Unloaded). This is to reflect that the destination can be any place and not just a terminal.

DAT(Delivered at Terminal)术语已被重命名为 DPU(Delivered at Place Unloaded)。这是为了反映作为目的地的交货地点可以是任何地方而不仅仅是运输终端。

f. An express allocation of security-related obligations has been added to A4 and A7 of each Incoterm, the costs of which are included in A9/B9. For example, A4 of the FOB Incoterm states "The seller must comply with any transport-related security requirements up to delivery". These provisions reflect the increasing prevalence of concerns relating to security in international trade.

每个国际贸易术语项下的 A4 和 A7 部分都明确规定了与安全有关的义务的分配规则，为履行该义务产生的费用的承担方式也在 A9/B9 部分载明。例如，FOB 术语项下的 A4 部分载明"卖方必须遵守任何与运输安全有关的要求，直至交付"。这些规定反映了当前国际贸易领域对安全问题日益增长的关注。

The following are 11 trade terms in INCOTERMS 2010.

下面是《2010 通则》的 11 个贸易术语。

(3) FOB, CFR and CIF 装运港交货的三种常用贸易术语

Among the 11 trade terms, FOB, CFR and CIF are the most commonly used ones. Nowadays, they are used as trade terms for symbolic delivery, which means documents sales replace goods sales, and the seller delivers the documents instead of the goods while the buyer pays according to the documents. Symbolic delivery is the basic of understanding modem international settlement and credit dealings.

在 11 个贸易术语中使用最多的贸易术语是 FOB、CFR、CIF。在现代国际贸易中，它们被用作象征性交货的贸易术语。所谓象征性交货，也就是以单据的买卖代替了货物的买卖，卖方以交单代替了交货，买方凭单付款。象征性交货是理解现代的国际结算、信用证交易的基础。

① FOB: Free On Board (...named port of shipment)船上交货(……指定装运港)

"Free On Board" means that the seller delivers the goods on board the vessel nominated by the buyer at the named port of shipment or procure the goods already so delivered. The risks of loss of or damage to the goods passes when the goods are on board the vessel, and the buyer bears all costs and risks from that moment onwards. The seller is required either to deliver the goods on board the vessel or to procure goods already so delivered for shipment. The reference to "procure" here caters for multiple sales down a chain (string sales), particularly common in the commodity trades.

This rule is used only for sea or inland waterway transport.

FOB may not be appropriate where goods are handed over to the carrier before they are on board the vessel, for example goods in containers, which are typically delivered at a container yard. In such situations, the FCA rule should be used.

"船上交货"是指卖方以在指定装运港将货物装上买方指定的船上或通过取得已交付至船上货物的方式。货物灭失或损害的风险在货物交到船上时转移，同时买方承担自那时起的一切费用和风险。卖方应将货物交到船上或取得已经这样交运的货物。此处使用的"取得"一词适用于商品贸易中常见的交易链中的多层销售(链式销售)。

该术语仅适用于海运或内河水运。

FOB 可能不适合货物在上船前已经交给承运人的情况，例如用集装箱运输的货物通常是在集装箱堆场交货。在此类情况下，应当使用 FCA 术语。

Obligations of the seller and the buyer 买卖双方的义务

A. The Seller's Obligations 卖方义务

a. The seller must deliver the goods either by placing them on board the vessel nominated by the buyer at the loading point, if any, indicated by the buyer at the named port of shipment or by procuring the goods so delivered. In either case, the seller must deliver the goods on board on the agreed date or within the agreed period and in the manner customary at the port.

b. The seller must give the buyer sufficient notice either that the goods have been delivered or that the vessel has failed to take the goods within the time agreed.

c. The seller must bear all costs and risks before the goods are loaded on board the ship.

d. The seller must obtain, at its own risk and expense, any export licence or other official authorization and carry out all customs formalities necessary for the export of the goods, and pay the costs of customs formalities necessary for export, as well as all duties, taxes and other charges payable upon export.

e. The seller must provide the commercial invoice in conformity with the contract of sale and any other evidence of conformity that may be required by the contract.

a. 卖方必须在指定的装运港内的装货点(如有的话)，将货物置于买方指定的船舶上，或以买方指定的方式交货。无论哪种情况，卖方都必须在约定的日期或期限内，按照该港的习惯方式交货。

b. 卖方必须就其已经交货或船舶未在约定时间内收取货物给予买方充分的通知。

c. 卖方必须承担货物装上船前的一切费用和风险。

d. 卖方必须自负风险和费用，取得任何出口许可证和其他官方授权，办理货物出口所需的一切海关手续，并且支付货物出口所需海关手续费用，以及出口应缴纳的一切关税、税款和其他费用。

e. 卖方必须提供符合买卖合同约定的商业发票，以及合同可能要求的其他与合同相符的证据。

B. The Buyer's Obligations 买方义务

a. The buyer must contract, at its own expense for the carriage of the goods from the named port of shipment, and give the seller sufficient notice of the vessel name, loading point and, where necessary, the selected delivery time within the agreed period.

b. The buyer must bear all costs and risks after the goods are loaded on board the ship.

c. The buyer must accept the proof of delivery and pay the price of the goods as provided in the contract of sale.

d. Buyer must obtain, at its own risk and expense, any import licence or other official authorization and carry out all customs formalities for the import of the goods and for their transport through any country, and pay all duties, taxes and other charges, as well as the costs of carrying out customs formalities payable upon import of the goods and the costs for their transport through any country.

a. 买方必须自付费用签订自指定的装运港起运货物的运输合同，并就船舶名称、装船点和在需要时其再约定期间内选择的交货时间向卖方发出充分的通知。

b. 卖方必须负责货物装上船后的一切费用和风险。

c. 买方必须接受和合同相符的交货凭证，并按照买卖合同约定支付价款。

d. 买方必须自负风险和费用，取得任何进口许可证或其他官方授权，办理货物进口和在必要时从他国过境所需的一切海关手续，并支付货物进口应缴纳的一切关税、税款和其他费用，及办理进口海关手续的费用和从他国过境运输费用。

When adopting the FOB terms, we shall pay attention to the following points:

a. Delivery of the goods on board the vessel.

b. Link-up of vessel and goods.

c. Expense for loading the goods on board the vessel.

INCOTERMS 2010 stipulates that the seller shall pay all related expenses until the goods are delivered either by placing them on board the vessel nominated by the buyer at the loading point, if any, indicated by the buyer at the named port of shipment or by procuring the goods so delivered. Generally, the seller is responsible for shipping charges; excluding stowage charges and trimming charges after the goods are loaded on board the ship.

d. The transfer of the risks.

It is a historic practice before INCOTERMS® 2010 to regard the rail as the boundary. INCOTERMS 2000 stipulates that under FOB term, the risk of loss of or damage to the goods is transferred from the seller to the buyer when these goods pass over the ship's rail at the named port of shipment. INCOTERMS 2010 specifies that the risk of loss of and damage to the goods passes when the goods are on board the vessel, and the buyer bears all costs from that moment onwards. It could be an engagement that both parties agree to regard boarding on ship as the boundary. The concept of "Cross the Ship's Rail" was cancelled thereafter.

使用 FOB 术语时要注意以下四点：

a. 船上交货的要求。

b. 船货衔接问题。

c. 货物装船的费用问题。

《2010 通则》中规定："卖方必须支付在指定的装运港内的装货点（如有的话），将货物置于买方指定的船舶上，或以买方指定的方式交货前与货物有关的一切费用"，这就说明了，在一般情况下，卖方要承担装船的费用，而不包括货物装上船的理舱费和平舱费。

d. 风险转移的问题。

以船舷作为划分风险的界限是《2010 通则》以前长期沿用的一种惯例。《2000 通则》就规定，在 FOB 术语下，货物灭失和损坏的风险自货物在指定装运港越过船舷时起由卖方转移至买方承担。《2010 通则》在关于 FOB 风险划分时就做了重新规定：货物的灭失和损坏的风险在货物装上船时起即由卖方转移至买方承担。取消了以船舷为界划分风险的概念，明确规定以货物装上船作为风险划分的界限。

② CFR: Cost and Freight (...Named Port of Destination) 成本加运费（……指定目的港）

"Cost and Freight" means that the seller delivers the goods on board the vessel or procures the goods already so delivered, The risk of loss of or damage to the goods passes when the goods are on board the vessel. The seller must contract for and pay the costs and freight necessary to bring the goods to the named port of destination.

This rule is to be used only for sea or inland waterway transport.

CFR may not be appropriate where goods are handed over to the carrier before they are on board the vessel, for example goods in containers, which are typically delivered at a container yard. In such circumstances, the CPT rule should be used.

"成本加运费"是指卖方在船上交货或以取得已经这样交付的货物方式交货，货物灭失或损坏的风险在货物交到船上时转移。卖方必须签订合同，并支付必要的成本和运费，将货物运至指定的目的港。

该术语仅用于海运或内河水运。

CFR 可能不适合于货物在上船前已经交给承运人的情况，例如用集装箱运输的货物通常是在集装箱货运站交货。在此类情况下，应当使用 CPT 术语。

Obligations of the seller and the buyer 买卖双方的义务

Except that the obligation of contracting for and paying the costs and freight necessary to bring the goods to the named port of destination is borne by the seller, not the buyer, both parties' obligations are just the same as that of FOB.

除了签订合同并支付必要的成本和运费将货物运至指定的目的港这项义务是由卖方负担，不由买方负担外，CFR 买卖双方义务基本上和 FOB 一样。

When adopting the CFR term, we shall pay attention to the following points:

a. Critical points

This rule has two critical points, because risk passes and costs are transferred at different places. While the contract will always specify a destination port, it might not specify the port of shipment, which is where risk passes to the buyer. If the shipment port is of particular interest to the buyer, the parties are well advised to identify it as precisely as possible in the contract.

b. Responsibilities of transportation.

INCOTERMS 2010 stipulates that the seller must contract or procure a contract for the carriage of the goods from agreed point of delivery, if any, at the place of delivery to the named port of destination or, if agree, any point at that port. The contract of carriage must be made on usual terms at the seller's expense and provide for carriage by the usual route in a vessel of the type normally used for the transport of the type of goods sold.

c. Bearing unloading expenses.

INCOTERMS 2010 also stipulates that the seller must pay the freight and all other costs resulting from contracting or procuring a contract for the carriage of the goods, including the costs of loading the goods on board and any charges for unloading at the agreed port of discharge that were for the seller's account under the contract of carriage; the buyer must pay all costs and charges relating to the goods while in transit until their arrival at the port of destination, and unloading costs including lighterage and wharfage charges, unless such costs and charges were for the seller's account under the contract of carriage. This means if the seller incurs costs under its contract of carriage related to unloading at the specified point at the port of destination, the seller is not entitled to recover such costs from the buyer unless otherwise agreed between the parties.

d. Shipping advice.

If the buyer fails to cover the risks as a result of deferred notice by the seller and once accidents happen, the seller is responsible.

使用 CFR 术语时要注意以下四点：

a. 关键点问题。

由于风险转移和费用转移的地点不同，该术语右两个关键点。虽然合同通常都会指定目的港，但不一定都会指定装运港，而这里是风险转移至买方的地方。如果装运港对买方具有特殊意义，特别建议双方在合同中尽可能准确地指定装运港。

b. 运输的责任。

《2010 通则》规定，卖方必须自负费用订立合同，将货物自交货地内的约定交货点(如有的话），运送至指定目的地或指定目的地内的约定(如有的话)。必须按照通常条件订立合同，由卖方支付费用，经由通常航线，由通常用来运输该类商品的船舶运输。

c. 卸货费用的负担。

《2010 通则》还规定，卖方必须支付按照上一条规定订立货物的运输合同所发生的货物装上船的运费和其他一切费用，包括将货物装上船和根据运输合同中规定的应由卖方支付的在约定卸货港的卸货费用；买方必须支付货物在运输途中直至到达约定目的港为止的一切费用，以及包括驳运费和码头费在内的卸货费，除非根据运输合同该费用应由卖方支付者除外。这是指如果卖方按照运输合同在目的港交付地点发生了卸货费用，则除非双方事先另有约定，卖方无权向买方要求补偿该项费用。

d. 装船通知。

如果卖方装船后没有及时通知买方，致使买方没有投保，一旦发生风险或事故，由卖方承担风险损失。

③ CIF: Cost, Insurance and Freight (...Named Port of Destination) 成本、保险费加运费（……指定目的港)

"Cost, Insurance and Freight" means that the seller delivers the goods on board the vessel or procures the goods already so delivered. The risk of loss of or damage to the goods passes when the goods are on board the vessel. The seller must contract for and pay the costs and freight necessary to bring the goods to the named port of destination. The seller also contracts for insurance cover against the buyer's risk of loss of or damage to the goods during the carriage and pay the costs of insurance.

This rule is to be used only for sea or inland waterway transport.

CIF may not be appropriate where goods are handed over to the carrier before they are on board the vessel, for example goods in containers, which are typically delivered at a container yard. In such circumstances, the CIP rule should be used.

"成本、保险费加运费"是指卖方在船上交货或以取得已经这样交付的货物方式交货。货物灭失或损坏的风险在货物交到船上时转移。卖方必须签订合同，并支付必要的成本和运费，将货物运至指定目的港。卖方还要为买方在运输途中货物的灭失或损坏风险办理保险，并支付保险费。

该术语仅用于海运或内河水运。

CIF 可能不适合于货物在上船前已经交给承运人的情况，例如用集装箱运输的货物通常是在集装箱堆场交货。此类情况下，应当使用 CIP 术语。

Obligations of the seller and the buyer 买卖双方的义务

Except that the obligation of contracting for insurance and paying the costs of insurance is borne by the seller, both parties' obligations are just the same as that of CFR.

除了签订保险合同并支付保险费这项义务是由卖方负担外，CIF 买卖双方义务基本上和 CFR 一样。

When adopting the CIF term, we shall pay attention to the following points:

a. Insurance coverage.

As explained by INCOTERMS 2010, the seller must obtain, at its own expense, cargo insurance complying at least with the minimum cover provided by Clauses (C) of the Institute Cargo Clauses (LMA/IUA) or any similar clauses. When required by the buyer, the seller shall, subject to the buyer providing any necessary information requested by the seller, provide at buyer's expense any additional cover, if procurable.

The insurance shall cover, at a minimum, the price provided in the contract plus 10% (i.e., 110%) and shall be in the currency of the contract.

b. Symbolic delivery.

CIF is a typical term for symbolic delivery, in comparison with physical delivery.

Physical delivery refers to that the seller delivers the goods to the buyer in due time and at due place as agreed in the contract.

Symbolic delivery refers to that the seller fulfills obligation on condition that the seller ships the goods on board the vessel as the contract stipulates at port of shipment within due time and delivers related entitled documents as stipulated on the contract. The risks are transferred when the goods are on board the vessel. The seller is liable for loading the goods in due time and has no guarantee for the arrival of goods. The core of symbolic delivery is the buying and selling of related documents instead of physical goods, in other words, delivering the documents is delivering goods by the seller to the buyer. The seller delivers the goods against documents and the buyer pays for the goods against the documents. As long as the seller provides all sets of qualified documents in due time and even if the goods are damaged or lost during shipment, the buyer shall pay. Reversely, if the seller provides wrong documents and even if the goods are in good shape, the buyer may refuse to pay.

使用 CIF 术语时要注意以下两点：

a. 保险险别问题。

按《2010 通则》解释，卖方必须自负费用取得货物保险。该保险需至少符合《协会货物保险条款》(Institute Cargo Clause, LMA/IUA)条款(C)或类似条款的最低险别。当买方要求且能够提供卖方所需的信息时，卖方应办理任何附加险别，由买方承担费用，如果能够办理。

保险最低金额是合同规定价格另加 10%(即 110%)，并采用合同货币。

b. 象征性交货问题。

CIF 贸易术语是一个典型的象征性交货(Symbolic Delivery)的贸易术语。所谓象征性交货是针对实际交货(Physical Delivery)而言的。

实际交货是指卖方要在合同规定的时间和地点,将符合合同规定的货物提交给买方或其指定的人,而不能以交单代替交货。

象征性交货是指卖方只要按照合同规定的时间在装运港把货物装上船并向买方提交了合同规定的代表货物所有权凭证的有关单据,就算完成了交货义务。风险在货物装上船时由卖方转移给买方,卖方只负责按时装运,无须负责保证到货。象征性交货的核心是单据的买卖,双方交易的是单据而不是货物,也就是说卖方只要向买方交单就是向买方交货。卖方是凭单交货,买方是凭单付款。只要卖方如期向买方提交了全套合格单据,即使货物在运输途中损坏或灭失,买方也必须履行付款义务。相反的,如果卖方提交的单据不符合要求,即使货物完好无损的到达目的地,买方仍有权拒绝付款。

FOB, CFR and CIF are classified into one group as they are alike in characters from the below six aspects:

a. They are used only for sea or inland waterway transport.

b. Place of delivery of the seller is on board a ship in the export country.

c. Risks are borne by the seller until the goods are on board the vessel.

d. Symbolic trade terms, or documents instead of goods dealing are the core of selling and buying.

e. The risks are transferred to the buyer once the seller delivers the goods on board the vessel.

f. Contracts signed under the above three terms are referred to shipment contracts, in other words, the seller is only responsible for punctual shipment and disregards when it arrives.

我们把 FOB、CFR、CIF 分为一组,是因为这三个贸易术语都有以下六个方面的特征:

a. 都仅适用于海运或内河水运。

b. 卖方的交货地点都是在出口国的装运港船上。

c. 风险的划分都是在出口国装运港以货物装上船为界。

d. 都是象征性交货的贸易术语,也就是说是以单据的买卖为核心,以交单代替了交货。

e. 卖方只要在装运港把货物装上船就完成了交货义务,风险就转移给了买方。

f. 以这三个贸易术语签订的买卖合同都是属于装运合同,也就是卖方只管按时装运,不管何时到达。

(4)FCA, CPT and CIP 向承运人交货的三种贸易术语

① FCA:Free Carrier (...named place of delivery) 货交承运人(……指定交货地点)

"Free Carrier" means that the seller delivers the goods to the carrier or another person nominated by the buyer at the seller's premises or another named place. The parties are well advised to specify as clearly as possible the point within the named place of delivery, as the risk passes to the buyer at that point.

If the parties intend to deliver the goods at the seller's premises, they should identify the address of those premises as the named place of delivery. If, on the other hand, the parties intend the goods to be delivered at another place, they must identify a different specific place of delivery.

FCA requires the seller to clear the goods for export, and the buyer to clear the goods for import, where applicable.

This rule may be used irrespective of the mode of transport selected and may also be used where more than one mode of transport is employed.

"货交承运人"是指卖方在卖方所在地或其他指定地点将货物交给买方指定的承运人或其他人。由于风险在交货地点转移至买方,特别建议双方尽可能清楚地写明指定交货地内的交付点。

如果双方希望在卖方所在地交货,则应当将卖方所在地址明确为指定交货地。如果双方希望在其他地点交货,则必须确定不同的特定交货地点。

如适用时,FCA要求卖方办理货物出口清关手续,买方办理货物进口清关手续。

该术语可适用于任何运输方式,也可适用于多种运输方式。

When adopting the FCA term, we shall pay attention to the following points:

A. The place of delivery and the responsibilities of loading and unloading.

As explained by INCOTERMS 2010, the seller must deliver the goods to the carrier or another person nominated by the buyer at the agreed point, if any, at the named place on the agreed date or within the agreed period. Delivery is completed: If the named place is the seller's premises, when the goods have been loaded on the means of transport provided by the buyer; In any other case, when the goods are placed at the disposal of the carrier or another person nominated by the buyer on the seller's means of transport ready for unloading.

This means that the seller shall load the goods on the means of transport provided by the buyer if the named place is the seller's premises; the seller does not have to unload the goods from his means of transport ready for unloading in any other case.

B. Comparison of FCA and FOB.

Common Points:

a. The buyer is responsible for shipment and covering insurance and the contracted price does not include shipping charges or insurance premium;

b. Port of loading is the place of delivery;

c. Contracts under these two terms are shipment contracts.

Differences:

a. FOB is used only for sea or inland waterway transport; FCA could be used in all means of transport including sea transport.

b. Places of delivery for FOB is on board the ship at named port of shipment; FCA is at named place of delivery.

c. Risks transfer when the goods are on board the vessel for FOB and when the goods are delivered to the carrier for FCA.

使用 FCA 术语时要注意以下两点：

A. 交货地点和装卸货的责任问题

按《2010 通则》解释，卖方必须在约定日期或期限内，在指定地点或指定地点的约定点(如有约定)，将货物交付给买方指定的承运人或其他人。以下情况，交货完成：若指定地点是卖方所在地，则当货物被装上买方提供的运输工具时；在任何其他情况下，则当货物在卖方的运输工具上可供卸载，并可由承运人或买方指定的其他人处置时。

这表明如果指定地点是卖方所在地，卖方需要将货物装上买方提供的运输工具完成交货；在任何其他情况下，卖方无需将货物从自己的运输工具上卸下，做好卸货准备即可完成交货。

B. FCA 与 FOB 的比较

相同点：

a. 都是由买方负责运输，买方负责保险。在价格构成上都不包含运费和保费。

b. 都属于出口国装运港(地)交货条件。

c. 以这两个贸易术语签订的买卖合同，都是装运合同。

不同点：

a. 适用的运输方式不同：FOB 只适用于海运或内河水运，FCA 适用包括海洋运输方式在内的一切运输方式。

b. 交货地点不同：FOB 是在指定装运港船上，FCA 是在出口国指定交货地点。

c. 风险划分的地点不同：FOB 以在装运港货物装上船为界；FCA 以出口国交货地货交承运人为界。

② CPT：Carriage Paid To (…named place of destination) 运费付至(……指定目的地)

"Carriage and Insurance Paid to" means that the seller delivers the goods to the carrier or another person nominated by the seller at an agreed place (if any such place is agreed between parties) and that the seller must contract for and pay the costs of carriage necessary to bring the goods to the named place of destination.

This rule may be used irrespective of the mode of transport selected and may also be used where more than one mode of transport is employed.

"运费付至"是指卖方将货物在双方约定地点(如果双方已经约定了地点)交给卖方指定的承运人或其他人。卖方必须签订运输合同并支付将货物运至指定目的地所需费用。

该术语可适用于任何运输方式，也可适用于多种运输方式。

When adopting the FCA term, we shall pay attention to the following points:

A. Critical points

This rule has two critical points, because risk passes and costs are transferred at different places. The parties are well advised to identify as precisely as possible in the contract both the place of delivery, where the risk passes to the buyer, and the named place of destination to which the seller must contract for the carriage. If several carriers are used for the carriage to the agreed destination and the parties do not agree on a specific point of delivery, the default position is that risk passes when the goods have been delivered to the first carrier at a point entirely of the seller's choosing and over which the buyer has no control. Should the parties wish the risk to pass at a later stage (e.g., at an ocean port or airport), they need to specify this in their contract of sale.

B. Responsibilities of transportation

INCOTERMS 2010 stipulates that the seller must contract or procure a contract for the carriage of the goods from the agreed point of delivery, if any, at the place of delivery to the named place of destination or, if agreed, any point at that place. The contract of carriage must be made on usual terms at the seller's expense and provide for carriage by the usual route and in a customary manner. If a specific point is not agreed or is not determined by practice, the seller may select the point of delivery and the point at the named place of destination that best suit its purpose.

If the seller incurs costs under its contract of carriage related to unloading at the named place of destination, the seller is not entitled to recover such costs from the buyer unless otherwise agreed between the parties.

C. Comparison of CPT and CFR

Common Points:

a. In both terms, the seller is obliged to arrange transport to the destination and bear related costs while the buyer covers insurance on himself.

b. Same delivery terms—Delivering the goods at port (place) of shipment.

c. Contracts under both terms are shipment contracts.

Differences:

a. CFR is used only for sea or inland waterway transport; CPT could be used in any mode of transport including sea transport.

b. Place of delivery for CFR is on board the ship at port of shipment, and for CPT is to the carrier at place of delivery in the exporting country.

c. Risks under CFR are transferred when the goods are on board the vessel at port of shipment in the exporting country, and risks under CPT are passed when the goods are delivered to the carrier at place of delivery in the exporting country.

A. 关键点问题

由于风险转移和费用转移的地点不同，该术语有两个关键点。特别建议双方尽可能确切地在合同中明确交货地点，风险在这里转移至买方，以及指定的目的地(卖方必须签订运输合同运到该目的地)。如果运输到约定目的地涉及多个承运人，且双方不能就交货点达成一致时，可以推定：当卖方在某个完全由其选择，且买方不能控制的点将货物交付给第一个承运人时，风险转移至买方。如双方希望风险晚些转移的话(例如在某海港或机场转移)，则需要在其买卖合同中注明。

B. 运输责任问题

卖方必须签订或取得运输合同，将货物自交货地内的约定交货点(如有的话)运送至指定目的地或该目的地的交付点(如有约定)。必须按照通常条件订立合同，由卖方支付费用，经由通常航线和习惯方式运送货物。如果双方没有约定特别的点或按照惯例也无法确定，卖方则可根据合同需要选择最适合其目的的交货点和指定目的地内的交货点。

如果卖方按照运输合同在指定的目的地卸货发生了费用，除非双方另有约定，卖方无权向买方要求偿付。

C. CPT 与 CFR 的比较

相同点：

a. 都是由卖方负责安排到目的地的运输，承担运费，买方自己投保，承担保费。

b. 都是装运港(装运地)交货条件。

c. 以这两个贸易术语签订的买卖合同都是装运合同。

不同点：

a. CFR 只适用于海运或内河水运，CPT 适用于任何一种运输方式，包括海运。

b. 交货地点不同：CFR 卖方在出口国装运港船上交货，CPT 在出口国装运地点货交承运人。

c. 风险划分不同：CFR 下风险在出口国装运港货物装上船后转移至买方，CPT 下风险在出口国装运地点货交承运人后转移至买方。

③ CIP: Carriage and Insurance Paid to (…Named Place of Destination) 运费和保险费付至(……指定目的地)

"Carriage and Insurance Paid to" means that the seller delivers the goods to the carrier or another person nominated by the seller at an agreed place (if any such place is agreed between the parties) and that the seller must contract for and pay the costs of carriage necessary to bring the goods to the named place of destination. The seller also contracts for insurance cover against the buyer's risk of loss of or damage to the goods during the carriage.

This rule may be used irrespective of the mode of transport selected and may also be used where more than one mode of transport is employed.

"运费和保险费付至"是指卖方将货物在双方约定地点(如双方已经约定了地点)交给其指定的承运人或其他人。卖方必须签订运输合同并支付将货物运至指定目的地的所需费用。卖方还必须为买方在运输途中货物的灭失或损坏风险签订保险合同。

该术语可适用于任何运输方式，也可适用于多种运输方式。

When adopting the CIP term, we shall pay attention to the following points:

A. Insurance coverage

As explained by INCOTERMS 2010, the seller must obtain, at its own expense, cargo insurance complying at least with the minimum cover provided by Clauses (C) of the Institute Cargo Clauses (LMA/IUA) or any similar clauses. When required by the buyer, the seller shall, subject to the buyer providing any necessary information requested by the seller, provide at buyer's expense any additional cover, if procurable. The insurance shall cover, at a minimum, the price provided in the contract plus 10% (i.e., 110%) and shall be in the currency of the contract.

But the above provision was revised in INCOTERMS 2020. As explained by INCOTERMS 2020, the seller must obtain, at its own expense, cargo insurance complying at least with the maximum cover provided by Clauses (A) of the Institute Cargo Clauses (LMA/IUA) or any similar clauses. When required by the buyer, the seller shall, subject to the buyer providing any necessary information requested by the seller, provide any cover lower than Clauses (A), if procurable.

B. Comparison of CIF and CIP

Common Points:

a. The contract price includes shipping charges and insurance premium, and the seller arranges transport to port (place) of destination and pays for related shipping charges and insurance premium.

b. Place of delivery is port (place) of shipment in the exporting country.

c. Contracts under both terms are shipment contracts.

Differences:

a. CIF is used only for sea or inland waterway transport; CIP could be used in any mode of transport including sea transport.

b. Place of delivery for CIF is on board the ship at port of shipment, and for CIP is to the carrier at place of delivery in the exporting country.

c. Risks transfer when goods are on board the vessel at port of shipment for CIF, and for CIP risks transfer when the goods are delivered to the carrier at place of delivery.

d. Insurance under CIF is purely ocean transport insurance; insurance under CIP may not only involve transport insurance but also inland or airway insurance.

使用 CIP 术语时要注意以下两点：

A. 保险险别问题

按《2010 通则》解释，卖方必须自负费用取得货物保险。该保险需至少符合《协会货物保险条款》(Institute Cargo Clause, LMA/IUA)条款(C)或类似条款的最低险别。当买方要求且能够提供卖方所需的信息时，卖方应办理任何附加险别，由买方承担费用，如果能够办理。保险最低金额是合同规定价格另加 10%(即 110%)，并采用合同货币。

但是上述规定在《2020 通则》里作了修订。按《2020 通则》解释，卖方必须自负费用取得货物保险。该保险需至少符合《协会货物保险条款》 (Institute Cargo Clause, LMA/IUA)条款(A)(Clause A)或类似条款的最高险别。当买方要求且能够提供卖方所需的信息时，卖方应办理任何比条款(A)(Clause A)更低级别的险别，如果能够办理。

B. CIF 与 CIP 的比较

相同点：

a. 价格构成中都包含了通常的运费和保费，卖方都要安排到目的港(目的地)运输，负责投保，支付有关运费和保费。

b. 交货地点都是在出口国装运港(装运地)。

c. 以这两个贸易术语签订的买卖合同均为装运合同。

不同点：

a. 适应运输方式不同：CIF 只适用于海运或内河水运，CIP 适用于任何一种运输方式，包括海运。

b. 交货地点不同：CIF 交货地点为出口国装运港船上，CIP 为出口国货交承运人。

c. 风险划分不同：CIF 以装运港货物装上船为界，CIP 以出口国装运地货交承运人为界。

d. 二者的保险不一样：CIF 单纯为海洋运输保险，CIP 可能涉及陆运或航空险。

The above three trade terms are used when the exporter delivers the goods to the carrier and share the following characters:

向承运人交货的贸易术语是 FCA、CPT、CIP。这三个贸易术语都是在出口国货交承运人时使用，有以下共同特征：

a. They are suitable for any means of transport including sea transportation.

b. Place of delivery of the seller is to the carrier in the exporting country.

c. Risk is transferred when the goods delivered to the carrier at place of delivery in the exporting country.

d. Contracts signed as per these three rules are all shipping contracts.

a. 都适合于包括海洋运输在内的任何一种运输方式。

b. 卖方交货的地点都是在出口国装运地货交承运人。

c. 风险划分都是以出口国装运地货交承运人为界。

d. 以这三个贸易术语签订的买卖合同都是装运合同。

(5) EXW and FAS 出口国交货的其他贸易术语

① EXW: EX Works (…named place of delivery) 工厂交货(……指定交货地点)

"Ex Works" means that the seller delivers when it places the goods at the disposal of the buyer at the seller's premises or at another named place (i.e. works, factory, warehouse, etc.). The seller does not need to load the goods on any collecting vehicle, nor does it need to clear the goods for export, where such clearance is applicable.

The parties are well advised to specify as clearly as possible the point within the named place of delivery, as the costs and risks to that point are for the account of the seller. The buyer bears all costs and risks involved in taking the goods from the agreed point, if any, at the named place of delivery.

This rule maybe used irrespective of the mode of transport selected and may also be used where than one mode of transport is employed. It is suitable for domestic trade, while FCA is usually more appropriate for international trade.

EXW represents the minimum obligation, costs and risks for the seller. The rule should be used with care as:

A. The seller has no obligation to the buyer to load the goods, even though in practice the seller may be in a better position to do so. If the seller does load the goods, it does so at the buyer's risk and expense. In cases where the seller is in a better position to load the goods, FCA, which obliges the seller to do so at its own risk and expense, is usually more appropriate.

B. A buyer who buys from a seller on an EXW basis for export needs to be aware that the seller has an obligation to provide only such assistance as the buyer may require to the effect that export: the seller is not bound to organize the export clearance. Buyers are therefore well advised not to use EXW if they cannot directly or indirectly obtain export clearance.

C. The seller has limited obligations to provide to the buyer any information regarding the export of the goods. However, the buyer may need this information for, e.g., taxation or reporting purposes.

"工厂交货"是指当卖方在其所在地或其他指定地点(如工厂、车间或仓库等)将货物交给买方处置时，即完成交货。卖方不需将货物装上任何前来接收货物的运输工具，需要清关时，卖方也无须办理出口清关手续。

特别建议双方在指定交货地点范围内尽可能明确具体交货点，因为在货物到达交货地点之前的所有费用和风险都由卖方承担。买方则需承担自此指定交货点(如有的话)受领货物所产生的全部费用和风险。

该术语可适用于任何运输方式，也可适用于多种运输方式。它适合国内贸易，而FCA一般则更适合国际贸易。

EXW术语是卖方承担责任、费用和风险最小的术语，使用时需注意以下问题：

A. 卖方对买方没有装货的义务，即使实际上卖方也许更方便这样做。如果卖方装货，也是由买方承担相关风险和费用。当卖方更方便装货物时，FCA 一般更为合适，因为该术语要求卖方承担装货义务，以及与此相关的风险和费用。

B. 以 EXW 为基础购买出口产品的买方需要明白，卖方只有在买方要求时，才有责任协助办理出口，即卖方无义务安排出口通关。因此，在买方不能直接或间接地办理出口清关手续时，不建议使用该术语。

C. 卖方仅有限度地承担向买方提供货物出口相关信息的责任。但是，买方则可能出于交税或申报等目的需要这方面的信息。

② FAS: Free Alongside Ship (…named place of shipment) 船边交货(……指定装运港)

"Free Alongside Ship" means the seller delivers when the goods are placed alongside the vessel (e.g., on a quay or a barge) nominated by the buyer at the named port of shipment. The risk of loss of or damage to the goods passes when the goods are alongside the ship, and the buyer bears all costs from that moment onwards.

This term requires the seller to clear the goods for export and the buyer to clear the goods for import.

This term can be only used for sea or inland water transportation. When adopting this term, the name of the port of shipment should be stated clearly after FAS.

Under FAS terms the seller's obligations are fulfilled when the goods have been placed alongside the vessel on the quay or in lighters. This means that the buyer has to bear all cost and risks of, losses of, or damage to the goods from that moment.

The parties are well advised to specify as clearly as possible the loading point at the named port of shipment, as the costs and risks to that point are for the account of the seller and these costs and associated handling charges may vary according to the practice of the port.

Where the goods are in containers, it is typical for the seller to hand the goods over to the' carrier at a terminal and not alongside the vessel. In such situations, the FAS rule would be inappropriate, and the FCA rule should be used.

"船边交货"是指当卖方在指定的装运港将货物交到买方指定的船边(例如，置于码头或驳船上)时，即为交货。货物灭失或损坏的风险在货物交到船边时发生转移，同时买方承担自那时起的一切费用。

该术语要求卖方办理货物出口清关，买方办理货物进口清关。

该术语仅适用于海运或内河水运。采用此术语时要在 FAS 后面注明装运港名称。

这一术语是指卖方在装运港将货物放置在码头买方所指派的船只的船边，即完成了交货。买方必须自该时刻起，负担一切费用和货物灭失或损坏的一切风险。

由于卖方承担在特定地点交货前的风险和费用，而且这些费用和相关作业费可能因各港口惯例不同而变化，特别建议双方尽可能清楚地注明指定的装运港内的装货点。

当货物装在集装箱里时，卖方通常将货物在集装箱码头移交给承运人，而非交到船边。这时，FAS 术语不适合，应当使用 FCA 术语。

Comparison of FAS and FOB　FAS 与 FOB 的比较

Common Points:

a. Both are only used for sea or inland water transportation.

b. The buyer arranges transport, covers insurance and bears shipping charges and insurance premium.

相同点：

a. 都仅适用于海运或内河水运。

b. 都是由买方安排运输、投保、承担运费和保险费。

Differences:

a. Place of delivery for FOB is on board the ship at named port of shipment, and for FAS is alongside the ship at named port of shipment.

b. Risks transfer when the goods are on board the vessel at named port of shipment for FOB, and when the goods are alongside the ship at named port of shipment for FAS.

c. The seller is responsible for loading the goods for FOB and the seller is free from shipping charges for FAS.

不同点：

a. FOB 中卖方交货的地点是在指定装运港的船上，而 FAS 是在指定装运港船边。

b. FOB 的风险划分是在指定装运港以货物装上船为界，而 FAS 的风险划分是在指定装运港的船边。

c. FOB 中由卖方负责装船，而 FAS 中卖方不承担装船费用。

(6)DAT, DAP and DDP 目的地交货的三种贸易术语

① DAT: Delivered at Terminal (…named terminal at port or place of destination) 运输终端交货(……指定港口或目的地的运输终端)

"Delivered at Terminal" means that the seller delivers when the goods, once unloaded from the arriving means of transport, are placed at the disposal of the buyer at a named terminal at the named port or place of destination. "Terminal", includes any place, whether covered or not, such as a quay, warehouse, container yard or road, rail or air cargo terminal. The seller bears all risks involved in bringing the goods to the unloading them at the terminal at the named port or place of destination.

This rule may be used irrespective of the mode of transport selected and may also be used where more than one mode of transport is employed.

The parties are well advised to specify as clearly as possible the terminal and, if possible, a specific point within the terminal at the agreed port or place of destination, as the risks to that point are for the account of the seller. The seller is advised to procure a contract of carriage that matches this choice precisely.

Moreover, if the parties intend the seller to bear the risks and costs involved in transporting and handling the goods from the terminal to another place, then the DAP or DDP rules should be used.

DAT requires the seller to clear the goods for export, where applicable. However, the seller has no obligation to clear the goods for import, pay any import duty or carry out any import customs formalities.

"运输终端交货"是指当卖方在指定港口或目的地的指定运输终端将货物从抵达的载货运输工具上卸下,交给买方处置时,即为交货。"运输终端"意味着任何地点,而不论该地点是否有遮盖,例如码头、仓库、集装箱堆积场或公路、铁路、空运货站。卖方承担将货物送至指定港口或目的地运输终端并将其卸下期间的一切风险。

该术语可适用于任何运输方式,也可适用于多种运输方式。

由于卖方承担在特定地点交货前的风险,特别建议双方尽可能确切地约定运输终端,或如果可能的话,约定在港口或目的地的运输终端内的特定点。建议卖方取得的运输合同应能与所做选择确切吻合。

此外,如果双方希望由卖方承担将货物由运输终端运输和搬运至另一地点的风险和费用,则应当使用 DAP 或 DDP 术语。

如适用时,DAT 要求卖方办理出口清关手续。但卖方无义务办理进口清关、支付任何进口税或办理任何进口海关手续。

The DAT rule has been renamed DPU [Delivered at Place Unloaded (…named place of destination)] in INCOTERMS 2020. "Delivered at Place Unloaded" means the seller has fulfilled its obligations when the goods are placed at the disposal of the buyer, unloaded from the means of transport at the agreed place of destination (this place may be a terminal, a warehouse or the buyer's premises). This revision is to reflect that the destination can be any place and not just a terminal.

在《2020 通则》里,DAT 术语已被重命名为 DPU[目的地卸货后交货(……指定目的地)]。"目的地卸货后交货"是指当卖方在指定目的地(这个地点可以是运输终端,仓库或买方的所在地)将货物从抵达的载货运输工具上卸下,交给买方处置时,即为交货。这个修订是为了反映作为目的地的交货地点可以是任何地方而不仅仅是运输终端。

② DAP: Delivered at Place (…named place of destination) 目的地交货(……指定目的地)

"Delivered at Place" means that the seller delivers when the goods are placed at the disposal of the buyer on the arriving means of transport ready for unloading at the named place of destination. The seller bears all risks involved in bringing the goods to the named place.

This rule may be used irrespective of the mode of transport selected and may also be used where more than one mode of transport is employed.

The parties are well advised to specify as clearly as possible the point within the agreed place of destination, as the risks to that point are for the account of the seller. The seller is advised to procure contracts of carriage that match this choice precisely. If the seller incurs costs under its contract of carriage related to unloading at the place of destination, the seller is not entitled to recover such costs from the buyer unless otherwise agreed between the parties.

DAP requires the seller to clear the goods for export, where applicable. However, the seller has no obligation to clear the goods for import, pay any import duty or carry out any import customs formalities. If the parties wish the seller to clear the goods for import, pay any import duty and carry out any import customs formalities, the DDP term should be used.

"目的地交货"是指当卖方在指定目的地将还在运抵运输工具上可供卸载的货物交由买方处置时，即为交货。卖方承担将货物运送到指定地点的一切风险。

该术语可适用于任何运输方式，也可适用于多种运输方式。

由于卖方承担在特定地点交货前的风险，特别建议双方尽可能清楚地订明指定的目的地内的交货点。建议卖方订立的运输合同应能与所做选择确切吻合。如果卖方按照运输合同在目的地发生了卸货费用，除非双方另有约定，卖方无权向买方要求偿付。

如适用时，DAP要求卖方办理出口清关手续。但是卖方无义务办理进口清关、支付任何进口税或办理任何进口海关手续。如果双方希望卖方办理进口清关、支付所有进口关税，并办理所有进口海关手续，则应当使用DDP术语。

③ DDP: Delivered Duty Paid (…named place of destination) 完税后交货(……指定目的地)

"Delivered Duty Paid" means that the seller delivers the goods when the goods are placed at the disposal of the buyer, cleared for import on the arriving means of transport ready for unloading at the named place of destination. The seller bears all the costs and risks involved in bringing the goods to the place of destination and has an obligation to clear the goods not only for export but also for import, to pay any duty for both export and import and to carry out all customs formalities.

This rule may be used irrespective of the mode of transport selected and may also be used where more than one mode of transport is employed.

The parties are well advised to specify as clearly as possible the point within the agreed place of destination, as the costs and risks to that point are for the account of the seller is advised to procure contracts of carriage that match this choice precisely. If the seller incurs costs under its contract of carriage related to unloading at the place of destination, the seller is not entitled to recover such costs from the buyer unless otherwise agreed between the parties.

DDP represents the maximum obligation, costs and risks for the seller.

The parties are well advised not to use DDP if unable directly or indirectly to obtain import clearance. If the parties wish the buyer to bear all risks and costs of import clearance, the DAP rule should be used. Any VAT or other taxes payable upon import are for the seller's account unless expressly agreed otherwise in the sale contract.

"完税后交货"是指当卖方在指定目的地将仍处于抵达的运输工具上，但已完成进口清关，且可供卸载的货物交由买方处置时，即为交货。卖方承担将货物运至目的地的一切风险和费用，并且有义务完成货物出口和进口清关，支付所有出口和进口的关税和办理所有海关手续。

该术语可适用于任何运输方式，也可适用于多种运输方式。

由于卖方承担在特定地点交货前的风险和费用，特别建议双方尽可能清楚地订明在指定目的地内的交货点。建议卖方订立的运输合同应能与所做选择确切吻合。如果按照运输合同卖方在目的地发生了卸货费用，除非双方另有约定，否则卖方无权向买方索要该费用。

DDP 术语是卖方承担责任、费用和风险最大的术语。

如卖方不能直接或间接地完成进口清关，则特别建议双方不使用 DDP。如双方希望买方承担所有进口清关的风险和费用，则应使用 DAP 术语。除非买卖合同中另行明确规定，任何增值税或其他应付的进口税款由卖方承担。

There are three terms in D group: DAT, DAP and DDP. The common points of them are:

A. The seller shall deliver the goods when the goods are placed at the disposal of the buyer at place of destination in the importing country.

B. They are used in physical delivery.

C. Risks transfer when the buyer takes hold of the goods at place of destination in the importing country.

D. Contracts under the terms are arrival contracts.

E. The seller shall bear shipping charges and insurance premiums which are both included in the contract price.

D 组贸易术语共 3 个：DAT、DAP 和 DDP。这三个贸易术语的共同点是：

A. 都是在进口国目的地交货的贸易术语，卖方的交货地点都是要把货物运到进口国目的地实际交给买方处置。

B. 都是实际交货的贸易术语。

C. 风险划分都是在进口国目的地货物处于买方处置之下时转移。

D. 以这三个贸易术语签订的买卖合同都是到达合同。

E. 运输和保险都由卖方来承担，在价格构成中都包含了运费和保费。

Section 2　Influencing Factors on Pricing
第2节　影响定价的因素

In foreign trade, we shall determine the appropriate prices for our commodities according to the international market price level, and based on the situations of different policies of various countries (regions) and purpose of business. As the components of price are different, the factors that affect the price change are also varied. Therefore, when we determine the prices of import and export commodities, we must fully consider the factors that affect the price, strengthen accounting of the cost, profit and loss, and pay attention to the reasonable price differences of same commodity in different circumstances.

The following factors should be taken into account in determining the prices of import and export commodities:

在对外贸易中，应根据国际市场价格水平，结合国别(地区)政策，并按照我们的经营意图确定商品的适当价格。由于价格构成因素不同，影响价格变化的因素也是多种多样的。因此，在确定进出口商品价格时，必须充分考虑影响价格的种种因素，加强成本和盈亏核算，并注意同一商品在不同情况下应有合理的差价。

确定进出口商品价格应考虑下列因素：

1. Needs 市场需求

As the world market may fluctuate with the change of supply and demand pattern, it is important to watch the change of supply and demand relationship and the trend of rising or falling of the market prices. Prices should be adjusted according to the changes in demand for commodities of the international market and the importing countries. If the commodities are in high demand and well selling, the prices should be raised correspondingly; if the commodities are in weak demand and poorly selling, the prices should be lowered correspondingly.

由于世界市场可能会随着供求格局的变化而波动，观察供求关系的变化和市场价格的涨跌趋势是很重要的。应根据国际市场和进口国对商品的需求变动调整价格，若是需求旺盛、畅销的商品，价格可相应提高，若是需求疲软、滞销的商品，则价格应相应降低。

2. Cost 商品成本

The price components of commodity usually includes the costs, expenses and profits. The costs directly determines the pricing of commodity. When determining the prices of import and export commodities, we should pay attention to strengthening cost accounting to improve economic benefits and prevent the bias of ignoring costs, profits and losses and simply pursuing trading volume.

商品的价格构成通常包括成本、费用和利润三个部分内容，商品成本直接决定了商品定价的高低。在确定进出口商品价格时，要注意加强成本核算，以提高经济效益，防止出现不计成本、不计盈亏，单纯追求成交量的偏向。

3. Quantity 订购数量

In principle, if the commodities are not in short supply, the deal quantity is smaller, the price is higher. Increasing quantity can be given appropriately discount, in order to encourage the merchants' motivation of managing our commodities.

原则上非紧俏商品的成交数量越小，价格越高，加大数量则可适当给予减价优惠，以鼓励客商经营商品的积极性。

4. Delivery 交货条件

In international goods trade, the sellers and buyers have different responsibilities, costs and risks due to differences in the place of delivery and the terms of delivery. These factors must be taken into account when determining the prices of imports and exports. If the seller bears more responsibilities, costs and risks under a particular term of delivery, the seller should quote a higher price. For example, the DAP price should be higher than the CIP price for the same commodity in the same quantity.

在国际货物贸易中，由于交货地点和交货条件的不同，买卖双方承担的责任、费用和风险有别，在确定进出口商品的价格时，必须考虑这些因素。如果在某一交货条件下卖方承担的责任、费用和风险较大，则卖方就应报高一些的价格，例如，就成交相同数量的同一商品，DAP 价就应高于 CIP 价。

5. Payment, Rate of Exchange and so on 支付条件、汇率风险等

Whether the terms of payment are beneficial affect directly the price of the goods. If payment is made by L/C at sight, we may consider giving the buyer appropriate price discount. On the other hand, if payment is by time L/C or documentary collection, the price level can be raised accordingly. Meanwhile, when determining commodity prices, we generally should strive to choose the currency favorable to us in transactions. If unfavorable currency has to be adopted in a transaction, the risks or losses that may arise from fluctuations in exchange rate should be taken into account in the price of commodity, that is, appropriate mark-up or mark-down.

支付条件是否有利，直接影响到商品的价格。如果以即期信用证方式付款，价格方面可以考虑给予一些优惠；反之，若以远期信用证付款或跟单托收方式，价格水平可相应调高。同时，在确定商品价格时，一般应当争取采用对自身有利的货币成交。如采用对自身

不利的货币成交时，应把汇率变动可能产生的风险或损失考虑到商品价格中去，即可以适当加价或降价。

Section 3　Money of Account, Money of Payment and Value Keeping Clause

第3节　计价货币、支付货币与保值条款

1. Money of Account, Money of Payment 计价货币与支付货币

(1) Money of Account　计价货币

Money of account is the currency specified in the contract to calculate the price. These currencies can be the currency of the export country, the currency of import country, or the currency of a third country.

The following factors should be taken into account when selecting the money of account:

A. Convertibility of Currency

When determining the money of account, the main choice should be made from the freely convertible currencies commonly used in the world.

B. Stability of Currency

Full consideration should be given to the risks that the fluctuations in exchange rate may bring. Try to choose the currency that is favorable to oneself. The general principle is that exports should choose "hard currency" (the value of which is more stable or floating upward), while imports should use "soft currency" (the value of which is floating downward).

计价货币是指合同中规定用来计算价格的货币。这些货币可以是出口国或进口国的货币，也可以是第三国的货币。

选择计价货币时应考虑以下因素：

A. 货币的可兑换性

在确定计价货币时，主要应从国际上通用的可自由兑换的货币中去选择。

B. 货币的稳定性

应充分考虑汇率波动可能带来的风险，尽量选用对自己有利的货币。一般原则是：出口应选择那些币值比较稳定或呈上浮趋势的"硬币"；进口应使用币值有下浮趋势的"软币"。

(2) Money of Payment　支付货币

Money of payment is the currency specified in the contract to pay the amount of the goods. If the price in the contract is expressed in a currency agreed upon by both parties and there is no stipulation of payment in other currencies, the currency specified in the contract is both the money of account and the money of payment. In the import and export business in China, account and payment adopt the same currency in most cases.

However, if it is stipulated that the price shall be denominated in one currency and the payment shall be made in another currency in the contract, it will bring different economic effects to both the seller and the buyer due to the difference of the hard and soft of the two currencies and the exchange rate at which the settlement shall be made. If the exchange rate of money of account and the exchange rate of money of payment are fixed at the time of contracting, then, in the case that the money of account is hard currency and the money of payment is soft currency, the quantity of hard currency received by the seller will decrease at the time of settlement. It is unfavorable to the seller. Conversely, if the money of account is soft currency and the money of payment is hard currency, the seller will receive more hard currency at the time of settlement than it converted at the exchange rate of the date of payment. It is favorable to the seller and unfavorable to the buyer.

支付货币是指合同中规定用来支付价款的货币。如合同中的价格是用一种双方当事人约定的货币来表示，没有规定用其他货币支付，合同中规定的货币既是计价货币，又是支付货币。在我国进出口业务中，多数情况下计价和支付采用同一种货币。

但如果合同中规定用一种货币计价，用另一种货币支付，由于这两种货币的软硬不一和按什么时候的汇率进行结算，会给买卖双方带来不同的经济效果。如果计价货币和支付货币的汇率在订约时已经固定，那么，在计价货币是硬币，支付货币是软币的情况下，卖方在结算时所收入的硬币量就会减少，这对卖方是不利的。反之，如果计价货币为软币，支付货币为硬币，那么，卖方结算时所收硬币就会比按付款日的汇率兑换所收的硬币量要多，这对卖方有利，而对买方不利。

2. Value Keeping Clause 保值条款

If unfavorable currency has to be adopted for the conclusion of a deal, we may seek to establish hedging clauses to avoid the risk of changes in the exchange rate of money of account.

Common hedging clauses include:

如果为达成交易而不得不采用对我方不利的货币，则可以争取订立保值条款，以避免计价货币汇率变动的风险。

常用的货币保值条款有：

(1) Gold Hedging Clause 黄金保值条款

Its specific method is: when concluding the contract, the amount of money of account is converted into a certain amount of gold at the gold price of the date of signing, then the specific amount of gold is converted into a certain amount of money of account at the gold price of the same date when making payment. If the price of gold goes up, the amount of money of account should increase, and vice versa.

The premise of applying gold hedging clause is that the price of gold remains stable. If the price of gold continues to fluctuate, this method cannot avoid risks.

其具体做法是：在订立合同时按签约日的黄金价格将计价货币的金额折合为若干一定数量的黄金，到支付日再将特定数量的黄金按当时的金价转换成一定数量的计价货币。如果黄金价格上涨，则支付货币金额要相应增加，反之，则相应减少。

实行黄金保值条款的前提是黄金价格保持稳定，若黄金价格不断波动，则此方法不能起到避免风险的作用。

(2) A Basket of Currency Hedging Clause 一篮子货币保值条款

Its specific method is: when concluding the contract, both parties shall negotiate to determine the exchange rate between the money of payment and a basket of hedging currencies, and stipulate the adjustment range of changes in exchange rate between various hedging currencies and the money of payment. If the changes in exchange rate are more than the specified range at the time of payment, it shall be adjusted according to the exchange rate stipulated in the contract so as to achieve the purpose of keeping value. As the exchange rates of currencies in a basket of currencies going up or down, the exchange risks are diversified. It can effectively avoid foreign exchange risks and limit relatively large foreign exchange risks within the specified range.

具体做法：在签订合同时，双方协商确定支付货币与一篮子保值货币之间的汇率，并规定出各种保值货币与支付货币之间汇率变动的调整幅度。如果到支付期时汇率的变动超过规定的幅度，则按合同中已规定的汇率调整，从而达到保值的目的。由于一篮子货币当中，货币的汇率有升有降，汇率风险分散化，这就可以有效避免外汇风险，把较大的外汇风险限制在规定的幅度内。

Section 4　Pricing Methods

第 4 节　定 价 方 法

1. Fixed Price 固定价格

The Seller delivers and the Buyer accepts the commodities at a fixed price agreed by both parties, neither party shall have the right to change the agreed price.

买卖双方按约定价格交接货物和收付货款，任何一方无权要求对约定价格进行变更。

2. Unfixed Price 非固定价格

In international sales of goods, the following methods of unfixed price can be used.

(1) Flexible pricing

The pricing time and the pricing method are specified in the price terms, for instance: "The price will be negotiated and decided by both parties 30 days before the shipment according to the international price level". Or only the pricing time is fixed, for instance: "To be priced on May 10th, 2019 by both parties".

(2) Partial fixed price and partial unfixed price

The parties concerned only fix the price for the commodities to be delivered recently, and leave the price of the commodities to be delivered in the long term open.

(3) Floating pricing

At the time of pricing, the price adjustment is also stipulated, for instance: "If the concluded price for other buyers is 5% higher or lower than the contract price, both parties will negotiate to adjust the contract price for the quantity of the contract".

在国际货物买卖中，可采取下列几种非固定价格的办法。

(1) 暂不固定价格

在价格条款中明确规定定价的时间和定价方法，如"在装船前 30 天，参照国际市场价格水平，协商议定正式价格"。或只规定作价时间，如"由双方在 2019 年 5 月 10 日商定价格"。

(2) 价格部分固定，部分不固定

交易双方只约定近期交货部分的价格，远期交货部分的价格，则待以后商定。

(3) 浮动价格

在规定价格的同时，还规定价格调整条款，如"如果卖方对其他客户的成交价高于或低于合同价 5%，对本合同的数量，双方协商调整价格"。

Section 5　Commission and Discount

第 5 节　佣金与折扣

1. Commission 佣金

(1) Definition 定义

Commission is the remuneration for the agents who provide service for principals. During trading, commission is usually in the form of remuneration which either side of a trade provides to the middleman. For example, exporters pay commission to sales agents, or importers pay commission to purchase agents. Therefore, commission applies to the contract signed by the exporter/importer and the agents. Certain trading occurs through middlemen or agents who need to be paid commission. If the ratio of commission is defined, we call it the defined commission; otherwise, we call it undefined commission which agents may require from both sides.

佣金指代理人或经纪人为委托人服务而收取的报酬。在货物买卖中，佣金常常表现为交易一方支付给中间商的报酬。例如，出口商支付佣金给销售代理人，或进口商支付佣金给采购代理人。因此，它适用于进出口商与代理人或佣金商签订的合同。有些交易是通过中间商、代理商进行的，这就要向其支付一定的酬金——佣金。凡货价中包含佣金的即为含佣金价。如明确规定佣金的百分比，则为明佣。如不标明百分比，甚至连佣金字样也不标示出来，则为暗佣，中间商有可能两头签佣。

(2) Defined Methods of Commission 佣金的规定方法

A. Labeled by words. e.g. This price includes 5 percent commission.

B. Trading terms: e.g. FOBC4 New York.

C. Defined by number: Commission: USD 20 per Metric Ton.

A. 文字说明。如：这一价格含5%的佣金。

B. 在贸易术语上表示。如：FOBC4 New York。

C. 绝对数表示。如：佣金：USD20每公吨。

(3) Calculation and Payment Methods of Commission 佣金的计算与支付方法

A. Calculation: by turnover value 计算方法：按成交金额计算

It should be defined in a contract whether commission is calculated on the basis of FOB or CIF. It is more sensible to adopt FOB which nevertheless cannot be accepted by agents. It is conventional that CIF serves as the basis of commission's calculation in a CIF contract. If it is not clearly defined in the contract, it usually turns to the invoice.

计算佣金的基数按 FOB 值还是 CIF 值应在合同中订明，按 FOB 值的基数计算佣金，这种计算方法比较合理，但是中间商往往不同意。按习惯做法如 CIF 合同就按 CIF 总值作为佣金计算的基数。如合同中未订明，通常按发票金额计算。

Formula

Commission=Price with Commission×Commission Rate

Net Price=Price with Commission−Commission per Unit

　　　　　=Price with Commission×(1−Commission Rate)

Price with Commission=Net Price / (1−Commission Rate)

e.g. Net price: 100 USD, CIF London commission rate: 5%. Calculate the price with commission: USD100/ (1−5%)=USD 105.26

计算公式:

佣金额=含佣价×佣金率

净价=含佣价-单位货物佣金额

   =含佣价×(1-佣金率)

含佣价=净价/(1-佣金率)

例:净价为 USD100,CIF London 佣金为 5%,则含佣价为:USD100/(1-3%)=USD105.26。

B. Payment methods of commission 佣金的支付方法

a. Remove from exporting/importing price.

b. Remittance from principals in a defined rate.

a. 中间商直接从货价扣除。

b. 委托人收清货款后再按约定佣金比率另行汇付。

2. Discount 折扣

Discount is aimed to motivate the initiatives of the buyer, which is provided by the seller as a concession in the contract.

The differentiation between the commission and the discount: commissions are offered by the seller to the middlemen, while discounts are concessions provided by the seller.

所谓折扣是指为了调动买方的积极性,在合同中订明卖方按原价给买方一定百分比的减让。

佣金与折扣的区别在于:佣金为卖方给第三者(中间商)的手续费,折扣为卖方直接给予买方的减让。

(1) Types of Discount 折扣的种类

A. Quantity Discount: discount offered if the amount purchased by buyers reaches certain quantity.

B. Special Discount: discount offered for frequent client

C. Defined Discount: defined discount rate in a contract

D. Undefined discount: not mentioned in a contract, but mentioned in other agreements.

A. 数量折扣:如买方购买达到一定的数量给予折扣。

B. 特别折扣:对于长年购买的老顾客给予价格优惠。

C. 明扣——在合同中明确规定折扣率。

D. 暗扣——合同中不标示出来,另有协议。

(2) Defined Methods of Discount 折扣的规定方法

A. Literally Defined 用文字明确表示

It is usual that the discount rate should be defined literally in a pricing terms. e.g., USD 1,000 per metric ton CIF Hamburg including 3% discount, or USD 1,000 per metric ton CIF

Hamburg less discount 3%.

在价格条款中，一般用文字明确表示给予折扣的比例。例如：CIF 汉堡每公吨 1000 美元，折扣 3%，或者写成：CIF 汉堡，每公吨 1000 美元，减 3%折扣。

B. Defined by determined number 用绝对数表示

e.g., USD l,000 per M/T less discount USD 10.00

例如：每公吨 1000 美元，减折扣 10 美元。

(3)Calculation and Payment Methods of Discount 折扣的计算与支付方法

Discount can be calculated on the basis of turnover value or invoice value.

Discount per Unit=Original Price×Discount Rate

Net Seller's Revenue=Original Price×(1－Discount Rate)

e.g., Original price: USD100.00/PC CIF Singapore. Discount rate: 2%. Discount offered by the seller to buyer: USD100.00×2%=USD2.00. Net revenue of the seller: USD100.00×(1－2%)=USD98.00. The payment method of discount can be offered directly during issuing; sellers remove the discount from the invoice value.

以成交额或发票金额为基础计算折扣额。

单位货物折扣额=原价×折扣率

卖方净收入=原价×(1－折扣率)

例如：原价 USD100.00/PC CIF Singapore，折扣为 2%，则卖方给买方的折扣为 USD100.00×2%=USD2.00，卖方的净收入为 USD100.00×(1－2%)= USD98.00。折扣的支付方法可在开证中直接扣除金额或开证为原价，卖方在发票中扣除折扣额。

Terminology 本章术语

1. trade terms 贸易术语
2. international trade customs 国际贸易惯例
3. INCOTERMS 国际贸易术语解释通则
4. FOB 船上交货
5. CFR 成本加运费
6. CIF 成本、保险费加运费
7. FCA 货交承运人
8. CPT 运费付至
9. CIP 运费保险费付至
10. EXW 工厂交货
11. FAS 船边交货

12. DAT 运输终端交货
13. DPU 目的地卸货后交货
14. DAP 目的地交货
15. DDP 完税后交货
16. money of account 计价货币
17. money of payment 支付货币
18. fixed price 固定价格
19. unfixed price 非固定价格
20. commission 佣金
21. discount 折扣

Exercises 本章练习

1. An exporter exports a batch of Christmas gifts to an English buyer with CIF London and as the Christmas gifts are seasonal, they contract that the buyer shall open a credit with the seller before the end of September and the seller shall ship the goods to Hamburg not later than 5th December. Or else, the buyer has the right to cancel the contract and get refund from the seller. So is the amended contract still a CIF contract? Why?

某进出口公司以 CIF 伦敦向英国某客商出售一批圣诞礼品，由于该商品的季节性较强，买卖双方在合同中规定：买方须于 9 月底将信用证开抵卖方，卖方保证不迟于 12 月 5 日将货物运抵汉堡，否则，买方有权撤销合同。如卖方已结汇，卖方须将货款退还买方。问：该合同是否还属于 CIF 合同？为什么？

2. An exporter in Beijing contracts with an English customer to export a lot of goods. After negotiating the price, our exporter insists on FCA Beijing while the English customer insists on FOB Tianjin. Please explain the reasons.

我北京某外贸公司与英商签订一批货物出口，在商谈好价格后，我北京公司坚持用 FCA 北京贸易术语，英商坚持用 FOB 天津贸易术语，试分析原因。

3. Our importer imports a batch of goods under FOB term. When the goods are being unloaded, a dozen of packages are found broken and soaked by seawater. After investigation, the goods are cast broken on deck and then soaked. Can our importer lodge a claim for the failure of the seller to fulfill obligation of delivery?

我国某外贸公司以 FOB 条件进口一批货物。在目的港卸货时，发现有几件货物外包装破裂，并且货物有被水渍的痕迹。经查证，货物是在装船时因吊钩不牢固掉在甲板上摔破的，因包装破裂导致里面的货物被水浸泡。试分析该外贸公司能否以对方未完成交货义务为由提出索赔？

4. Our exporter exports a batch of clothes to Europe under CIF. The contract specifies that insurance is to be covered by the exporter against all risks with CICC and pay with credit. Our exporter ships the goods in nominated port of shipment within specified time and the shipping company signs bills of lading, and then our exporter negotiates with Bank of China. The second day, our exporter are informed that the shipping vessel catches fire on the sea and all the clothes are burnt down. The buyer requires our exporter to lodge a claim with CICC, or else to refund. Our exporter absolutely refuses this requirement and puts forward settlements, distinguishing both parties' obligations and finally settles this case.

我国某外贸公司按 CIF 条件向欧洲某国进口商出口一批服装。合同中规定由我方向中国人民保险公司投保了一切险，并采用信用证方式支付。我出口公司在规定的期限、指定的我国某港口装船完毕，船公司签发了提单，然后在中国银行议付了款项。第二天，出口公司接到客户来电称：装货的海轮在海上失火，服装全部烧毁，客户要求我公司出面向中国人民保险公司提出索赔，否则要求我公司退回全部货款。我方果断拒赔，并提出了解决的办法，区分了买卖双方的责任，解决了此案。

Answers for Reference 参考答案

1.Analysis: The contract is not a CIF contract because:

(1) CIF contracts are shipment contracts, according to which the seller should deliver the goods on board the nominated ship at port of loading for shipment to the destination within specified time and bear no risks or expenses during the shipment of the goods. In the above case, the seller shall ship the goods to Hamburg not later than 5th December or else, the buyer has the right to cancel the contract. This substantially alters the character of shipment contracts.

(2) CIF is used for symbolic delivery in which the seller delivers the goods against documents while the buyer pays against documents. In the above case, the seller shall refund to the buyer if settlements have been made. This alters the characters of symbolic delivery.

In conclusion, contract in the above case is not a shipment contract any more.

分析：本案中的合同性质已不属于 CIF 合同。因为：

(1) CIF 合同是"装运合同"，即按此类销售合同成交时，卖方必须在合同规定的装运期内在装运港将货物交至运往指定目的港的船上，即完成了交货义务，对货物运输途中发生灭失或损坏的风险以及货物交运后发生的事件所产生的费用，卖方概不承担责任。而本案的合同条款规定："……卖方保证不得迟于 12 月 5 日将货物运抵汉堡，否则，买方有权撤销合同……"该条款意指卖方必须在 12 月 5 日将货物实际运抵汉堡，其已改变了"装运合同"的性质。

(2) CIF 术语是典型的象征性交货，在象征性交货的情况下，卖方凭单交货，买方凭单付款，而本案合同条款规定："……如卖方已结汇，卖方须将货款退还买方。"该条款已改变了"象征性交货"下卖方凭单交货的特点。因而，本案的合同性质已不属于 CIF 合同。

2. Analysis: (1) The seller insists on FCA Beijing as he fulfills obligation once he delivers the goods to the carrier in Beijing and risks are transferred to the buyer. However, if FOB Tianjin is adopted, the seller has to bear shipping charges and risks from Beijing to Tianjin. (2) The seller shall get documents for negotiation after he delivers the goods to the carrier under FCA Beijing, however, the seller shall load the goods on board the ship to get documents for negotiation under FOB Tianjin.

In conclusion, the exporter insists on FCA Beijing while the English customer insists on FOB Tianjin.

分析：(1)卖方坚持用 FCA 北京，卖方在北京货交承运人，卖方的交货义务就算完成。风险也就转移给了买方，如果采用 FOB 天津，而卖方还要多承担北京到天津的运输和风险。(2)FCA 北京，卖方货交承运人后，即可取得单据，交单议付。而 FOB 天津，卖方要到天津装船后才能取得单据议付货款。所以买方坚持要用 FOB 天津，卖方坚持用 FCA 北京。

3. Analysis: Our importer has the right to lodge a claim to the seller. According to INCOTERMS 2020, risks transfer from the seller to the buyer when the goods are on board the vessel at port of shipment. In the above case, before the goods are on board the vessel, the packages get broken as the lift hooks get loosened, as a consequence, costs and expenses are to be borne by the seller.

分析：该外贸公司不能向对方索赔。根据《2020 通则》的规定，卖方承担货物的风险从货物于装运港装上船时开始转移给买方，就本案例看，在货物置于船舶之上前，因装船时吊钩不牢导致货物摔下包装物破裂，该项损失按风险划分界限，应该由卖方承担。

4. Analysis: According to INCOTERMS 2020, risks transfer to the buyer after the goods are on board the vessel. The goods are lost during shipment and are to be borne by the buyer. The goods were lost during the sea voyage, so the risk of the loss of the goods should be borne by the buyer and the buyer also should make a claim to the insurance company against insurance policy by himself. In addition, CIF is used for symbolic delivery in which documents are presented against goods. Thus the buyer shall not refuse to pay once the seller presents right documents, even if the goods get lost or damaged during shipment.

Hints: (1) In CIF contracts, the seller fulfills obligation as long as he ships the goods within specified time and presents right documents including entitlement to the goods to the buyer. There is no need for the seller to ensure arrival of the goods. (2) In CIF contracts, the seller delivers the goods against the documents and the buyer pays against documents. As long as the seller presents whole set of documents stipulated by the contract in due time and even if the goods get lost or damaged during shipment, the buyer should pay.

分析：上述案例中的合同属 CIF 性质，根据《2020 通则》的规定，双方有关货物风险的划分，是以货物在约定的装运港装上船时为界。凡是货物在装上船后发生的风险，应当由买方负责。既然，货物是在运输途中损失，该风险应由买方承担，并由买方持卖方转让给其的保险单证向保险公司提出索赔。另外，CIF 术语是象征性交货，它的特点是"凭单据履行交货义务，并凭单据付款"。只要卖方按照合同的规定将货物装船并提交齐全的、正确的单据，即使货物已在运输途中遭受丢失，买方也不能拒收单据或向卖方索要支付的货款。

启示：(1)在 CIF 合同中卖方只要按期在约定地点完成装运，并向买方提交合同规定的、包括物权凭证在内的有关单据，就算完成了交货义务，而无须保证到货。(2)在 CIF 合同中，卖方是凭单交货，买方是凭单付款。只要卖方如期向买方提交了合同规定的全套合格单据，即使货物在运输途中损坏或丢失，买方也必须履行付款义务。

Appendix: INCOTERMS 2020 Rules

Trade terms	Full name	Chinese name	Place of delivery	Risks transfer	Foreign freight	Insurance premium	Export duty	Import duty	Means of transport
EXW	Ex Works	工厂交货	Ex works ... named place	Delivered to the buyer	Buyer	Buyer	Buyer	Buyer	All modes
FCA	Free Carrier	货交承运人	Free carrier ... named place	Delivered to the carrier	Buyer	Buyer	Seller	Buyer	All modes
FAS	Free Alongside Ship	船边交货	Alongside the ship at port of shipment	Alongside the ship at port of shipment	Buyer	Buyer	Seller	Buyer	Sea and inland waterway
FOB	Free on Board	船上交货	On board the ship	Delivered on board The vessel	Buyer	Buyer	Seller	Buyer	Sea and inland waterway
CFR	Cost and Freight	成本加运费	On board the ship	Delivered on board The vessel	Seller	Buyer	Seller	Buyer	Sea and inland waterway
CIF	Cost, Insurance and Freight	成本、保险费加运费	On board the ship	Delivered on board The vessel	Seller	Seller	Seller	Buyer	Sea and inland waterway

续表

Trade terms	Full name	Chinese name	Place of delivery	Risks transfer	Foreign freight	Insurance premium	Export duty	Import duty	Means of transport
CPT	Carriage Paid to	运费付至	To the carrier in export country	Delivered to the carrier	Seller	Buyer	Seller	Buyer	All modes
CIP	Carriage and Insurance Paid to	运费、保险费付至	To the carrier in export country	Delivered to the carrier	Seller	Seller	Seller	Buyer	All modes
DPU	Delivered at Place Unloaded	目的地卸货后交货	To deliver at named place of destination	Delivered to the buyer at place of destination	Seller	Seller	Seller	Buyer	All modes
DAP	Delivered at Place	目的地交货	To deliver at place of destination	Delivered to buyer at place of destination	Seller	Seller	Seller	Buyer	All modes
DDP	Delivered Duty Paid	完税后交货	To deliver at named place of destination	Delivered to buyer at named place of destination	Seller	Seller	Seller	Seller	All modes

附表：国际贸易术语解释通则 2020

贸易术语	全称	中译名	交货地点	风险转移	运费	保险费	出口报关	进口报关	运输方式
EXW	Ex Works	工厂交货	出口国工厂	出口国工厂货交买方	买方	买方	买方	买方	任何方式
FCA	Free Carrier	货交承运人	出口国内指定地点货交承运人	出口国内货交承运人	买方	买方	卖方	买方	任何方式
FAS	Free Alongside Ship	船边交货	装运港船边	装运港货交船边	买方	买方	卖方	买方	海洋运输
FOB	Free on Board	船上交货	装运港船上	货物装上船	买方	买方	卖方	买方	海洋运输
CFR	Cost and Freight	成本加运费	装运港船上	货物装上船	卖方	买方	卖方	买方	海洋运输

续表

贸易术语	全称	中译名	交货地点	风险转移	运费	保险费	出口报关	进口报关	运输方式
CIF	Cost, Insurance and Freight	成本、保险费加运费	装运港船上	货物装上船	卖方	卖方	卖方	买方	海洋运输
CPT	Carriage Paid to	运费付至	出口国内货交承运人	出口国内货交承运人	卖方	买方	卖方	买方	任何方式
CIP	Carriage and Insurance Paid to	运费、保险费付至	出口国内货交承运人	出口国内货交承运人	卖方	卖方	卖方	买方	任何方式
DPU	Delivered at Place Unloaded	目的地卸货后交货	指定目的地	指定目的地买方处置货物后	卖方	卖方	卖方	买方	任何方式
DAP	Delivered at Place	目的地交货	指定目的地约定点	指定目的地买方处置货物后	卖方	卖方	卖方	买方	任何方式
DDP	Delivered Duty Paid	完税后交货	指定目的地约定点	指定目的地买方处置货物后	卖方	卖方	卖方	卖方	任何方式

Chapter 4　Payment of Goods

第 4 章　国际货物贸易货款支付

　　In international trade, how to pay for import and export goods is a complicated problem, which is also one of the important issues concerned by both buyers and sellers. It needs the certain operation process and handover procedure during the goods from the exporting country to the importing country, and exists the certain risks. As the buyers and sellers are located in two places, it is difficult to make delivery and payment strictly at the same time as sane as domestic retail trade. Moreover, the two countries have differences in legal system, financial management, monetary system and foreign exchange control. At the same time, the settlement of the payment often requires the involvement of the banks or other financial institutions other than the buyer and the seller, so the relationship is complicated. In order to ensure the smooth progress of the transaction and the safe receipt and payment of the goods, the buyer and the seller must make specific arrangements regarding the time and place of payment, the way and method of payment, and the currency used for payment and a series of other issues related to payment.

　　In a transaction, the process of choosing and determining the time and place of payment and the currency of payment is actually a process in which both parties adjust and compromise these contradictions through negotiation according to their respective trade policies, market status and business intentions. This also decides the diversity of payment tools and payment methods in international trade.

　　国际贸易中，进出口货款如何支付是一个复杂的问题，也是买卖双方密切关心的重要问题之一。货物从出口国到进口国需要有一定的运转过程和交接手续，存在着一定的风险；买卖双方又分处两地，很难与国内零售贸易那样，严格地做到交货和付款同时进行。而且双方国家在法律体制、金融管理、货币制度、外汇管制方面，都存在差别。同时，由于货款的结算往往还需要除买卖双方之外的银行或其他金融机构介入，关系复杂。为了保证交易的顺利进行，货款的安全收付，买卖双方必须就货款支付的时间、地点，付款的途径与方法，以及用于支付的货币等一系列与支付有关的问题，做出具体安排。

　　在一笔交易中，有关支付的时间和地点及支付货币的选择和确定过程，实际上是双方根据各自的贸易政策、市场地位、经营意图，通过磋商谈判，采用各种方式，就这些矛盾进行调整、妥协而达到统一的过程。这也就决定了国际贸易货款支付工具以及支付方式的多样性。

Section 1　Instruments of Payment

第1节　支付工具

1. Cash 现金

Cash can be used as a means of valuation, settlement and payment in international trade. However, in international trade, the use of cash as an instrument of payment is rare. Because the use of cash to pay off international claims and debts involves not only the dangers and inconveniences caused by the direct transfer of large amounts of cash, but also the slow turnover of funds. Therefore, the case of use of cash as an instrument of payment in the settlement of modern international trade is an exception.

Bill is a frequently used instrument of payment in international trade. It is a kind of security which is often used as a substitute for cash in circulation. The three mainly adopted bills and notes are bill of exchange (draft), promissory note and cheque (check).

现金在国际贸易中可作为计价、结算和支付的手段。但是在国际贸易中以现金作为支付工具的情形，却不多见。因为以现金清偿国际债权债务，不仅涉及直接运送大量现金所引起的各种危险和不便，而且产生资金周转的缓慢。所以，现代国际贸易的结算，以现金作为支付工具的情形，可说是例外。

票据是在国际贸易中经常使用的一种支付工具。它是一种可以代替现金流通的有价证券，在国际贸易中，主要使用的有三种票据：汇票、本票和支票。

2. Bill of Exchange 汇票

(1) Definition of Bill of Exchange 汇票的定义

In Bills of Exchange Act 1882 in the UK, the bill of exchange is defined as "an unconditional order in writing, addressed by one person (drawer) to another (drawee), signed by the person giving it, requiring the person to whom it is addressed to pay on demand, or at a fixed or determinable future time, a sum certain in money, to or to the order of, a specified person (payee), or to bearer".

In Negotiable Instruments Law of the People's Republic of China, the draft is a bill signed by the drawer, requiring the entrusted payer to make unconditional payment in a fixed amount at the sight of the bill or on a fixed date to the payee or the holder.

在《1882年英国汇票法》中，汇票是一个人向另一个人签发的、要求见票时或在将来的固定时间或可以确定的时间，对某人或其指定的人或持票人支付一定金额的无条件的支付命令。

在《中华人民共和国票据法》中，汇票是出票人签发的，委托付款人在见票时或者在指定日期无条件支付确定金额给收款人或持票人的票据。

(2) Contents of Bill of Exchange 汇票的内容

In Negotiable Instruments Law of the People's Republic of China, the draft is regarded as being invalid in case that the following items are not stated on the draft: a. the word "draft"; b. unconditional appointment; c. definite sum; d. name of payer; e. name of payee; f. draft issuance date; g. signature of drawer. However, in addition to the above particulars, the tenor of payment, the place of issue and other necessary information are usually written on the draft.

根据《中华人民共和国票据法》，下述规定事项未记载的，汇票无效：a.表明"汇票"字样；b.无条件支付委托；c.确定的金额；d.付款人名称；e.收款人名称；f.出票日期；g.出票人签章。但汇票上除记载以上事项以外，通常还会写明付款期限、出票地点等其他需要记载的内容。

① The words of "Bill of Exchange", or "Draft" are required to be on the draft, to distinguish from other paying instruments (Promissory Note, Check), but it is not required in Bills of Exchange Act.

应载明"汇票"字样，以示与其他票据支付工具(本票、支票)相区别，但《英国汇票法》无此要求。

② It is an unconditional pay order in writing, with the unlimited payment, without proviso.
表明无条件支付的书面命令，支付不受限制，不附带条件。

③ A certain sum, which is indicated in Arabic numbers and words in a definite currency including the interest, not allowed to be described with ambiguous words and approximate sum.

确定的金额。表明以一定的货币表示的确切数目，不能用大约或模棱两可的描述，要用文字大写、数字小写分别列明金额。

④ Drawee: the person to whom the order is addressed by the drawer and who is to pay the money. The drawee of a commercial draft can be the buyer, importer or bank, the drawee of the banker's draft is definitely a bank.

受票人，即付款人，出票人命令付款的人。商业汇票的受票人可以是买方、进口人或银行，银行汇票的受票人为银行。

⑤ Payee: the person to whom the payment is ordered to be made. In the import and export business, he can be an exporter, seller, an appointed bank or a normal holder of the draft.

受款人，又称收款人，受领汇票所规定金额的人，进出口业务中可以是出口商、卖方、指定的银行或正当持票人。

There are three kinds of ways to fill up the payee:

A. Restrictive payee

Writing the words on the draft, like "pay to ×× Co. only", or "pay to ×× Co., not negotiable". This type of draft is not transferable, and only the payee is qualified to accept the payment.

B. Demonstrative Order

Writing the words on the draft like "pay to ×× Co. or order" or "pay to the order of ×× Co.". This type requires endorsement when negotiation.

C. Pay to Bearer

Writing the words on the draft like "pay to bearer" or "pay to holder". It is transferable with the draft without endorsement.

受款人一栏(俗称"抬头")的填写方法有三种做法：

A. 限制性抬头

在汇票上注明："仅付××公司"或"付××公司，不准转让"。此种汇票不能流通转让，仅限指定的××人或××公司收取货款。

B. 指示性抬头

在汇票上注明："付××公司或其指定的人"或"付××公司指定的人"；这种汇票除××公司可以收取货款外，也可以经过其背书转让给第三者。

C. 持票人或来人抬头

在汇票上注明："付来人"或"付持票人"。这种抬头的汇票无须背书，仅交付汇票即可转让。

⑥ Drawer, the person who issues the draft. The property of the draft is different according to different drawers. The drawer of a commercial draft is an exporter while the drawer of the banker's draft is a bank. After signing the draft, the drawer assumes the responsibility of guaranteeing that the draft will be paid or accepted, that is, he becomes the main debtor of the draft. If the signature is fake or not authorized, the draft is invalid.

出票人，即签发汇票的人。出票人不同，汇票的性质不同。商业汇票的出票人为出口商，银行汇票的出票人为银行。出票人签字后，就承担担保汇票必获付款或承兑的责任，即成为汇票的主债务人。如果伪造签字，或未经授权人的签字均视为无效。

⑦ The Date of Issuance 出票日期

The issuance date must be written on the draft so as to confirm the qualification of the drawer and calculate the payment date.

汇票上必须记载出票日期，以便凭以确定出票人在签发汇票时有无行为能力。以出票日作为计算付款日。

⑧ The Tenor of Payment 付款期限

A. Regulation of Payment Time 规定付款期限的方法

a. At Sight

Payment at sight refers to that the payment is made immediately by the payer at sight of the draft, and the due date is the day that the payee presents the draft to the payer.

b. Payable ×× Days after Sight

The draft holder makes presentation of the draft to the payer, demanding the payer to accept the draft and make payment on the due date. The due date is confirmed according to the presentation date.

c. Payable ×× Days after Issuance Date

e.g., payable within 60 days after the date of draft.

d. Payable ×× Days after Date

e.g., payable within 30 days after the date of B/L.

e. Fixed Date

Payable on a fixed date. e.g., payable on December 10th, 2019.

a. 见票即付

见票即付又称即期付款，即付款人见票即付，受款人向付款人提示汇票的当天作为到期日。

b. 见票后××天付

持票人向付款人提示付款，要求承兑，根据提示见票日确定付款到期日。

c. 出票后××天付

从出票之日的第二天起算直至第××天付款。例如，出票日后60天付款。

d. 特定日期后××天付

从指定的特定日期起算直至第××天付款。例如，提单日后30天付款。

e. 定日付款

定日付款指定确定的日期付款。例如，在2019年12月10日付款。

B. Payment time stipulated in the Negotiable Instruments Law of the People's Republic of China《中华人民共和国票据法》规定的付款期限

a. Payable at sight

b. Payable on a fixed date

c. Payable on a fixed date after the draft is issued

d. Payable on a fixed date after the sight of the draft

a. 见票即付

b. 定日付款

c. 出票后定期付款

d. 见票后定期付款

C. Methods of Calculation of Payment Time 付款时间的计算方法

The tenor is not including the sight date, the issuance date or B/L date. According to

Negotiable Instruments Law of the People's Republic of China, the draft without the specific payment time requirement will be regarded as being payable at sight.

付款期限均不包括见票日、出票日或提单日，算尾不算头。《中华人民共和国票据法》规定：未规定付款日期的，即视为见票即付。

⑨ The Place of Draft Issuance and Payment 出票地点和付款地点

The place of draft issuance also is written next to the date. It is necessary to write the issuance place in order to confirm the applicable law. According to Negotiable Instruments Law of the People's Republic of China, the issuance place must be written on the draft, which can be the business operation place, the habitation, or the regular dwelling place of the drawer.

The place of payment is written next to the name of the payer, namely the place of making payment against the draft. According to Negotiable Instruments Law of the People's Republic of China, the payment place can be the business operation place, the habitation, or the regular dwelling place of the drawer in case that the specific payment place is not written on the draft.

出票地点通常写在出票日期的旁边。载明出票地点的必要性：确定以哪个国家的法律为依据。我国《票据法》规定：汇票上应该载明出票地点，若未载明，则出票人的营业场所、住所或经常居住地为出票地。

付款地点指付款人名字旁边的地点，即汇票金额支付地。《中华人民共和国票据法》规定：未记载付款地的付款人的营业场所、住所或经常居住地为付款地。

⑩ Other Items Maybe Written on the Draft 任意记载事项

A. The draft is issued in duplicate, the drawee makes payment against one draft, and then the other one is cancelled accordingly.

B. Consideration clause, for value received.

A. "付一不付二。"汇票一般做成两张，受票人对其中一张付款，另一张自动作废。

B. 对价条款，对价收讫。

(3) The Classification of the Draft 汇票的种类

① According to the different drawer 按出票人不同来分

A. Banker's draft 银行汇票

The draft is drawn by a bank, and the drawer is a bank. It is mainly used in remittance. A banker's draft is sent to payee by remitter, with which the payee can exchange the money from the payer (the bank).

The characteristics of banker's draft: both the drawer and the drawee are banks.

银行汇票是由银行开出的汇票，出票人为银行，主要用于汇付，通常交由汇款人寄给受款人或亲自交给受款人，凭票向付款人(银行)兑取票款。

银行汇票的特点：出票人和受票人都是银行。

B. Commercial draft 商业汇票

If the drawer is a commercial concern, the bill is called a commercial draft. It is often used in foreign trade finance. The characteristics of commercial draft: The drawer is a firm or an individual, the payer (the drawee) is a firm, an individual, or a bank.

商业汇票是由工商企业开出的汇票,它经常用于对外贸易的资金融通。商业汇票的特点：出票人是商号或个人,付款人(即受票人)可以是商号、个人,也可以是银行。

② According to the documents accompanied 按流通转让时有无随附单据来分

A. Clean draft 光票

In the transfer of the bill of exchange, if the draft of exchange is not accompanied with shipping documents, it is a clean draft. The banker's draft is usually a clean draft.

汇票流通时,不随附货运单据的汇票,称为光票。银行汇票多为光票。

B. Documentary draft 跟单汇票

If the draft is accompanied with shipment documents, it is documentary draft. This draft is guaranteed by exporter's credit as well as the goods. The commercial draft is usually a documentary bill. In international trade, mostly it is the documentary bill that is used, occasionally the clean draft is used to collect payment in small or sundry charges, such as commission, interest, sample fee and cash in advance, etc.

随附货运单据的汇票,这种汇票既有人的信用担保,又有物的担保。商业汇票多为跟单汇票。在国际贸易中的货款结算,大多数使用跟单汇票。如果是小额费用或杂费时,如收取佣金、利息、样品费和代垫费用等,偶尔使用光票。

③ According to payment time 按付款时间不同来分

A. Sight draft 即期汇票

A sight draft demands immediate payment by the drawee at the sight of the draft.

汇票上规定见票后立即付款的称为即期汇票。

B. Time draft or usance draft 远期汇票

In case of a time draft, the drawee is required to accept it first and pay it at a fixed or determinable future time, in other words, it requires acceptance before payment.

汇票上规定受票人先承兑,然后在指定的或将来一个可确定的日期付款的,换句话说,要求先承兑后付款的称为远期汇票。

(4) Acts Relating to a Bill of Exchange 汇票的票据行为

① Issuance 出票

Issuance is to fill up by the drawer the particulars in a bill of exchange the date of drawing. The name of the drawee, the time and amount of the payment, etc. The draft is signed by the drawer and then sent to the payee.

出票是指出票人在汇票上填写付款人、付款金额、付款日期和地点以及受款人等项目,经签字后交给受款人的行为。

② Presentation 提示

The holder of the draft presents the draft to the drawee, asking for the acceptance or payment. It is called at sight or demand when the drawee sees the draft.

A. Presentation for Payment.

The draft holder presents the draft to the payer asking for the sight payment.

B. Presentation for Acceptance.

For a time draft, the draft holder presents the draft to the payer asking for the acceptance at sight of the draft and payment on the maturity time.

提示指持票人将汇票提交受票人，要求承兑或付款的行为。受票人看到汇票叫见票。

A. 提示付款

持票人向付款人提交汇票，要求付款。

B. 承兑提示

远期汇票持票人向付款人提交汇票，付款人见票后办理承兑手续，到期时付款。

③ Acceptance 承兑

It is a promise made by the payer that it will make payment against a time draft. The payer writes the word "acceptance" on the bill remarking the acceptance date and affixes its signature, then returns the draft to the draft holder. The payer is regarded as the acceptor after making acceptance for the draft. The first debtor of the draft is the drawer before making acceptance, and it changes into the payer after making acceptance while the drawer becomes the second debtor.

承兑是指远期汇票的付款人对远期汇票表示承担到期付款责任的行为。付款人在汇票上写明"承兑"字样，注明承兑日期，并签字，交还持票人。付款人对汇票做出承兑，即成为承兑人。汇票在付款人承兑前，主债务人是出票人，在付款人承兑后，主债务人是付款人，出票人成为从债务人。

④ Payment 付款

For the sight payment, the payer shall make payment against the presentation of the draft; for the time draft, the payer makes payment on the maturity time after the acceptance. All the debts on the draft come to an end after the payment.

对即期汇票，在持票人提示汇票时，付款人即应付款；对远期汇票，付款人经过承兑后，在汇票到期日付款。付款后，汇票的一切债务即告终止。

⑤ Endorsement 背书

In international market, the draft is a kind of transfer instrument, which is negotiable and transferable in the bill market. The endorsement is one legal procedure of transferring the draft, that is to say, the holder of draft signs its name on the back of the bill or adding the name of the bearer (endorsee), and then transfers the draft to the bearer. After the endorsement, the claim for the payment is transferred to the bearer, too.

The draft can be transferred again and again after endorsements. For the endorsee, all the endorsers and the drawers are its remote holders; for the endorser, all the bearers after its endorsement and transferring are its subsequent parties. The remote holders are committed to the guaranty responsibility of the payment for the subsequent party.

Generally speaking, there are three main kinds of endorsement.

在国际市场上，汇票是一种流通工具，可以在票据市场上流通转让。背书是转让汇票权利的一种法定手续，就是由汇票持有人在汇票背面签上自己的名字，或再加上受让人(被背书人)的名字，并把汇票交给受让人的行为。经背书后，汇票的收款权利便转移给受让人。

汇票可以经过背书不断转让下去。对于受让人来说，所有在他以前的背书人以及原出票人都是他的前手；对于出让人来说，所有在他让与以后的受让人都是他的后手。前手对于后手负有担保汇票必被偿付的责任。

汇票背书主要有以下三种：

A. Restrictive Endorsement 限制性背书

The endorser may write clearly on the upper part of the signature on the back of the draft the endorsee with restrictive conditions. A restrictive endorsement is one which limits the draft for further negotiation, such as "Pay ×× only" or "Pay ×× non-transfer". Once the draft is restrictively endorsed, it cannot be transferred any more.

背书人在汇票背面其签字的上方写明被背书人，并加上限制性条件。例如"仅付××"或"付××不准转让"。汇票经限制性背书后，就不能再流通转让了。

B. Demonstrative Endorsement 指示性背书

A demonstrative endorsement is one which specifies the person to whom, or to whose order, the bill is to be payable, such as "Pay ×× or to order of".

背书人在汇票背面其签字的上方写明被背书人，但允许其继续转让。例如"付给××或其指定人"。

C. Blank Endorsement 空白背书

A blank endorsement, or endorsement in blank, is one which specifies no payee. The effect of a blank endorsement is to make the bill payable to bearer and to make delivery and without additional endorsement. The bearer or holder of a draft so endorsed may sometimes required, however, to place his endorsement upon it at the time of making a further negotiation

它指的是背书人只在汇票背面签字而不注明被背书人的名字，亦称"不记名背书"。汇票经空白背书后，受让人或持票人根据情况的需要，再转让时可通过自己的背书把汇票转成记名背书，此后的被背书人又可将其恢复为空白背书继续转让。

⑥ Discounting 贴现

Discounting means that the usance draft after the acceptance but undue is sold to a bank or a discounting house for the immediate payment with the discounting interest deducted from the payment sum based on a certain discounting rate.

In the international market, in order to receive the payment immediately, a time draft holder may transfer the draft to the others by making endorsement before the draft is mature.

贴现是指远期汇票承兑后,尚未到期,由银行或贴现公司从票面金额中扣除按一定贴现率计算的贴现息后,将余款付给持票人的行为。

在国际市场上,一张远期汇票的持票人如想在付款人付款前取得票款,可以通过背书转让汇票,即可将汇票进行贴现。

⑦ Dishonor 拒付

It is called the dishonor by non-acceptance or by non-payment in case that the draft is not accepted or not paid when the draft is presented by the bill holder for the acceptance. Dishonor also happens when the payer returns the draft, keeps away from the draft, dies, or is bankrupted.

The bill holder has the right of recourse in case that the draft is not accepted when it is presented within a reasonable time or it is not paid on the maturity date. The bill holder has the right to claim against the endorser and drawer.

持票人提示汇票要求承兑时,遭到拒绝承兑,或遭到拒绝付款,均称为拒付。付款人避不见票、死亡、破产,也称拒付。

汇票的持票人有权对合理期限内提示而遭到拒付的汇票或未在到期日付款的汇票行使追索权,持票人有权向背书人和开票人进行索偿。

⑧ Recourse 追索

Upon the dishonor, the bill holder has the right to claim for the settlement of the payment and the relevant charges against the prior endorser (or the drawer).

To exercise the right of recourse, the bill holder shall present the protest (or certificate of dishonor). The protest is an official document made by the local notary public, bank, chamber of commerce or court testifying that the draft has been dishonored. It is the legal proof with which the bill holder can take the right of the recourse against the prior endorser. If the dishonored draft has been accepted, the bill holder can go to court claiming for the payment against the acceptor.

汇票遭到拒付,持票人对其前手(即背书人、出票人)有请求其偿还汇票金额及费用的权利。

在行使追索权时,持票人必须提供拒绝证书(或拒付证书)。拒绝证书可以由付款地法定公证人,如银行、商会、法院,做出证明拒付事实的文件,这是持票人凭以向其"前手"进行追索的法律依据。如被拒付的汇票已经承兑,出票人可凭以向法院起诉,要求承兑人付款。

The order of making recourse is as follows:

A. According to the law of Britain: The bill holder can exercise the recourse against anyone of his prior endorsers or drawers.

B. According to the law of Germany: The bill holder can only exercise the recourse against the direct endorser, and then the endorser further takes recourse against his prior endorser in turn.

C. According to Negotiable Instruments Law of the People's Republic of China, the bill holder shall present the relevant proof about the refusal of the acceptance or payment when it exercises the recourse right, and the acceptor or payer shall be committed to the civil obligation due to the dishonor unless it presents the reason letter for the dishonor of the bill. The bill holder is allowed to get other relevant proofs legally.

进行追索的顺序如下：

A. 英国相关法律法规规定：持票人可直接找出票人或者任何前手追索。

B. 德国相关法律法规规定：持票人只能找直接背书人，依次向前手追索。

C. 《中华人民共和国票据法》规定，持票人行使追索权时，应提供被拒绝承兑或被拒付的有关证明，承兑人或付款人必须出具拒绝证明或提出退票理由书，否则应承担由此产生的民事责任。持票人可以依法取得其他有关证明。

The draft without recourse: To avoid the obligation of settling the recourse claim, the drawer or endorser of the bill remarks the word like "without recourse", which kind of draft is hardly discounted or transferred in market. According to the laws, the payer of the draft cannot exercise the recourse after the payment even though the payment is wrong.

"不受追索权"的汇票：这种汇票的出票人或背书人为了避免承担被追索的责任，在出票时或背书时加注"不受追索"字样，这种汇票在市面上难以贴现或转让。按各国票据法，汇票的付款人一经付款，即使付款有误，也不能向受款人追索。

3. Check (Cheque)支票

(1) Definition of Check 支票的定义

It is stipulated in The Bills of Exchange Act of UK that a check is a sight draft with the bank as the payer, that is to say, it is an unconditional order drawn on a banker by the drawer, requiring the banker to pay on demand a sum certain in money to or to the order of a specified person or to the bearer.

In Negotiable Instruments Law of the People's Republic of China, a check means a bill issued and signed by the drawer, appointing the bank or other financial institutes to make payment of a sum certain in money unconditionally to the payee or the check holder.

The key elements in a check according to Negotiable Instruments Law of the People's Republic of China are as follows:

A. The words of "check" or "cheque"

B. Unconditional payment promise

C. A sum certain in money

D. The name of payee

E. The issuance date

F. The signature of the drawer

The check without any one of stipulated elements is regarded as invalid.

在《1882年英国票据法》中，支票是以银行为付款人的即期汇票，即存款人要求银行无条件支付一定金额的委托或命令。

《中华人民共和国票据法》规定：支票是出票人签发的，委托办理支票存款业务的银行或者其他机构在见票时无条件支付确定金额给收款人或持票人的票据。

《中华人民共和国票据法》规定的支票要项包括：

A. 表明"支票"字样

B. 无条件支付委托

C. 确定的金额

D. 收款人名称

E. 出票日期

F. 出票人签字

未记载如上规定事项之一的支票无效。

The drawer writes a sum certain in money on the check and draws on a banker requiring the banker to pay the sum to the specified person or to the bearer. The drawer shall be committed to the obligation for the check and on the law. The obligation of the check means that the drawer shall take the responsibility of making payment to the payee; the legal obligation refers to that the drawer shall keep an account in the paying bank with the deposit not lower than the sum on the check. If the deposit is less, the check will be dishonored when the bearer presents the check to the paying bank for the payment. In this case, the drawer shall be held for the legal responsibility. The check is only at sight.

出票人在支票上签发一定的金额，要求受票的银行见票即付一定金额给特定人或持票人。出票人在签发支票后，应负票据上的责任和法律上的责任。前者是指出票人对收款人担保支票的付款；后者是指出票人签发支票时，应在付款的银行存有不低于票面金额的存款。如存款不足，支票持有人在向付款银行提示支票要求付款时，就会遭到拒付，这种支票叫空头支票。开出空头支票的出票人要负法律上的责任。支票只有即期，没有远期。

(2) Classification of Check 支票的种类

According to the relevant law of China, checks are classified into cash check and transfer check.

In other countries, checks are divided into crossed check and uncrossed check. The crossed check is crossed with two parallel lines on the up-left of the check, and the payee cannot cash the check but receive the payment through the bank transfer. The uncrossed check can both cash the money and make transfer.

《中华人民共和国票据法》规定：支票可分为现金支票和转账支票。

在其他国家，支票可分为划线支票和未划线支票。划线支票在支票左上角被划上两道平行线，受款人只能通过银行代为收款转账，不能提取现金。未划线支票既可转账也可提取现金。

4. Promissory Note 本票

(1) Definition of Promissory Note 本票的定义

In Bills of Exchange Act 1882 of the United Kingdom, the promissory note is an unconditional promise in writing made by one person (the maker) to another (the payee) and signed by the maker engaging to pay on demand or at a fixed or determinable future time a sum certain in money to or to the order of a specified person or bearer.

In accordance with Convention on the Unification of the Law Relating to Bills of Exchange and Promissory Notes, the promissory note shall include the following contents:

A. The words of "promissory note"

B. Unconditional payment promise

C. The payee or the specified person by the payee

D. The drawer

E. The date and place of the issuance

F. A period for payment

G. A sum certain in money

H. The payment place

在《1882年英国票据法》中，本票是一个人向另一个人签发的，保证即期或定期或在可能确定的将来时间，对某人或其他持票人支付一定金额的无条件承诺。即本票是出票人对受款人承诺无条件支付一定金额的票据。

根据《日内瓦统一汇票、本票法》，本票必须包括以下各项内容：

A. 写明其"本票"字样

B. 无条件支付承诺

C. 收款人或其指定的人

D. 出票人

E. 出票日期、地点

F. 付款期限

G. 一定金额

H. 付款地点

In the Negotiable Instruments Law of the People's Republic of China, the promissory note is the note issued by the drawer, promising to make unconditionally a definite sum of money to the payee or the note holder at sight of the note. It is stipulated in Negotiable Instruments Law of the People s Republic of China that the promissory note is named as the bank promissory note, issued and signed by the central bank of China or other financial institutions. There are only bank promissory notes in China but no commercial promissory notes.

The key elements in the promissory note are as follows:

A. The words of "promissory note"

B. Unconditional payment promise

C. A sum certain in money

D. The name of payee

E. The issuance date

F. The signature of the drawer

在《中华人民共和国票据法》中，本票是出票人签发的、承诺自己在见票时无条件支付确定的金额给收款人或者持票人的票据。该法规定：本票称为银行本票，由中国人民银行或其他金融机构签发。我国只有银行本票，没有商业本票。

我国《票据法》规定的本票要项包括：

A. 表明"本票"字样

B. 无条件支付承诺

C. 确定金额

D. 收款人名称

E. 出票日期

F. 出票人签字

(2) Classification of the Promissory Notes 本票的种类

Commercial promissory notes are also called general promissory notes, drawn by the commercial firms. The commercial promissory notes are divided into sight promissory note and time promissory note.

Bank promissory notes are issued and signed by banks. The bank promissory notes are sight, which are mostly adopted in international trade.

商业本票也称为一般本票，由工商企业签发。商业本票可分为即期商业本票与远期商业本票。

银行本票是由银行签发的本票。银行本票都是即期的。国际贸易中使用的本票大都是银行本票。

(3) The Involved Parties to the Promissory Notes 本票的当事人

There are two parties usually: the drawer and the payee. The payer of the promissory note is the drawer himself. The time promissory notes needn't the acceptance.

Some banks issue the promissory note which is at sight, without stating the payee or the words of "to the order". The kind of promissory note is equal to the currency circulated in the market.

主要有两个当事人：出票人和受款人。本票的付款人即出票人本人。远期本票不需承兑。

有的银行发行见票即付、不记载收款人的本票或来人抬头的本票，这种本票相当于纸币在市场上流通。

(4) The Differences of the Promissory Note and the Bill of Exchange 本票与汇票的区别

① The promissory note is a promise made by the drawer to make payment to the note holder; the draft is an order made by one party to the other party requiring it to make payment.

② There are only two parties in a promissory note, but three parties in a draft.

③ The drawer of a promissory note is the payer, and a time promissory note needn't the acceptance; the drawee of a draft is the payer.

④ In whatever situation, for a promissory note, the drawer is the first debtor. For a draft, the drawer is the first debtor before the bill is accepted, the acceptor becomes the first debtor after the acceptance and the drawer turns into the second debtor.

⑤ The promissory note is made out in only one original; the draft is made out in duplicate.

① 本票是出票人承诺自己向持票人付款，汇票是一个人向另一个人发出的支付命令。

② 本票只有两个当事人，汇票有三个当事人。

③ 本票的出票人即是付款人，远期本票不需承兑；汇票的受票人是付款人。

④ 本票在任何情况下，出票人都是主债务人；汇票在付款人承兑前，出票人是它的主债务人，在承兑后，承兑人是主债务人，出票人成为从债务人。

⑤ 本票只能开出一张，汇票可开出两张。

Section 2　Modes of Payment

第 2 节　支 付 方 式

1. Remittance 汇付

(1) Definition of Remittance 汇付的定义

Remittance refers to that the payer makes payment to the payee through a bank or other institutions. For the remittance in the international trade, the buyer makes payment to the seller by bank according to the conditions and the payment time stipulated in the contract.

汇付是指付款人主动通过银行或其他途径将款项汇交收款人。国际贸易货款采用汇付，一般是由买方按合同约定条件(如收到单据或货物)和时间，将货款通过银行汇交给卖方。

(2) Involved Parties in the Remittance 汇付的当事人

Four parties are involved in the remittance business: the remitter, the payee, the remitting bank and the paying bank.

Remitter is the party who makes payment by remittance. Usually the importer or the buyer is the remitter.

Payee or Beneficiary is the party who receives payment. Usually the seller is the payee or beneficiary.

Remitting Bank is the bank which issues a remittance instruction at the request of the buyer. Usually, the remitting bank is the bank in the importer's country.

Paying Bank is the bank that transfers the money to the account of the seller following the instruction of the remitting bank. The paying bank is usually the bank in the exporter's country.

The application form of remittance is a contract concluded between the buyer and the remitting bank, and the paying bank is the agency bank of the remitting bank, committed to the obligation of making payment.

在汇付业务中，通常有四个当事人：汇款人、收款人、汇出行和汇入行。

汇款人，即汇出款项的人，一般为进口人、买方。

收款人，即为收取款项的人，在进出口业务中一般为卖方。

汇出行，即接受买方的委托汇出款项的银行，通常是进口地银行。

汇入行，即解付汇款的银行，一般是出口地银行。

汇款申请书是买方与汇出行之间的一项合同，汇出行与汇入行是代理合同，承担解付汇款的义务。

(3) Classification and Procedure of Remittance 汇付的种类及其业务程序

① Mail Transfer (M/T) 信汇

Mail Transfer refers to that the remitting bank sends a remittance instruction letter by mail to the paying bank at the request of the payer, authorizing the paying bank to make payment of a sum of money to the payee. The procedure of M/T can be seen in the following figure (Fig. 4-1).

Advantages: Low cost. Disadvantages: Long time for receiving the payment.

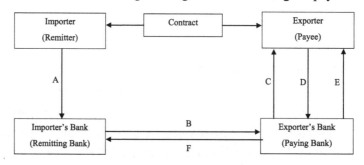

Fig. 4-1　Procedure of M/T

Remarks:

A. The importer submits the application for mail transfer to the remitting bank and pay the amount specified in the contract and the charge for mail transfer.

B. The remitting bank, in accordance with the application for mail transfer, sends the remittance instruction to the importing bank by airmail, instructing it to pay the exporter.

C. The paying bank sends the remittance advice to the exporter.

D. The exporter comes to the paying bank for getting payment against the remittance advice.

E. The paying bank makes payment to the exporter.

F. The paying bank sends the debit advice to the remitting bank.

信汇是指汇出行应汇款人申请，将信汇委托书寄给汇入行，授权解付一定金额给收款人的付款方式。信汇程序如图 4-1 所示。

优点：费用低廉。缺点：收取汇款时间长。

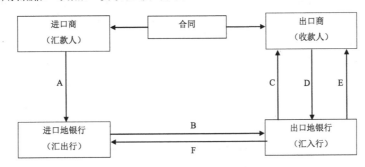

图 4-1　信汇程序

说明：

A. 进口商向汇出行提交信汇申请书，并按合同规定金额缴款和支付信汇手续费。

B. 汇出行按照信汇申请书，用航空信函发汇款指令给汇入行，指示其对出口商付款。

C. 汇入行向出口商发送汇款通知书。

D. 出口商凭汇款通知书到汇入行取款。

E. 汇入行向出口商交款。

F. 汇入行向汇出行发送付讫借记通知。

② Telegraphic Transfer (T/T) 电汇

Telegraphic Transfer refers to that the remitting bank sends the remittance instruction to the paying bank by telex, tele-transmission or SWIFT at the request of the payer. The procedure of T/T can be seen in the following figure (Fig. 4-2).

Advantages: Speedy, beneficial to the seller's capital running as it can receive the payment in a short time. Disadvantages: High cost.

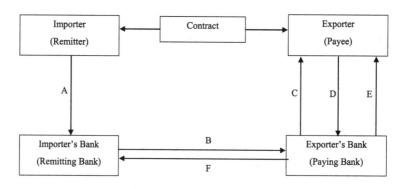

Fig. 4-2 Procedure of T/T

Remarks:

A. The importer submits the application for telegraphic transfer to the remitting bank and pay the amount specified in the contract and the charge for telegraphic transfer.

B. The remitting bank, in accordance with the application for telegraphic transfer, sends the remittance instruction to the paying bank by means of telecommunications, instructing it to pay the exporter.

C. The paying bank sends the remittance advice to the exporter.

D. The exporter comes to the paying bank for getting payment against the remittance advice.

E. The paying bank makes payment to the exporter.

F. The paying bank sends the debit advice to the remitting bank.

电汇是指汇出行应汇款人的申请，拍发加押电报或电传或 SWIFT 给另一个国家的分行或代理行(汇入行)，指示解付一定金额给收款人的付款方式。电汇程序如图 4-2 所示。

优点：速度快，卖方能尽快收到货款，有利于卖方资金周转。缺点：费用高。

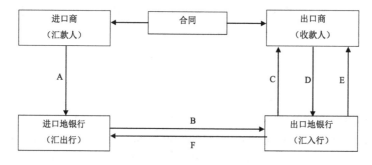

图 4-2　电汇程序

说明：

A. 进口商向汇出行提交电汇申请书，并按合同规定金额缴款和支付电汇手续费。

B. 汇出行按照电汇申请书，用电讯手段发汇款指令给汇入行，指示其对出口商付款。

C. 汇入行向出口商发送汇款通知书。

D. 出口商凭汇款通知书到汇入行取款。

E. 汇入行向出口商交款。

F. 汇入行向汇出行发送付讫借记通知。

③ Demand Draft (D/D) 票汇

Demand Draft (D/D) is a process that the remitting bank, at the request of the remitter, draws a demand draft on its branch or correspondent bank instructing it to make a certain amount of payment to the payee on behalf of the remitter. The remitter sends the draft to the payee. The payee gets the payment from the paying bank with draft. The procedure of D/D can be seen in the following figure (Fig. 4-3).

Advantages: Low cost and flexible withdrawal. Disadvantages: The drafts are easy to lose.

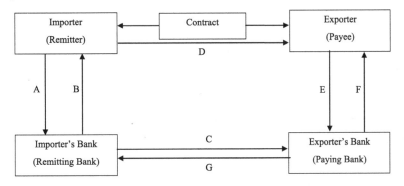

Fig. 4-3 Procedure of D/D

Remarks:

A. The importer submits the application for D/D to the remitting bank and pay the amount specified in the contract and the charge for D/D.

B. The remitting bank, in accordance with the application for D/D, issues a banker's sight draft to the importer.

C. The remitting bank sends the payment note of D/D (counterfoil) to the paying bank.

D. The importer sends the banker's sight draft to the exporter.

E. The exporter endorses the draft and hands it to the paying bank for payment.

F. The paying bank checks the draft and makes payment to the exporter at sight.

G. The paying bank sends the debit advice to the remitting bank.

票汇是汇出行应汇款人的申请，代替汇款人开立的以其分行或代理行为解付行、支付一定金额给收款人的银行即期汇票，由汇款人自行将汇票寄交收款人，收款人凭以向汇入行取款的付款方式。票汇程序如图 4-3 所示。

优点：费用低廉，取款灵活。缺点：汇票易遗失。

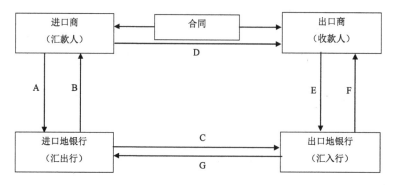

图 4-3 票汇程序

说明：

A. 进口商向汇出行提交票汇申请书，并按合同规定金额缴款和支付票汇手续费。

B. 汇出行按照票汇申请书，开出银行即期汇票给进口商。

C. 汇出行向汇入行寄票汇委托付款通知书(票根)。

D. 进口商自行将银行即期汇票寄送出口商。

E. 出口商将汇票背书后交汇入行要求付款。

F. 汇入行核对汇票，见票即期付款。

G. 汇入行向汇出行发送付讫借记通知。

(4) Advantages and Disadvantages of Remittance 汇付的利与弊

In international trade, most of transactions are paid through M/T and T/T if remittance is used. T/T is beneficial to the seller because it enables him to obtain money promptly, accelerate the turnover of funds, increase the income of interests and avoid the risks of fluctuation in exchange rate. But it is disadvantageous to the buyer in that he has to bear more cable expenses and bank charges. In practice, if T/T is not definitely stipulated in transaction, the buyer had better make payment by M/T. When the amount of payment is comparatively large, or the money market fluctuates greatly, or the currency of settlement being used is likely to devaluate, it is wise for the buyer to use T/T. In a word, the choice of T/T or MIT should be clearly stipulated in the contract according to specific situation. As far as D/D is concerned, it is transferable, which is different from M/T and T/T.

国际贸易中，如果使用汇付时，大多数交易是通过信汇和电汇来完成的。电汇对卖方有利，使其可以较快地收到货款，加速资金周转，增加利息收入和避免汇率变动的风险，但买方却要多付电报费用和银行费用。在实际业务中，除非明确规定要使用电汇，买方最好通过信汇付款。有时，当款项的金额较大或因货币市场动荡，使用的结算货币有贬值的可能时，通过电汇付款是买方明智的选择。总之，是用电汇还是信汇要根据实际情况在合同中明确规定。就票汇来说，它是可以转让的，这一点与信汇和电汇不同。

(5) Usage of the Remittance 汇付的应用

The remittance can be divided into the following two kinds:

汇付还可分为货到付款和预付货款两种：

① Cash on Delivery (COD)货到付款

The buyer will make payment on receipt of the documents or goods from the seller. Actually, it is a kind of credit offered by the seller to the buyer as well as a kind of Open Account Transaction (O/A). For the seller, the risk of it is the greatest. It totally depends on the credit of the buyer whether the seller will be paid after the delivery of the goods.

买方在收到卖方的单据或货物后，再付款。实际上是卖方向买方提供的一种信用，也是一种赊销(O/A)，对卖方来说风险最大，卖方交货以后，能否得到偿付，全凭买方个人信用，也称为商业信用。

② Payment in Advance 预付货款

The buyer will make payment prior to the seller's delivery of the goods. In this way, the buyer offers credit to the seller while the buyer takes some risks. It is sometimes called Cash with Order (CWO). The buyer will make payment to the seller by T/T or M/T in a few days after the conclusion of the contract.

在卖方还未生产交货时，买方预付货款，这种方式买方向卖方提供了信用，买方存在一定的风险，这种做法可以称为随订单付现(CWO)。或者在合同签订后若干天，买方即将货款电汇或信汇给卖方。

2. Collection 托收

(1) Definition of Collection 托收的定义

Collection is an arrangement whereby the seller (principal) draws a draft on the buyer (payer) and authorizes its bank to collect.

The definition of the International Chamber of Commerce (ICC) URC 522: The collection is the handling by banks, on instructions received, of documents (financial documents and/or commercial documents), in order to: a. obtain acceptance and/or, as the case may be, payment, or b. deliver commercial documents against acceptance and/or, as the case may be, against payment, or c. deliver documents on other terms and conditions.

托收是指卖方(委托人)出具汇票，委托银行向买方(付款人)收取货款的一种支付方式。

国际商会《托收统一规则》(URC522)给托收下的定义：托收是指由接到托收指示的银行根据所收到的指示处理金融单据以便取得付款或承兑，或凭付款或承兑交出商业单据，或凭其他条款或条件交出单据。

(2) Involved Parties in Collection 托收的当事人

① Principal 委托人

Usually, the principal is the seller.

委托人也称本人，通常是卖方。

② Remitting Bank 托收银行

The bank in the exporter's country is authorized by the principal to effect the collection on behalf of the principal.

托收银行是指出口地银行接受委托人委托，办理托收业务的银行。

③ Collecting Bank 代收行

The bank in the importer's country who receives the authorization from the remitting bank to collect the funds from the payer.

代收行是指接受托收行的委托，向付款人收取货款的进口地银行。

④ Payer 付款人

The payer is the buyer, who is also the drawee.

付款人是买方，也是汇票的受票人。

⑤ Presenting Bank 提示行

The bank who presents the shipment documents with draft to the payer.

向付款人做出提示汇票和单据的银行。

(3) Types and Procedure of Collection 托收的种类及其业务程序

The collection is classified into two kinds: clean collection and documentary collection.

Clean collection means the collection of financial documents without accompany by commercial documents (Financial documents means bills of exchange, promissory notes, checks, payment receipts or other similar instruments used for obtaining the payment of money; Commercial documents means invoices, shipping documents, documents of title or other similar documents or any other documents whatsoever, not being financial documents).

Documentary collection means the collection accompanied with commercial documents. The documentary collection is divided into Documents against Payment (D/P) and Documents against Acceptance (D/A).

托收可分为光票托收和跟单托收两种。

光票托收是指资金单据的托收，不附有商业单据(资金单据是指汇票、期票、支票、付款收据或其他用于取得付款的类似凭证，商业单据是指发票、装运单据、所有权单据或其他类似的单据，或一切不属于资金单据的其他单据)。

跟单托收是指附有商业单据的托收。跟单托收又可分为付款交单和承兑交单。

① Documents against Payment (D/P) 付款交单

The document against payment refers to that the seller delivers the documents upon receipt of the payment from the buyer (importer). The buyer cannot get the documents until it makes the payment to the seller. According to the different time of payment, document against payment can be further divided into D/P at sight and D/P after sight.

付款交单指卖方的交单是以买方(进口商)的付款为条件。先付款后交单，以付款为交单的前提条件。根据付款时间不同，付款交单可分为即期付款交单和远期付款交单。

A. D/P at sight 即期付款交单

After the shipment, the seller draws a sight draft and makes presentation of it with the full set of shipment documents to the buyer through the banks, and the buyer makes the payment at sight of the bill. The bank releases the documents to the buyer on receipt of the full payment from the buyer. The procedure of D/P at sight can be seen in the following figure (Fig. 4-4).

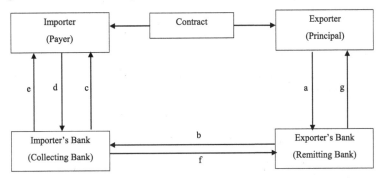

Fig. 4-4　Procedure of D/P at sight

Remarks:

a. According to the contract, the exporter ships the goods and draws a sight draft, then submits the draft together with commercial documents to the remitting bank for collecting a documentary draft on his behalf.

b. The remitting bank sends the sight draft together with commercial documents to the collecting bank for collecting money.

c. The collecting bank represents the sight draft and documents to the importer for payment.

d. The importer checks the documents and makes payment at sight.

e. The collecting bank hands over the documents to the importer.

f. The collecting bank notifies the remitting bank of crediting the money to their account.

g. The remitting bank makes payment to the exporter.

卖方装运后开具即期汇票，随附全套单据，通过银行向买方提示，买方见票后立即付款，买方付清货款后取得全套单据。银行向买方交单是以买方先付款为条件。即期付款交单程序如图 4-4 所示。

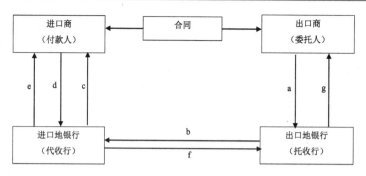

图 4-4 即期付款交单程序

说明：

a. 出口商根据合同规定装运货物后，开立即期汇票，连同商业单据交托收行办理托收。

b. 托收行将汇票连同商业单据一起寄交代收行委托代收。

c. 代收行向进口商提示即期汇票与单据。

d. 进口商自行检查单据无误后，于见票时即期付款。

e. 代收行交单据给进口商。

f. 代收行办理转账并通知托收行款已收妥。

g. 托收行向出口商交款。

B. D/P after sight 远期付款交单

After the shipment, the seller draws a time draft and makes presentation of it with the full set of shipment documents to the buyer through the banks, and the buyer accepts the bill after confirming it and makes the payment on the mature date. Then the bank releases the documents to the buyer. The procedure of D/P at sight can be seen in the following figure (Fig. 4-5).

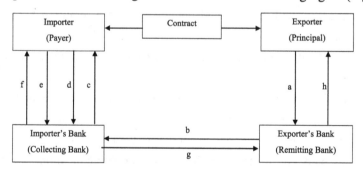

Fig. 4-5 Procedure of D/P after sight

Remarks:

a. According to the contract, the exporter ships the goods and draws a time draft, then submits the draft together with commercial documents to the remitting bank for collecting a documentary draft on his behalf.

b. The remitting bank sends the time draft together with commercial documents to the collecting bank for collecting money.

c. The collecting bank represents the time draft and documents to the importer for acceptance.

d. The importer checks the documents and accepts the time draft, then the collecting bank takes back the draft and documents.

e. The importer makes payment when the time draft falls due.

f. The collecting bank hands over the documents to the importer.

g. The collecting bank notifies the remitting bank of crediting the money to their account.

h. The remitting bank makes payment to the exporter.

The above shows that only after the payment has been made can the buyer obtain the shipping documents, and take delivery of or resell the goods, whether it is D/P sight or D/P after sight. Therefore, using D/P sight or D/P after sight represent less risk for the seller compared to using remittance.

卖方装运后开出远期汇票，随附商业单据，通过银行向买方提示，买方审核单据无误后，即在汇票上承兑，于汇票到期日付清货款后，银行向其交单。远期付款交单程序如图 4-5 所示。

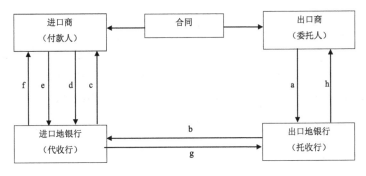

图 4-5 远期付款交单程序

说明：

a. 出口商根据合同规定装运货物后，开立远期汇票，连同商业单据交托收行办理托收。

b. 托收行将汇票连同商业单据一起寄交代收行委托代收。

c. 代收行向进口商提示远期汇票与单据。

d. 进口商自行检查单据无误后，承兑远期汇票，然后代收行收回汇票和单据。

e. 进口商于远期汇票到期时付款给代收行。

f. 代收行交单据给进口商。

g. 代收行办理转账并通知托收行款已收妥。

h. 托收行向出口商交款。

以上说明，不论是即期付款交单还是远期付款交单，都是买方付清货款后才能取得代表货物所有权的单据，才能提货或转售货物。所以，与汇付相比，托收中的付款交单的风险对卖方来说略小。

For D/P after sight, there are two methods to get the documents in advance for the buyer, which are as follows:

a. To make payment before the mature date.

b. With Trust Receipt (T/R), to borrow the documents from the bank before the payment. The trust receipt is a kind of credit guarantee document in written form issued by the buyer. If the collecting bank accepts the trust receipt and lends the documents to the buyer by itself, the collecting bank shall commit to the obligation of compensation to the seller in case that the buyer fails to pay.

在远期付款交单中，如果买方想提前取得单据，通常有两种做法：

a. 付款到期日之前提前付款获取单据。

b. 凭借信托收据(T/R)，在付款前向银行借出单据。信托收据是一种买方出具的书面信用担保文件。如代收行以信托收据的方式自行向买方借出单据，一旦买方不能付款，代收行对卖方承担赔偿责任。

② Documents against Acceptance (D/A) 承兑交单

After the shipment, the seller draws a time draft and makes presentation to the buyer through banks with the full set of documents, the collecting bank releases the documents to the buyer upon receipt of the acceptance of the buyer. The seller will fulfill the payment when the bill falls due. The procedure of D/A can be seen in the following figure (Fig. 4-6).

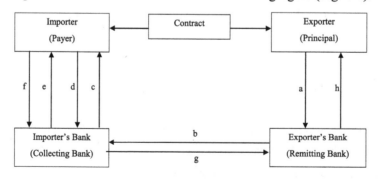

Fig. 4-6　Procedure of D/A

Remarks:

a. According to the contract, the exporter ships the goods and draws a time draft, then submits the draft together with commercial documents to the remitting bank for collecting a documentary draft on his behalf.

b. The remitting bank sends the time draft together with commercial documents to the collecting bank for collecting money.

c. The collecting bank represents the time draft and documents to the importer for acceptance.

d. The importer checks the documents and accepts the time draft.

e. The collecting bank takes back the draft and hands over the commercial documents to the importer documents.

f. The importer makes payment when the time draft falls due.

g. The collecting bank notifies the remitting bank of crediting the money to their account.

h. The remitting bank makes payment to the exporter.

Documents against Acceptance means that the buyer obtains the ownership of cargo before making payment and thus the seller is put into a great risk. The seller will get into the loss of goods and money in case of the buyer's failure in payment. Therefore, the international trade companies in our country are very cautious to the payment by D/A.

卖方在装运后开出远期汇票，随附全套单据，通过银行向买方提示，买方承兑汇票后，代收行即将全套单据交给买方。在汇票到期时，买方再来履行付款义务。承兑交单程序如图 4-6 所示。

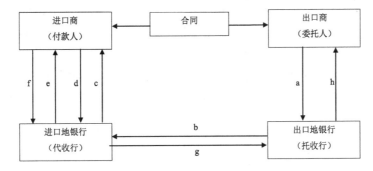

图 4-6　承兑交单程序

说明：

a. 出口商根据合同规定装运货物后，开立远期汇票,连同商业单据交托收行办理托收。

b. 托收行将汇票连同商业单据一起寄交代收行委托代收。

c. 代收行向进口商提示远期汇票与单据。

d. 进口商自行检查单据无误后，承兑远期汇票。

e. 代收行收回汇票，交商业单据给进口商。

f. 进口商于远期汇票到期时付款给代收行。
g. 代收行办理转账并通知托收行款已收妥。
h. 托收行向出口商交款。

承兑交单实际上是买方先取得货物所有权,以后再来付款,所以对卖方来说风险非常大。一旦买方到期不付款,卖方就会遭到货款两空的损失。因此,现在我国的外贸公司对使用承兑交单非常谨慎。

(4) Nature, Advantages and Disadvantages of Collection 托收的性质和利弊

Collection is a kind of commercial credit, offered to each other by firms and merchants. The collection bank acts only as collector of funds on behalf of the seller and is not committed to the obligation whether the buyer makes payment or not. It is dependent on the commercial credit of the buyer if the seller will be paid after the delivery of goods.

Collection is in favor of the buyer. The payment by collection needn't go through as complicated procedures as the L/C, without the requirement of bank deposit, with lower bank service charges, and not occupying capital.

The collection transaction puts the seller under a great risk. The remitting banks and collecting banks are not committed to the obligation of payment, and thus it is completely dependent on the buyer's credit whether the seller can receive payment or not. The seller is in the risk of failure or delay of being paid in case that the buyer goes bankruptcy, loses the ability of discharging debt or refuses to pay in purpose. Although D/P is to deliver the documents on receipt of payment, the buyer may refuse to make payment and give up the documents when the market is shrinking. In this case, the seller will bear the loss of money and goods as well. The banks are not committed to the obligation of keeping and delivery of the shipment, but the seller has to pay for the settlement charges of delivery, customs clearance, warehouse storage, insurance, resale, auction or shipping back, etc. . For the payment by D/A, the risk for the seller is larger.

托收是一种商业信用,也就是商人之间互相提供的信用。通过银行办理托收,银行属于代办性质,对买方是否付款不承担责任。卖方交货后能否收回货款,完全要看买方个人的信誉。托收虽然通过银行办理,但银行只是代收代付,并不承担付款责任。

托收对买方有利,它不需要像信用证那样办理烦琐的手续,不需银行押金,减少费用支出,不占压资金。

托收对卖方存在较大的风险。银行并不承担付款的责任,卖方能否收到货款完全依赖买方的个人信用。如买方破产或丧失清偿债务的能力或有意赖账,出口人则有可能收不回或延迟收回货款。虽然付款交单是以买方首先付款为条件,但在市场情况下跌时,信誉不好的买方可能溜之大吉,既不赎单,也不付款,那么卖方同样要遭受货款两空的损失。在这种情况下,银行没有义务代为保管或提取货物,出口人还要承担在进口地办理提货、缴

纳进口关税、存仓、保险、转售以及货物被低价拍卖或运回国内的损失。在承兑交单的情况下，卖方的损失会更大，风险也更大。

(5) The Rules of Uniform Rules for Collections 522 (URC522) 国际商会《托收统一规则522号》(URC522)的有关规定

① The instructions of Collection shall write the words like "keep to URC522, and D/P after sight is not advisable".

② The time draft is not allowed and the commercial documents shall be delivered after the payment. For the D/P after sight, it shall be remarked with documents against payment or documents against acceptance.

③ The consignee shall not be the banks or to order of bank; banks are only in charge of documents, not responsible for the goods.

④ Banks are not responsible for the verification of documents, but in charge of confirming if the quantity of documents is the same as indicated in the collection instruction.

⑤ The presenting bank shall send the advice of dishonor to the remitting bank in case that the collection is dishonored.

① 托收指示中注明"遵循 URC522，不提倡使用 D/P 远期"。

② 不应含有远期汇票，同时规定商业单据要在付款后才交付，如果是远期付款交单，应注明单据是付款后交单，还是仅凭承兑后交单。

③ 银行及其指定人不应为收货人，银行只管单不管货。

④ 银行不负责核实单据，只负责审核单据的所列份数是否与托收指示相符。

⑤ 托收如被拒付，或拒绝承兑，提示行应向托收行发出拒付通知。

(6) Points for Attention for Collection 使用托收方式应注意的问题

The seller shall make a detailed investigation about the credit of the buyer before accepting the payment by Collection.

For the countries that are strict on foreign exchange, it is not advisable to adopt Collection as the payment method.

The seller shall have a full understanding of the commercial regulations of the import country. For example, in some Latin American countries, the shipping documents will be released to the buyer on receipt of the acceptance for D/P after sight, it makes no difference with D/A. For these countries, it is not advisable to accept D/P after sight as the payment term.

The exporter shall try to conclude the contract with CIF term if the payment term is by Collection. The risk is larger with FOB or CFR in case that the buyer refuses to pay as the seller does not hold the insurance policy, For the exports with FOB or CFR, the seller shall insure for the export credit.

For the Collection, the seller shall have a wholesome accounting system with regular examination, urge and settle the unpaid business in prevention of the possible loss.

在决定用托收付款方式前，卖方应对客户的资信做详细的调查和了解。确实资信可靠，才可采用。

对于某些外汇管制较严的进口国，不宜采用托收的方式。

要了解进口国的商业惯例。例如，某些拉美国家按当地的法律和习惯，对于远期付款交单，进口人承兑汇票后，即向买方交单，与D/A没有区别。对于这些国家，我们不宜接受远期付款交单的方式。

如果采用托收的付款方式，签合同时应争取以CIF成交。因为用FOB或CFR，万一买方拒绝付款赎单，卖方手中没有掌握保险单，风险更大。如用FOB或CFR出口，卖方应投保出口信用险或卖方利益险。

采用托收方式时，卖方要有健全的财务管理制度，定期检查，及时催收清理，以免发生损失。

3. Letter of Credit 信用证

Letter of credit (L/C) is a payment term mainly used in international trade. Under the circumstance that the seller and the buyer don't know much of each other, lacking mutual trust, the payment term of L/C is a good solution to this difficult problem, which replaces commercial credit with bank credit, getting a bank involved in the payment obligation. The availability of the payment promise to the seller from a bank before the delivery of goods helps the transactions go well, further boosting the development of international trade.

L/C payment is in favor of buyers, too. In a sales transaction by L/C, the buyer can restrict the seller with the clauses of L/C to the fulfillment of the contract, ensuring the quality, quantity and delivery time of the goods. The seller cannot be paid if it breaches the contract.

信用证结算是目前我国外贸进出口结算的一种主要方式，它以银行信用取代商业信用，以银行的付款责任取代买方的付款责任，在买卖双方缺乏信任、互不熟悉的情况下，信用证的付款方式很好地解决了支付中的难题，使卖方在交货以前就能得到银行付款的承诺，使交易得以顺利进行，有利于国际贸易的快速发展。

在信用证交易中，买方也有得天独厚的好处，它可以利用信用证条款约束卖方履行合同，保证所购买货物的品质、数量、交货期符合合同的规定，卖方如果违约将得不到偿付。

(1) Definition of L/C 信用证的定义

Letter of Credit is a kind of conditional document in written form, opened by a bank, with a promise to make payment. To be more specific, it is a kind of warrant issued by a bank at the request of the buyer, addressed to the exporter, in a certain amount, under a certain condition, promising to make payment. The said "certain amount, certain condition,, means that the payment made by the opening bank is under the condition that the seller presents the documents complying with the L/C clauses.

According to The Uniform Customs and Practice for Documentary Credits, 2007 Revision, ICC Publication No. 600 ("UCP600"), documentary credit means any arrangement, however named or described, that is irrevocable and thereby constitutes a definite undertaking of the issuing bank to honor a complying presentation. "To honor" means: a. to pay at sight if the credit is available by sight payment. b. to incur a deferred payment undertaking and pay at maturity if the credit is available by deferred payment. c. to accept a bill of exchange ("draft") drawn by the beneficiary and pay at maturity if the credit is available by acceptance. The payment by letter of credit refers to the credit given by banks, it is not money, but the issuing bank or the bank concerned promise to make payment by banks' credits. The issuing banks provide credits, not money.

信用证是一种银行开立的、有条件的、承诺付款的书面文件。具体地说，就是银行(开证行)应进口人的请求和指示，向出口人开立的、一定金额的、在一定条件下保证付款的凭证。所谓"一定金额，一定条件"，是指开证行的付款是以卖方提交符合信用证的单据为条件。

国际商会《跟单信用证统一惯例(2007年修订版)》(UCP600)给信用证的定义是：信用证是指一项不可撤销的安排，无论其名称或描述如何，该项安排构成开证行对相符交单予以承付的确定承诺。承付是指：a. 如果信用证为即期付款信用证，则即期付款。b. 如果信用证为延期付款信用证，则承诺延期付款并在承诺到期日付款。c. 如果信用证为承兑信用证，则承兑受益人开出的汇票并在汇票到期日付款。信用证支付方式是银行的信用，而不是资金。开证行或相关银行以自己的信用做出付款保证。开证行提供的是信用，不是资金。

(2) Parties Involved in L/C 信用证的当事人

① Opener/Applicant 开证申请人

Opener is the party which applies to the bank for the opening of a Letter of Credit, namely, the importer or the buyer under a contract.

开证申请人是向银行申请开立信用证的人，即进口人或买卖合同中的买方。

② Issuing/Opening Bank 开证行

Issuing Bank is the bank which issues a credit to the seller, usually, the bank located in the country of the importer.

开证行是受开证人委托，向卖方开立信用证的银行，一般为进口人所在地银行。

③ Beneficiary 受益人

Beneficiary is the party entitled to be reimbursed under a credit and specified in the credit, usually the exporter.

受益人是信用证上所指定的有权使用该证得到偿付的人，一般为出口商。

④ Advising/Notifying Bank 通知行

Advising/Notifying Bank is the bank nominated by the issuing bank to transfer a credit to the bank of the exporter's country, usually the branch bank or the correspondent bank abroad of the issuing bank.

通知行是受开证行的委托，将信用证转交出口商的银行，出口地银行通常是开证行在国外的分行或代理行。

⑤ Negotiating Bank 议付行

Negotiating Bank is the bank which is ready to purchase or discount the documentary bill presented by the beneficiary under a Letter of Credit. It may be a bank designated by the issuing bank or another bank which is able to negotiate under the credit. Negotiation means that, after confirming the documents in compliance with the L/C, the negotiating bank discounts the documentary bill and pays for the shipping documents under the L/C according to the L/C clauses, and the reimbursement sum is the balance after the interests accrued from the negotiation date to the estimated payment date are deducted. Negotiation is actually a kind of financing way for the beneficiary; after negotiation the bank becomes the holder of the draft with recourse.

议付行是愿意买入或贴现受益人交来跟单汇票的银行，可以是由开证行指定的银行，也可以是公开议付的银行。议付又称押汇、买单，是指议付行在审单无误的情况下，按信用证的条款贴现受益人的汇票，买入信用证项下的货运单据，从票面金额中扣除从议付日到估计收到票款之日的利息，将余款先行支付给受益人。议付实际上是银行向受益人先行垫付资金，银行在议付之后就成为汇票的正当持票人，具有追索权。

⑥ Paying/Drawee Bank 付款行

Paying Bank is the bank which is specified in an L/C, usually an issuing bank, or a branch bank/correspondent bank of the issuing bank. Due to the transfer of money, the issuing bank will nominate another bank as the paying bank. The paying bank and issuing bank are on the same legal status, without recourse.

付款行是信用证上指定的付款银行，一般是开证行，也可以是开证行以外的分行或代理行。由于资金调拨的原因，开证行可以指定另一家银行为付款银行。付款行与开证行具有同等的法律地位，都是终局性的，没有追索权。

⑦ Reimbursing Bank 偿付行

Reimbursing Bank is the bank which is specified in an L/C to make reimbursement on behalf of the issuing bank or paying bank. The bank is not committed to check the documents but makes payment upon the authorization of the issuing bank, and the payment is final. The reimbursing bank is requested to fulfill the payment resulting from the capital of the issuing bank deposited in the third party country.

偿付行是信用证指定的代开证行或付款行清偿货款的银行，其不负责审单，只根据开证行的授权付款,付款也是终局性的。偿付行的出现,往往是由于开证行的资金调度或集中在该银行的缘故,要求该银行代为偿付信用证规定的款项。

⑧ Confirming Bank 保兑行

Confirming Bank is the bank which adds the confirmation to a Letter of Credit at the request of the issuing bank. The confirming bank is responsible for the L/C separately with the commitment of making payment or negotiation. The confirming bank holds the same obligation and status as the opening bank. The confirming bank can be the advising bank at the same time. It can be acted by Advising/Notifying Bank or other kinds of banks.

保兑行是根据开证行的请求,在信用证上加具保兑的银行。保兑行在信用证上加具保兑后,即对信用证独立负责,承担必须付款或议付的责任。保兑行具有与开证行相同的责任和地位。保兑行可以由通知行兼任,也可由其他银行加具保兑。

(3) Procedures of L/C Payment 信用证支付的一般程序

① Application for L/C 开证人申请开立信用证

During international sales transactions, the applicant is usually the importer. After the conclusion of the sales contracts, the buyer (L/C applicant) applies to the opening bank for the L/C. The L/C applicant fills out the application form at first based on the sales contract. The buyer shall apply for L/C according to the clauses of sales contract without changing the terms and conditions and obligations in the contract. Once the L/C is opened, the beneficiary shall effect the fulfillment of documents presentation according to the L/C terms, upon which the opening bank makes payment.

The L/C applicant shall pay some margin to the opening bank, usually ×× percent of the L/C amount. The applicant shall also pay L/C opening charges and correspondence charges to the L/C opening bank.

在国际贸易的货物买卖中,开证人一般为进口人。买卖合同订立后,买方(开证申请人)向开证行申请开立信用证,开证人申请开证时,应填写开证申请书,开证申请书的内容实际上完全反映了买卖合同的内容,虽然银行开立信用证是根据买方的开证申请书,但信用证开立的基础却是买卖合同。买方申请开立信用证必须完全遵循买卖合同的条款和义务,不得利用开证的机会,擅自改变合同的条款。信用证一旦开立,受益人就必须按照信用证的条款履行交单义务,这也是开证行履行付款的依据。

开证人申请开立信用证,应向开证行交付一定比率的押金,一般为信用证金额的百分之几到几十。开证人还应按规定向开证行支付开证手续费和邮电费。

② Issuance of L/C 开证行开立信用证

The issuing bank issues the L/C at the request of the L/C applicant. The clauses of the L/C shall be in compliance with the contents of L/C application form. The issuing bank then undertakes the payment responsibility to the beneficiary after opening the L/C.

开证行根据开证人的申请向受益人开立信用证。所开信用证的条款必须与开证申请书所列一致。开证行开立信用证后，对受益人承担了付款责任。

③ Advice of L/C 通知行通知信用证

After receiving L/C from the opening bank, the advising bank notifies the L/C beneficiary contact required by the opening bank. The advising bank shall deliver it to the L/C beneficiary promptly after verifying the test key and the signature in the L/C.

通知行收到开证行开来的信用证后，通知行通知开证行要求的收件人。它应立即将信用证的密押和签字印鉴进行核对，在核对无误后，立即交信用证的受益人。

④ Verification and Modification of L/C 审证与修改信用证

The beneficiary shall verify the L/C firstly after receiving it, confirming that the L/C contents are in compliance with the sales contract. In case of any discrepancies, unacceptable L/C clauses or soft clauses, the beneficiary shall notify the buyer to amend the L/C.

It is stipulated in UCP600 as follows: "an issuing bank is irrevocably bound by an amendment as of the time it issues the amendment"; "a credit can neither be amended nor cancelled without the agreement of the issuing bank, the confirming bank, if any, and the beneficiary"; "the terms and conditions of the original credit (or a credit incorporating previously accepted amendments) will remain in force for the beneficiary until the beneficiary communicates its acceptance of the amendment to the bank that advised such an amendment. The beneficiary should give notification of acceptance or rejection of an amendment. If the beneficiary fails to give such notification, the shipping documents presented are consistent with the L/C and any not yet accepted amendment, the beneficiary will be deemed to have given such notification of acceptance of such amendment. As of that moment the credit will be amended".

受益人接到信用证后应首先审核信用证，检查买方开证时是否与买卖合同相符。如发现不符或某些条款不能接受或有软条款，应立即通知买方修改信用证。

UCP600 中规定："开证行自发出修改之时起，即不可撤销地受其约束"；"未经开证行、保兑行(如有的话)及受益人同意，信用证既不得修改，也不得撤销"；"在受益人告知通知修改的银行其接受该修改之前，原信用证(或含有先前被接受的修改的信用证)的条款对受益人仍然有效。受益人应提供接受或拒绝修改的通知。如果受益人未能给予通知，当交单与信用证以及尚未表示接受的修改的要求一致时，即视为受益人已做出接受修改的通知，并且从此时起，该信用证被修改"。

⑤ Presentation and Negotiation 交单议付

The beneficiary may prepare the goods and arrange for the shipment according to the clauses in the L/C after receiving the L/C and the confirmation of it or the amendment notification.

The beneficiary may go to a local bank for negotiation when obtaining the fall set of documents after the shipment. The local bank advances funds to the beneficiary after deducting the bank interest which is calculated from the advance date to the reimbursement date, offering a financing to the beneficiary, and gaining interests and service charges.

受益人收到信用证，经审查无误，或收到修改通知书认可后，即可根据信用证规定的条款进行备货和安排出运。

受益人在装船后取得全套单据，可以据以向所在地银行进行押汇，也称为议付。即由当地银行将出运货物的货款扣除预计收到货款的这段时间的利息后先行给付受益人，以给受益人资金融通，银行从中赚取利息和手续费。

⑥ Honor and Payment 开证申请人付款赎单

The opening bank shall notify the applicant to make payment for the documents after transferring the funds to the negotiating bank. The applicant shall go to the opening bank and check the shipment documents on receipt of the notification from the opening bank. After verifying the documents, the applicant settles all payment including the charges involved and gets the documents. The deposit, if any, will be deducted from the payment; the collateral shall be returned to the applicant too after paying off. Then, the relationship between the applicant and the opening bank due to the L/C comes to an end.

开证行将全部票款拨还议付银行后，应立即通知开证人付款赎单。开证人接到开证行通知后，也应立即到开证行核验单据，认为无误后，将全部票款及有关费用一并向开证行付清并赎取单据。如申请开证时曾交付押金，付款时可扣除押金；如申请开证时曾递交抵押品，则在付清票款和费用后，抵押品由开证行发还。此时，开证人与开证行之间由于开立信用证所构成的权利义务关系即告终结。

To sum up, we can see the procedures of L/C payment are as follows (See Figure 4-7).

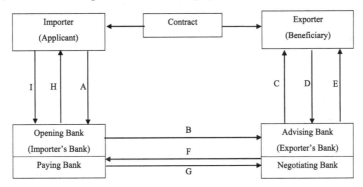

Fig. 4-7　Procedure of L/C payment

Remarks:

A. The buyer makes application for a letter of credit with his bank and signs the opening bank's agreement form. The opening bank approves the application and issues the actual L/C document.

B. The opening bank forwards the L/C to the advising bank.

C. The advising bank delivers the L/C to the beneficiary.

D. Having examined the letter of credit, the beneficiary (exporter) ships the goods. After that, the beneficiary prepares the documents specified in the L/C, draws a draft and presents them to an exporter's bank for negotiation.

E. The negotiating bank negotiates the documents and pays money to the beneficiary in accordance with the L/C.

F. The negotiating bank forwards the documents to the opening bank.

G. The opening bank receives the documents and checks them. If the documents are in order and comply with the L/C, the opening bank credits the negotiating bank's account.

H. The opening bank notifies the buyer to make payment for documents.

I. After making payment, the buyer receives the documents and take delivery of the goods.

综上可知，信用证支付的程序如图 4-7 所示。

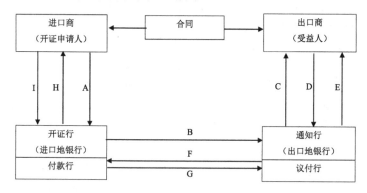

图 4-7　信用证支付的程序

说明：

A. 进口商向当地银行(开证行)申请开立信用证，并与开证行签订协议。开证行同意其申请后开出信用证。

B. 开证行将信用证寄给通知行。

C. 通知行将信用证转递给受益人。

D. 受益人(出口商)经审核信用证认可后，即装运货物。受益人发货后，备妥信用证规定的单据，送交出口地银行办理议付。

E. 议付行确认单据后，按照信用证规定将垫款给受益人。

F. 议付行将单据寄给开证行索款。

G. 开证行经审核单据无误后，付款给议付行。

H. 开证行通知进口商付款。

I. 进口商付款后取得单据，即可提货。

(4) Nature and Characteristics of Letter of Credit 信用证方式的性质和特点

① Nature 性质

A. Reverse Remittance 逆汇法

The payment by Letter of Credit is a kind of reverse remittance.

信用证付款方式是一种逆汇法。

B. Bank Credit 银行信用

With the payment obligation of importer transferred to a bank through L/C payment, a bank is undertaking an absolute responsibility for payment.

信用证把原来由进口人履行的凭单付款责任转由银行来履行，在商业信用之上加上银行信用，银行负绝对责任。

There are three important legal principles as follows:

a. Undertaking an absolute responsibility, a bank is in the first place to make payment.

b. Being an independent instrument, L/C is a promise or contract independent from the sales contract.

c. With the principle of strict compliance, a bank makes payment upon the strict compliance of documents with L/C.

信用证交易的性质有三个非常重要的法律原则：

a. 银行承担的是绝对责任，超越担保原来的责任，银行承担第一位的责任。

b. 自足文件，信用证是独立于买卖合同的一种契约。

c. 严格相符原则，单据和信用证严格相符，也是银行付款的依据。

② Characteristics 特点

A. Opening Bank Undertaking the Responsibility of the First Payer 开证行承担第一性的付款责任

It is a kind of absolute and primary responsibility of payment. That is to say, after opening an L/C, the L/C opening bank has to fulfill the payment according to L/C terms whether the buyer is bankrupt, with a solvency or not, dead. Without the consent of the beneficiary, an L/C cannot be revoked or revised.

这种责任是一种绝对的责任、第一位的付款责任。也就是说，只要卖方提交了符合信用证规定的单据，无论买方是否破产、死亡都与卖方无关，开证行必须按照信用证的承诺对卖方付款，未经受益人同意，开证行不得撤销或者更改信用证。

B. An Independent Instrument 信用证是一种自足文件

A letter of credit is another contract, which is issued based on the sales contract, but independent from the sales contract and application form. A letter of credit is a contract between the issuing bank and the beneficiary. The rights and obligations of the parties involved in an L/C are subject to the L/C, not bound by the sales contract. Therefore, a payment or acceptance promise made by a bank is not bound by the restriction of the claims or defenses between the L/C applicant and the issuing bank or the beneficiary based on the existing relationships.

It's written in Clause 4 (a) in UCP600 as follows: "A credit by its nature is a separate transaction from the sales contact or other contract on which it may be based. Banks are in no way concerned with or bound by such a contract, even if any reference whatsoever to it is included in the credit. Consequently, the undertaking of a bank to honor, to negotiate or to fulfill any other obligation under the credit is not subject to claims or defenses by the applicant resulting from its relationships with the issuing bank or the beneficiary." "A beneficiary can in no case avail itself of the contractual relationships existing between banks or between the applicant and the issuing bank."

信用证是基于买卖合同为基础开立的，但是信用证一旦开立就独立于买卖合同、独立于开证申请书，成为与买卖合同无关的另一个契约，信用证实际上是开证行与受益人之间的一个合同。信用证的各方当事人的权利、义务都以信用证为准，不受买卖合同的约束。因此，一家银行做出付款、承兑的承诺，不受申请人与开证行或与受益人之间在已有关系上产生索偿或抗辩的制约。

UCP600 第 4 条(a)款规定："就其性质而言，信用证与可能作为其开立基础的销售合同或其他合同是相互独立的交易，即使信用证中含有对此类合同的任何援引，银行也与该合同无关，且不受其约束。因此，银行关于承付、议付或履行信用证项下其他义务的承诺，不受申请人基于与开证行或与受益人之间的关系而产生的任何请求或抗辩的影响。""受益人在任何情况下不得利用银行之间或申请人与开证行之间的合同关系。"

C. L/C is a Kind of Transaction of Documents 信用证业务是一种单据的买卖

Under a letter of credit, a bank makes payment against documents. A bank makes payment depending on the documentary compliance with the shipping documents and credit, which is neither concerned with the goods, nor sales contract despite the truth or falsity of documents.

It is stipulated in Article 34 of UCP600 as "A bank assumes no liability or responsibility for the form, sufficiency, accuracy, genuineness, falsification or legal effect of any document, or for the general or particular conditions stipulated in a document or superimposed thereon; nor does it assume any liability or responsibility for the description, quantity, weight, quality, condition, packing, delivery, value or existence of the goods, services or other performance represented by any document, or for the good faith or acts or omissions, solvency, performance or standing of the consignor, the carrier, the for-warder, the consignee or the insurer of the goods or any other person".

Under a letter of credit, with the principle of strict compliance, the documents must comply with credit as well as each other. The paying bank must make payment as long as a presentation of documents is complying even though the actual shipment has something wrong. The paying bank can refuse payment too if a presentation is not complying even though the shipment is right. In case that the goods have something wrong or the seller is deceiving, the solution to make refusal of payment is to find out the documentary discrepancies.

在信用证项下，银行实行的是凭单付款的原则，银行付款的依据仅仅是单据和信用证的规定表面相符，银行与货物无关，与买卖合同无关，与单据的真假无关。

UCP600 第 34 条规定："银行对任何单据的形式、充分性、准确性、内容真实性、虚假性或法律效力，或对单据中规定或添加的一般或特殊条件，概不负责；银行对任何单据所代表的货物、服务或其他履约行为的描述、数量、重量、品质、状况、包装、交付、价值或其存在与否，或对发货人、承运人、货运代理人、收货人、货物的保险人或其他任何人的诚信与否、作为或不作为、清偿能力、履约或资信状况，也概不负责。"

在信用证条件下实行严格相符的原则，不仅要做到单证一致，还要做到单单一致。在信用证项下，只要交单正确，即使货物有假，银行也必须付款。如果单据有错误，即使货物正确，银行可以拒付。如果发现货物有假或者卖方存在欺诈行为，买方如果想让银行拒付，唯一的办法就是寻找单据的不符点。

(5) Forms of Opening Letter of Credit 信用证的形式

① Open by Airmail 信开本

The issuing bank will type the credit on a preprinted form with details transmitted from the application form and send it to the advising bank by registered airmail service.

信开本是指开证银行采用印就的信函格式的信用证，开证后以航空邮寄送通知行。

② Open by Cable 电开本

The issuing bank transmits the full credit information through cable, telex, fax or SWIFT to the advising bank.

电开本是指开证行使用电报、电传、传真、SWIFT 等各种电讯方法将信用证条款传达给通知行。

③ SWIFT L/C SWIFT 信用证

Currently, SWIFT is the main way to transmit L/C in international trade.

"SWIFT" (namely BIC) is the abbreviation of Society for Worldwide Interbank Financial Telecommunication. The organization is a non-profitable international cooperation organization of international banks, established in May of 1973 in Belgium, with membership management, and including more than 200 countries, over 3,000 banks, over 8,000 working sites. Each member bank of the association has its own code, namely SWIFT code, equaling to the identification card of the bank. In order to ensure a speedy and accurate payment transfer to the payee5s account, the applicant of remittance by cable fills the SWIFT code of the payee bank.

The swift code can be searched out through the Internet. Most of China's banks are the members of the association. For a credit with SWIFT, the credit must be issued according to the regulations in the SWIFT manual, adopting the tag stipulated in the SWIFT manual, and the undertaking clauses of banks can be omitted in the credit but the undertaking of bank cannot be exempted according to UCP600.

Before the SWIFT L/C, the credits are issued through cable or telex with different bank criteria, in different clauses and forms, and in complex words. Since SWIFT is adopted, L/C is issued in standard, fixed, and unified form, with speedy transmission and low cost; therefore, SWIFT has been widely used in European countries, American countries and Asian countries.

For the time being, the SWIFT format code is MT700 and MT701, and the revision of L/C is transmitted through SWIFT standard format MT707.

目前，在国际贸易中以SWIFT传递信用证是一种主要形式。

"SWIFT"(又称BIC)是环球银行金融电讯协会的简称。该组织是一个国际银行同业间非营利性的国际合作组织，于1973年5月在比利时成立，采用会员制，目前已有200多个会员国家和地区、3 000多个会员银行、8 000多个站点。凡该协会的成员银行都有自己的代码，即SWIFT code，相当于银行的身份证。电汇申请人在电汇时填写收入行SWIFT code能保证汇款快速准确地到达收款人账户。如不清楚对方银行的SWIFT code可上网查询。我国的主要银行大都是该协会会员。采用SWIFT信用证，必须遵守SWIFT使用手册的规定，使用SWIFT手册规定的代号(tag)，信用证必须按国际商会制定的UCP600的规定，在信用证中可以省去银行的承诺条款，但不能免去银行所应承担的义务。

过去进行全电开证时，都采用电报或电传开证，各国银行标准不一，条款格式也各不相同，而且文字烦琐；采用SWIFT开证后，使信用证具有标准化、固定化、统一格式的特性，而且传递速度快，成本低，现在已被西北欧、美洲、亚洲等国家银行广泛使用。

目前开立的SWIFT格式信用证代号为MT700和MT701，如对开出的SWIFT信用证进行修改，则采用MT707标准格式传递信息。

(6) Contents of Letter of Credit 信用证的内容

① General Information of L/C 对信用证本身的说明

The general information of a credit is mainly as follows: A. Whether the credit is confirmable or not, and transferrable or not; the conception of revocable credit has been deleted from UCP600, and all credits are irrevocable; B. credit number; C. sum, currency, and spelling in words and figures; D. expiry date and place; E. whether there is an expiry date outside territory.

The expiry date of an L/C is the deadline for the seller to deliver documents to the bank, and the date when the opening bank guarantees payment. An L/C can do without the time of shipment, but an L/C is invalid without the expiry date. In Clause 6 of UCP600, it is written as follows: "A deadline of presenting documents must be specified. The specified deadline for the honoring and negotiating will be regarded as the last day for presenting documents."

In practice, the expiry date of an L/C is 15 or 21 days after the shipment. The expiry place of an L/C must be clearly stipulated: Generally, the beneficiary's country is the expiry place of an L/C. An accepted expiry place of an L/C can be "at Beneficiary's country" "at your country" or "in China". An expiry place of an L/C outside territory is not accepted.

对信用证本身的说明主要包括：A. 信用证是否可保兑、是否可转让，UCP600 取消了可撤销信用证的概念，所有信用证都是不可撤销的；B. 编号；C. 金额、货币、单词、数字拼写；D. 有效期及到期地点；E. 是否有境外有效期。

信用证的有效期是卖方向银行交单的最后期限，也是开证行保证付款的期限。一个信用证可以没有装期，但不能没有有效期；一个信用证没有有效期则本身无效。UCP600 第 6 条中规定："信用证必须规定一个交单的截止日。规定的承付或议付的截止日将被视为交单的截止日。"

按照惯例，信用证有效期的到期日是装船后的 15 天，也可规定为 21 天。信用证有效期的到期地点在信用证中必须明确规定，一般是受益人所在国为信用证的有效期到期地点。可接受的信用证规定的到期地点如 "at Beneficiary's country" "at your country" "in China"。不接受境外到期。

② Information Required on the Draft 对汇票的要求

Under a letter of credit with draft, the information about drawer, drawee, payee, sum, and other main terms must be specified in the draft. In Clause 6 (c) of UCP600, it is written as follows: "A credit must not be issued available by a draft drawn on the applicant."

Usually, it is stipulated in a credit for a draft as follows: "We hereby open our irrevocable letter of credit in your favor which is available by your drafts at sight drawn on us for full invoice value accompanied by the following documents."

在信用证项下，如使用汇票，要明确汇票的出票人、受票人、受款人、汇票金额、主要条款等内容。UCP600 第 6 条 c 款规定："信用证不得开成凭以申请人为付款人的汇票兑用。"

通常信用证中对汇票是这样规定的："我们兹开出以你方为受益人的不可撤销信用证，本证凭你方按发票金额开出的以我行为付款人的即期汇票付款，并随附下列单据。"

③ Description of the Goods 对货物的说明

The details including name, types, specification, quantity, packing, price must be stated in a credit, as well as the contract which the credit is subject to.

在信用证中要注明货物的名称、品种、规格、数量、包装、价格，并注明根据某某买卖合同。

④ Shipment Clauses 对装运的要求

In a credit, the details of loading port (place), destination port (place), time of shipment and partial shipment/transshipment or not, etc. must be specified.

在信用证中应列明装运港(地)、目的港(地)、装运期限以及可否分批、转运等项内容。

⑤ Documents 对单据的要求

In a credit, the documents required shall be specified as follows:

在信用证中应列明所需的各种货运单据，主要有以下几种：

A. Documents about the Goods 货物单据

They include invoice, packing list, certificate of origin, inspection certificate, etc..

It is written in UCP600 that a commercial invoice "must appear to have been issued by the beneficiary" "must be made out in the name of the applicant" "must be made out in the same currency as the credit" "The description of the goods, services or performance in a commercial invoice must correspond with that appearing in the credit".

包括发票、装箱单(包装清单)、产地证、商检证明书等。

UCP600 规定，商业发票"必须看似由受益人出具""必须出具成以申请人为抬头""必须与信用证的货币相同""商业发票上的货物、服务或履约行为的描述应该与信用证中的描述一致"。

B. Shipping Documents 运输单据

The most important one is the ocean bill of lading, which is the warrant of cargo ownership.

Usually, a bill of lading is described in a credit as: "Full set clean on board ocean bills of lading, made out to order and blank endorsed, marked freight prepaid and notify applicant."

其中最重要的是海运提单，它是货物所有权的凭证。

通常对提单的描述为："全套清洁的已装船提单，凭指定和空白背书，注明运费已付和通知申请人。"

C. Insurance Polices 保险单据

In UCP600, it is written as follows: "An insurance document, such as an insurance policy, an insurance certificate or a declaration under an open cover must appear to be issued and signed by an insurance company, an underwriter or their agents or their proxies." "When the insurance document indicates that it has been issued in more than one original, all originals must be presented." "Cover notes will not be accepted." "An insurance policy is acceptable in lieu of an insurance certificate or a declaration under an open cover." "The date of the insurance document must be no later than the date of shipment, unless it appears from the insurance document that the cover is effective from a date not later than the date of shipment." "The insurance document must indicate the amount of insurance coverage and be in the same currency as the credit." "If there is no indication in the credit of the insurance coverage required, the amount of insurance coverage must be at least 110% of the CIF or CIP value of the goods."

UCP600 规定："保险单据，例如保险单或预约保险项下的保险证明书或者声明书，必须看似由保险公司或承保人或其代理人或代表出具并签署。""如果保险单据表明其以多份正本出具,所有正本均须提交。""暂保单将不被接受。""可以接受保险单代替预约保险项下的保险证明书或声明书。""保险单据日期不得晚于发运日期,除非保险单据表明保险责任不迟于发运日生效。""保险单据必须表明投保金额并以与信用证相同的货币表示。""如果信用证对投保金额未做规定,投保金额须至少为货物的 CIF 或 CIP 价格的 110%。"

⑥ Special Clause 特殊条款

It means some special instruction or special requirement for the negotiation, or payment route, or confirmation or not.

银行对议付或付款路线或是否保兑,做出特别指示,或有特别要求。

⑦ Bank's Promise of Payment 银行保证付款的承诺

For example, we hereby agree with the drawers, endorsers and bona fide holders of drafts drawn under and in compliance with the terms of this credit that such drafts will be duly honored on due presentation to the drawee if negotiated on or before expiry date and paid on maturity.

The advising bank is requested to notify the beneficiary without adding their confirmation.

例如:我们兹向根据本证开出并符合本证条款的汇票的出票人、背书人和正当持票人承诺,只要你们在本证的效期内向付款行提示或议付(远期汇票在汇票的到期日向付款行提示),将立即得到付款。

请通知行通知受益人本证未加以保兑。

⑧ A Declaration to Subject to UCP600 声明本证遵循惯例 UCP600

For example, this credit is subject to the Uniform Customs and Practice for Documentary Credit 2007 Revision by ICC (International Chamber of Commerce) and Publication No. 600.

例如:本证遵循国际商会 2007 年修订本第 600 号出版物规定的《跟单信用证统一惯例》。

(7) Types of Letter of Credit 信用证的种类

① Irrevocable L/C 不可撤销信用证

Before the publication of UCP600, credits are classified into being revocable and irrevocable. Since UCP600 was put into effect on 1st July, 2007, the conception of revocable credit is deleted, that is to say, "a credit is irrevocable even if there is no indication to that effect."

An irrevocable letter of credit means that the issuing bank is irrevocably bound to honor as of the time it issues the credit. That is to say, an issuing bank cannot amend or revoke a credit without the approval of the party involved; an issuing bank must effect payment so long as the beneficiary makes a presentation of flawless documents.

在 UCP600 之前,信用证还区分为可撤销和不可撤销信用证。在 UCP600 于 2007 年 7 月 1 日生效之后,已经没有了可撤销信用证的概念:"凡是信用证都是不可撤销的,即使未如此表明。"

所谓不可撤销信用证，是指开证行自开立信用证之时起即不可撤销地承担承付责任。也就是说，未经信用证的有关当事人同意，开证行不得片面修改和撤销信用证，只要受益人提交了符合信用证的单据，开证行必须履行付款义务。

② Sight L/C 即期信用证

Sight letter of credit means under sight L/C, the issuing bank or paying bank effects payment immediately upon the presentation of the documentary draft and shipping documents complying with the letter of credit by the beneficiary. The payment in this way is speedy and safe, in favor of capital turnover.

In sight letter of credit, T/T Reimbursement Clause is also added sometimes, which means the issuing bank allows the negotiating bank to notify the issuing bank or the nominated paying bank by cable or fax that the documents presented are complying with the L/C clauses, and the issuing bank is responsible for effecting payment to the negotiating bank by T/T upon receipt of the above-mentioned notification.

即期信用证是指开证行或付款行收到符合 L/C 条款的跟单汇票或装运单据后，立即履行付款义务的信用证。这种方式收汇迅速、安全，有利于资金周转。

在即期信用证中，有时还加列电汇索偿条款，表明开证行允许议付行用电报或电传通知开证行或指定付款行，说明各种单据与信用证要求相符，开证行接到电报或电传通知后，有义务立即用电汇将货款拨交议付行。

③ Sight Payment L/C 即期付款信用证

It is a letter of credit with payment to be made immediately upon a presentation of flawless documents, remarked with the words such as "Available by Payment" in the credit, and generally not demanding the beneficiary to issue a draft. The paying bank of sight payment L/C may be the issuing bank itself the advising bank or the nominated bank in a third country

A sight payment L/C taking the bank of exporter's country as the paying bank, and with the maturity place of presentation in the export place, is most favorable to the beneficiary as the payment can be made promptly. If the paying bank is the issuing bank or the bank in a third country, usually the presentation is required to be made in the place where the paying bank is located.

即期付款信用证是指采用即期兑现方式的信用证,证中通常注明"付款兑现"字样，一般不要求受益人开立汇票。即期付款信用证的付款行可以是开证行本身，也可以是出口地的通知行或指定的第三国银行。

以出口地银行为付款人的即期付款信用证的交单到期地点在出口地，可以及时得到偿付，对受益人最为有利。付款行为开证行本身或第三国银行，交单也是通常规定在付款行所在地。

④ Usance L/C 远期信用证

A usance L/C is a letter of credit under which the payment is made by the issuing bank or paying bank within the stipulated time upon receipt of documents. A time draft is issued by the beneficiary. There are three types of usance L/C.

远期信用证指开证行或付款行收到信用证的单据时，在规定期限内履行付款义务的信用证。受益人开出的是远期汇票，远期信用证主要有三种。

A. Acceptance L/C 承兑信用证

It is a letter of credit accepted by a bank, that is to say, the nominated bank will make acceptance upon receipt of the shipping documents with a time draft drawn on which by the beneficiary, and make payment on the maturity date.

For the draft under the credit, the bank, based on the rights and obligations subject to the credit before the acceptance, undertakes payment to the bill drawer, holder, or endorser after the acceptance. This kind of credit is also referred to as bank acceptance L/C.

承兑信用证指由某一银行承兑的信用证，即当受益人向指定银行开具远期汇票并提示时，指定行即进行承兑，并于汇票到期日履行付款。

这种信用证项下的汇票，在承兑前，银行对出口商的权利义务以信用证为准，承兑后，银行作为汇票承兑人对出票人、持票人、背书人承担付款责任。这种信用证也称为银行承兑信用证。

B. Deferred Payment L/C 延期付款信用证

It is stipulated in a letter of credit by the issuing bank that the payment is to be made within ×× days after shipment or on receipt of documents. Under the kind of L/C, the exporter is not required to issue a draft, so the exporter cannot discount draft to get money in advance, but pays for the goods itself or borrows money from bank. In export businesses, the price of goods under the kind of L/C will be a little higher than the bank acceptance L/C in order to balance the difference between the interest rate and discount rate. For a transaction in large amount, it is better to combine the kind of L/C payment with the export loan of government.

延期付款信用证指开证行在信用证中规定，货物装船后若干天付款，或开证行收到单据后若干天付款的信用证。这种信用证不要求出口商开立汇票，所以出口商不能利用其贴现市场资金，只能自己垫付或向银行借款。在出口业务中，使用这种信用证的货价应比银行承兑信用证高些，以便拉平利息率与贴现率之间的差额。成交金额较大时，要与政府的出口信贷结合起来使用。

C. Usance L/C Payable at Sight 假远期信用证

It is also named as "buyer's usance L/C. In this kind of L/C, a usance draft is drawn by the beneficiary, and discounted by the paying bank, with all interests paid by the importer. The kind of credit appears to be a usance L/C, but actually the exporter can receive the payment in full amount at sight. So, it is called usance L/C payable at sight.

假远期信用证也称"买方远期信用证"。信用证规定受益人开立远期汇票,由付款行负责贴现,并规定贴现利息和费用由进口商承担。这种信用证表面上看是远期信用证,但从上述条款规定来看,出口商可以即期收到全额货款,因此被称为"假远期信用证"。

⑤ Transferable L/C 可转让信用证

It can be divided into transferable L/C and non-transferable L/C according to the beneficiary's right of transferring L/C.

Transferable Letter of Credit is a credit under which the beneficiary (first beneficiary) may request the bank authorized to pay, incur a deferred payment undertaking, accept or negotiate (the transferring bank), or in the case of freely negotiable credit, the bank specifically authorized in the credit as a transferring bank, to make the credit available in whole or in part to one or more other beneficiary(ies) (second beneficiary(-ies)). In UCP600, it's stipulated that "transferrable credit means a credit that specifically states it is transferable". A transferable credit may be made available in whole or in part to another beneficiary ("second beneficiary") at the request of the beneficiary ("first beneficiary").

According to the stipulation in UCP600, a credit is not transferable unless the word "transferable" is specifically stated in the credit by the issuing bank. Transferable credit can only be transferred once, i.e. it can only be transferred by the first beneficiary to the second beneficiary who shall not have the right to transfer the credit to any third beneficiary.

根据受益人对信用证的权利可否转让,信用证分为可转让信用证和不可转让信用证。

可转让信用证是指信用证的受益人(第一受益人)可以要求授权付款、承担延期付款责任、承兑议付的银行(统称"转让银行"),或当信用证是自由议付时,可以要求信用证中特别授权的转让银行,将信用证全部或部分转让给一个或数个受益人(第二受益人)使用的信用证。UCP600 规定:"可转让信用证系指特别注明'可转让'字样的信用证。可转让信用证可应受益人(第一受益人)的要求转为全部或部分由另一受益人(第二受益人)兑用。"

根据 UCP600 的规定,唯有开证行在信用证中明确注明"可转让",信用证方可转让。可转让信用证只能转让一次,即只能由第一受益人转让给第二受益人,第二受益人不得要求将信用证转让给其后的第三受益人。

⑥ Revolving L/C 循环信用证

A credit is established for a certain sum and quantity of goods with a provision that when a shipment has been made and documents presented re-available in its original from and another shipment can be made so on until to the stipulated time or total amount.

Revolving L/C can be divided into by time and by amount. A revolving L/C by time means that the beneficiary can draw money by L/C repeatedly in a certain period. A revolving L/C by amount means that the foil amount will be automatically re-available for negotiation and payment again after the L/C negotiation until the preset total amount is used up.

循环信用证是指信用证被全部或部分使用后，其金额又恢复到原金额，可再次使用，直至达到规定的次数或规定的总金额为止。

循环信用证又分为按时间循环的信用证和按金额循环的信用证。按时间循环的信用证是受益人在一定的时间内可多次支取信用证规定的金额；按金额循环的信用证是信用证金额议付后，仍恢复到原金额可再次使用，直到用完规定的总额为止。

⑦ Reciprocal L/C 对开信用证

A reciprocal L/C is that two parties open letters of credit in favor of each other. The features of reciprocal L/C: the drawer and beneficiary of one L/C are usually the drawee and payer of another one; the opening bank of one L/C is the advising bank of another one. The amount of the two credits is the same or almost the same. The two credits can be opened to each other at the same time or one by one. Reciprocal L/C is often used in barter trade, processing trade etc.. Both parties are afraid that the counterpart will not fulfill the obligation of import or export after one party has exported or imported by the first credit, then they can restrict each other in the way of being mutually involved and conditioned.

对开信用证是指两张信用证的开证申请人互以对方为受益人而开立的信用证。对开信用证的特点是第一张信用证的受益人(出口商)和开证申请人(进口商)就是第二张信用证的申请人和受益人，第一张信用证的通知行通常就是第二张信用证的开证行。两张信用证的金额相等或大体相等，两证可同时互开，也可先后开立。对开信用证多用于易货贸易或进料加工贸易方式，交易的双方都担心对方凭第一张信用证出口或进口后，另外一方不履行进口或出口的义务，于是采用这种互相联系、互为条件的开证办法，彼此得以约束。

⑧ Back to Back L/C 背对背信用证

Back to back letter of credit means that beneficiary requires the advising bank of the original credit or other bank to issue a new credit with similar contents on the basis of the original L/C. The beneficiary of back to back L/C can be a foreign or domestic player. A back to back letter of credit must be irrevocable.

Back to back letter of credit is usually opened for the resale of goods by middleman to make profit or in case that direct trade business is not allowed in two countries and a third party is needed to link up the transaction. In this case. The trade is on the basis of two sales contracts signed by exporter, middleman and importer. The original L/C is the first credit based on the contract signed by middleman and importer, and the back to back credit is second credit based on the contract signed by middleman and exporter, namely subsidiary L/C. The beneficiary of the original L/C is the applicant of the back to back L/C. The original credit is still valid after the second L/C is issued.

The contents of a back to back credit are as same as the contents of the original credit except for the applicant, opening bank, beneficiary, sum, price, shipment time, and valid time. The price in the original credit is higher than the price of a back to back credit, the difference of the two prices is the profit or commission of middleman. About the shipment time, the shipment time of the back to back L/C is earlier than that of the original L/C. The issuing bank of back to back credit makes payment upon the presentation of the documents by the beneficiary of back to back credit, then the issuing bank requires immediately the beneficiary of the original L/C to supply the commercial invoice and draft complying to the original L/C clauses in order to replace the commercial invoice and draft offered by the beneficiary of back to back L/C, then send the documents including the shipment documents to the issuing bank of the original L/C for collection.

背对背信用证又称转开信用证，是指受益人要求原证的通知行或其他银行以原证为基础，另开一张内容相似的新信用证。背对背信用证的受益人可以是国外的，也可以是国内的。背对背信用证的开证银行只能根据不可撤销信用证来开立。

背对背信用证的开立通常是当中间商转售他人货物，从中图利，或两国不能直接办理进出口贸易时，通过第三者以此种方法来沟通贸易。这种贸易是由三方即出口商、中间商、进口商签订两份买卖合同，按照中间商与进口商签订的第一份合同开出的信用证称为原信用证；按照中间商与出口商签订的第二份合同开出的第二张信用证称为背对背信用证，也称从属信用证。原信用证的受益人就是背对背信用证的开证申请人。新证开出后，原证仍然有效。

背对背信用证的内容除开证人、受益人、金额、单价、装运期限、有效期限可有变动外，其他条款一般与原证相同。原信用证价格高于背对背信用证的价格，高低的差额就是中间商赚取的利润或佣金。关于装运期限，背对背信用证的装运期应早于原信用证的规定。背对背信用证的受益人按规定履行交单，开证行对受益人付款后，便立即要求原证的受益人提供符合原证条款的商业发票和汇票，以便调换背对背信用证受益人提供的商业发票及汇票，然后附上货运单据寄往原证的开证行收汇。

⑨ Confirmed L/C 保兑信用证

There are two kinds of credits, which are confirmed L/C and unconfirmed L/C.

A confirmed L/C is a credit issued by the issuing bank, and guaranteed by another bank to fulfill the payment for the consistent presentation of documents. The bank who adds its confirmation to the credit is called as Confirming Bank.

In UCP600, it is written as follows: "Provided that the stipulated documents are presented to the confirming bank or to any other nominated bank and that they constitute a complying presentation, the confirming bank must…" "A confirming bank is irrevocably bound to honor or negotiate as of the time it adds its confirmation to the credit."

A new regulation in UCP600 about the nature of confirming bank for L/C amendment are as follows: "An issuing bank is irrevocably bound by an amendment as of the time it issues the amendment. A confirming bank may extend its confirmation to an amendment and will be irrevocably bound as of the time it advises the amendment. A confirming bank may, however, choose to advise an amendment without extending its confirmation and, if so, it must inform the issuing bank without delay and inform the beneficiary in advice."

As an independent principal, a confirming bank is responsible independently for the beneficiary, undertaking the obligation of payment to beneficiary in the first place. That is to say, like the issuing bank, a confirming bank undertakes the payment obligation in the first place. A confirmed L/C is a credit with double guaranty, which is most favorable to exporter. A confirming bank is usually the advising bank, or the other bank in the exporter's country or the bank of the third country. The confirmation is effected through adding confirmation words to the credit by the confirming bank.

An unconfirmed credit means that the credit issued by the issuing bank is not confirmed by another bank. An unconfirmed credit is usually issued when the issuing bank is with a good reputation or the L/C amount is small.

信用证按是否有另一家银行加保兑，可以分为保兑信用证和不保兑信用证。

保兑信用证是指开证行开出的信用证，由另一家银行保证对符合信用证条款规定的单据履行付款义务。对信用证加保兑的银行，叫作保兑行。

UCP600 规定："只要规定的单据提交给保兑行，或提交给其他任何指定银行，并且构成相符交单，保兑行必须承付……""保兑行自对信用证加具保兑之时起即不可撤销地承担承付或议付的责任。"

UCP600 对修改信用证时保兑行的性质有新的规定："开证行自发出修改之时起，即不可撤销地受其约束。保兑行可将其保兑扩展至修改，并自通知该修改时，即不可撤销地受其约束。但是，保兑行可以选择将修改通知受益人而不对其加具保兑。若然如此，其必须毫不延误地将此告知开证行，并在其给受益人的通知中告知受益人。"

保兑行以独立的"本人"身份对受益人独立负责，并对受益人负首先付款责任。也就是说，保兑行同开证行一样，承担第一性的付款责任。这是一种双重保证的信用证，对出口商最为有利。保兑行通常可以由通知行来承担，也可以是出口地的其他银行或第三国银行。保兑的手续一般是由保兑行在信用证上加列保兑文句。

不保兑信用证是指开证银行开出的信用证没有经另一家银行保兑。当开证银行资信较好或成交金额不大时，一般都使用这种不保兑的信用证。

⑩ Standby L/C 备用信用证

It is also called Commercial Paper L/C or Guarantee L/C, which is a guaranty issued by the opening bank on behalf of the applicant declaring that the bank will undertake certain obligations. That is to say, the opening bank guarantees that when the applicant fails to fulfill its obligation that has to be done, the beneficiary can make a bill of exchange on the applicant according to the stipulations of the standby letter of credit or present to the opening bank the statements or evidence papers which can testify the applicant's failure to fulfill his obligations to effect the payment.

备用信用证又称商业票据信用证、担保信用证或保证信用证，是指开证行根据开证申请人的请求对受益人开立的承诺承担某项义务时，受益人只要凭备用信用证的规定向开证行开具汇票(或不开汇票)，并提交开证申请人未履行义务的声明或证明文件，即可取得开证行的偿付。备用信用证属于银行信用，开证银行保证在开证申请人未履行其义务时，即由开证银行付款。因此，备用信用证对受益人来说是备用于开证申请人发生违约时，取得赔款的一种方式。备用信用证下，银行承担的也是第一位的责任。

⑪ Soft Clause L/C 软条款信用证

It is a credit with some special clauses added by the L/C applicant, appearing to be an irrevocable credit, but an invalid credit actually, and cannot be utilized by the beneficiary smoothly.

In legal sense, a credit with soft clauses is against the nature and principle of L/C with fraud. It is also called as trap L/C. In the actual operation on L/C service, we must examine the credit, and require the L/C applicant to delete the soft clauses which the beneficiary hardly meets, or refuses to accept.

由于信用证的开证申请人在信用证中加列了某些特殊条款，使受益人无法利用信用证，表面上的不可撤销信用证实际上是无效的信用证。

从法律上说，软条款信用证从根本上违反了信用证的性质和原则，带有某些欺诈性质，有人把它称为陷阱信用证。我们在实际业务中，要仔细审证，如遇到信用证中某些加列的条款，是受益人主观努力所无法做到的，对这样的条款要坚决要求开证人删除，否则不要轻易接受这类信用证。

(8) Letter of Guarantee (L/G) 银行保函

In international trade, the lack of mutual understanding and trust between both parties in a transaction causes obstacles to conclude deals and fulfill contracts smoothly. In order to solve these problems, the banks and other financial institutions with excellent credit offer the service of letter of guarantee, through which, the warrantor promises the L/G applicant will fulfill the liability or obligation under the concerning business contract or other economic contracts, further in favor of the transaction's fulfillment.

在国际经济贸易中，交易双方往往缺乏了解和信任给达成交易和履行合同造成一定障碍。为了解决这些问题，就出现了由信誉卓著的银行以及其他金融机构办理的保函业务，担保人保证申请人履行双方签订的有关商务合同或其他经济合同项下的某种责任或义务，从而有利于交易的顺利进行。

① Definition and Nature of L/G 银行保函的定义及其性质

Letter of Guarantee is a guaranty in written form issued by bank, insurance company, guarantee company or individual upon request of the applicant, promising to fulfill the payment or compensation to some extent in a certain amount of money in case that the applicant fails to fulfill the obligation. Bank's L/G is a kind of guaranty issued by bank, undertaking the obligation of payment. Under a bank's L/G the bank undertakes absolute payment obligation according to the regulation of L/G.

According to the payment conditions under the L/G, the L/G can be divided into the following two kinds:

银行保函(简称 L/G)又称保证书，是指银行、保险公司、担保公司或个人(保证人)应申请人的请求，向第三方(受益人)开立的一种书面信用担保凭证，保证在申请人未能按双方协议履行其责任或义务时，由担保人代其履行一定金额、一定期限范围内的某种支付责任或经济赔偿责任。银行保函是由银行开立的、承担付款责任的一种担保凭证。银行根据保函的规定承担绝对付款责任。

在保函项下，受益人在什么条件下才能取得保证人的偿付，按索偿条件分，通常可分为两种：

A. Demand L/G 见索即付保函

Demand L/G is also named as unconditional L/G, with bank's undertaking of the payment in the first place, which is a kind of independent warranty separated from the basic contract, with the rights and liabilities of beneficiary subject to the contents of L/G, not limited by the basic contract. The guarantor must fulfill payment so long as the beneficiary presents the documents complying with the requests of L/G. All letters of guarantee are irrevocable. Letter of guarantee is in form of writing, including telecommunication messages with encrypted EDI information.

见索即付保函又称无条件保函，银行承担的是第一性的责任，是一种与基础合同相脱离的独立性担保文件，受益人的权利与担保人的义务完全以保函所载内容为准，不受基础合同的约束。受益人只要提交了符合保函要求的单据，担保人就必须付款。所有保函均为不可撤销的文件。保函必须是书面的，"书面"包括有效的电讯信息加密押的 EDI 信息。

B. Conditional L/G 有条件保函

A conditional L/G means guarantor makes payment to beneficiary conditionally, and guarantor will fulfill payment only under the condition of complying with the regulation of L/G. So, the guarantor of a conditional L/G is undertaking a subordinate payment obligation.

有条件保函是指保证人向受益人付款是有条件的，只有在符合保函规定的条件下，保证人才予付款。可见，有条件保函的担保人承担的是第二性的附属的付款责任。

② Types of L/G 银行保函的种类

Letter of guarantee is widely used in the practical operation of business, applicable to the transactions of goods as well as other economic fields, such as the international construction contracts, bid and loan businesses. According to the usage, letter of guarantee can be divided into tender L/G, performance L/G and repayment L/G.

银行保函在实际业务中的使用范围很广,它不仅适用于货物的买卖,而且广泛适用于其他国际经济领域。例如,在国际工程承包、招标与投标以及借贷业务中都有使用。银行保证书按其用途可分为投标保证书、履约保证书和还款保证书。

A. Tender Guarantee 投标保证书

A tender guarantee means bank, insurance company or other involving party (guarantor) makes promise to beneficiary (tenderee), sometimes according to the instruction of the authorized bank by the guarantee applicant, that guarantor shall fulfill payment with the stipulated sum in case that applicant (tender) fails to fulfill the obligation resulting from his tender.

A tender guarantee mainly guarantees that tender will not revoke or revise the tender without the agreement with tenderee, and will sign the contract paying the fulfillment deposit after winning the bid. Otherwise, the bank will be committed to the compensation for the loss of the tenderee.

投标保证书是指银行、保险公司或其他当事人(保证人)向受益人(招标人)承诺,或由按照担保申请人所授权的银行的指示向受益人(招标人)承诺,当申请人(投标人)不履行其投标所产生的义务时,保证人应在规定的金额限度内向受益人付款。

投标保证书主要担保投标人在开标前不撤销投标和片面修改投标条件,中标后要保证签约和交付履约金。否则,银行负责赔偿招标人的损失。

B. Performance Guarantee 履约保证书

A performance guarantee is a promise made by a guarantor, that a guarantor will make payment to beneficiary with the agreed sum in case that guarantee applicant (contractor) fails to fulfill the contract concluded by beneficiary (owner) and contractor.

Performance guarantee is widely used in the normal import and export businesses. Performance guarantees are divided into Import Performance Guarantee and Export Performance Guarantee.

履约保证书是指保证人承诺,如果担保申请人(承包人)不履行他与受益人(业主)之间订立的合同,应由保证人在约定的金额限度内向受益人付款。

履约保证书的适用范围很广泛,在一般货物进出口交易中也有使用。履约保证书可分为进口履约保证书和出口履约保证书。

a. Import Performance Guarantee 进口履约保证书

It is a guarantee issued by guarantor (bank) upon request of importer to exporter (beneficiary). It is stipulated in the guarantee that the bank is committed to making compensation for payment if the importer fails to make payment in a timely manner after exporter fulfills the delivery of goods as requested in the contract. The kind of guarantee is a convenient, prompt and assured guarantee for the exporter.

进口履约保证书是指保证人(银行)应进口商的申请开给出口商(受益人)的保证书。保证书规定,如出口商按合同交货后,进口商未能按期付款,由银行负责偿还。这种履约保证书对出口商来说,是一种简便、及时和确定的保障。

b. Export Performance Guarantee 出口履约保证书

It is a guarantee issued by guarantor (bank) upon request of exporter to importer (beneficiary). It is stipulated in the guarantee that the bank is committed to making compensation for the loss of the importer if the exporter fails to make delivery of goods on time as requested in the contract. The importer is ensured by the kind of guarantee.

出口履约保证书是指保证人(银行)应出口商的申请开给进口商(受益人)的保证书。保证书规定,如出口商按合同未能按期交货,银行负责赔偿进口商的损失。这种履约保证书对进口商是有保障的。

C. Repayment Guarantee 还款保证书

Repayment guarantee is a guarantee issued by bank, insurance company or other involving party upon request of the application of one party of a contract to the other party of a contract. It is stipulated in the repayment guarantee that the bank is committed to making reimbursement in case that the applicant fails to fulfill the obligation agreed in the contract, not returning or repaying the deposit or paid amount to the beneficiary.

A repayment guarantee used in an international project contract is offered by a contractor to the project owner through a bank, As stipulated in the guarantee, the bank is committed to making reimbursement in case that the applicant fails to fulfill the obligation agreed in the contract, not returning or repaying the deposit or paid amount to the beneficiary.

Repayment guarantee is also applicable in the import and export business of goods, service trade, technology trade etc.. For example, in a contract of whole set equipment and large vehicles with the payment by installment or deferred payment usually adopted, a performance guarantee is issued by the importer to the exporter after signing the contract, in which the importer is ensured by a bank to make payment as requested in the contract. At the same time, a repayment guarantee is issued by the exporter to his counterpart, in which the bank promises to make reimbursement of the principle paid by the importer and the related interests if the exporter fails to make delivery on time.

还款保证书是指银行、保险公司或其他当事人应合同一方当事人的申请,向合同另一方当事人开立的保证书。保证书规定,如申请人不履行他与受益人订立的合同的义务,不将受益人预付、支付的款项退还或还款给受益人,银行则向受益人退还或支付款项。

还款保证书在国际承包业务中使用时,由承包人通过银行向业主提供。保证书规定,如申请人不履行他与受益人订立的合同的义务，不将受益人预付、支付的款项退还或还款给受益人，则由银行向受益人退还该款项。

还款保证书还适用于货物进出口、劳务使用和技术贸易等业务。例如，在成套设备及大型交通工具的合同中，通常采用带有预付性质的分期或延期支付部分价款。在这种交易中，进口商在签订合同后，向出口商开立履约保证书，由银行保证进口商按合同规定按期支付价款，同时，出口商也向对方开立还款保证书。如出口商不能按期交货，银行保证及时偿还进口商已付款项的本金及所产生的利息。

In addition to the above mentioned guarantees, there are also other kinds of guarantees according to different functions and usages, such as technology imported guarantee, processing with imported materials guarantee, tender guarantee, offset trade guarantee, financial leasing guarantee, loaning guarantee, deferred payment guarantee under trade, etc.

除上述几种保函外，还可以根据其他功能和应用的不同，分为其他种类，如技术引进保函、来料加工保函、投标保函、补偿贸易保函、融资租赁保函、借款保函、贸易项下的延期付款保函等。

Section 3　Payment Terms in The Contract

第3节　合同中的支付条款

1. Payment Terms for Different Payment Methods 不同支付方式的支付条款

(1) Payment Terms by Remittance 汇付支付条款

In order to clarify the responsibilities and prevent the importer from delaying the remittance, we shall clearly specify the time, specific method and amount of remittance in the contract for the transaction settled by remittance.

For instance:

① The Buyers shall pay the total value to the Sellers in advance by T/T (M/T or D/D) not later than…

② …% of the total contract value as advance payment shall be remitted by the Buyer to the Seller through T/T within one month after signing this contract.

为明确责任，防止进口商拖延汇款时间，对于使用汇付方式结算的交易，在合同中应当明确规定汇付的时间、具体的汇付方法和金额等内容。

例如：

① 买方应不晚于×年×月×日将全部货款用电汇(信汇或票汇)方式预付给卖方。

② 买方同意在本合同签字之日起1个月内将本合同总金额×%的预付款，以电汇方式

汇交卖方。

(2) Payment Terms by Collection 托收支付条款

When the seller and the buyer agree to make payment through collection, the payment terms in the contract must specify the method of presentation, the time of payment or acceptance, etc.

For instance:

在买卖双方约定通过托收支付货款时，合同的支付条款必须订明交单方式、付款或承兑的期限等内容。

例如：

① Payment Terms by D/P at Sight 即期付款交单条款

Upon first presentation the Buyer shall pay against documentary draft(s) drawn by the Seller at sight. The shipping documents are to be delivered against payment only.

买方应凭卖方开具的即期跟单汇票于见票时立即付款，付款后交单。

② Payment Terms by D/P after Sight 远期付款交单条款

The Buyer shall duly accept the documentary draft(s) drawn by the Seller at…days after sight upon first presentation and make payment on its maturity. The shipping documents are to be delivered against payment only.

买方对卖方开具的见票后×天付款的跟单汇票，应于提示时即予承兑，并应于汇票到期日即予付款，付款后交单。

③ Payment Terms by D/A 承兑交单条款

The Buyer shall duly accept the documentary draft(s) drawn by the Seller at …days after sight upon first presentation and make payment on its maturity. The shipping documents are to be delivered against acceptance of the draft(s).

买方对卖方开具的见票后×天付款的跟单汇票，应于见票时即予承兑，并应于汇票到期日即予付款，承兑汇票后交单。

(3) Payment Terms by Letter of Credit 信用证支付条款

Payment terms by letter of credit in a contract of international goods sales are more complicated. In the case of settlement by letter of credit, it is generally stipulated in the payment terms of the contract, such as the time of opening L/C, opening bank, type of L/C, amount, time of shipment, expiry date, etc..

For instance:

在国际货物买卖合同中，信用证支付条款比较复杂。如果采用跟单信用证方式结算，一般应在买卖合同的支付条款中，就开证时间、开证银行、信用证种类、开证金额、装运期、到期日等做出明确规定。

例如：

① Payment Terms by Sight L/C 即期信用证条款

The Buyer shall arrange with … bank for opening an irrevocable letter of credit in favor of the Seller before… (or within … days after receipt of the Seller's advice or within … days after signing of this contract). The said letter of credit shall be available by sight draft(s) for full invoice value and remain valid for negotiation in China until the 15th day after date of shipment.

买方应于×年×月×日前(或接到卖方通知×天内或签约后×天内)通过××银行按全部发票金额开立以卖方为受益人的不可撤销即期信用证，直至装运日期后15天在中国议付有效。

② Payment Terms by Time L/C 远期信用证条款

The Buyers shall arrange with … bank for opening an irrevocable banker's acceptance letter of credit in favor of the Sellers before …. The said letter of credit shall be available by draft(s) at … days after sight for full invoice value and remain valid for negotiation in China until the 15th day after the aforesaid time of shipment.

买方应于×年×月×日前通过××银行按全部发票金额开立以卖方为受益人的不可撤销的见票后×天付款的银行承兑信用证，信用证议付有效期延至上述装运期后15天在中国到期。

2. Combination of Payment Modes 各种支付方式的结合

In order to meet the demands in our country5s international trade development, we shall adopt different payment terms flexibly based on the research of those used widely in international market. In the practical operation of international trade, in order to conclude the deal, both parties may adopt two or more payment terms combined together if they fail to reach agreement on a certain payment term. The frequently used combination of payment terms are listed as follows:

为了适应我国外贸发展的需要，必须在认真研究国际市场各种惯用的支付方式的基础上，灵活地加以运用。实践中，有时为了促成交易，在双方未能就某一种支付方式达成协议时，也可以采用两种或多种方式结合使用的方式，常见的有以下几种：

(1) Combination of Letter of Credit and Remittance 信用证与汇付相结合

It means that the payment is partially made by L/C and the balance is paid by remittance. For example, for the transaction of ores, both parties may agree that ×× percent of the invoice amount is paid by L/C with presentation of the shipment documents, the balance is paid by remittance according to the goods inspection result and the actual quality or weight after the arrival of the goods.

这种方式是指部分货款用信用证支付，余数用汇付方式结算。例如，对于矿砂等初级产品的交易，双方约定，信用证规定凭装运单据先付发票金额的若干成，余数待货到目的地后，根据检验的结果，按实际品质或重量计算出确切的金额，另用汇付方式支付。

(2) Combination of Letter of Credit and Collection 信用证与托收相结合

It means that the payment is made partially by L/C and the balance by collection. It is usually operated in the way as follows: Two bills of exchange are issued under the credit, the payment by L/C is made with the clean draft and the payment by collection is made by sight or time D/P with the presentation of the full set of documents. For the sake of safety, the clause such as "the documents delivered upon the full payment" must be stated in the letter of credit.

这种方式是指部分货款用信用证支付，余数用托收方式结算。一般做法是，信用证规定出口人开立两张汇票，属于信用证部分的货款凭光票付款，而全套单据附在托收部分汇票项下，按即期或远期付款交单方式托收。但信用证上必须订明"在发票金额全部付清后才可交单"的条款，以确保安全。

(3) Combination of Collection and Standby L/C or L/G 托收与备用信用证或银行保函相结合

Collection is a kind of commercial credit putting great risk on the seller. However, collection is in favor of the buyer as it is of low cost and with simple procedures. To promote its products, the seller may adopt the collection combining with L/G, which is in favor of the buyer as well as avoiding risks. The specific operation is that the exporter may collect the payment from the bank with clean bill and L/G after receiving the standby L/C and L/G complying with the contract.

Before the seller makes delivery, the buyer issues a standby L/C or L/G in advance. For example, under collection, the bank is committed to fulfilling payment if the buyer fails to make payment. Through the settlement method, the expiry date of standby L/C or L/G shall be after the expiry date of collection so that the seller has sufficient time to claim for reimbursement against the bank after the collection is refused.

托收是一种商业信用，对卖方来说风险较大。但是，托收对买方而言费用较低、手续简便。卖方为了推销商品可以采用托收和银行保函相结合的方法，既给买方优惠，又避免了风险。其具体做法是，出口人在收到符合合同规定的备用信用证或银行保函后，就可凭光票与声明书向银行收回货款。

卖方在交货前，买方先开立一份备用信用证或保函。如托收项下，买方不能够履行付款义务，则由银行承担付款义务。使用这种结算方式，备用信用证或保函的有效期应当迟于托收付款期限的一定时间，以便托收被拒付后，卖方有足够的时间向银行追偿货款。

(4) Combination of Remittance, Collection and L/C 汇付、托收、信用证三者相结合

For the transaction of whole set equipment, large mechanical products and vehicles, due to the large contract sum and long production cycle of the product, the payment is usually made by installment according to the project schedule and delivery schedule.

在成套设备、大型机械产品和交通工具的交易中，因为成交金额较大，产品生产周期较长，一般采取按工程进度和交货进度分若干期付清货款，即分期付款和延期付款的方法，采用汇付、托收和信用证相结合的方式。

(5) Pay by Installments 分期付款

With the payment by installments, the payment is settled upon the goods that are delivered to the buyer. Without interests involved in the transaction, to some extent, the seller makes use of the capital of the buyer. The details are as follows:

It is agreed by both the seller and the buyer in the contract that the buyer may pay part of payment as deposit to seller through remittance before the production, and the seller shall offer the photocopy of export license and letter of guarantee issued by bank to the buyer before the deposit is paid. Except for the deposit, the balance payment may be paid by installments, with letter of credit at sight issued by the buyer, and the balance of payment is usually paid off on the delivery time of goods or the expiry time of seller's quality warranty. The ownership of the goods will be transferred when the balance of payment is paid off. With the payment by installments, the payment will be paid off or almost paid off on the delivery time. Therefore, the contract with payment by installments is a contract with payment at sight.

采用分期付款，卖方在交货时，买方的货款基本付清。这种交易不涉及利息，在某种意义上，卖方甚至利用了买方的资金。其具体做法是：

买卖双方在合同中规定，在产品投产前，买方可采用汇付方式，先交部分货款作为订金，卖方在买方付出订金前，应向买方提供出口许可证影印本和银行开具的保函。除订金外，其余货款可按不同阶段分期支付，买方开立不可撤销的信用证，即期付款，但最后一笔货款一般是在交货或卖方承担质量保证期满时付清。货物所有权则在付清最后一笔货款时转移。在分期付款的条件下，货款在交货时付清或基本付清。因此，按分期付款条件签订的合同是一种即期合同。

(6) Deferred Payment 延期付款

With this payment term, most of payment will be paid in the future years or by installment within a long future period after the goods are delivered to the buyer. So, the transaction is a credit sale with the buyer utilizing the capital of the seller, so the interests shall be added to the price of goods. The details are as follows:

For the transaction of the whole set equipment and in large sum, the deferred payment is adopted as the buyer hardly pays off once for all. After signing the contract, the buyer will make a small part of payment as deposit. It is also stipulated in some contracts that, part of payment will be paid according to project schedule or delivery schedule, but most of the payment will be paid by installments in the following years after the delivery of goods, namely by the usance L/C. The payment term means a commercial credit offered to the buyer by the seller, so the buyer shall undertake the interests of the deferred payment. The ownership will be transferred upon the delivery.

采用这种支付方式，在卖方交货时，买方大部分货款要在将来若干年或相当长的一段时间分期摊付，属于一种赊销性质的交易。买方实际上是占用了卖方的资金，在货价中要加上利息的成本。具体做法是：

在成套设备和大宗交易的情况下，由于成交金额较大，买方一时难以付清全部货款，可采用延期付款的办法。买卖双方签订合同后，买方一般要预付一小部分货款作为订金。有的合同还规定，按工程进度和交货进度分期支付部分货款，但大部分货款是在交货后若干年内分期摊付，即采用远期信用证支付。这种支付方式等于是卖方给买方提供的商业信贷，因此，买方应承担延期付款的利息。在延期付款的条件下，货物所有权一般在交货时转移。

Terminology 本章术语

1. instruments of payment 支付工具
2. bill of exchange (draft) 汇票
3. sight draft 即期汇票
4. time draft (usance draft) 远期汇票
5. documentary draft 跟单汇票
6. issuance 出票
7. presentation 提示
8. acceptance 承兑
9. endorsement 背书
10. discounting 贴现
11. dishonor 拒付
12. recourse 追索
13. promissory note 本票
14. commercial promissory note 商业本票
15. bank promissory note 银行本票
16. check (cheque) 支票
17. remittance 汇付
18. mail transfer (M/T) 信汇
19. telegraphic transfer (T/T) 电汇
20. remittance by banker's demand draft (D/D) 票汇

21. collection 托收
22. clean collection 光票托收
23. documentary collection 跟单托收
24. cocuments against payment (D/P) 付款交单
25. D/P at sight 即期付款交单
26. D/P after sight 远期付款交单
27. documents against acceptance (D/A) 承兑交单
28. letter of credit (L/C) 信用证
29. irrevocable L/C 不可撤销信用证
30. sight L/C 即期信用证
31. sight payment L/C 即期付款信用证
32. usance L/C 远期信用证
33. negotiation L/C 议付信用证
34. acceptance L/C 承兑信用证
35. deferred payment L/C 延期付款信用证
36. usance L/C payable at sight 假远期信用证
37. transferable L/C 可转让信用证
38. revolving L/C 循环信用证
39. reciprocal L/C 对开信用证
40. back to back L/C 背对背信用证
41. confirmed L/C 保兑信用证
42. standby L/C 备用信用证
43. letter of guarantee (L/G) 银行保函

Exercises 本章练习

1. A Chinese exporter received one set of irrevocable L/C from abroad with the China branch of a foreign bank as the advising bank and confirming bank. After the shipment, at the time that the exporter was to present the shipment documents to the bank for negotiation, the exporter was suddenly notified by the foreign bank that the bank would not accept the negotiation of the documents and make payment since the issuing bank has declared bank corruption, but the foreign bank agreed to make collection against the buyer with the nomination of the exporter. What do you think of it? Please give an explanation in brief.

我国某外贸公司收到国外开来的不可撤销信用证一份,由设在我国境内的某外资银行通知并加保兑。我方在货物装运后,正拟将有关单据交银行议付时,忽接该外资银行通知,由于开证行已宣告破产,该行不承担对该信用证的议付或付款责任,但可接受我出口公司委托向买方直接收取货款的业务。对此,你认为我方应如何处理?简述理由。

2. A Chinese exporter reached a contract with a UK buyer about some commodities in a large quantity in terms of CIF and irrevocable sight L/C payment, stipulating the shipment shall be effected in November in the contract, but no specific L/C issuing date mentioned therein, Later, the UK buyer delayed the issuance of L/C because of the decrease of market price of the commodity. To avoid the delay of the shipment, the exporter had urged the buyer to issue L/C for many times since the middle of OCT., the buyer finally issued the L/C up to 8th Nov. However, it is too late for the exporter to arrange for the shipment as scheduled, who therefore required the buyer to extend the shipment time and the L/C negotiation expiry date for one more month. The UK buyer refused the requirement, and cancelled the contract unilaterally excusing that the exporter failed to effect shipment on time. The exporter did nothing but accepted it, Please make analysis and comment about it: Had the exporter settled the matter in a proper way? And what lessons shall we learn from it?

我国某外贸公司与英商就某商品按 CIF、即期信用证付款条件达成一项数量较大的出口合同,合同规定 11 月装运,但未规定具体开证日期,后因该商品市场价格趋降,外商便拖延开证。我方为防止延误装运期,从 10 月中旬起即多次电催开证,终于使该商在 11 月 8 日开来了信用证。但由于该商品开证太晚,使我方安排装运发生困难,遂要求对方对信用证的装运期和议付有效期进行修改,分别推迟一个月。但英商拒不同意,并以我方未能按期装运为由单方面解除合同,我方也就此作罢。试分析我方如此处理是否适当?应从中吸取哪些教训?

3. An exporter makes an offer to a Japanese client in terms of payment by D/P at sight, and the clients reply is that the offer is acceptable in terms of the payment by D/P in sight of 90 days and collection by Bank A nominated by the client. Please make an analysis of the reason why the Japanese client brings about the requirement.

我某公司向日本某商 D/P 见票即付式推销某商品,对方答复:如我方接受 D/P 见票后 90 天付款,并通过他指定的 A 银行代收则可接受。请分析日方提出此项要求的出发点。

4. In a business talk between a Chinese exporter and a HK buyer in a trade fair about the export of sneakers, the HK buyer claimed that the import quota is needed as the final destination of goods is USA, while the expiry time of the quota owned by the buyer is at the end of June, so the shipment must be made by the end of June otherwise the HK buyer has to take responsibility of contract breach. As the term of the contract, the exporter was required to pay USD 300,000 as a guaranty deposit, and the client promised to issue an irrevocable L/C from a well-known HK bank. The exporter overlooked the clause saying "one shipment approval certificate signed by the

L/C applicant must be presented with shipment documents", in the credit when it received the L/C. When the exporter made presentation of shipment documents to the bank, the exporter was aware of the term and required the HK buyer to cancel the clause or issue the concerning certificate, but the HK buyer always put it off. At last, the exporter couldn't make presentation and lost the deposit. Please make an explanation of what we can learn from the case.

我某出口企业在交易会与某港商洽谈一批运动鞋出口,港商声明该批运动鞋最终目的地是美国,需用配额。港商手中的配额为 6 月底到期,如我出口企业要接受该订单,要保证在 6 月底前交货。如延期不能交货,港商也无法出口至美国,要承担违约责任。作为签约时的条件,要求我出口企业先交 30 万美元的保证金,客户承诺开来香港某知名银行的不可撤销信用证,出口企业在收到信用证时,未察觉到交单时应提交"由开证申请人签署的允许装船的批准书"的条款。出口企业在生产完毕制单结汇时,发现了这一条款,要求港商删除该条款或出具批准书,但港商百般推脱。最后致使我出口企业无法出运并结汇,损失保证金。请说明,在此案例中,我方应接受的教训是什么?

Answers for Reference 参考答案

1. Analysis: The exporter shall make shipment as stipulated and make document presentation to the foreign bank for the payment. In accordance with UCP600, the confirming bank and the issuing bank are both taken as the first payers with responsibility of making payment to the beneficiary, which is irrevocable without the permit of the beneficiary. The confirming bank is required to make negotiation and payment so long as the beneficiary makes presentation to the confirming bank with the documents complying with the L/C.

分析:我方应按照规定交货并向该保兑外资银行交单,要求付款。因为根据《跟单信用证统一惯例》(UCP600),信用证一经保兑,保兑行与开证行同为第一性的付款人,对受益人就要承担保证付款的责任,未经受益人的同意,该保证不得撤销。只要受益人在信用证的有效期内将符合 L/C 规定的单据递交保兑行,保兑行必须议付、付款。

2. Analysis: The exporter did not settle it properly, the lessons we shall take are as follows: ①The issuance time of L/C shall be stipulated in the contract. ②In accordance with the international usual practice, the buyer shall issue the L/C before the shipment month even though the issuance date is not mentioned in the contract; the exporter shall keep the claim right against the buyer for the buyer's failure of issuing L/C on time. ③As to the buyer cancelling the contract unilaterally without the permit of exporter, the exporter shall not let it be.

分析:我方处理不恰当。应吸取的教训:①在合同中未规定信用证开到日期不妥;②按照惯例,即使合同未规定开证期限,买方也应于装运月前开到信用证,买方未及时开到信用证，我方应保留索赔权；③对于外商以我方未能按时装运为由，单方面宣布解除合同，我方不能就此作罢。

3. Analysis: Obviously, the Japanese client tends to put off the payment time through changing the D/P at sight into D/P in sight of 90 days, which is in favor of his capital running. The nomination of collecting bank is for buyer's borrowing shipment documents from the bank which is also in benefit to the buyer. In a usance D/P business, the collecting bank usually will not allow the payer to borrow the documents. So, the Japanese client is supposed to have financial relationship with bank A, and then he is permitted to borrow the documents from the bank in order to make foil use of the exporter's capital.

分析：日商提出将 D/P 即期改为 90 天远期，很显然旨在推迟付款，以利其资金周转。而日商指定 A 银行作为该批托收业务的代收行，则是为了便于向该银行借单，以便早日获取经济利益。在一般的远期付款交单托收业务中，代收行在未经授权的情况下通常是不会轻易同意付款人借单的。该日商之所以提出通过 A 银行代收货款的原因，肯定是该商与 A 银行有既定融资关系，从中可取得提前借单的便利，以达到进一步利用我方资金的目的。

4. Analysis: It is a case about the cheat of the exporter's deposit. On receipt of an L/C, the exporter must examine the credit carefully to avoid the soft clause like the above-mentioned clause showed in the L/C. The soft clause resulted in the exporter's failure to make presentation of complying documents to bank for payment, The shipment of exporter is an obligation stipulated in the sales contract, which doesn't need the approval of the buyer, therefore, it is an unreasonable requirement for the exporter to make shipment on receipt of the approval of the buyer and exporter shall refuse to pay deposit.

分析：这是买方骗取保证金的案例。在收到信用证时，必须谨慎审核信用证，港商先骗出口企业保证金，后又在信用证中设入"由开证申请人签署的允许装船的批准书"的软条款，使得出口企业无法获得该批准书，也就无法向银行交单结汇。卖方的装船行为完全是按照买卖合同的一种义务，无须通过买方允许，所以出口企业的装船以买方批准为前提是无理的要求，并且不能同意缴纳保证金。

Chapter 5　Delivery of Goods

第 5 章　国际货物贸易运输

In international trade, the seller delivers the goods in exchange for the buyer's payment. It is the seller's basic duty to deliver the goods to the buyer or load the goods on the earner as nominated at the time, place and with the mode of transport specified in the contract after signing it.

In common law, according to the cases over the past years, common law countries regard quality clauses, quantity clauses and time of delivery as the fundamentals of the contract. The consequences could be very serious once the rules are broken. In this chapter, time of delivery is the priority of shipment clauses. Time of shipment and time of delivery are totally different concepts, but under FOB, CFR and CIF terms, the seller delivers the documents instead of the goods, which means, once the goods are delivered on board the ship or shipping conveyance at the loading port, the seller's duty to deliver goods is accomplished. The date indicated by the earner on the shipping documents is the time of delivery and the place of shipment is rightly the place of delivery. That is to say, under CIF, FOB and CFR trade terms which indicate symbolic delivery, shipment just means delivery and time of shipment is rightly time of delivery.

国际贸易中，卖方交付货物是以买方支付货款为交换条件。买卖合同签订后，按照合同规定的时间、地点和方式将货物运交买方或装上指定的承运工具，是卖方所承担的基本义务。

在英美法中，根据历年的判例，英美法的国家把品质条款、数量条款、交货期作为合同的要件条款。如果违反了要件条款，后果十分严重。在本章中，装运条款首先要讲到装运期。装运期和交货期是两个不同的概念，但是在 FOB、CFR、CIF 条件下，卖方以交单代替了交货，也就是说只要把货交到装运港的船上或运输工具上，卖方的交货义务就算完成，承运人在运输单据上所注明的日期即作为交货日期，货物的装运地点即作为交货地点。也就是说，在 CIF、FOB、CFR 象征性交货的贸易术语下，"装运"就意味着交货，交货期等于装运期。

Section 1 Modes of Transport

第 1 节 运输方式

In international trade, there are various kinds of modes of transportation: ocean transportation, rail transportation, air transportation, river transportation, postal transportation, road transportation, channel transportation, container transportation, international multimodal transportation and continental-bridge transportation, etc., of which ocean transportation is the most important, traditional and time honored means of transport. Currently, as the most preferred mode of transport, ocean transportation accounts for 80% of the total capacity. We'll introduce a few significant means of transportation in international trade hereinafter.

在国际贸易中，运输方式有许多种，如海洋运输、铁路运输、航空运输、河流运输、邮政运输、公路运输、管道运输、集装箱运输、国际多式联运、大陆桥运输等。其中，最重要的方式是海洋运输，海洋运输是国际贸易中历史最悠久的一种传统的运输方式。目前，在国际货物运输总量中，海洋运输占 80% 以上，是目前国际贸易中最重要的一种运输方式。以下我们主要介绍国际贸易中比较重要的几种方式。

1. Ocean Marine Transport 海上运输

Ocean marine transport is mostly preferred due to its large capacity, low cost, massive passing ability and freedom from road and railway limitations, while it's comparatively slow, risky and vulnerable to bad weather.

There are two main types of ocean transportation: liner transportation and charter transportation.

海洋运输有以下特点：通过能力大、运量大、运费低、不受道路、轨道限制。缺点是受自然条件影响较大，航行速度较慢，风险较大。

海洋运输方式主要有两种：班轮运输和租船运输。

(1) Liner Transport 班轮运输

A liner is a vessel with regular sailings and arrivals and sails on a fixed (regular) sailing route and calls at fixed (regular) base ports. It adopts a comparatively fixed timetable and charges at comparatively fixed rates. Liner transport is suitable for goods in small lots and high frequency. Most goods are transported through liner transport in international trade.

班轮运输又称定期船运输，简称班轮，指船舶按照预定的航行时间表，在固定的航线和港口往返航行，从事客货运输业务并按事先公布的费率收取运费。班轮运输适合批量小、次数多的商品。国际贸易中大部分的货物还是采用班轮运输。

① Characteristics of Liner Transport 班轮运输的特点

A. Fixity, namely fixed routes, fixed ports of call, fixed dates and comparatively fixed rates.

"四固定",即固定的航线、固定的停靠港、固定的船期和相对固定的运费率。

B. Responsibility: Goods are subject to the loading and unloading by the liners and handling charges are already included in the freight. Liners and the consignor are free from handling charges, demurrage charges and dispatch money.

责任：货物由班轮公司负责配载和装卸，装卸费已包含在运费内，班轮公司和托运人双方不计装卸费、滞期费和速遣费。

C. Liabilities, obligations and exemptions of liners and the shipper are all on the basis of the bill of lading issued by liners, In terms of goods with large transport volume and low value like grains, beans, mines and coals, the price is negotiated by both parties.

承运人和托运人双方的权利、义务和责任豁免均以班轮公司签发的提单条款为依据。对某些运量大、货价低的货物，如粮食、豆类、矿石、煤炭，由船货双方协商定价。

② Freight of Liners 班轮运费

Freight is the remuneration payable to the carrier for the carriage of goods. The freight paid for the carriage by a liner differs in the way of calculating from that paid under a charter party.

Freight=Fb+$\sum S$

Fb——Basic freight

S——Surcharge

运费是指因运输货物而付给承运人的报酬。付给班轮运输费用与付给不定期船的费用是不一样的。

班轮运费=Fb+$\sum S$

Fb——基本运费

S——附加运费

A. The Basic Standards for Calculating Freight 计算基本运费的标准

a. According to gross weight in terms of weight ton, which is indicated by "W" in the tariff. 1 M/T is to be considered as 1 weight ton. Heavy cargo is usually charged on this basis.

按货物毛重计收，即以重量吨为计算单位计收运费，在运价表内用"W"表示。一重量吨为 1 公吨(1 000 kg)。笨重的货物一般都采用这种方法。

b. According to volume, i.e., measurement ton, which is indicated by "M" in the tariff. It is 40cubic feet or one cubic meter that constitutes one measurement ton. Often light cargoes are charged on this basis.

按货物体积计收，即以尺码吨为计算单位计收运费，在运价表内用"M"表示。一尺码吨为1立方米或 40 立方英尺。通常轻型货物用这种方法。

c. According to value of the cargo, i.e., a certain percentage of FOB price which is indicated by "A.V." (Ad Valorem) in the liner freight tariff. Usually a percentage between 1% and 4% is charged on the value of such goods as gold, silver, precious stones, and valuable drawings and paintings.

按商品的价格计收，如按 FOB 价的一定百分比计收，称从价运费，用"A.V."或"Ad-Val"表示。此项计算标准适用于贵重或高价商品，如金、银、宝石和宝贵的从价百分比一般为 1%~4%。

d. According to gross weight or volume, i.e., choosing the higher rate between the two, which is indicated by "W/M" in the tariff.

按货物的毛重或体积两者中选收费较高的一种计收运费，在运价表中用"W/M"表示。

e. According to gross weight or volume or A.V., i.e., at the discretion of the carrier, choosing the highest rate of the three, which is indicated by "W/M or A.V." In this case, it is up to the carrier to decide to charge whichever of the three that produces the highest rate of freight.

选择货物的毛重或体积或价值三者中收费最高的一种计收运费，在运价表中用"W/M or A.V."表示。在此方式中，由承运人从三者中选择最高的那一种计收运费。

f. According to gross weight or volume, and then plus a certain percentage of A.V., which is indicated by "W/M plus A.V.".

按货物的毛重或体积，再加上货物价值的一定百分比计收运费，在运价表中用"W/M plus A.V."表示。

g. According to the number of the cargo. For example, a freight of so much is for one truck or one head of live animal.

按货物的件数计收。例如，卡车按每辆(Per Unit)、活牲畜按每头(Per Head)计收。

h. According to the temporary/interim or special agreement entered into between the ship-owner and the consignor.

按船主与托运人之间临时签订的协议计收运费。

B. Surcharges 附加运费

The main surcharges are shown as follows:

主要附加运费如下：

a. Heavy lift additional 超重附加费

b. Long length surcharge 超长附加费

c. Direct additional 直航附加费

d. Transshipment surcharge 转船附加费

e. Port congestion surcharge (PCS) 港口拥挤附加费

f. Port surcharge 港口附加费

g. Bunker surcharge or bunker adjustment factor (BAF) 燃油附加费

h. Optional fees 选港费

i. Alternation of destination surcharge 变更港口附加费

j. Deviation surcharge 绕航附加费

k. Yard Surcharges (YAS) 码头附加费

l. Peak Season Surcharges (PSS) 旺季附加费

m. Equipment Position Surcharges (EPS) 设备位置附加费

n. Currency Adjustment Factor (CAF) 货币贬值附加费

In addition to the above-mentioned surcharges, ice surcharge, cleaning tank surcharge, fumigation surcharge, etc. are sometimes included.

除了上述提到的附加费外，还有冷冻附加费、清理附加费、熏舱附加费等。

C. The Way to Calculate Freight 运费计算方法

a. First translate the English name of the commodity, find out the freight standard of calculating or the freight grade.

b. Find out the basic freight rate in the route freight tariff according to the grades and purpose sea route, then the relative surcharges for the suitable route and basic port.

c. The basic freight rate plus various additional surcharges is the freight per freight ton.
Total freight amount=[basic freight rate×(1+ $\sum$ surcharge rate)+ $\sum$ surcharges] ×total freight

a. 首先译出托运货物的英文名称，在"货物分级表"中查出该商品所属的等级和计算标准。

b. 根据等级和目的港航线，查出基本运费率和附加费率或附加费额。

c. 商品的基本费率加各种附加费，即为该商品每一运费吨的单位运价。用公式表示：
商品运费总额=[基本费率×(1+ $\sum$ 附加费率)+ $\sum$ 附加费额]×总运费吨

(2) Shipping by Charter 租船运输

Charter transport refers to a cargo ship not operating on regular routes and schedules. A ship may be hired wholly or just some shipping space for transportation.

Contrary to a liner, a charter vessel does not follow a fixed route, freight rate or timetable and has no fixed ports of call.

租船运输又称不定期船运输，指包租整船或部分舱位进行运输。

与班轮运输相反，租船运输有"四不固定"：航线不固定、停靠港不固定、船期不固定、运费率不固定。

① Types of Charter 租船运输的种类

Charter vessels fall into three types: voyage charter, time charter and bare boat charter.
租船运输又分为程租船、期租船和光租船。

A. Voyage Charter 定程租船

Voyage charter is also named irregular charter, which is the hire of a ship for the carriage of goods from one specified port to another, or for a round trip, and is characterized by shipping low-value and bulk commodities like grains, coals, wood, and mines. It can be divided into one-way charter, round-way charter and consecutive voyage charter according to the way of financing leasing.

Under a voyage charter, payment by the charterer is usually based on an agreed rate per ton for a "full and complete cargo". Should he fail to provide sufficient cargo to fill the ship he is liable for what is termed dead freight, a prorate payment for the space not used. A voyage charter also stipulates the number of days known as lay days, for loading and unloading. Should these be accessed, the charter is liable for a demurrage charge for each day in excess, and conversely is entitled to dispatch money for each day not taken up. The liability of the shipowner is to provide a ship that is seaworthy and to avoid unjustifiable deviation on voyage.

定程租船又称为程租船、不定期船、航次租船，是指由船舶所有人负责提供船舶在指定港口之间进行一个航次或数个航次承运指定货物的租船运输。特点是：以运输价值较低廉的粮食、煤炭、木材、矿石等大宗货物为主。程租船按其租赁方式的不同，可分为单程租船、来回航次租船、连续航次租船。

在定程租船情况下，租船人常常按议定的每吨装满货物的费率支付费用。如果他不能使船只载满，空舱费用由租船人按载重吨支付。定程租船还规定了装卸货的受载日期。如果受载日期超过规定，租船人须付每天超期的滞期费。反之，船方支付在受载日期内提前完成装卸每天的速谴费。船方的责任是保证船舶的适航性，并避免航途中不必要的绕航。

B. Time Charter 定期租船

The time charter, also called transport vessel or vehicle charter is a kind of transport based on affixed period instead of on a certain number of voyages or trips. The charterer charters the ship for a period of time during which the ship is deployed and managed by the charterer. What concerns the charterer most is the period, not the voyage. The chartering may be for a period of one year or of several years.

During the period of chartering, the ship is managed, deployed and used by the charterer. A series of work, such as loading, unloading, stowing and trimming and the so caused fuel expenses, port expenses, loading and unloading expenses, etc., should be borne by the charterer. The ship-owner should bear the wages and board expenses of the crew, and be responsible for seaworthiness during the period of chartering and the so-caused expenses and the vessel insurance premium.

定期租船又称期租船、期限租船，是以期限为基础的租船方式，而不是以某一航线或航程为基础。船舶所有人将船舶出租给租船人使用一定期限，在此期限内由租船人自行调度和经营管理。租用时间可以是一年或数年。

在租船期间，货船的经营、管理和使用权都归承租人。同时，由于装卸货物、平仓理仓等引起的燃油费、港口费、装卸费等也都由承租人负担。船东要负责支付船员的工资，并保证在租用期间货船适合海洋运输及相关费用和货船的保险费。

The Difference between voyage charter and time charter: Ship-owner of a voyage charter is responsible for hiring the crew and providing fuel while the charterer is in the latter case; Ship-owner of a voyage charter takes on sailing and maintaining of the ship while the charterer does in the latter case.

程租船与期租船的区别：程租船时船员、燃料配备都由船方负责，期租船时由租方负责；船舶经营调度，程租船时由船方负责，期租船时由租方自己负责。

C. Demise Charter 光船租船

Demise charter, is also called bare-boat charter, the charterer takes a lease of the entire ship for an agreed time. So demise charter belongs to time charter, but there are some differences: as to time charter, during the period of chartering, the ship-owner provides the charterer with a crew, while as to bare-boat charter, the ship-owner only provides the charterer with a bare-boat, the charterer shall employ the crew and pay the crew's wages and provisions, ship's maintenance and stores, etc. by himself, apart from those expenses he is responsible for under the time charter.

光船租船是承租人按约定时间租赁整艘船，也是期租。所不同的是，在定期租船方式下，船主不仅提供货船，还有船员，而在光船租船方式下，船主不提供船员，只有一条船交给租方使用，由租方自行配备船员，负责船舶的经营管理和航行各项事宜(如船舶的维护、修理及机器的正常运转等)。

② Charter Party 租船合同

The charter party is a contract concluded between the ship-owner and the charterer when the latter charters the ship or booking shipping space from the former. It stipulates the rights and obligations of the two parties. The main terms on the charter party include the interested parties, name and flag of the ship, description and quantity of the shipments, time of chartering, freight, loading and unloading expenses, time limit of loading and unloading, demurrage and dispatch money.

租船合同是租船人和船舶所有人之间订立的载明双方权利、义务的契约。租船合同的主要条款中包括有关当事人、船名和货船标识、装运货物的名称和数量、租期、运费、装卸费、装卸时限、滞期费、速遣费。

The freight may be stipulated in the charter party as follows:

a. Freight can be paid in advance.

b. Freight can be paid after the goods have arrived at the port of destination.

c. Part of freight is paid in advance, the rest of which is paid after the goods have arrived at the port of destination.

Before the charterer pays off freight and other charges, the ship-owner is entitled to refuse to deliver the goods, this kind of right is called lien.

租船合同中有关运费的规定如下：

a. 运费预付。

b. 货到目的港时再付运费。

c. 已付部分运费，余下的货到目的港之后再付。

在租船人付清运费之前，船主有权拒绝交付货物，这称对留置权。

When discussing the problem of whom will be responsible for the charges of loading and unloading, both the ship-owner and the charterer should make it very clear in the charter party. There are five methods to be used to stipulate the expenses of loading and unloading:

在签订程租船合同时，必须明确装卸费用是由承租人还是船东负担。对这个问题有五种规定方法：

a. Liner terms/gross terms/berth terms 班轮条件

The ship-owner bears loading and unloading cost.

船方负担装卸费。

b. Free in and out (FIO) 船方不管装，不管卸

The ship-owner does not bear loading and unloading cost.

船方不负担装卸费。

c. Free in (FI) 船方管卸不管装

The ship-owner is only responsible for unloading cost.

船方只承担卸货费。

d. Free out (FO) 船方管装不管卸

The ship-owner is only responsible for loading cost.

船方只承担装船费。

e. Free in and out, stowed and trimmed (FIOST) 船方不管装、不管卸、不管理舱、不管平舱

The ship-owner does not bear loading and unloading cost, not even bear the expenses of stowing and trimming.

船方不承担装卸费，也不承担理舱费和平舱费。

In voyage charter transport, the lay time is directly related to the operating cycles and benefits of the ship-owner, so lay time should be stipulated in detail when both parties come into a contract. If the charterer fails to finish loading the goods within the limited time resulting in extended staying time and trip time, it would increase expenses as well as decrease cycling rates for the ship-owner. So lay time stipulations are closely related to the benefits of both parties. Therefore, it is the main clause specified in the charter party. The time limit of loading and unloading may be indicated by:

程租船运输方式，货物在装卸港口装卸时间长短直接关系到船舶的使用周期和船方的

利益。租方在和船方签订租船合同时，要就船舶在港装卸的时间做出具体的规定。如租船人未能在约定的装卸时间内将货物装完或卸完，而延长了船舶在港停留时间，从而延长了航次时间，这对船舶所有人来说，既可能因增加船舶在港口停泊的时间而增加了港口费用的开支，又因航次时间延长而降低了船舶的周转率。装卸时间的规定直接关系到船方和租方的切身利益。所以，装卸时间是租船合同的主要条款，装卸时限的规定方法有：

a. 在一定天数内装卸完毕。

b. 规定装卸速度。

c. 按惯常的速度装卸。

During the time limit of loading and unloading, in case the charterer does not finish the work of loading and unloading, in order to compensate the ship-owner for his losses, the charterer should pay certain amount of fine for the exceeding time, this is the so-called demurrage.

During the time limit of loading and unloading, in case the charterer finishes the work of loading and unloading ahead of schedule, then the ship-owner shall pay certain amount of bonus to the charterer, this is the so-called dispatch money.

在规定的装卸时限内，如果租船人没有完成货物的装卸工作，租船人就必须因此而向船主支付一定数目的过期费，这就是滞期费。

在规定的装卸时限内，如果租船人提前完成了货物的装卸工作，船主就必须因此而向租船人支付一定数目的奖励费，这就是速遣费。

2. Land Transport 陆路运输

Land transport includes rail transport and road transport. In international transportation, the importance of rail transport is only secondary to the maritime transportation; moreover, the cargo imported or exported by ship are mostly distributed or collected overland by rail. Rail transport has the characteristics of large carrying load, high speed, and low risk.

For China with a vast territory, the cargoes imported by ships are usually transported by rail to the consumers across the country, and most of cargoes for export are pooled to the ports by rail. Therefore, railway plays an important role in the distribution or collection of goods in China for international trade. The movement of the raw materials, semi-final products, and packing materials for international trade throughout the country are mainly by rail, too. Generally speaking, the railway is one of the necessary parts in international transport chains.

陆路运输包括铁路运输和公路运输。在国际货物运输中，铁路运输是一种仅次于海洋运输的主要运输方式，海洋运输的进出口货物，也大多是靠铁路运输进行货物集中和分散的。铁路运输具有运量大、速度快、风险小的特点。

由于我国幅员辽阔，海运进口货物大部分利用铁路运往内地各用货单位，海运出口货物也多是通过铁路向港区集中，因此，铁路运输是我国国际贸易货物集散的重要工具。国内各省和地区调运外贸物资、各种原料、半成品和包装物料，也主要是依靠铁路运输来完成。我国国际贸易进出口货物运输一般都要通过铁路这一环节，铁路运输在国际货物运输中发挥着重要作用。

(1) International Carriage of Goods by Rail 国际铁路货物联运

With one set of uniform transportation documents, the goods are moved through two or more countries by rail as a whole, without the involvement of the consigner and consignee when the goods are delivered from one country to the other country.

For the transport mode, the goods are free from the check-in again at the frontier office, and carried over the frontier by train. It benefits to the international trade and transaction, urging the development of the integrative economy.

凡是使用一份统一的国际联运票据由铁路负责经过两国或两国以上铁路的全程运送，并由一国铁路向另一国铁路运送货物时，不需要发货人和收货人参加的这种运输称为国际铁路货物联运。

国际铁路货物联运免除了货物在国境站重新办理托运的手续，火车可以直接过轨运输；有利于各国之间的国际贸易和经济交往，加速了经济一体化的发展。

(2) National Rail Transport 国内铁路运输

The mode of national rail transport means the transportation is made by rail in one country according to the concerning rules and regulation of the country. In China, the transportation by rail to the loading port for the goods to be exported or from the discharging port to throughout the country for the imported goods both fall in the mode. The transportation by rail for the cargo or goods supplied to HK and Macao is also included in the mode, which comprises two parts, one is national rail transport and the other is HK or Macao rail transport. The detailed processes are as follows: After the goods are carried to Shenzhen station by rail with the consignee named as a transportation agent in Shenzhen such as SINOTRANS Shenzhen, SINOTRANS Shenzhen will get through the concerning customs procedures and transit the goods to HK, when the goods arrive in HK, the HK agent will take the goods and send them to Kowloon station of Hong Kong.

The above-mentioned shows that the characteristics of the rail transport for HK or Macao is two parts of rail transport linked by chartering. The national transportation documents cannot be taken as the documents for payment, but the carrier's cargo receipt issued by the SINOTRANS local branch as the document for payment presented to bank.

In China, there are three lines destined to HK and Macao which are No.751, 753 and 755. The goods are sent to Shenzhen station by the consigner or exporter, then have the local transportation agent in Shenzhen (such as SINOTRANS) to get through the customs procedures and transit the goods to the agent in HK or Macao who will deliver the goods to the final buyer in

HK or Macao, and the exporter makes collection with the cargo receipt issued by the transportation agent.

国内铁路运输是指仅在本国范围内按《国内铁路货物运输规程》的规定办理的货物运输。我国出口货物经铁路运至港口装船及进口货物卸船后经铁路运往各地，均属国内铁路运输的范畴。供应港、澳地区的物资经铁路运往香港、九龙，也属于国内铁路运输的范围。它的全过程由两部分组成，即内地段铁路运输和港、澳段铁路运输，货车到达深圳后，要过轨至香港，继续运送至九龙车站，内地铁路与香港铁路不办理直通联运，因此，就形成了现行的这种运输方式：发送地以内地运输向铁路部门办理托运至深圳北站，收货人为深圳外运分公司，深圳外运分公司作为各外贸发货单位的代理与铁路部门办理租车手续，并付给租车费，然后租车去香港，货车过轨后，香港中国旅行社则作为深圳外运分公司的代理在港段重新起票托运至九龙。

由此可见，对香港、澳门地区的铁路运输的特色是租车方式两票运输。内地运单不能作为结汇的凭证，目前，由各地外运公司以运输承运人的身份向外贸单位提供经深圳中转香港货物的承运货物收据，作为向银行结汇的凭证。

我国开辟 751、753、755 三趟快车往港澳运输：由发货人将货物托运到深圳北站，由当地外贸运输公司再办理港段铁路托运手续，由香港中国旅行社收货后转交香港或澳门的买主，出口企业凭外贸运输公司出具的承运货物收据办理收汇手续。

3. Air Transport 航空运输

As a modern transportation mode, air transport has developed rapidly with the advantages of being speedy, exact, safe and convenient. At the same time, the drastic growth of the goods adapted to air transport also pushes the development of air industry. More and more modern and big airplanes, big airports with perfect facilities and modern telecommunication facilities are produced and constructed to meet the demand of air transportation in international trade. In this way, international trade and air industry boost each other with the advancement of air technology and air transportation. For the time being, the proportion of air transportation occupied in the whole international transportation is increasing with the growing quantity of cargo transported by air.

The goods which are the most adapted to air transport are including urgent cargo, fresh and alive products, precise appliances, valuables, putrescible and seasonal items etc.

Since 1974, China has joined International Civil Aviation Organization (ICAO).

航空运输是一种现代化的运输方式。由于航空运输具有速度快、准确、安全、方便等优点，航空货物运输在世界范围内得到迅速发展。同时，国际贸易中适合于航空运输的货物大量增加，促进了航空事业的发展。航空事业的发展又给航空运输提供了现代化、大型化的飞机，机场规模宏大，设施完善，航空公司不断增加，通信手段现代化，这些都为国际贸易货物的空运提供了更为便利的条件，促进了国际贸易的发展。国际贸易与航空业务互相促进，航空技术与航运共同发展。目前，在整个国际贸易运输中，航空货物运输所占的比重不断增加，货运量也越来越大。

航空运输最适合运输急需物质、鲜活产品、精密仪器、贵重物品、易腐、季节性强的货物。

我国于1974年加入国际民航组织(ICAO)。

(1) Classification of Air Transport Modes 航空运输的主要方式

① Scheduled Airline 班机运输

Scheduled airline refers to the airlines that transport regularly by fixed route, between fixed departure and destination at fixed time schedule. Usually this kind of flights uses passenger-cargo airplane, some bigger air companies have opened up regular full air cargo flight. With the advantage of its fixed time, route and stop station, the scheduled airline is more suitable for the transport of emergency items, fresh and live produce or seasonal commodities.

班机是指在固定时间、固定航线、固定始发站和目的站运输的飞机，通常班机是使用客货混合型飞机，一些大的航空公司也有开辟定期全货机航班的。班机因有定时、定航线、定站等特点，因此适用于运送急需物品、鲜活商品以及节令性商品。

② Chartered Carrier 包机运输

Chartered earner refers to the airplane that is hired by one consigner or share-hired by several consigners (or air-freight service agency). Thus, chartered carrier could be divided into two kinds: whole-hired and share-hired. The former kind is suitable for transporting goods in large quantity, and the latter one is suitable for goods to be delivered to the same destination by different consigners.

包机是指包租整架飞机或由几个发货人(或航空货运代理公司)联合包租一架飞机来运送货物。因此，包机又分为整包机和部分包机两种形式，前者适用于运送数量较大的商品，后者适用于多个发货人，但货物到达站又是同一地点的货物运输。

③ Consolidation 集中托运

Consolidation is usually utilized by air-freight service agency, who combines scattered goods into one batch, with the airway bills for each shipment issued respectively for each consignor, then makes delivery of the whole batch of goods to the scheduled destination with one set of chief airway bill. After the arrival, the goods are cleared, sorted out and dispatched to the actual consignees respectively by the local agency of air-freight carrier. The price of consolidation flight is usually 7%-10% lower than that of scheduled airliner fixed by International Air Transportation Association. For this reason, the consignors are more willing to commit the goods to air-freight agency for delivery.

集中托运是指航空货运公司把若干单独发运的货物(每一货主的货物要出具一份航空

运单)组成一整批货物，用一批总运单(附分运单)整批发运到预定目的地，由航空公司在那里的代理人收货、报关、分拨后交给实际收货人。集中托运的运价比国际空运协会公布的班机运价低 7%～10%，因此发货人比较愿意将货物交给航空货运公司安排。

④ Air Express Service 航空急件传递

Air Express is the fastest one in the current international air transportation modes. Differing from air paravion and air freight, air express service is operated by the organizations specialized in this business field, who is in a close cooperation with airline companies, with urgent mails transferred by specially-assigned person, between consignor, airport and consignee at the fastest speed. It is most suitable for delivery of medicine and medical equipment in urgent needs, valuables, blue print documents and other goods and documents, therefore it is called "Desk to Desk Service".

航空急件传送是目前国际航空运输中最快捷的运输方式。它不同于航空邮寄和航空货运，而是由一个专门经营此项业务的机构与航空公司密切合作，设专人用最快的速度在货主、机场、收件人之间传送急件，特别适用于急需的药品、医疗器械、贵重物品、图纸资料、货及单证等的传送，被称为"桌到桌运输"。

(2)Air Carrier 航空运输承运人

① Airline Company 航空运输公司

Airline company is the actual earner of the goods transported by air, who is in charge of the whole transportation.

航空运输公司是指航空运输的实际承运人，对全程运输负责。

② Air Freight Logistics or Agent 航空货运代理公司

It is the agent of the consignor and airline company as well. It is usually nominated by the consignor or consignee to offer the services including booking flights, chartering and the like works as well as the movement and delivery of the goods, making documents, customs clearance and getting through inspection etc.

航空货运代理公司既是货主代理，也是航空公司代理。接受收、发货人的委托，代办进出口货物的航空定舱、包机等业务，并代办发运、接交、制单、报关和报验等工作。

(3) Air Freight Rates 航空运价

The rate of air freight is the freight from the departure airport to the arrival airport, not including other extra expenses for the services like picking up, storage etc.. The rate is calculated generally as per weight (kg) or volumetric weight (6,000 CBCM converted to 1 kg), whichever is higher. The rate of the air freight is fixed according to general cargo rates (GCR), specific commodity rates (SCR) and commodity classification rates (CCR).

航空运输货物的运价是指从起运机场至目的机场的运价，不包括其他额外费用(如提货、仓储费等)。运价一般是按重量(千克)或体积重量(6 000 立方厘米折合 1 千克)计算的，以两者中高者为准。空运货物是按一般货物、特种货物和货物的等级规定运价标准。

4. Postal Transport and Courier Service 邮政运输和快递运输

(1) Postal Transport 邮政运输

According to international trade practice, the seller fulfils the duty of delivery only if he delivers the parcel to the post office, pays off the postage, and gets the receipt. The post office is responsible for the delivery of the goods to the destination, and the consignee goes to the post office responsible for the delivery of the goods to the destination, and the consignee goes to the post office for picking up his goods. Postal transport falls into two kinds: regular mail and air mail.

This method is simple and convenient, and delivery is made simply when a receipt of the goods posted is obtained. It is a kind of international and "door-to-door" transport. According to the postal regulations of the world, the longest length of each parcel limits to one meter, and the weight under 20 kilograms. The restriction of the size and weight on the parcels limits the practicality of this mode, it is only suitable for exactitude instruments, machinery components, bullion ornaments, material medical and other small sized and precious goods.

邮包运输是托运人在托运地邮局办理邮件托运手续后，由邮局负责将邮件传递到目的地，收货人直接在目的地邮局提取邮件的一种运输方式。邮包分为普通邮包和航空邮包两种。

这种运输方式的特点是手续简便，费用不太高，具有广泛的国际性和"门到门"的运输性质。根据各国邮政的规定，国际邮包运输限定每件长度不能超过 1 米，重量不能超过 20 千克，所以邮包运输只适用于量轻体小的商品，如精密仪器、机器零件、金银首饰、药品以及各种样品和零星物品等。

(2) Courier Service 快递运输

International express is mainly refers to UPS, Fedex, DHL, TNT –the four giants, including UPS and Fedex headquarters located in the United States, DHL headquarters in Germany, TNT based in the Netherlands. International express has a very high demand of delivery of information, collection and management, supported by global self-built network and international information systems.

Currently, there are five kinds of mode for cross-border e-commerce logistics operation as follows: express, postal packets, overseas warehouse, special Courier, central railway multimodal transport.

国际快递主要是指 UPS、Fedex、DHL、TNT 这四大巨头，其中，UPS 和 Fedex 总部位于美国，DHL 总部位于德国，TNT 总部位于荷兰。国际快递对信息的提供、收集与管理有很高的要求，以全球自建网络以及国际化信息系统为支撑。

目前，跨境电子商务的物流运作方式主要有以下五种模式：快递、邮政小包、海外仓、专线速递、中欧铁路多式联运。

5. Pipeline Transport 管道运输

Pipeline transportation is a mode of transportation by pipeline used for transporting commodities, such as gas, liquid and powder solids, which is produced with the production of petroleum and crude oil. The form of pipeline transportation is different from that of transportation of ordinary cargos. General cargo transport is transported to the destination with the movement of the means of transport, while the pipeline itself which is the means of pipeline transport is fixed, and only the goods themselves move within the pipeline. Pipeline transportation is a special mode of transportation in which the transportation channels and means of transportation are combined into one.

At present, pipeline transportation accounts for a large proportion in the transportation of global energy products (petroleum crude oil, refined oil, natural gas, associated gas from oil fields, coal water slurry, etc.). In recent years, pipeline transportation has also been further studied and developed for bulk materials, pieces of goods, packaging materials transportation, and the system of container pipeline transportation are developed. Pipeline transportation is one of the important components of comprehensive transportation in national economy, and it is also a characteristic to measure whether the industry of energy and transportation are developed in a country. At present, the long-distance and large-diameter pipelines of oil and gas are operated and managed by independent companies.

管道运输是利用管道输送气体、液体和粉末状固体的一种运输方式，它随着石油原油的生产而产生。管道运输与普通货物运输的形态不同。普通货物运输是随着运输工具的移动，被运送到目的地，而作为管道运输的运输工具本身的管道是固定不变的，只是货物本身在管道内移动。管道运输是运输通道和运输工具合而为一的专门的运输方式。

目前，在全球能源产品(石油原油、成品油、天然气、油田伴生气、水煤浆等)的运输中，管道运输占有较大的比重。近年来，管道运输也被进一步研究开发用于散状物料、成件货物、集装物料运输，并发展了容器式管道输送系统。管道运输是国民经济综合运输的重要组成部分之一，也是衡量一个国家的能源业与运输业是否发达的一个特征。目前，长距离、大管径的油气管道均由独立的运营管理企业负责经营和管理。

6. Container Transport 集装箱运输

Container, in a literal sense, it is a kind of tremendous holder with sort of intensity (most containers are made of steel now) for cycling and easy to be mechanically operated.

Container transport is a method of distributing merchandise in unitized form adopting an inter-modal system which provides a possible combination of sea, road and other modes of transportation.

集装箱又称"货箱""货柜"。按原文字面的含义，它是一种"容器"，必须具有一定的强度(现在集装箱多为钢制)，是专供周转使用、便于机械操作的大型货物容器。

所谓集装箱运输的概念就是将一定数量的单件货物装入按标准规格特制的集装箱内，并以该箱作为运送单位的一种现代化的运输方式。它可适用于各种运输方式的单独运输和不同运输方式的联合运输。

(1) Types and Specifications of Container 集装箱的种类和规格

The most widely adopted sizes are twenty-foot equivalent unit (TEU) and forty-foot equivalent unit (FEU). But recently, containers are becoming lager and lager. For instance, American President Lines adopt 53-foot container. The generally adopted sizes in China are:

$8' \times 8' \times 20'$　twenty-foot equivalent unit (TEU)

$8' \times 8' \times 40'$　forty-foot equivalent unit (FEU)

In the metric system:

① twenty-foot equivalent unit (TEU):

5.925m (length) × 2.34m (width) × 2.379m (height) = 33m^3

The real volume is 25m^3

The door: 2.286m (width) × 2.278m (height)

Dead weight: 1.9M/T

Carrying capacity: 22.1M/T

② forty-foot equivalent unit (FEU):

12.043m (length) × 2.336m (width) × 2.379m (height) = 67m^3

The real volume is 55m^3

The door: 2.286m (width) × 2.278m (height)

Dead weight: 3.48M/T

Maximum Carrying capacity: 27.59M/T

目前在国际航运上使用的集装箱多为 20 英尺和 40 英尺集装箱。但近年来，集装箱向大型化方向发展，如美国总统轮船公司采用 53 英尺型集装箱。我国通常采用的规格为：

$8' \times 8' \times 20'$　20 英尺集装箱

$8' \times 8' \times 40'$　40 英尺集装箱

换算为公制：

① 20 英尺柜：(长)5.925 米×(宽)2.34 米×(高)2.379 米=33 立方米

实际装箱时有效容积为 25 立方米

箱门：(宽)2.286 米×(高)2.278 米

自重：1.9 公吨

载重：22.1 公吨

② 40 英尺柜：(长)12.043 米×(宽)2.336 米×(高)2.379 米=67 立方米

实际装箱时有效容积为 55 立方米

箱门：(宽)2.286 米×(高)2.278 米

自重：3.48 公吨

最大载重：27.59 公吨

(2) Goods Handing over of Container Transportation　集装箱运输货物的交接

① Types of Goods　集装箱货物的分类

A. Full Container Load (FCL)　整箱货

The FCL consignments are packed into the container as one unit by the consigner for shipment. This means is adopted when the goods are of a container load or many containers load. Except that some consignors have containers, others generally lease a few to send to the production side or the warehouse, and then under the customs official's supervision, the consignor pack the goods into the container, after locking and sealing up the container, getting the dock receipt (D/R) in exchange for bills of lading or shipping documents.

这种装箱方式是指货主自行将货物装满整箱后，以箱为单位向承运人进行托运。这种情况是货主有足以装满一个或几个整箱的货源时所采用的装箱方式。除有些货主自己备有集装箱外，一般都是货主向承运人或集装箱租赁公司租用一定数量的集装箱，当空箱运到货主的工厂或仓库后，在海关人员的监督下，由货主把货物装入箱内，加锁铅封后交给承运人并取得场站收据(Dock Receipt, D/R)，凭此换取提单或运单。

B. Less than Container Load (LCL)　拼箱货

LCL stands for less than container load or partial container load as opposite to FCL. LCL consignments are first sent to the container freight station or inland container depot where the carrier can consolidate and pack the goods into containers according to the nature, destination, and weight and so on and then send the containers to the container yard for shipment.

这种装箱方式是指承运人(或其代理人)接受货主托运的数量不足装满整箱的小票货运后，根据货物性质和目的地进行分类整理，把去同一目的地的货物，集中到一定数量，拼装入箱。由于箱内不同货主的货物拼装在一起，所以叫拼箱货。这种方式在一个货主的货物不足装满整箱的情况下采用。拼箱货的分类、整理、集中、装箱(拆箱)、交货等均由承运人在码头集装箱货运站或内陆集装箱转运站进行。

② Expressions Indicated on the Bills of Lading　在提单上注明集装箱货物运输方式

FCL/FCL—full container load, full container delivery, one consignor and one consignee.

FCL/LCL—full container load, less than full container received, one consignor and more than one consignee.

LCL/FCL—less than full container load, full container load, more than one consignor but one consignee.

LCL/LCL—less than full container load, less than full container load and more than one consignor and consignee.

FCL/FCL——整箱装、整箱交，发货人一个，收货人一个。

FCL/LCL——整箱装、拼箱接，发货人一个，收货人多个。

LCL/FCL——拼箱装、整箱接，发货人多个，收货人一个。

LCL/LCL——拼箱装、拼箱接，发货人和收货人都是多个。

③ Container Yard (CY) and Container Freight Station (CFS) 集装箱堆场与集装箱货运站

The FCL and LCL consignments are delivered from different locations.

CY is for the delivery of a whole container while CFS is for the delivery of loose cargo.

So the above FCL/FCL can be expressed as CY/CY and LCL/LCL is CFS/CFS. The former means the FCL received by the carrier is packed at the shipper's or the forwarder^ premises, and delivery of that same FCL to the consignee's premises; and the latter means the loose cargo first delivered to the carrier's container freight station at the port of origin is packed into the whole container, and that same whole container is emptied at the carrier's container freight station at the port of destination.

集装箱运输整箱货与拼箱货是在不同的场地集中分拨。

集装箱堆场是整箱货直接运交集装箱堆场集中待运，集装箱货运站是专门集中分拨拼箱货的场所。

所以上述 FCL/FCL 也可表述为 CY/CY。LCL/LCL 也可写成 CFS/CFS。前者意为在出口国装运港整箱装，在目的地整箱交；后者意为在出口国拼箱装，在目的地拼箱接。

7. Combined Transport/Multimodal Transport 多式联运

International multimodal transport involves the transportation of freight in an international container or vehicle, using multiple modes of transportation (rail, ship and truck), without any handling of the freight itself when changing modes.

The practice is the multimodal transport operator (MTO) taking the cargo from the place of sellers in one country to the site of the buyers in another country by at least two modes of transportation on the basis of a multimodal transportation contract.

The characteristics is that only one carriage contract, one freight rate and one multimodal transport document are required no matter how long the distance is and no matter how complex the procedures are. The only one multimodal transport operator is responsible for the entire journey in case that the goods are lost or damaged. However, the combined bill of lading in ocean transport is only responsible for the first part of the journey.

国际多式联运是在集装箱运输的基础上发展起来的一种综合性的连贯运输方式,它把过去的那种海、陆、空、公路、江河等互不关联的单一运输有机地结合起来,以完成一票进口或出口货物在国际之间的运输。

具体做法:由多式联运经营人(MTO)根据多式联运合同以至少两种不同的运输方式将货物从一国境内接管地运至另一国境内指定交货地点。

其特点是:不管路途多远、手续多复杂,货主只办理一次托运、支付一笔运费、取得一张多式联运单据,如货物在途中发生灭失、货损之类问题,只找一个多式联运经营人解决,对全程负责。注意:海运中联运提单只对第一程负责。

Section 2 Transport Documents

第2节 运 输 单 据

Shipping documents refer to the evidence of the cargo on board the ship or under the supervision of the earner after getting receipt of it. The shipping documents are of great significance as they are proof of receiving the cargo, dealing with claims and making settlements.

运输单据是指承运人收到货物后证明货物已装上运输工具,已发运或已由承运人接受监管的单据。它是交接货物、处理索赔与理赔及向银行结算货款的重要凭据。

1. Bill of Lading 海运提单

A bill of lading (B/L), most commonly used in international trade, is a document issued by a carrier to a shipper, signed by the captain, agent, or owner of a vessel, stating the conditions in which the goods are to be transported to the specified port of destination to the lawful holder of the bill of lading. It is also a document of title to the goods, enabling the consignor to get receipt of the goods from shipping company or its agent at the port of destination.

海运提单(B/L)简称提单,是目前海运业务使用最为广泛和主要的运输单据。它是由船长或船公司或其代理人签发的,证明已收到特定货物,允诺将货物运至指定的目的港,并交付给收货人的凭证。海运提单也是收货人在目的港据以向船公司或其代理提取货物的凭证。

(1) Natures and Functions of Bill of Lading 海运提单的性质和作用

① It is a receipt issued by a carrier evidencing that a consignment of goods has been received at his disposal.

海运提单是承运人或其代理人签发的货物收据,证明承运人已按提单所列内容收到货物。

② It is a document of title to the goods; that is, the legal owner of a bill of lading holds legal possession of the goods described in it. The legal holder is given the right to obtain delivery of the goods. Because of this, it can be transferred, pledged or negotiated by banks before the arrival at the destination.

海运提单是物权凭证。海运提单是代表货物所有权的凭证。收货人或提单的合法持有人，有权凭提单向承运人提取货物。由于提单是一种物权凭证，因而在国际市场上，提单可以在载货船舶到达目的港交货之前办理转让，或凭以向银行办理押汇、议付或抵押贷款。

③ It is an evidence of a contract of carriage between the consignor and consignee. Clauses printed in the overleaf stipulate both parties' rights and liabilities and are regarded as proof for treatment of disputes.

海运提单是托运人和承运人之间运输契约的证明。提单的背面条款规定了双方的权利、义务、责任，作为双方处理纠纷的依据。

④ A bill of lading functions as evidence of loading, unloading, transferring, dispatching, claiming, and freight collecting by the carrier.

海运提单是作为承运人收取运费的证明，以及在运输过程中办理货物装卸、转船、发运、交接以及最后索赔的依据。

(2) Contents of Bills of Lading 海运提单的格式和内容

① The Face of the Bill 提单正面的内容

A. Column 1 on the left is written with name of exporting commodity

B. Column 2 is the title of consignee, or, the owner of the bill

C. Column 3 is written with name and address of the buyer

The rest of the bill is written with:

D. Place of receipt or shipment

E. Port of destination or unloading

F. Name of ocean vessel and Voyage No.

G. Shipping marks and articles No.

H. Name of commodity and No. of containers or packages

I. Weight and volume

J. Freight prepaid or freight to be collected

K. Copies of original bills of lading

L. Signature of shipping company or its agent

M. Date and place of issue

A. 提单左边第一栏为托运人栏，也称发货人栏，一般填写出口商名称。

B. 第二栏为收货人栏，也称抬头，是提单的所有权人栏。

C. 第三栏为通知收货人栏，此栏注明买方名称、地址。

提单正面其他各栏分别注明：

D. 装货地或装货港。

E. 目的地或卸货港。

F. 船名及航次。

G. 唛头及件号。

H. 货名及件数。

I. 重量和体积。

J. 运费已付或运费到付。

K. 正本提单的份数。

L. 船公司或其代理人的签章。

M. 签发提单的日期及地点。

② The Overleaf of the Bill 提单背面条款

Rights, liabilities and exemptions of both parties which are main evidence of dealing with disputes are printed on the overleaf.

提单背面印定的条款规定了承运人与货方之间的权利、义务和责任豁免，是双方当事人处理争议时的主要法律依据。

(3) Types of Bills of Lading 海运提单的种类

① According to whether the goods are loaded on board the vessel, B/L can be classified as follows:

根据是否装船可分为：

A. On Board B/L; Shipped B/L 已装船提单

On board B/L refers to the one that shall be issued after the cargo has been actually shipped on board the vessel. It is issued by the shipping company or its agent, on which both the loading date and the name of the vessel shall be indicated in detail. UCP600 states, "A bill of lading indicates that the goods have been shipped on board a named vessel at the port of loading stated in the credit by an on board notation indicating the date on which the goods have been shipped on board." As a bill of lading is the receipt of cargo, the seller must provide on board bills of lading.

已装船提单是指承运人已将货物装上指定船舶后所签发的提单，其特点是提单上必须以文字表明货物已经装某某船上，并表明装船日期，同时还应由船长或其代理人签字。根据《跟单信用证统一惯例》(UCP600)的规定，"提单，通过以下方式表明货物已在信用证规定的装货港装上具名船只：已装船批注注明货物的装运日期"。因为提单是代表货物所有权的凭证，所以卖方所提供的提单必须是已装船提单。

B. Received for Shipment B/L 备运提单，又称收讫待运提单

Received for shipment B/L is the one that acknowledges that goods have been received for shipment but not been loaded on board the carrying vessel yet. The consignor could exchange it for on board B/L, or turn it to be on board B/L on condition that the earner or agent adds an on board notation on received for shipment B/L indicating the name of the vessel and shipping date, and sign his or her name.

备运提单是指承运人已收到托运货物等待装运期间所签发的提单。在签发备运提单情况下，发货人可在货物装船后凭以调换已装船提单；也可经承运人或其代理人在备运提单上批注货物已装上某具名船舶及装船日期，并签署后使之成为已装船提单。

② According to the apparent condition of the received cargo, B/L can be classified as follows:

根据提单上有无不良批注可分为：

A. Clean B/L 清洁提单

A clean bill of lading refers to the one that does not contain any notation declaring a defective condition of the exterior packing of goods. UCP600 states, "Banks favor only clean bills of lading, and a clean bill of lading refers to the one that does not contain any notation declaring a defective condition of the exterior packing of goods."

清洁提单是指货物在装船时表面状况良好，船公司在提单上未加任何有关货物受损或包装不良等批注的提单。《跟单信用证统一惯例》(UCP600)规定："银行只接受清洁运输单据。清洁运输单据指未载有明确宣称货物或包装有缺陷的条款或批注的运输单据。"

B. Unclean B/L; Foul B/L 不清洁提单

Unclean B/L or Foul B/L is the one that contains unfavorable notation about the apparent condition of the cargo. e.g. "packages in damaged condition" "iron strap loose or missing". An unclean B/L is not acceptable to banks.

不清洁提单是指船公司在提单上对货物表面状况或包装加有不良或存在缺陷等批注的提单。例如，提单上批注"包装损坏""铁条松散或丢失"等。银行不接受不清洁提单。

③ According to the title, B/L can be classified as follows:

根据提单抬头的不同可分为：

The title of the bill refers to the consignee who is entitled to take delivery of the goods. Different title means different means of transferring title of goods. It is of great importance to learn about different types of bills according to the title and choose different means of transaction and payment in order to get the goods safely exchanged and obtain bank financing.

所谓提单的抬头，就是指提单的收货人，有权凭提单向承运人提货的人。因为提单的抬头做法不同，关系到物权和物权转移的方法问题，为了使货物安全交接，卖方安全收汇，必须了解各种不同抬头提单的做法和本身的意义，如何转让提单的所有权，并根据不同交易方式和付款方式选用不同抬头的提单。

A. Straight B/L 记名提单

It is the one that is made out to a designated consignee. Only the named consignee at the destination is entitled to take delivery of the goods under the B/L, not to any other party through endorsement. A straight B/L is non-negotiable.

Straight B/Ls avoid the probable risks in the process of transferring. The goods remain in the ownership of the consignor, yet the bills are non-negotiable and inconvenient for buying and selling goods by exchanging bills. Banks are unwilling to accept straight B/Ls as documents for negotiation. Straight B/Ls were rarely used in international trade unless they were used in transferring valuables and materials for aid. But recently, with the increasing use of EDI, straight B/L tends to become popular in the ocean shipping in order to get rid of fraud with false documents and to facilitate the importer to take delivery of the goods immediately.

记名提单指在提单的收货人栏(抬头栏)内直接打出收货人的名称，这就表明该提单项下的货物只能由该特定收货人提取，不能用背书的方式转让给第三者，因此记名提单不能流通转让。

记名提单避免了在转让过程中可能带来的风险，使货物始终掌握在货主手中，但也失去了物权凭证可以流通转让的性质及在市场买卖单据就可以达到买卖货物的便利。因此在做议付时，银行也不愿意接受记名提单作为议付的单据。记名提单过去在国际贸易中较少使用，一般只在运送贵重物品、援外物资时才用。但近年来，由于 EDI 技术在国际贸易中的发展，为了防止假单诈骗和便于进口商及时提货，记名提单在近海运输的交易中有渐渐流行的趋势。

B. Blank B/L; Bearer B/L; Open B/L 不记名提单

It refers to the bill in which the name of a definite consignee is not mentioned. The area in B/L calling for the name of the consignee is left blank, with neither the name of the consignee nor the phraseology of "to order" filled in. Any one who holds the B/L is entitled to the goods. This kind of B/L can be transferred/ negotiable without endorsement. There usually appear in the box of consignee words like "to bearer" and holder of the B/L can take delivery of the goods against the surrender of B/L, i.e., ownership of the goods passes when the bill is handed over to anyone。

不记名提单是指提单收货人栏内没有指明任何收货人，既没有收货人的名称，也没有"凭指示"，即仅填写"来人"或空着不填。这种提单的特点：提单的持有人即收货人。这种提单不经背书即可以转让，这样，谁持有提单，谁就可以提货，承运人交货也只凭单，不凭人。因此，采用这种提单风险大，一般不予使用。

C. Order B/L 指示提单

It is issued "to order" or "to the order of … (any person named)" in the box of consignee. The consignee is for the ratification of owner of B/L (consignor). Order B/Ls, widely used in international trade, are transferable and the shipper or the transferor should endorse the bill at the overleaf of the B/L to transfer the title to the goods.

Order B/L with blank endorsement is the most commonly requirement for bills of lading in terms of payment by letters of credit. Endorsement is a legal process during which the holder of the documents transfers the title to another party. In detail, the documents holder, the endorser signs or stamps the endorsee's name on the back of the B/L, and this is also called special endorsement. The blank endorsement carries only the signature of the endorser and does not specify in whose favor it is made. In practice, to facilitate the transfer of B/Ls in each stage, for instance, B/Ls are firstly transferred to the negotiation bank, the blank endorsement is usually used.

B/L made out to order and blank endorsement refers to the B/L in which the name of a definite consignee is not mentioned and only marked "to order". The seller keeps in possession of the goods before the buyer dominates a consignee, but after blank endorsement by the consignor, the bona fide holder is entitled to take delivery of the goods from the shipping company. B/Ls under collection should stick to order B/Ls endorsed by the seller.

指示提单是指提单的收货人栏内只填写"凭指定"(to order)或"凭某人指示"(to order of ××)字样。这种提单的特点：收货人尚待提单所有人(发货人)确定。发货人或转让人可以通过背书转让提单的所有权，也就是转让提单的提货权，所以这种提单又称可转让提单，在国际贸易中广泛使用。

"空白抬头，空白背书"的提单又是在信用证方式下对提单的形式要求，最普遍、使用最广泛的一种。背书是单据(或票据)的所有人转让单据所有权的一种法律手续。具体说，就是单据的所有人，在提单的背面签名或盖章。他就称为背书人，再写上受让人的名字。受让人称为被背书人，通过这种方式就把提单的所有权(具体地说是提货权)从背书人手中转移给被背书人(受让人)。这也叫作记名背书。如果只有背书人在提单背面签名，而不写受让人的名字，就称为"空白背书"。在国际贸易中为了方便提单在各个环节的转让，比如提单先转让给议付行，通常采用"空白背书"。

"空白抬头"也就是"凭指示"的指示提单，习惯上把这种提单称为"空白抬头，空白背书"的提单。凭指定提单在发货人(出口人)未指定收货人之前，卖方仍保持货物的所有权。如经发货人在提单上空白背书后，即成为凭单提货的单据，合法持有这种提单的人就有权向船公司提货。凡是以托收方式出口的提单必须坚持使用卖方背书的指示提单。

④ According to the validity, B/L can be classified as follows:

根据提单的效力可分为：

A. Original B/L 正本提单

It is legally valid and signed and dated by either the shipping company or by a duly authorized agent. Original bills of lading should be marked "original" on their face. Bills of lading are usually made out in two copies or three copies and when one of the originals is used for taking delivery of the goods, the others automatically become null and void. According to

UCP600, if letters of credit require bills of lading "in duplicate" "in two fold" or "in two copies", at least one original should be presented unless documents have other requirements. The only original or the only set of originals, as the case may be, is the whole set required by the bill of lading.

正本提单是指提单上有承运人、船长或其代理人签名盖章并注明签发日期的提单。这种提单在法律上是有效的单据。正本提单上必须标明"正本"字样。正本提单一般签发一式两份或三份，凭其中的任何一份提货后，其余的即作废。《跟单信用证统一惯例》(UCP600)规定：信用证规定的每一种单据须至少提交一份正本。如果信用证使用诸如"一式两份""两份""两套"等用语要求提交多份单据，则提交至少一份正本，其余使用副本即可满足要求，除非单据本身另有说明。唯一的正本单据，或如果以多份正本出具，为提单中表明的全套正本。

B. Copy B/L 副本提单

A copy B/L, without carrier's signature or stamps, is just the opposite of an original bill and only for reference. For easy distinction, a copy bill of lading is marked "copy" "duplicate" or "not negotiable".

副本提单是指与正本提单相对的提单，即提单上没有承运人签字盖章，只供参考使用。副本提单上一般都印有"Copy""Duplicate"或"Non-negotiable"字样，以示与正本提单相区别。

⑤ According to means of transportation, B/L can be classified as follows:

根据运输方式分为：

A. Direct B/L 直达提单

Direct B/L means the B/L in which the goods are shipped directly from the port of loading to the port of destination without involving transshipment.

轮船从装运港装货后，中途不经过换船而直接驶往目的港卸货的称为直达。签发这种运输方式的提单叫作"直达提单"。

B. Transshipment B/L 转船提单

Transshipment B/L indicates the goods need to be transshipped at an intermediate port as there is no direct service between the shipment port and the destination port. It is sometimes necessary to employ two or more carriers to get the goods to the final destination.

转船运输是指货运全程由至少两艘轮船承运。就是说，从装运港装货的轮船，不直接驶往目的港，需要在中途港换装另一只船运往目的港，有时甚至换船不止一次。在这种情况下，就要签发"转船提单"。

C. Through B/L 联运提单

Through B/L is issued by the first carrier and acted as documents of title of the goods using more than two different means of transportation from origin to destination.

联运提单是指须经两种或两种以上的运输方式联运的货物,由第一程海运人所签发的,包括运输全程并能在目的港或目的地凭以提货的提单。

⑥ According to the contents, B/L can be classified as follows:

根据提单内容繁简分为:

A. Long Form B/L 全式提单

A long form B/L refers to the B/L on the back of which all the detailed terms and conditions about the rights and obligations of the carrier and the consignor are listed as an integral part of the bill. It is more frequently used.

全式提单又称繁式提单,是指提单背面列有承运人和托运人权利、义务的详细条款的提单。

B. Short Form B/L 简式提单

A short form B/L is a document which omits the terms and conditions on the back of B/L.

简式提单又称略式提单,是指提单上略去背面条款,而只列出提单正面的必须记载事项。

⑦ Stale B/L 过期提单

B/Ls presented to the consignee or buyer after the stipulated expiry date of presentation or after the goods are at the port of destination are described as "stale B/L". In the former case, the buyer presents the B/Ls for negotiation beyond the time of presentation of documents stipulated in L/C. According to UCP600, banks would decline shipping documents presented more than 21 days after the issue date. In the latter case, the bill fails to arrive before the arrival of the goods. This case often appears in short sea voyages, so it is necessary to add a clause of "stale B/L acceptable" in short sea voyages.

过期提单是指错过规定的交单日期或者晚于货物到达目的港日期的提单。前者是指卖方超过信用证规定的交单期才交到银行议付的提单。根据《跟单信用证统一惯例》(UCP600)规定,如信用证无特殊规定,银行将拒绝接受在运输单据签发日后超过21天才提交的单据。后者是指货已到达但提单未到。这是在近洋运输时容易出现的情况,故在近洋国家间的贸易合同中,一般都订有"过期提单可以接受"的条款。

⑧ Antedated B/L 倒签提单

It refers to a bill of lading issued by the carrier prior to the actual date of shipment of the goods after the goods have been loaded.

倒签提单是指货物装船完毕后,承运人签发的以早于货物实际装船日期为签单日期的提单。

⑨ Advanced B/L 预借提单

It refers to a bill of lading borrowed by the shipper from the carrier prior to or before shipment for the purpose of settlement with bank in time.

The issuance of antedated B/L and advanced B/L is both breach of contract and illegal behavior. It is regarded as the seller and the ship's joint fraud in many countries. Once found, the carrier will have to compensate the consignee for the loss suffered.

预借提单是指货物在装船前或装船完毕前,托运人为及时跟银行结汇向承运人预先借用提单。

签发预借提单和倒签提单都是既违约又违法的行为,在许多国家都被视为卖方和船方的共同欺诈,一经发现,承运人将不得不共同赔偿收货人因此遭受的损失。

2. Road Consignment Note 铁路运单

(1) International Railway Through Transport Bill 国际铁路联运运单

It does not represent the title of the goods, and is non-transferable. International railway through transport bill and its copies are shipping contract between the railway and the consignor and are of legally binding force to the railway, the consignor and the consignee. When the consignor submits all goods to the starting station, and the starting station dates and stamps the transport bill and its copies to testify all goods are received by the shipper, that is to say, transporting contract comes into effect.

国际铁路联运运单,不是代表货物所有权的凭证,不可转让。铁路运单和运单副本是国际联运中铁路与货主之间的运输契约,对收货人、发货人和铁路都具有法律约束力。当发货人向始发站提交全部货物,始发站在运单和运单副本上加盖注明日期的印章证明货物已被接受承运,即认为运输契约已经生效。

(2) Cargo Receipt 承运货物收据

It is the shipping contract between the carrier and the consignor, which is issued by the earner and is used under special circumstances. The cargoes transported by road from inland to Hong Kong and Macao are usually entrusted to Chinese foreign trade transportation corporations. When cargoes are loaded and dispatched, Chinese foreign trade transportation corporations immediately issue a copy of cargo receipt to the consignor as evidence to deal with settlement of exchange. Cargo receipt is also a certificate for the consignee to take delivery of the cargo.

承运货物收据是在特定运输方式下所使用的一种运输单据,它是承运人出具的货物收据,也是承运人与托运人签订的运输契约。我国内地通过铁路运往港、澳地区的出口货物,一般多委托中国对外贸易运输公司承办。当出口货物装车发运后,对外贸易运输公司即签发一份承运货物收据给托运人,以作为对外办理结汇的凭证。它还是收货人凭以提货的凭证。

3. Airway Bill 空运单

It does not represent the title of the goods and is non-transferable. It is cargo receipt issued by the carrier after receiving the goods. The carrier sends out an arrival notice and the consignee takes delivery of the goods by virtue of arrival notice and identification. So, airway bill is not title of goods and shall not be transferred or financed. However, it is a formal proof evidencing the consignor has already taken delivery of the goods, with which the consignor could make a settlement with the consignee.

航空运单不是代表货物所有权的凭证,不可转让。航空货运单是承运人收取货物后签发的货物收据。货抵目的地后,承运人向收货人发出到货通知,收货人凭到货通知和身份证明提取货物。所以,航空货运单并非物权凭证,也不能转让和凭以向银行融通资金,但它是证明发货人业已交运货物的正式凭证,发货人可凭以向收货人结算货款。

4. Postal Receipt and Courier Receipt 邮政收据和快递单

Postal receipt is the main document of parcel transport, which is used for the transport of small pieces of goods. It is the certificate issued by the post office after receiving the parcel from the sender, and also the certificate of the transport contract between the post office and the shipper, but it cannot be used to pick up the goods.

Courier receipt is a receipt that the express company signs and gives to the sender after receiving the parcel, sample, document and other articles sent abroad. It is one of the simplest proof of delivery and receipt of goods by both buyer and seller.

The air express has its own unique transport documents——proof of delivery (POD). The proof of delivery is in quadruplicate. The first copy remains at the place of origin and is used for export declaration. The second copy is attached to the surface of the goods and accompanied by the goods. The recipient may sign this copy to indicate that he has received the goods (hence the name of the delivery certificate), but usually the recipient of the express mail signs on the delivery record provided by the courier company and keeps this copy. The third copy serves as the basis for internal settlement of the express company. The fourth copy shall be retained at the addressor's place as a proof of delivery, which printed the clauses on the back, and shall be used as a basis for determining the rights and interests of the parties and resolving the dispute in the event of a dispute. POD is equivalent to the waybill used in air transport of general cargo, but is more versatile than airline waybills.

邮政收据(Postal Receipt)是邮包运输的主要单据,用于小件货物的运输,它既是邮局收到寄件人的邮包后所签发的凭证,也是邮局方和发货方之间运输契约的凭证,但不能据以提货。

快递收据(Courier Receipt)是快递公司在收受对外寄发的包裹、样品、单据等物品后签章交给邮寄人的收据凭证。它是一种最简单的买卖双方对物品的交货和收货凭据。

航空货运使用的是航空运单,邮政使用的是包裹单,航空快递业也有自己的独特的运输单据——交付凭证(proof of delivery, pod)。交付凭证一式四份。第一联留在始发地并用于出口报关；第二联贴附在货物表面，随货同行，收件人可以在此联签字表示收到货物(交付凭证由此得名)，但通常快件的收件人在快递公司提供的送货纪录上签字，而将此联保留；第三联作为快递公司内部结算的依据；第四联作为发件凭证留存发件人处，同时该联印有背面条款，一旦产生争议时可作为判定当事各方权益，解决争议的依据。POD 相当于普货空运中的分运单，但比航空公司分运单的用途更广泛。

5. Combined Transport Document/Multimodal Transport Document 多式联运单据

An international multimodal transport operator shall issue a multimodal transport document (MTD) by himself or a person authorized by him when receiving container cargo. A multimodal transport document is not a contract of international multimodal transport, but a proof of the contract of international multimodal transport. This document shall be a negotiable document (Negotiable MTD) or a non-negotiable document (Non-Negotiable MTD) of the shipper's option. Non-negotiable MTD are cannot be transferred. Negotiable MTD are as negotiable as bills of lading, which is one of the main marks that distinguish such documents from other transport documents.

According to the Convention on Multimodal Transport, if the shipper requests the multimodal transport operator to issue transferable multimodal transport documents, the method of transfer shall be specified on such documents. If the delivery is specified to order, the transfer should be made after endorsement. If the delivery is specified to the holder, the transfer may be made without endorsement. In addition, if more than one set of originals is issued, the number of originals should be indicated. If multiple copies are issued, each copy should be marked "non-transferable copy". For the issuance of more than one set of negotiable multimodal transport documents, the words "non-negotiable copies" shall be indicated. In the case of the issuance of more than one original set of negotiable multimodal transport documents, the multimodal transport operator has fulfilled its obligation to deliver if he or his representative has delivered in accordance with one of the original sets.

Currently in the field of ocean shipping, some companies like China Ocean Shipping Company established "combined transport bill of lading (CTB/L)", which can be used both in port-to-port transportation and inter-modal transportation between ocean transportation and other kinds of transportation.

国际多式联运经营人在接收集装箱货物时，应由本人或其授权的人签发国际多式联运单据(MTD)。国际多式联运单据并不是国际多式联运合同，而是国际多式联运合同的证明，同时也是国际多式联运经营人收到货物的收据和凭其交货的凭证。这种单证应发货人的选择可以是可转让单证(Negotiable MTD)，也可以是不可转让的单证(Non-Negotiable MTD)。

不可转让的国际多式联运单证没有流通性。可转让的国际多式联运单证和提单一样具有流通性，这是此类单证区别于其他运输单证的主要标志之一。

《多式联运公约》规定，如果发货人要求国际多式联运经营人签发可以转让的国际多式联运单证，则应在此类单证上列明转让方法。如列明按指示交付，需经背书后转让；如列明向持票人交付，无须背书即可转让。此外，如签发一套一份以上的正本，应注明正本份数；如签发多份副本，每份副本均应注明"不可转让副本"字样。对于签发一套一份以上的可转让国际多式联运单证正本的请注明"不可转让副本"字样。对于签发一套一份以上的可转让国际多式联运单证正本的情况，如国际多式联运经营人或其代表已按照其中一份正本交货，该国际多式联运经营人便已履行其交货责任。

目前在航运界，一些船公司如中国远洋运输公司制定了一种"联合运输提单(CTB/L)"，既可以用于一般港到港的运输，也可用于海运与其他运输方式的联运。

Section 3　Clauses of Shipment

第3节　装运条款

Shipment clauses include time of shipment, port of shipment and port of destination, partial shipment and transshipment, demurrage, dispatch and so on.

装运条款包括装运时间、装运港和目的港、分批装运、转运、滞期、速遣条款等内容。

1. Time of Shipment　装运时间

Time of shipment is the deadline by which the seller makes shipment of the contracted goods or delivers them to the carrier.

装运时间也称装运期，指卖方按合同规定的时间，将货物装上运输工具或交给承运人。

(1) Shipment and Delivery　装运期与交货期

Shipment and delivery are two totally different concepts, but under CIF, CFR, CIP, CPT, FCA and FOB trade terms, they have the same meaning. As we often refer shipment to delivering and most contracts are under the above six terms, it tends to regard these two concepts as one.

Quality clauses, quantity clauses and time of shipment are fundamentals of the sales contract in Common Law. The consequences could be so serious that the buyer has the right to reject the goods, terminate the contract and claim for compensation if the seller breaks any one of the three clauses. As a result, the seller should deliver the goods strictly according to the contract.

装运与交货是两个不同的概念，但在CIF、CFR、FOB象征性交货的贸易术语(也包括CIP、CPT、FCA)中，二者是一致的，平常所说的装运期也就是交货期，又由于买卖合同大部分是用上述六个贸易术语，人们习惯上已经把二者视为一体。

英美法把品质条款、数量条款和交货期作为合同的要件，如违反这三个要件之一，买方有权拒收货物、解除合同，同时要求损害赔偿，后果是十分严重的。因此，卖方一定要严格按照合同规定的时间交货，也就是装运。

(2) Stipulating "Time of Shipment" 装运时间的规定方法

① Ways of Stipulating 规定方法

A. Specifying a fixed period of time or a deadline, e.g. Shipment during June, 2019.

规定某年、某月份装运。例如：2019 年 6 月份装运。

B. Specifying the end of one month, e.g. Shipment before the end of June, 2019.

规定某年某月底前装运。例如：2019 年 6 月底前装运。

C. Specifying the date, e.g. Shipment before 30th June, 2019.

规定某年某月某日前装运。例如：2019 年 6 月 30 日前装运。

D. Specifying two or more than two months, e.g. Shipment during May/June, 2019.

规定跨月装运，规定某两个月或某几个月内装运。例如：2019 年 5/6 月份装运。

E. Specifying a period upon receipt of payment, e.g. Shipment within 30 days after receipt of L/C.

规定在收到信用证后若干天(若干月)内装运，例如：收到信用证后 30 日内装运。

② Some Wrong Stipulations 装运时间的错误规定方法

A. Specifying one fixed date for shipment, which is unattainable for the seller.

规定具体某日装运。这是卖方自缚手脚，无法做到的。

B. Ambiguous stipulations like immediate shipment, prompt shipment, and shipment as soon as possible, which could cause misunderstanding and arguments so as to delay shipment.

笼统规定。例如：立刻装运、迅速装运、尽快装运。对这些表述，各国理解、解释不同，容易发生纠纷，耽误装运。

2. Port (Place) of Shipment and Port (Place) of Destination 装运港(地)和目的港(地)

Port of shipment and port of destination should be clearly specified in the contract when both parties come into agreement. Generally, port of shipment is put forward by the seller for the buyer's confirmation while port of destination is put forward by the buyer for the seller's confirmation.

凡涉及运输的合同均需规定装运港和目的港，必须在磋商交易时就达成一致。一般来说，装运港由卖方提出，经买方同意后确认。目的港由买方提出，卖方确认。

(1) Port (Place) of Shipment 装运港(地)

It is the port where the goods are shipped and depart from. In the case of FOB, CIF and CFR, the delivery of the goods is fulfilled when the goods are loaded on board the vessel or to the carrier nominated by the buyer and at the same time the seller submits the shipping documents.

Hence, port of shipment should be clearly stated in the contract so that the seller could deliver the goods to the carrier.

In export trade, it is the usual practice to designate only one port of shipment in. one transaction, but exceptionally, when large amounts of goods are involved and, in particular, the goods are stored at different places, two or more ports of shipments are also specified, such as "Shanghai and Guangzhou" "Dalian/ Qingdao/ Shanghai". Sometimes, as the port of shipment is not yet determined at the time the transaction is being concluded, a general clause like "China ports" may be used.

装运港是货物起始装运的港口。以 FOB、CIF、CFR 为例,卖方按合同规定在装运港将货物装上船或买方指定船只并提交运输单据,就算完成了交货义务,因此,在买卖合同中必须明确规定装运港。

在出口贸易中,习惯做法是只规定一个港口为装运港,并列明具体港口名称。但如果该批货物太多,特别是分放在几个地方,这时候可以破例规定两个或三个装运港,如"装运港上海和广州""装运港大连、青岛和上海"。有时在签订合同时装运港口还没有定下来,也可以规定为"在中国港口装运"。

(2) Port (Place) of Destination 目的港(地)

It is the port at which goods are ultimately discharged. Port of destination should closely follow CIF and CFR terms and CIP and CPT should indicate the final destination after delivery.

The stipulation on the port of destination shall be definite and specific. We should not use ambiguous terms, such as "main ports in Europe" or "main ports in Africa". In case the middleman abroad has not found a proper buyer when the contract is concluded, in order to make it convenient for him to sell the cargo afloat, the "optional port" may be accepted upon request of the foreign party, the buyer is allowed to choose one from the several ports of destination provided.

目的港是最终卸货的港口。CIF、CFR 都必须在贸易术语后规定目的港,CIP、CPT 需规定发货后最终运达的目的地。

对于目的港的规定必须明确具体,最好不用模棱两可的措辞,如"欧洲主要港口""非洲主要港口"等。如果在签订合同时,国外的中间商未能找到合适的买家,为了便于该中间商销售货售货物,可以根据外国客户的要求,接受买方的"选择港口"条件,但必须是合同中规定的那几个港口。

3. Partial Shipment and Transshipment 分批装运和转运

One of the most important issues in the contract is whether partial shipment and transshipment are allowed as it directly affects the benefits of both parties. The buyer hopes to receive the goods at one time to decrease the cost and keep safety while the seller hopes that partial shipment and transshipment are allowed in consideration of production cycle and convenient conveyance.

能否分批装运和转运直接关系到买卖双方的切身利益，是买卖合同中的重要内容。买方希望直运，希望一次交货，降低成本，保护货物安全。卖方考虑生产周期、运输方便，最好是"允许分批，允许转船"。

(1) Partial Shipment 分批装运

It means the commodities are to be shipped in more than one lot. The reason for allowing partial shipment may be: The lack of means of conveyance or shipping space; the limitations of loading and unloading facilities; the restriction of market capacity and production ability. However, the buyer may require shipment in one lot in consideration of decreasing costs and expenses. Generally, "Partial Shipment Allowed" is beneficial to the seller.

According to the contract law of some countries, if there is no stipulations about partial shipment and both parties have no conventions or customs, partial shipment shall not be deemed allowed.

分批装运又称分期装运，是指一个合同项下的货物分若干批或若干期装运。凡成交数量较大，受货源、运输、销售、资金等条件限制，有必要分期分批发货的，通常在买卖合同中规定"允许分批"。买方为了减少提货手续，节省费用开支，在进出口业务中往往要求出口商一次装运货物，则在合同中规定"不准分批装运"。一般来说，规定"允许分批装运"对卖方比较有利。

按某些国家的合同法规定，如合同中未对分批装运做出规定，买卖双方事先也没有特别约定或习惯做法，则卖方不得分批装运。

UCP600 states:

A. Unless otherwise stipulated, partial shipment is allowed.

B. Paragraph B, Article 31 in UCP600 states, "...Transportation documents, which appear on their face to indicate that shipment commencing on the same means of conveyance and for the same journey, provided they indicate the same destination, will not be regarded as covering a partial shipment, even if they indicate different dates of shipment, different ports of loading, or places of dispatch." That is to say, the goods under the same one contract and loaded on the same vessel will not be regarded as covering a partial shipment.

C. Article 32 in UCP600 states, "If a drawing or shipment by installments within given periods is stipulated in the credit and any installment is not drawn or shipped within the period allowed for that installment, the credit ceases to be available for that and any subsequent installment."

For instance，the L/C stipulated "shipment during May/June/July, with first shipment 100M/T during May, second shipment 200M/T during June, and third shipment 300M/T during

July." the beneficiary should strictly deliver 100 M/T in May, 200 M/T in June and 300 M/T in July. Once one lot failed to be shipped punctually, the credit ceases to be available for this lot and the rest lots and the bank is entitled to dishonor.

《跟单信用证统一惯例》(UCP600)规定：

A. 除非信用证另有规定，允许分批装运。

B. UCP600 第 31 条(b)款规定："如果运输单据表明使用同一运输工具并经由同一路线运输的，而且运输单据注明的目的地相同，那么即使运输单据上表明的装运日期不同和/或装运港、接管地、发运地不同，也不视为分批装运。"也就是说，装于同一航次同一条船上的同一合同项下的货物，即使装运的地点、时间不同，只要运往同一目的地，也不视为分批装运。

C. UCP600 第 32 条规定："信用证规定在指定的时间段内分期付款或分期发运，任何一期未按信用证规定期限支取或发运时，信用证对该期及以后各期均告失效。"也就是说，限期限量分批装运的货物只要其中有一批未按时装运，信用证对该批和以后各批均告无效。

例如，信用证规定："在 5 月/6 月/7 月间装运，第一批在 5 月间装运 100 公吨，第二批在 6 月间装运 200 公吨，第三批在 7 月间装运 300 公吨。"受益人交货必须严格按照 5 月 100 公吨，6 月 200 公吨，7 月 300 公吨装运，只要其中有一批未按时装运，则信用证对该批及以后各批均告无效，银行有权拒付货款。

(2) Transshipment 转运、转船

Transshipment is adopted when ships sailing directly to the port of destination are not available or direct sailings to the destinations are few and far between. Transshipment is allowed in UCP600 unless otherwise stipulated in the credit.

Goods are subject to loss or damage during the journey in case of transshipment, which would increase costs and expenses and extend the time of arrival. But transshipment is inevitable when there is no direct sailing to the destination. Therefore, it is essential for both parties to make it clear in the contract.

With the development of means of transportation such as super vessels, container vessels, ro-ro ship and barge carrier, and especially the increasing use of multi-modal transportation, transshipment is widely used in international trade practice. UCP600 states, "Transshipment means a transfer and reloading during the course of carriage from one conveyance or vessel to another conveyance or vessel, with the same mode of transport or from one mode of transport to another." "A bill of lading may indicate that goods will or may be transshipped provided that the entire carriage is covered by one and the same bill of lading." "A transport document indicating that transshipment will or may take place is acceptable provided that the goods are transported by container, trailer or barge earner, even if the credit prohibits transshipment."

In brief, transshipment is prohibited in case of port-to-port ocean transportation and the non-container transportation.

驶往目的港没有直达船或航班间隔太长,则在合同中应订明"允许转船"。《跟单信用证统一惯例》(UCP600)准许转运,除非信用证另有规定。

货物在运输途中转运,容易受损或散失,而且会增加费用和支出,延迟到达目的地的时间。但在无直达运输工具的情况下,转运就不可避免。是否允许转运关系到买卖双方切身利益,有必要在买卖合同中明确规定。

但是随着运输工具的不断改进和大型船、集装箱船、滚装船、母子船的涌现和推广使用,以及各种新的运输方式尤其是多式联运方式日益广泛运用,转运在实际业务中几乎已成为经常发生,甚至不可避免的事。《跟单信用证统一惯例》(UCP600)对转运做出新的规定:"转运是指在信用证规定的装货港到卸货港之间的运输过程中,将货物从一船卸下并再装上另一船的行为。""提单可以表明货物将要或可能被转运,只要全程运输由同一提单涵盖。""即使信用证禁止转运,注明将要或可能发生转运的提单仍可接受,只要其表明货物由集装箱、拖车或母子船运输。"

简言之,真正被禁止的转运,仅指海运中港至港和非集装箱货物运输的转运。

Terminology 本章术语

1. ocean marine transport 海上运输
2. rail transport 铁路运输
3. air transport 航空运输
4. postal transport 邮政运输
5. express transport 快递运输
6. pipeline transport 管道运输
7. container transport 集装箱运输
8. international multimodal transport 国际多式联运
9. liner transport 班轮运输
10. charter shipping 租船运输
11. bill of lading (B/L) 海运提单
12. on board B/L 已装船提单
13. clean B/L 清洁提单
14. order B/L 指示提单
15. original B/L 正本提单
16. stale B/L 过期提单
17. antedated B/L 倒签提单

18. advanced B/L 预借提单
19. cargo receipt 承运货物收据
20. airway bill 航空运单
21. multimodal transport documents (MTD) 多式联运单据
22. partial shipment 分批装运
23. transshipment 转运

Exercises 本章练习

1. A Chinese foreign trade exporter exported 30,000 boxes of goods to America, contracting to ship the goods in each lot during March to August, 5,000 boxes each month, payment by confirmed irrevocable letter of credit. The customer duly sent letter of credit on which the total amount are in conformity with the contract, but the shipping clauses indicated "the latest date of shipment is 31st, August, by partial shipment". Our exporter dispatched 5,000 boxes in March, 6,000 boxes in April, 10,000 boxes in May and 9,000 boxes in June. The customer raised an objection to this. Are we right to do this? Why?

我国某外贸公司向美国出口商品30 000箱，合同规定3月至8月按月等量装运，每月装运5 000箱，凭保兑不可撤销信用证付款，客户按时开来信用证，证上总金额与总数量均与合同相符，但装运条款规定"最迟装运期8月31日，分数批装运"。我方3月装出5 000箱，4月装出6 000箱，5月装出10 000箱，6月装出9 000箱。客户发现后向我方提出异议。我们这样做是否可以？为什么？

2. A Chinese exporter exported 1,000 tons of tungsten ore to Canada. The letter of credit stipulated "partial shipment is not allowed". Later, the exporter loaded 500 tons each on the same ship on the same voyage number in Fuzhou and Xiamen. And the bill of lading also indicated different ports of loading and dates of shipment. Does this act beak the rule?

我国某外贸公司对加拿大出口1 000公吨乌沙，国外来证规定"不允许分批装运"，结果出口方在规定的期限内分别在福州、厦门各装500公吨于同一航次的同一船上，提单上也注明了不同的装货港和不同的装货日期，问这是否违约？

3. Our exporter exported a batch of timber handicraft to Spain in CIF prices. The contract and letter of credit stipulated shipment during May/June, 2016. However, we had difficulty chartering a vessel, and adopted partial shipment in two to three lots. In this case, did we break the stipulations of letter of credit?

我国某外贸公司对西班牙按CIF价格出口树脂工艺品一批。合同规定装运期为5月/6月，国外开来的信用证规定2016年5月/6月装船。当我方在租船订舱时发生困难，一时租不到足够的仓位，要分两到三次装运，这种情况是否构成违反信用证的条款？

Answers for Reference 参考答案

1. Analysis: Only in order to get payment in due time, we were supposed to do this. As credit is independent of the contract and once the credit and the relating documents are in conformity, the exporter can get payment. The letter of credit generally indicates that "the latest date of shipment is 31st, August, in partial shipments". So our exporter was right. But the buyer can lodge claim to the seller acceding to the delivery inconformity with the contract. So our exporter was not right. In case of trouble in the following days, the exporter shall adopt partial shipment in equal lots, which is corresponding to the contact and letter of credit.

分析：仅从信用证项下我方能否如期收回货款考虑，卖方这样做可以。因为信用证一经开立就成为独立于合同之外的法律文件，只要单证一致，即可收取货款。信用证中笼统规定"最迟装运日期8月31日，分数批装运"，所以我方的做法是可以的。但买方可依据交货不符合同向卖方提出索赔，所以出口商的做法不可以。为防日后麻烦，出口商应该等量分批装运，这既符合了合同规定，又满足了信用证的要求。

2. Analysis: According to UCP600, "Transportation documents, which appear on their face to indicate that shipment commencing on the same means of conveyance and for the same journey, provided they indicate the same destination, will not be regarded as covering a partial shipment, even if they indicate different dates of shipment, different ports of loading, or places of dispatch." Thus, it was not partial shipment and didn't break the clauses in the L/C and the bank shall not refuse to pay.

分析：根据《跟单信用证统一惯例》(UCP600)规定："如果运输单据表明使用同一运输工具并经由同一路线运输的，而且运输单据注明的目的地相同，那么即使运输单据上表明的装运日期不同和/或装运港、接管地、发运地不同，也不视为分批装运。"因此，上述做法不被视为分批装运，没有违反信用证条款，银行不得拒绝议付。

3. Analysis: So long as we ship all the goods during May to June, the letter of credit has not to be amended. According to UCP600 Section 31(a), "Unless there are other stipulations, transshipment and partial shipment is allowed."

分析：只要5月/6月将货装运完毕，可以不要求修改信用证。UCP600第31条(a)款规定："除非信用证另有规定，否则允许分批支款及/或分批装运。"

Chapter 6 Cargo Transport Insurance
第 6 章 国际货物贸易运输保险

  Insurance is a kind of economic compensation system, which collects insurance premium from most units and individuals. It is the practice of sharing among many persons, risks of life or property that would otherwise be suffered by only a few. This is effected by each person paying a sum of money called a premium, which is put into a "pool" or insurance fund, out of which money is paid to those who suffer loss. Legally speaking, it is a compensational contract, that is, the insured pays a sum of consideration (premium) to the insurance company and the insurance company will, according to the terms indicated in the insurance contract, indemnify the insured of any loss that occurs within the scope of the coverage.

  In international buying and selling of goods, there are a number of risks, which, if they occur, will involve traders in financial losses. For instance cargoes in transit may be damaged due to breakage of packing, clash or fire, etc. These hazards, and many others, may be insured against. Every year, a certain amount of cargo was destroyed or damaged by perils of the sea in transit, but whichever particular cargo it would be it cannot be anticipated. All cargo owners take the risk of loss through the perils. However, foreign traders can insure themselves against many of these risks. Insurance is a process for spreading risk, so that the burden of any loss is borne not by the unfortunate individual directly affected but by the total body of person under consideration. In return for a payment known as a premium paid by the insured, an insurance company will agree to compensate the insured in the event of losses arising from the risks covered during the period of insurance.

  保险是一种经济补偿制度，它按科学的方法计收保险费，集中多数单位和个人的保险金建立保险基金，"利用分散危险分摊损失"的办法，对参加保险的少数被保险人由于特定灾害事故所遭受的损害或责任给予经济补偿或对人身伤亡给付保险金。从法律角度看，它是一种补偿性契约行为，即被保险人向保险人提供一定的对价(保险费)，保险人则对被保险人将来可能遭受的承保责任范围的损失负赔偿责任。

  国际贸易货物的买卖存在着各种各样的风险，这些风险的发生将会给有关的商人们带来经济损失。例如，货物在运输途中由于包装破损、碰损或火灾等原因而损坏等。这些风险以及其他一些风险都可以通过保险来加以防范。虽然，每一年都有一定数目的货物在运输途中不可避免地要遭受到海上风险而被摧毁或受损，但是灾难会降临到哪一批货上事先是无法预知的。所有的货主都要冒货物灭失的危险。然而，从事国际贸易的商人可以通过保险来防止很多风险。保险的目的是将风险分摊，这样风险发生时，就可以由所有的相关人员分摊而不是由直接遭遇方单独承担。当投保人交付保险费后，如在保险期内发生承保范围内的风险所致的损失，保险公司将同意向被保险人赔付该损失。

Section 1　Ocean Marine Cargo Transport Insurance

第1节　海运货物保险

1. Things Covered by Marine Insurance 海运货物保险的保障范围

The insurance company covers three aspects, i.e. risks, losses and expenses, and compensates for the losses according to different risks. Risks, losses and coverage are closely related to one another. Risks lead to losses and the insurance company makes indemnity on the basis of different coverage, that is, the insurance company does not hold responsibility for all risks and all losses.

保险公司保障的范围包括三个方面：风险、损失及发生的费用。保险公司按照不同险别所包含的风险所造成的损失承担赔偿责任。风险、损失和险别三者有着紧密的联系。风险引起损失，险别则是保险公司对风险和损失的承保责任范围，也就是说，保险公司并不是对所有的风险、所有的损失都承担赔偿责任，而是根据险别不同，决定保险公司责任的大小。

(1) Risks 保障的风险

Risks include two kinds: Perils of the Sea and Extraneous Risks. (See Table 6-1)

Table 6-1　Risks

Risks	Perils of the Sea	1. Natural Calamities: heavy weather, thunder and lightening, flood, earthquake, tsunami, etc.
		2. Fortuitous Accidents: grounding, stranding, sunk, collision, fire, explosion, missing, etc.
	Extraneous Risks	1. General Extraneous Risks: theft, breakage, clashing, leakage, fresh and/or rain water damage, contamination, sweating and/or heating, taint of odor, rusting, hook damage, shortage in weight, etc.
		2. Special Extraneous Risks: war, strike, non-delivery of cargo, refusal to receive cargo, etc.

风险包括两大类：海上风险和外来风险(见表 6-1)。

表 6-1　风险

风险	海上风险	1. 自然灾害：恶劣气候、雷电、洪水、地震、海啸等
		2. 意外事故：搁浅、触礁、沉没、互撞、失火、爆炸、失踪等
	外来风险	1. 一般外来风险：偷窃、破碎、碰损、渗漏、淡水雨淋、玷污、受潮受热、串味、生锈、钩损、短量等
		2. 特殊外来风险：战争、罢工、交货不到、拒收等

① Perils of the Sea 海上风险

Perils of the sea are those caused by natural calamities and fortuitous.

Natural calamities: Disasters such as heavy weather, thunder and lighting, tsunami, earthquake, floods, etc.

Fortuitous accidents refer to the accidents caused by unexpected haphazard, such as ship stranded, striking upon the rocks, ship sinking, ship collision, colliding with icebergs or other objects, fire, explosion, ship missing, etc. Marine insurance business covers not only marine accidents, but also road accidents as well.

海上风险是由自然灾害和意外事故引起的风险。

自然灾害：是指恶劣气候、雷电、海啸、地震、洪水等灾难。

意外事故是指由于偶然的非意料之中的原因造成的事故，如船舶搁浅、触礁、沉没、船舶互撞、与流冰或其他物体相撞、起火、爆炸以及船舶失踪等事故。海上保险业务中的意外事故，并不局限于发生在海上，也包括发生在陆地上的意外事故。

② Extraneous Risks 外来风险

Extraneous Risks are the unexpected risks resulting in losses other than Perils of the Sea, including general extraneous risks and special extraneous risks.

General Extraneous Risks include: theft or pilferage, breakage, clashing, leakage, fresh and/or rain water damage, contamination, sweating and/or heating, taint of odor, rusting, hook Damage, shortage in weight, etc.

Special Extraneous Risks include: war, strike, non-delivery of cargo, refusal to receive cargo, Emergence of aflatoxin, etc.

外来风险是指海上风险以外的其他外来原因所造成的风险。外来原因是指事先难以预料的、致使货物受损的某些外部因素。外来风险分为一般外来风险和特殊外来风险。

一般外来风险包括：偷窃、破碎、碰损、渗漏、淡水雨淋、玷污、受热受潮、串味、生锈、钩损、短量等。

特殊外来风险包括：战争、罢工、交货不到、拒收、产生黄曲霉素等。

(2) Losses 保障的损失

Marine Losses refer to any loss or damage due to natural calamities and fortuitous accidents and the related cost incurred in the process of transit, both on ocean-connected inland and in the river. According to the extent of damage, losses in marine insurance fall into two types: total loss and partial loss. The former may be subdivided into actual total loss and constructive total loss; the latter may be subdivided into general average and particular average. (See Table 6-2)

Table 6-2　Losses

Losses	Total Loss	1. Actual Total Loss 2. Constructive Total Loss
	Partial Loss	1. General Average 2. Particular Average

海上损失指被保险货物在海洋运输途中，因遭遇海上风险所引起的损坏或灭失，还包括与海运连接的陆上运输和内河运输过程中遭受的损坏或灭失。根据损失的不同程度可分为全部损失和部分损失。前者可再分为实际全损和推定全损。后者可分为共同海损和单独海损(见表 6-2)。

表 6-2　损失

损失	全部损失	1. 实际全损 2. 推定全损
	部分损失	1. 共同海损 2. 单独海损

① Total Loss 全部损失

It refers to the loss of the entire value of the subject matter to the insured, normally involving the maximum amount for which a policy is liable. Total Loss can be subdivided into actual total loss and constructive total loss.

全部损失简称全损，是指被保险货物由于承保风险造成的全部灭失或完全变质或不可能归还被保险人的损害。全损分为实际全损和推定全损两种。

A. Actual Total Loss 实际全损

It means that the cargo has been totally lost or has been damaged to the extent that it has lost its original usage. It includes:

a. The subject matter of insurance has been completely lost.

b. The subject matter of insurance completely loses its original form and utility.

c. The ownership of insured to the subject matter of insurance has been irreparably and completely derived.

d. The carrying ship has missed to a certain period and there is still no message.

实际全损是指货物完全灭失或变质而失去原有用途，即货物的全部损失已经发生或不可避免。具体包括：

a. 保险标的已经完全灭失。

b. 保险标的完全失去原有的形状、效用。

c. 被保险人对保险标的的所有权已无可挽回地被完全剥夺。

d. 载货船舶失踪达到一定时期仍无音讯。

B. Constructive Total Loss 推定全损

It means the subject matter of insurance is not totally lost, but the actual total loss shall be unavoidable or the costs to be incurred in salvaging, recovering and reconditioning the goods together with the forwarding charges to the destination named in the policy would be exceed the insured value or the value of the goods on arrival.

In the case of constructive total loss, the insured may obtain partial compensation for the loss or full compensation for the loss. If the insured wishes to obtain full compensation for the loss, the insured must unconditionally surrender the subject matter insured to the insurer. Abandonment refers to behavior that the insured transfers all the rights of subject matter insured to the insurer and ask him to compensate for total loss. If the insured does not dispatch notice of abandonment, the insurer makes for partial indemnity and the insured is entitled to take over the cargo residue.

推定全损是指保险标的遭遇风险受损后，并未完全灭失，但实际全损不可避免，或进行抢救、修理和恢复原状所需要的费用再加上续运货物至目的地的费用总和超过保险价值或货物到达目的地后的价值。

在推定全损的情况下，被保险人可以获得部分损失的赔偿，也可获得全部损失的赔偿。如果被保险人想获得全部损失的赔偿，被保险人必须无条件地把保险标的委付给保险人。委付是指被保险人将保险标的的一切权利转让给保险人，并要求保险人按全损给予赔偿的行为。如被保险人不提出委付通知，保险人只能按部分损失给予赔偿，被保险人拥有残余物所有权。

② Partial Loss 部分损失

It means a partial damage to or the total loss of part of the insured goods. According to different causes, partial loss can be either general average or particular average.

部分损失是指被保险货物的损失没有达到全部损失的程度。根据损失产生的原因不同，部分损失可分为共同海损和单独海损。

A. General Average (G.A.) 共同海损

It is defined as a deliberate and reasonable sacrifice of the ship, freight, cargo, or the additional expenses incurred to rescue a ship and its cargo from impending danger or for the common safety of the adventure under a peril of the sea or some other hazards.

There are four conditions constituting G.A.:

a. The danger that threats the common safety of cargo and/or vessel shall be materially existent and is not foreseen.

b. The measures taken by the master shall be conscious and reasonable, which means, G.A. is man-made but not an accidental loss.

c. The sacrifice shall be specialized and not caused by perils directly and the expense incurred shall be additional expense which is not within the operation budget.

d. The actions of the ship's master shall be successful in saving the voyage.

The loss of sacrifice as well as the expenses incurred in a general average shall be shared among all parties, including the ship owner, all cargo owners and carrier, in proportion to their respective interested value benefited from the general average, and such proportion is called a general average contribution. As to each party involved, the amount benefited from G.A. may be less than the intrinsic value of the vessel, cargo and transportation costs. So G.A. belongs to partial loss.

载货船舶在海运途中遇到海上风险或其他灾难时,船长为了维护船舶和所有货物的共同安全或使航程得以继续完成,有意并且合理做出的某些牺牲或支出的特殊费用。

构成共同海损的条件包括：

a. 船方在采取紧急措施时,必须确有危及船、货共同安全的事先未预见到的危险存在。

b. 船方所采取的措施必须是有意识的、合理的。所谓有意识的,是指共同海损的发生必须是人为的,有意识行为的结果,而不是一种意外的损失。

c. 所做出的牺牲或支出的费用必须是非常性质的。所谓非常性质,是指这种牺牲或费用不是通常业务中所必然会遇到或支出的。

d. 构成共同海损的牺牲和费用支出,最终还必须是有效的。

共同海损的牺牲和费用应由船、货或运费三方按最后获救的价值共同按比例分摊,称为共同海损的分摊。对个别有关当事人而言,分摊到的金额均小于船、货、运费的本身价值,因此从这个意义上说,共同海损属于部分损失。

B. Particular Average (P.A.) 单独海损

It is a partial loss of the subject matter insured, caused directly by an event that has been insured against. It falls entirely upon the particular owner of the property which has suffered the damage. For instance, collision or breakage is irrelevant to cargo owners and ship owners and it caused only partial loss, which is called particular average.

单独海损是指货物由承保风险直接导致损失,未达到全损程度,而是单独一方的利益受损并只能由该利益所有者单独负担的一种部分损失。如碰撞、破碎,与其他货主、船主无关,而损失又未达到全损程度,称为单独海损。

The differences between P.A. and G.A. are as follows:

a. P.A. is caused directly by risks; G.A. is man-made loss in order to remove or alleviate risks.

b. The damaged party is responsible for losses incurred in a P.A.; the loss of sacrifice as well as the expenses incurred in a G.A. shall be shared among all parties.

单独海损与共同海损的区别如下:

a. 单独海损是风险直接导致的损失;共同海损是为了解除或减轻这些风险而人为造成的损失。

b. 单独海损的损失由受损方自己承担;共同海损由受益各方按受益大小的比例分摊。

(3) Expenses 保障的费用

Marine Cargo Insurance covers the expenses incurred to avoid or reduce the damage to or loss of the subject matter insured. There are mainly four types.

保障的费用指保险标的发生保险事故后,为减少货物的实际损失而支出的费用,可由保险公司赔付。保障的费用有四种。

① Sue and Labor Charges 施救费用

They are extraordinary expenses made in a time of peril by the insured to act to avert or minimize any loss of or damage to the subject matter insured.

在遭遇保险责任范围内的灾害事故时,被保险人或其代理人、雇佣人员和保险单证的受让人等为抢救保险标的物以防止其损失扩大所采取的措施而支出的费用。

② Salvage Charges 救助费用

They are expenses resulting from measures properly taken by a third party other than the insured and insurer to preserve maritime property from perils at sea.

保险标的物遇到上述灾害事故时,由保险人和被保险人以外的第三方采取救助行为后向其支付的报酬。

③ Forwarding Charges 续运费用

They refer to the additional charges such as discharge expenses and storage expenses of the insured goods and forwarding charges to the destination in the insurance policy when the transportation of the insured goods terminates at the port or place not specified in the policy caused by the risks insured.

续运费用是指因保险单承保风险引起的被保险货物的运输在非保险单载明的目的地港口或地方终止时,被保险货物的卸货费用、仓储费用,以及继续运往保险单载明的目的地港口的费用等额外费用。

④ Extra Charges 额外费用

They refer to the charges paid to prove the establishment of the claim for loss, including the expenses paid to inspect, survey, notarize, adjust or auction the damaged goods after the subject matter of the insurance is damaged. Only when claim is tenable, the insurer will compensate for extra charges. But if notarization and/or survey are carried out by the authorization of insurer, no matter claim is tenable, the insurer still needs to assume the extra charge(s).

额外费用是指为了证明损失索赔的成立而支付的费用，包括保险标的受损后，对其进行检验、查勘、公证、理算或拍卖受损货物等支付的费用。一般只有在索赔成立时，保险人才对额外费用负赔偿责任，但如果公证、查勘等是由保险人授权进行的，不论索赔是否成立，保险人仍须承担该项额外费用。

2. Coverages of Marine Insurance Clauses 海运货物保险的险别

(1) Ocean Marine Cargo Insurance Clauses of China Insurance Company 中国海运货物保险险别

China Insurance Clauses (CIC) are constituted according to both practices and conventions in the international insurance market and China's real needs for insurance. Insurance coverage refers to the scope of responsibility the insurer takes and it is the basis of not only performing rights and obligations, but also the basis of collecting insurance premium.

According to Insurance Company of China Ocean Marine Cargo Clauses of PICC, the insurance coverage is mainly classified into two groups: Basic Insurance Coverage and Additional Insurance Coverage.

中国人民保险公司根据我国保险业务的实际需要并参照国际保险市场的习惯做法制定了各种不同运输方式的货物运输保险条款以及附加险条款，总称"中国保险条款"。保险险别是保险人对风险和损失的承保责任范围，它是保险人与被保险人履行权利与义务的基础，也是保险人承保责任的大小和被保险人缴付保险费多少的依据。

根据中国人民保险公司《海洋运输货物保险条款》，保险险别分为两大类：基本险和附加险。

① Basic Insurance Coverage 基本险

A. Free from Particular Average (F.P.A.) 平安险

Free from particular average originally means the compensation does not cover Particular Average. It mainly covers total loss due to natural disasters and total or partial loss caused by fortuitous accidents. F.P.A. is not free of all the partial loss due to natural disasters. In fact, F.P.A. covers sacrifice in and contribution to General Average and salvage charges, that is, F.P.A is not responsible for Particular Average due to natural disasters.

F.P.A. insurance covers:

a. Actual total loss or constructive total loss of the consignment caused by natural calamities such as heavy weather, thunder and lightening, tsunami, earthquake, flood, etc.;

b. Total loss or partial loss caused by fortuitous accidents such as stranding, striking upon the rocks, icebergs or other objects, collision, fire and explosion;

c. Partial loss of the insured cargo attributable to heavy weather, lightening, and/or tsunami, where the conveyance has been grounded, stranded, sunk or burnt irrespective of whether the event or events took place before or after such accidents;

d. Partial or total loss resulting from the falling of entire package or packages into sea during loading, transshipment or discharge;

e. Reasonable cost incurred by the insured on salvaging the cargo or averting or minimizing a loss recoverable under the policy, provided that such cost shall not exceed the sum insured of the consignment;

f. Losses attributable to discharge of the insured cargo at a port of distress following a sea peril as well as special charges arising from loading, warehousing and forwarding of the cargo at an intermediate port of call or refuge;

g. Sacrifice in and contribution to general average and salvage charges;

h. Such proportion of losses sustained by the ship owners is to be reimbursed by the cargo owner under the Contract of Affreightment "Both to Blame Collision" clause.

平安险起初译为"单独海损不赔"。其责任范围主要包括自然灾害导致的全部损失和意外事故造成的全部损失或部分损失。平安险并不是对自然灾害造成的部分损失都不赔，实际上部分损失中的共同海损以及共同海损的牺牲和分摊及救助费用和对受损保险货物进行施救的费用等，是保险公司的赔偿责任范围。也就是说平安险只是对自然灾害造成的单独海损不赔。

投保了平安险，保险公司对下列损失负赔偿责任：

a. 被保险的货物在运输途中由于恶劣气候、雷电、海啸、地震、洪水等自然灾害造成整批货物的全部损失或推定全损。

b. 由于运输工具遭到搁浅、触礁、沉没、互撞，与流冰或其他物体碰撞以及失火、爆炸等意外事故所造成的货物全部或部分损失。

c. 在运输工具已经发生搁浅、触礁、沉没、焚毁等意外事故的情况下，货物在此前后又在海上遭受恶劣气候、雷电、海啸等自然灾害所造成的部分损失。

d. 在装卸或转船时由于一件或数件甚至整批货物落海所造成的全部或部分损失。

e. 被保险人对遭受承保责任内的危险货物采取抢救、防止或减少货损的措施所支付的合理费用，但以不超过该批被毁货物的保险金额为限。

f. 运输工具遭遇海难后，在避难港由于卸货引起的损失，以及在中途港或避难港由于卸货、存仓和运送货物所产生的特殊费用。

g. 共同海损的牺牲、分摊和救助费用。

h. 运输契约中如订有"船舶互撞责任"条款，则根据该条款规定应由货方偿还船方的损失。

B. With Particular Average/ With Average (W.P.A./W.P.) 水渍险

Aside from the risks covered under F.P.A. conditions as above, this insurance also covers partial losses of the insured goods caused by natural calamities such as heavy weather, thunder and lightening, tsunami, earthquake or flood.

水渍险直译为"单独海损也赔"，水渍险的责任范围除了包括平安险的全部责任范围外，还负责被保险货物在运输途中由于恶劣气候、雷电、海啸、地震、洪水等自然灾害造成的部分损失。

C. All Risks (A.R.) 一切险

Aside from the risks covered under the F.P.A and W.P.A. conditions as above, All Risks insurance also covers all risks of loss of or damage to insured goods whether partial or total, arising from general extraneous risks in the course of transit. The cover of All Risks is the most comprehensive of the three. It covers 11 additional risks. It should be noted that "All Risks" does not, as its name suggests, really cover all risks.

除了包括上述平安险和水渍险的各项责任以外，该保险还负责被保险货物在运输途中由于一般外来风险所致的全部或部分损失。在三种基本险别中，一切险承保的范围最为广泛。一切险承保责任已包含 11 种一般附加险。也就是说，一切险是平安险、水渍险、一般附加险的总和。需要注意的是，一切险并不是像其名称所说的那样，承保所有的风险。

Exclusions of Basic Insurance Coverage 基本险的除外责任

The three coverages, i.e. F.P.A. and W.P.A. and All Risks do not cover:

a. Loss or damage caused by the intentional act of fault of the insured;

b. Loss or damage falling under the liability of the consignor;

c. Loss or damage arising from the inferior quality or shortage of the insured goods prior to the attachment of this insurance;

d. Loss or damage arising from normal loss, inherent vice or nature of the insured goods, loss of market and/or delay in transit and any expenses arising therefore;

e. Risks and liabilities excluded by the ocean marine cargo war risks clauses and strike, riot and civil commotion clauses of CIC.

上述三种基本险别对下列损失不负赔偿责任：

a. 被保险人的故意行为或过失所造成的损失。

b. 属于发货人的责任所造成的损失。

c. 在保险责任开始前，被保险货物已存在的品质不良或数量短量所造成的损失。

d. 被保险货物的自然损耗、本质缺陷或本身特性以及市价跌落、运输延迟所引起的损失或费用。

e. 属于海洋运输货物战争险和罢工险条款规定的责任范围和除外责任。

Commencement and Termination of Basic Insurance 保险责任期限(保险责任的起讫)

The commencement and termination of basic insurance are usually stipulated by adopting the customary "Warehouse to Warehouse Clause (W/W Clause)" clause.

W/W Clause indicates that the insurance company undertakes an insurance liability over the insured cargo from the warehouse or the place of storage of the shipper named in the policy until the cargo has arrived at the warehouse or the place of storage of the receiver named in the policy. The insurance liability terminates once the cargo arrives at the warehouse of the receiver.

If the insured cargo is unloaded from the ship but does not arrive at the warehouse of the receiver immediately:

a. The insurance shall be limited to sixty days after completion of discharge of the insured goods at the final port of discharge before they reach the above mentioned warehouse of storage.

b. The cargo shall be transshipped from the destination not indicated in the policy. Then the insurance shall terminate when transshipment begins.

In the international insurance business, the insurance company does not hold W/W liabilities in the insurance contract. As the sole characteristics of the insurance, the ownership of the cargo is constantly changing, which requires that the buyer shall hold insurance benefit to the insurance subject when asking for claims. At this time, the right of the recourse is transferred to the buyer. Under the FOB, CFR, FCA and CPT contracts, the seller delivers the cargo at the port of shipment. Thus, their insurance liability is from Ship to Warehouse.

保险责任期限是指保险人承担保险责任的起讫时限。按照国际保险业的习惯，采用的是"仓至仓条款"。

仓至仓条款是保险责任起讫的条款。它是指自被保险货物运离保险单所载明的起运地发货人的仓库时生效，包括正常的运输过程，直至该货物运交保险单所载明的目的地收货人的仓库时为止。当货物一进入收货人的仓库，保险责任即行终止。

如货物卸离海船后，没有马上进入收货人仓库：

a. 保险公司的责任延续60天。如果在60天内某日进入仓库，保险责任也即行终止。

b. 如在上述60天内被保险货物需转运至非保险单所载明的目的地时，则以该项货物开始转运时终止。

在国际保险业务中，保险公司并不是对所有保险合同都承担仓至仓责任的。因为由于海上货物运输保险本身的特殊性质，货物的所有权在不断的转让之中，它仅要求在保险标的发生损失，买方索赔时必须具有保险利益。此时保险单的求偿权已转移给买方。具体到贸易术语，如FOB、CFR、FCA、CPT术语订立的买卖合同，卖方在装运港船上交货，所以，以上贸易术语的保险责任起讫实际上是"船至仓"。

② Additional Risks 附加险别

Additional Risks cover losses caused by Extraneous Risks and Extraneous Risks include General Extraneous Risks and Special Extraneous Risks, so Additional Risks are divided into General Additional Risks and Special Additional Risks. Additional Risks include General Additional Risks and Special Additional Risks.

附加险承保的是外来风险造成的损失，而外来风险又有一般外来风险和特殊外来风险之分，所以附加险也可分为一般附加险和特殊附加险。

A. General Additional Risks 一般附加险

a. Theft, Pilferage and Non-delivery (T.P.N.D.) 偷窃、提货不着险

b. Fresh Water Rain Damage (F.W.R.) 淡水雨淋险

c. Risk of Shortage 短量险

d. Risk of Intermixture & Contamination 混杂、玷污险

e. Risk of Leakage 渗漏险

f. Risk of Clash & Breakage 碰撞、破碎险

g. Risk of Odor 串味险

h. Damage Caused by Heating & Sweating 受热、受潮险

i. Hook Damage 钩损险

j. Loss or Damage Caused by Breakage of Packing 包装破裂险

k. Risks of Rust 锈损险

General Additional Risks shall go with F.P.A. and W.P.A. according to the characteristics of the cargo. All Risks cover all these eleven general additional risks; therefore, it is not necessary to insure General Additional Risks if All Risks are obtained.

一般附加险不能作为一个单独的项目投保，而只能在投保平安险或水渍险的基础上，根据货物的特性和需要加保一种或若干种一般附加险。一般附加险包括在一切险的承保范围内，故在投保一切险时，不存在再加保一般附加险的问题。

B. Special Additional Risks 特殊附加险

Special Additional Risk differs from general addition risk in that the former covers loss or damage caused by some special extraneous reasons such as politics, law, regulations and war. On the other hand, like general additional risk, special additional risks cannot be used to insure goods alone either.

Special Additional Risks include:

a. War Risk 战争险

War Risk is one of the main types of Special Additional Risks. Though it cannot be solely insured, it is more independent than other additional risks. It includes Insurance Coverage,

Exclusions, and Commencement and Termination.

战争险是特殊附加险的主要险别之一,它虽然不能独立投保,但对其他附加险而言又有很强的独立性,其内容包括责任范围、除外责任、责任起讫等。

Insurance Coverage of War Risk 战争险的承保责任范围

War Risk covers: Losses caused by war, war-like events, armed conflicts or piratical behaviors; Damage resulting from arrest, detain, inhibition or seizure caused by the above mentioned reasons; Losses caused by regular arms such as torpedo and bombs; General average or expenses caused by coverage under this clause.

战争险负责赔偿:直接由于战争、类似战争行为、敌对行为、武装冲突或海盗行为等所造成运输货物的损失;由于上述原因所引起的捕获、拘留、扣留、禁制、扣押等所造成的运输货物的损失;各种常规武器(水雷、炸弹等)所造成运输货物的损失;由本险责任范围所引起的共同海损牺牲、分摊和救助费用。

Exclusions of War Risk 战争险的除外责任

War Risk does not cover loss, damage, or expenses arising from any hostile use of atomic or nuclear weapons of war.

Exceptions are losses or damage caused by atomic bomb, hydrogen bomb, detention and seizure by the administrative authority.

战争险对由于敌对行为使用原子弹或热核制造的武器导致被保险货物的损失和费用不负责赔偿。

例外条款:原子弹、氢弹、执政当局命令、扣押或拘留引起的损失。

Commencement and Termination of War Risk 战争险的保险责任起讫

It is based on "ocean" clauses and limited to ocean risks, which is totally different from Warehouse to Warehouse Clauses. That is to say, the insurer's coverage begins when the cargo is loaded at the port of shipment dominated by the insurance policy and ends when the cargo is unloaded at the port of destination. If the cargo fails to be unloaded at the port of destination, then the war coverage automatically ends by 15 days after the cargo arrives at the port of destination; if transshipment happens, whether or not the cargo is unloaded locally, the insurance coverage ends by 15 days after the cargo arrives at the port of destination and once the cargo is loaded on another ship, the insurance coverage continues to be valid.

战争险的责任起讫与基本险所采用的"仓至仓"条款不同,而是采用"水面"条款,以"水上危险"为限,是指保险人的承保责任自货物装上保险单所载明的起运港的海轮或驳船开始,到卸离保险单所载明的目的港的海轮或驳船为止。如果货物不卸离海轮或驳船,则从海轮到达目的港当日午夜起算满 15 日之后责任自行终止;如果中途转船,不论货物在当地卸货与否,保险责任以海轮到达该港可卸货地点的当日午夜起算满 15 日为止,等再装上续运海轮时,保险责任才继续有效。

b. Strikes Risk 罢工险

It covers loss of or damage to the cargo insured directly caused by acts of strikers and locked-out workmen. But it does not cover loss of or damage to the cargo caused by lack of labor force or failure to apply the workforce. For instance, cargo suffers losses without fuel added or due to the malfunction of the air-conditioner caused strike, so the insurer doesn't compensate for them.

According to the international insurance practice, the insured shall not be charged with any other expense as long as the insured has already covered War Risk and generally War Risk is covered together with Strikes Risk.

罢工险是指对罢工人员行为所造成的损失进行保险，但对由于罢工而造成的劳力不足或不能运用劳力而造成的货物受损不赔。例如，因罢工导致无人加油或空调不工作造成的货物受损，保险人不予赔偿。

根据国际保险业的惯例，投保罢工险时，只要投保人已投保战争险，保险人就不再另收保费，而且一般都是与战争险同时承保。

c. Failure to Delivery Risk 交货不到险

d. Import Duty Risk 进口关税险

e. On Deck Risk 舱面险

f. Rejection Risk 拒收险

g. Aflatoxin Risk 黄曲霉素险

h. Fire Risks Extension Clause (for Storage of Cargo at destination Hongkong, including Kowloon or Macao) 出口货物到香港(包括九龙)或澳门存仓火险责任扩展条款

③ Special Risks of Ocean Marine Cargo Insurance 海运货物保险专门险

Special Risks of Ocean Marine Cargo Insurance are special risks covered according to the characteristics of ocean marine cargo and can be covered separately.

海运货物保险专门险是根据海洋运输货物的特性而承保的专门险别，可以单独投保。

A. Ocean Marine Insurance Clause (Frozen Products) 海洋运输冷藏货物保险条款

a. Risks for Shipment of Frozen Products 冷藏险

Aside from the risks covered under W.P.A. conditions as above, this insurance also covers spoilage or loss of the insured goods due to the failure of the cold storage machinery to work for a continuous period of more than 24 hours.

冷藏险的责任范围，除负责水渍险承保的责任外，还负责赔偿由于冷藏机器停止工作连续达24小时以上所造成的被保险货物的腐败或损失。

b. All Risks for Shipment of Frozen Products 冷藏一切险

Aside from the risks covered under Risks for Shipment of Frozen Products conditions as above, this insurance also covers all risks of loss of or damage to insured goods arising from general extraneous risks in the course of transit.

冷藏一切险的责任范围，除包括冷藏险的各项责任外，还负责赔偿被保险货物在运输途中由于一般外来风险所造成的腐败或损失。

B. Ocean Marine Insurance Clause (Woodoil Bulk) 海洋运输散装桐油保险条款

This insurance covers losses due to shortness, leakage, contamination or deterioration of the insured woodoil in bulk, regardless of the cause.

海洋运输散装桐油保险条款是保险人承保不论何种原因造成的被保险散装桐油的短少、渗漏、玷污或变质的损失。

C. Livestock & Poultry Insurance 活牲畜、家禽运输保险

The insurance covers loss due to the death of live livestock or poultry in the course of transit, but doesn't cover loss due to the death of live livestock or poultry the death caused by the following cases: The death of insured live livestock or poultry arising from the poor health prior to the commencement of the insurance; The death of insured live livestock or poultry due to pregnancy, vaccination or vaccination; The death of insured live livestock or poultry caused by the slaughter ordered by the administering authority due to infectious diseases or sick; The death of insured live livestock or poultry arising from lack of feed; The death of insured live livestock or poultry caused by prohibitions on import or export or discrepancies in inspection, etc.

活牲畜、家禽运输保险是保险人对于活牲畜、家禽在运输途中的死亡负责赔偿，但对下列原因造成的死亡，不负赔偿责任：在保险责任开始前，被保险活牲畜、家禽健康状况不好；或被保险活牲畜、家禽因怀恶、防疫注射或接种所致的死亡；或因传染病、患病，经管理当局命令屠杀；或因缺乏饲料而致的死亡；或由于被禁止进口或出口或检验不符而引起的死亡；等等。

(2) Institute Cargo Clauses 伦敦保险协会海运货物保险险别

Insurance business originating from England enormously affects the whole world. The Institute Cargo Clauses (I.C.C.) were initially published by the Institute of London Underwriters in 1912 and were revised in 1981 and the newest clauses came into effect on Jan.1, 1982. Currently, almost 2/3 of the countries follow Institute Cargo Clauses in the insurance business, which has a great effect in the world. We shall accept Institute Cargo Clauses if foreign clients demand.

Institute Cargo Clauses is mainly composed of the following six clauses. The first five kinds can be independently covered without being attached to any other particular coverage. Meanwhile, ICC(A) clauses include malicious damage clauses, but malicious damage clauses should be attached to ICC(B) or ICC(C) clauses.

英国的保险业历史悠久，对世界各国影响很大。英国伦敦保险协会的货物条款制定于1912年，最近的一次修订完成于2009年，并于2009年1月1日起开始施行。目前，世界

上有 2/3 的国家在海上保险业务中采用了该协会货物条款，它对世界保险业的发展产生很大的影响。我国保险公司承保的业务，如果外商要求按 ICC 条款投保，则我方可以接受。

协会货物保险条款主要有以下 6 种。前 5 种险别条款可以单独投保。另外，ICC(A)险中包括恶意损害险，但在投保 ICC(B)险或 ICC(C)险时，应另行投保恶意损害险。

① Institute Cargo Clauses A (ICC(A)) 协会货物条款(A)

Institute Cargo Clauses A adopt the method of "all risks except for exclusions", that is to say, except for exclusions, the insurer is responsible for the rest risks. It is similar to that of All Risks under China Marine Cargo Insurance Clauses.

Exclusions include:

A. General Exclusions: Willful misconduct of the assured; ordinary leakage, ordinary loss in weight or volume, ordinary wear and tear; unsuitable packing; inherent vice; delay; insolvency or financial default of the owners, managers, characters or operators of the vessel; any weapon or device employing atomic or nuclear fission and/or fusion.

B. Exclusions of Unseaworthiness and Unfitness: Unseaworthiness and unfitness of vessel for the safe carriage of the subject-matter insured, where the insured know the breach of implied undertaking of the seaworthy and fitness, at the time the subject-matter insured is loaded; unfitness of container or conveyance for the safe carriage of the subject-matter insured.

C. Exclusions of War: The losses caused by war, civil war, revolution, rebellion, insurrection, civil strife, or any hostile act by or against a belligerent power; capture, seizure, arrest, restraint or detainment (excluding pirates), and the consequence thereof or any attempt thereat; derelict mines, torpedoes, bombs or other derelict weapons of war.

D. Exclusions of Strikes: The losses caused by strikers, locked-out workmen, or persons taking part in labor disturbances, riots or civil commotions; strikes, lock-outs, labor disturbances, riots or civil commotions; any act of terrorism being an act of any person acting on behalf of, or in connection with, any organization; any person acting from a political, ideological or religious motive.

ICC(A)采取"一切风险减除外责任的方法"，即除了"除外责任"项下所列的风险，保险人不予负责外，其他风险均予负责。ICC(A)相当于我国海洋货物运输保险条款的一切险。

除外责任包括：

A. 一般除外责任包括：归因于被保险人故意的不法行为造成的损失或费用；自然渗漏、重量或容量的自然损耗或自然磨损；包装或准备不足或不当所造成的损失或费用；保险标的内在缺陷或特性所造成的损失或费用；直接由于迟延所引起的损失或费用；由于船舶所有人、经理人、租船人或经营破产或不履行债务造成的损失或费用；由于使用任何原子或热核武器所造成的损失或费用。

B. 不适航和不适货除外责任是指在装船时，如被保险人或其受雇人已经知道船舶不适航，以及船舶、装运工具、集装箱等不适货。如违反适航、适货的默示保证为被保险人或其受雇人所知道。

C. 战争除外责任是指由于战争、内战、敌对行为等造成的损失或费用；由于捕获、拘留、扣留等(海盗除外)所造成的损失或费用；由于漂流水雷、鱼雷等造成的损失或费用。

D. 罢工除外责任是指由于罢工者、被迫停工工人等造成的损失或费用；由任何恐怖主义者或处于政治动机而行动的人所造成的损失或费用。

② Institute Cargo Clauses B [ICC(B)] 协会货物条款(B)

Institute Cargo Clauses B list all risks covered. Namely, it specifies insurable risks one by one for the insured's choice and is convenient for settlement of compensation. ICC(B) cover the loss of or damage of subject matter insured arising from the following cause:

A. Fire or explosion;

B. Vessels or barges being stranded, grounded, sunk, capsized;

C. Overturning or derailment of land conveyance;

D. Collision or contact of vessel, barge or conveyance with any external object other than water;

E. Discharge of cargo at a port of distress;

F. Earthquake, volcanic eruption or lightening;

G. General average sacrifice;

H. Jettison and washing overboard;

I. Entry of sea, lake or river water into vessel, barge, conveyance, container, lift van or place of storage;

J. Total loss of any package lost overboard or dropped when loading on to, or unloading from vessel or barge.

In addition, the insurer covers general average contributions and salvage charges, provided that the cause of general average is not the risks other than ICC(B).

Exclusions of ICC(B): In addition to the exclusions of ICC(A), it shall not cover deliberate damage to or deliberate destruction of the subject-matter insured or any part thereof by the wrongful act of any person or persons.

Thus, ICC(B) mainly covers loss caused by natural disasters and fortuitous accidents, as well as sacrifice in and contribution to general average and salvage charges. It is similar to W.P.A. Clauses of C.I.C..

ICC(B)采用"列明风险"的方式。列明风险，即将承保范围内风险一一罗列出来，便于投保人选择险别，又便于保险公司处理损害赔偿。ICC(B)对因下述原因所致的保险标的的损失和损害负责赔偿：

A. 火灾或爆炸；

B. 船舶或驳船触礁、搁浅、沉没或倾覆；

C. 陆上运输工具倾覆或出轨；

D. 船舶、驳船或运输工具与水以外的任何外界物体碰撞或接触；

E. 在避难港卸货；

F. 地震、火山爆发、雷电；

G. 共同海损牺牲；

H. 抛货和浪击落海；

I. 海水、湖水或河水进入船舶、驳船、运输工具、集装箱、吊装车厢或储存处所；

J. 货物在装卸时落水或坠落而造成的整件货物的全部损失。

此外，保险人还承保共同海损分摊和救助费用，但导致共同海损的原因必须不是ICC(B)所除外的风险。

ICC(B)的除外责任包括了ICC (A)的除外责任的内容，另外加上对海盗造成的损失和对第三方的恶意损害。

由此可见，ICC(B)主要承保自然灾害和意外事故所致的损失，同时还承保共同海损的牺牲、分摊和救助费用，类似于我国《海洋运输货物保险条款》中的水渍险。

③ Institute Cargo Clauses C [ICC(C)] 协会货物条款(C)

Institute Cargo Clauses C only cover losses caused by important events and is not liable for unimportant accidents and natural calamities. ICC(C) cover the loss of or damage of subject matter insured arising from the following cause:

A. Fire or explosion;

B. Vessels or barges being stranded, grounded, sunk, capsized;

C. Overturning or derailment of land conveyance;

D. Collision or contact of vessel, barge or conveyance with any external object other than water;

E. Discharge of cargo at a port of distress;

F. General average sacrifice;

G. Jettison.

In addition, the insurer covers general average contributions and salvage charges, provided that the cause of general average is not the risks other than ICC(C).

The exclusions of ICC(C) are the same as that of ICC(B). ICC(C) is similar to F.P.A. Clauses of C.I.C..

ICC(C)只赔重大意外事故造成的损失，对非重大意外事故和自然灾害造成的损失都不予赔偿。ICC(C)对因下述原因所致的保险标的的损失和损害负责赔偿：

A. 火灾或爆炸；
B. 船舶或驳船触礁、搁浅、沉没或倾覆；
C. 陆上运输工具倾覆或出轨；
D. 船舶、驳船或运输工具与水以外的任何外界物体碰撞或接触；
E. 在避难港卸货；
F. 共同海损牺牲；
G. 抛货。

此外，保险人还承保共同海损分摊和救助费用，但导致共同海损的原因必须不是 ICC(C) 所除外的风险。

ICC(C)的除外责任与 ICC(B)的除外责任一样。ICC(C)相当于我国保险条款的平安险。

④ Institute War Clauses (Cargo) 协会战争险条款(货物)

Institute War Clauses (Cargo) cover losses of subject matter of insurance caused by: War, civil war, revolution, rebellion, insurrection or the resulting civil strife, or any hostile act of belligerent states or aiming at belligerent states; Arrest, detain, inhibition or seizure caused by the above mentioned reasons and its consequences, or any related attempt to do so; Abandoned mines, torpedoes, bombs, or other abandoned weapons of war; Losses caused by regular arms such as torpedo and bombs; General average or expenses caused by coverage under this clause.

The exclusions of Institute War Clauses (Cargo) are almost same as the "General Exclusions" and "Exclusions of Unseaworthiness and Unfitness" of ICC(A).

The commencement and termination of Institute War Clauses (Cargo) subject to "water borne only". That is to say, the insurer's coverage begins when the cargo is loaded at the port of shipment dominated by the insurance policy and ends when the cargo is unloaded at the port of destination. If the cargo fails to be unloaded at the port of destination, then the war coverage automatically ends by 15 days after the cargo arrives at the port of destination; if transshipment happens, whether or not the cargo is unloaded locally, the insurance coverage ends by 15 days after the cargo arrives at the port of destination and once the cargo is loaded on another ship, the insurance coverage continues to be valid.

协会海运货物战争险主要承保由于下列原因造成保险标的的损失：战争、内战、革命、叛乱、造反或由此引起的内乱，或交战国或针对交战国的任何敌对行为；由于上述承保风险引起的捕获、拘留、扣留、禁止或扣押及其后果，或任何进行这种行为的有关企图；遗弃的水雷、鱼雷、炸弹或其他遗弃的战争武器；由本险责任范围所引起的共同海损牺牲、分摊和救助费用。

协会货物战争险条款的除外责任与 ICC(A)的"一般除外责任"及"不适航、不适货除外责任"基本相同。

协会货物战争险的责任起讫以"水上危险"为限，即保险责任自货物装上海轮时开始，直到卸离海轮时终止，若货物未及时卸离海轮，以海轮到达最后港口或卸货港当日午夜起满15天为限，保险责任终止；如果在中途港转运，也以到港15天为限。

⑤ Institute Strikes Clauses (Cargo) 协会罢工险条款(货物)

Institute Strikes Clauses (Cargo) cover: Loss caused by strikers, forced workers, or persons involved in industrial unrest, riots, or civil disobedience; Loss or damage caused by any terrorist or any person acting for political purposes; General average or expenses caused due to avoiding the above insured risks.

The exclusions of Institute Strikes Clauses (Cargo) are almost same as the "General Exclusions" and "Exclusions of Unseaworthiness and Unfitness" of ICC(A). However, as Institute Strikes Clauses (Cargo) are only responsible for the loss directly caused by the strike and other risks covered, the insurer shall not be liable for the following losses and expenses: Loss or expense arising from lack of or distrain of labor force caused by strikes, lockouts, strike movements, riots and civil commotions, etc.; Loss resulting from setbacks in voyage; Loss or expense resulting from war, civil war, revolution, rebellion, insurrection or the resulting civil strife, or any hostile act of belligerent states or aiming at belligerent states.

协会货物罢工险承保：罢工者、被迫停工工人或参与工潮、暴动或民变人员所造成的损失；任何恐怖分子或任何出于政治目的采取行为的人引起的灭失或损害；为了避免以上承保风险所造成的共同海损牺牲、分摊和救助费用。

协会货物罢工险的除外责任与ICC(A)的"一般除外责任"及"不适航、不适货除外责任"基本相同，但由于协会货物罢工险只负责由于罢工等风险直接造成的损失，对于下列损失与费用，保险人不负赔偿责任：由于罢工、停工、工潮、暴动和民变等造成劳动力缺乏、缺少或扣押所引起的损失或费用；由于航程挫折而引起的损失；由于战争、内战、革命、叛乱或由此引起的内乱，或交战国或针对交战国的任何敌对行为所造成的损失或费用。

⑥ Malicious Damage Clauses 恶意损害险条款

Malicious Damage Clauses cover loss of or damage to the insured cargo caused by acts of vandalism by the person other than the insured (e.g. the captain, crew, etc.). However, if malicious damage caused by behaviors of the person acting for politically motivated purpose, it is not covered by the clauses, but can be covered by Institute Strikes Clauses (Cargo).

协会货物恶意损害险承保的是被保险人以外的其他人(如船长、船员等)的故意破坏行为所致被保险货物的灭失或损害。但是，恶意损害如果出于有某种政治动机的人的行为，便不属本险别的承保风险，但可以在协会货物罢工险条款中得到保障。

Section 2 Cargo Transport Insurance of Other Transport Modes

第 2 节 其他运输方式货物保险

1. Insurance of Land Transport 陆路运输货物保险

According to Overland Transportation Cargo Insurance Clauses of PICC, overland transport insurance covers rail and road transportation.

根据中国人民保险公司《陆上运输货物保险条款》规定，责任范围仅限于火车和汽车运输。

(1) Basic Coverage of Overland Transportation Insurance 陆路运输货物保险的基本险别

① Overland Transportation Risks 陆运险

The risks covered under Overland Transportation Risks are somewhat similar to those under W.P.A. for marine cargo insurance. It covers total or partial loss of the insured cargo caused by natural calamities, such as storm, thunder, flood and earthquake, or resulted from the clashing, overturning, and derailing of the transportation in transit. It also covers total or partial loss of the insured cargo due to the lightening transportation being grounded, stranded, sunk or clashed in the course of lightening. It covers total or partial loss of the insured cargo caused by accidents, such as tunnel wrack, cliff crack, fire or explosion, too. In addition, the insurance covers the reasonable cost incurred by the insured on salvaging the cargo or averting or minimizing a loss recoverable under the policy, provided that such cost shall not exceed the sum insured of the consignment.

陆运险的承保责任范围与海洋运输货物保险条款中的"水渍险"相似。保险公司负责赔偿被保险货物在运输途中遭受暴风、雷电、洪水、地震等自然灾害，或由于运输工具遭受碰撞、颠覆、出轨，或在驳运过程中因驳运工具遭受搁浅、触礁、沉没、碰撞，或由于遭受隧道坍塌、崖崩或失火、爆炸等意外事故所造成的全部或部分损失。此外，被保险人对遭受承保责任内危险的货物采取抢救、防止或减少货损的措施而支付的合理费用，保险公司也负责赔偿，但以不超过该批被救货物的保险金额为限。

② Overland Transportation All Risks 陆运一切险

The risks covered under Overland Transportation All Risks are somewhat similar to those under All Risks for marine cargo insurance. Aside from the risks covered under Overland Transportation Risks, this insurance also covers all risks of loss of or damage to the insured goods, whether partial or total, arising from external causes in transit.

The exclusions of overland transportation insurance are just the same as that of marine cargo insurance.

陆运一切险的承保责任范围与海上运输货物保险条款中的"一切险"相似。保险公司除承担上述陆运险的赔偿责任外,还负责保险货物在运输途中由于一般外来原因所造成的全部或部分损失。

陆上运输货物险的除外责任与海洋运输货物险的除外责任相同。

(2) Commencement and Termination of Overland Transportation Insurance 陆路运输货物保险的保险责任起讫期限

It also follows the W/W clause. The insurance company undertakes an insurance liability over the insured cargo from the warehouse or the place of storage of the shipper named in the policy until the cargo has arrived at the warehouse or place of storage of the receiver named in the policy. The insurance shall be limited to sixty days after completion of discharge of the insured goods at the final port of discharge before they reach the above mentioned warehouse of storage.

陆上运输货物险的责任起讫也采用仓至仓责任条款。保险人负责自被保险货物运离保险单所载明的起运地仓库或储存处所开始运输时生效,包括正常运输过程中的陆上和与其有关的水上驳运在内,直至该项货物运达保险单所载目的地收货人的最后仓库或储存处所或被保险人用作分配、分派的其他储存处所为止。如未运抵上述仓库或储存处所,则以被保险货物运抵最后卸载的车站满60天为止。

(3) Overland Additional Risks 陆运附加险

It includes Overland General Additional Risks and Overland Special Additional Risks.

Attention should be paid to the following:

A. One or more types of General Additional Risks and Special Additional Risks could be covered together with Overland Transportation Risks;

B. If the added risks are War Risk, the coverage shall be limited to the railway, and the duration does not follow W/W clause but is limited by the time when the cargo is loaded on the transportation.

C. If there is no transshipment, the duration is 48 hours after the cargo arrives at the destination; if there is transshipment, the duration is 10 days and the coverage continues to be valid once the cargo is loaded on the transportation.

陆运附加险包括陆运一般附加险和陆运特殊附加险。需要注意以下问题:

A. 在投保陆运险的基础上可加保一种或若干种一般附加险和特殊附加险。

B. 投保陆运一切险时,如加保战争险则仅以铁路运输为限,其责任起讫不是"仓至仓"条款,而是以货物置于运输工具时为限。

C. 从货物装上车开始至卸车时为止;如果不卸车,则从货物到站当日午夜起满48小时为止；如中途转车，不论卸车与否以 10 天为限，装上车续运则继续有效。

2. Insurance of Air Transport 航空运输货物保险

(1) Basic Coverage of Air Transportation Insurance 航空运输货物保险的基本险别

① Air Transportation Risk 航空运输险

The coverage of Air Transportation Risk is almost as extensive as that of W.P.A. in marine cargo insurance according to Air Transportation Cargo Insurance Clauses of PICC. It covers total or partial loss of or damage to the insured cargo caused in transit by lightening, fire, explosion, jettison due to the aircraft encountering bad weather or other perils, collision, overturning, crashing or missing and other accidents.

根据中国人民保险公司《航空运输货物保险条款》，航空运输险的承保责任范围与海洋货物运输保险条款中的"水渍险"相似，包括被保险货物在运输途中遭受雷电、火灾、爆炸或由于飞机遭受恶劣气候或其他危难事故而被抛弃，或由于飞机遭受碰撞、倾覆、坠落或失踪等自然灾害和意外事故所造成的全部或部分损失。

② Air Transportation All Risks 航空运输一切险

In addition to what are covered under Air Transportation Risks, the coverage of Air Transportation All Risks also covers total loss or partial loss of or damage to the insured cargo arising from external causes in transit.

航空运输一切险的承保责任范围与海洋运输保险条款中的"一切险"相似，除包括航空运输险的各项责任外，还包括被保险货物由于一般外来原因所造成的全部或部分损失。

(2) Commencement and Termination of Air Transportation Insurance 航空运输货物保险的保险责任起讫期限

It follows W/W clauses, but the insurance shall be limited to 30 days after completion of discharge of the insured cargo from the aircraft at the final airport of discharge. And if the cargo shall be transferred to the destination not indicated in the insurance policy, the insurance liability ends when transferring begins.

虽然航空运输货物险的责任起讫也采用"仓至仓"条款，但不同的是如果货物运达保险单所载明的目的地而货物未进仓，以货物在最后卸载地卸离飞机后满 30 天为止。如在上述 30 天内，该保险货物需转运到非保险单所载明的目的地时，保险责任以该项货物开始转运时终止。

(3) Air Transportation Cargo War Risk 航空运输货物战争险

It is one type of Additional Risks to Air Transportation Risk based on Air Transportation Risk and Air Transportation All Risks.

The insurance company undertakes loss of or damage to the cargo caused by war, military events, armed conflicts, regular weapons and bombs, excluding losses caused by atomic or heated nuclear weapons.

Commencement and Termination of Air Transportation Cargo War Risk: from charging the cargo on the plane to discharging from the plane at the destination indicated in the policy. But the insurance shall be limited to 15 days after the cargo arrives at the final airport of discharge. If the cargo is transferred during the trip, the insurance shall be limited to 15 days after the cargo arrives at the transshipment point. The insurance continues to be valid once the cargo is reloaded on the plane.

航空运输货物战争险是航空运输货物险的一种附加险，只有在投保了航空运输险或航空运输一切险的基础上方可加保。

加保航空运输货物战争险后，保险公司承担赔偿在航空运输途中由于战争、敌对行为或武装冲突以及各种常规武器和炸弹所造成的货物损失，但不包括因使用原子或热核制造的武器所造成的损失。

航空运输货物战争险的责任起讫期间从被保险货物装上飞机开始，直到卸离保险单所载明的目的地的飞机时为止。如不卸机，则以载货飞机到达目的地的当日午夜起计算满15天为止。如被保险货物在中途转机，保险责任以飞机到达转运地当日起满15天为止。重新装上飞机保险责任恢复有效。

Terminology 本章术语

1. natural calamities 自然灾害
2. fortuitous accidents 意外事故
3. general extraneous risk 一般外来风险
4. special extraneous risk 特殊外来风险
5. actual total loss 实际全损
6. constructive total loss 推定全损
7. general average 共同海损
8. particular average 单独海损
9. Free from Particular Average (F.P.A.) 平安险
10. With Particular Average/With Average (W.P.A./W.A.) 水渍险
11. All Risks 一切险
12. Theft, Pilferage and Non-delivery (T.P.N.D.) 偷窃、提货不着险
13. Fresh Water Rain Damage (F.W.R.) 淡水雨淋险
14. Risk of Shortage 短量险
15. Risk of Intermixture & Contamination 混杂、玷污险

16. Risk of Leakage 渗漏险
17. Risk of Clash & Breakage 碰撞、破碎险
18. Risk of Odor 串味险
19. Damage Caused by Heating & Sweating 受热、受潮险
20. Hook Damage 钩损险
21. Loss or Damage Caused by Breakage of Packing 包装破裂险
22. Risks of Rust 锈损险
23. War Risk 战争险
24. Strike Risk 罢工险
25. Failure to Delivery Risk 交货不到险
26. Import Duty Risk 进口关税险
27. On Deck Risk 舱面险
28. Rejection Risk 拒收险
29. Aflatoxin Risk 黄曲霉素险
30. Institute Cargo Clauses A ICC(A) 协会货物条款(A)
31. Institute Cargo Clauses B ICC(B) 协会货物条款(B)
32. Institute Cargo Clauses C ICC(C) 协会货物条款(C)
33. Institute War Clauses (Cargo) 协会战争险条款(货物)
34. Institute Strikes Clauses (Cargo) 协会罢工险条款(货物)
35. Malicious Damage Clause 恶意损害险条款
36. Overland Transportation Risks 陆运险
37. Overland Transportation All Risks 陆运一切险
38. Air Transportation Risk 航空运输险
39. Air Transportation All Risks 航空运输一切险

Exercises 本章练习

1. Our exporter exported a load of cargo to a Middle-east country under CIF terms and covered WPA in addition to T.P.N.D., but the vessel was detained as a result of the Iran-Iraq war. The importer lodged a claim to the insurance company. Can the importer be compensated?

我国某外贸公司按 CIF 条件向中东某国出口一批货物，根据合同投保了水渍险附加偷窃提货不着险(T.P.N.D.)，但在海运途中，因两伊战争船被扣押，进口商以提货不着向保险公司索赔，问是否能得到赔偿？

2. In the previous case, which type of insurance should be covered so that the insurance

shall make indemnity?

上例应投保什么险，保险公司方予赔偿？

3. Our exporter exported 1,000 bales of gray cloth to Australia, covering W.P.A.. 100 bales were wetted as a result of leakage of the pipe during transit. Should the insurance company make indemnities?

我国某外贸公司向澳大利亚出口坯布 100 包，投保水渍险，货在海运途中因船舱使用水管漏水，致使该批货中 100 包浸水渍，问保险公司是否赔偿？

4. A vessel collapsed with flowing icebergs on the sea and a crack was founded on one side of the vessel. Sea water flooded in and part of the cargo was wet. The captain had to call at the nearest port to drain off water and afterwards threw off some bulky goods into the sea to make the vessel floating. Which part belongs to general average and which belongs to particular average?

有一货轮在海中与流冰相撞，船身一侧裂口，海水涌进，舱内部分货物遭浸泡，船长不得不将船就近驶上浅滩，进行排水，修补裂口，而后为了起浮又将部分笨重货物抛入海中，问哪些是单独海损？哪些是共同海损？

5. A vessel with Compartment A and Compartment B caught a fire during the trip and Compartment A was on fire. However, the captain mistakenly thought both compartments were on fire and ordered the crew to put out the fire with water cannons. Losses are:(1)the main engine was damaged;(2)two lots of goods in Compartment A, one lot was burned down partially and the other was water logging. Which belongs to particular average and which belongs to general average?

某货轮有甲乙两舱，船在航行途中发生火灾，火灾蔓延到甲舱。船长误以为甲乙两舱都着火，命令对两舱同时高压水龙灭火施救，损失情况：(1)主引擎烧坏；(2)甲舱两批货，一批货物部分被火烧毁，另一批灭火时遭水浸。问哪些是单独海损？哪些是共同海损？

6. A vessel was caught in a storm during the trip and water came into the compartments, resulting in USD 6,000 of losses. This lot of goods valued at USD 18,000 was covered with F.P.A.. Three days later, the vessel caught a fire. Shall 6,000 dollar of losses be indemnified by the insurance company?

一货轮在航行途中遇风暴，船上货舱进水，一批货投保平安险，共 18 000 美元，棉坯布部分遇水浸，损失 6 000 美元左右。三天后船又遭受火灾。问该批货 6 000 美元损失保险公司是否应赔偿？

7. An importer imported a batch of china, in case of collision and breakage, covering all risks additional with risk of clash and breakage. Is this right?

某公司进口一批瓷器，为防碰撞、破碎，投保了一切险另加碰撞险，是否正确？

8. Our exporter imported a batch of cargo from abroad under CFR Shanghai, covering WPA

with PICC according to shipping advice provided by the seller. Then our exporter advised the earner to unload the goods at Huangpu port Guangzhou as a result of the alter of the domestic user. However, during the trip from Huangpu to Nanjing, the train caught a mountain torrent so that the cargo was damaged partially. Our exporter claimed compensations to the insurance company and was refused. Is the insurance company justified to disclaim the indemnity? And please explain the reasons.

我国某外贸公司以 CFR 上海从国外进口一批货物，并据卖方提供的装船通知及时向中国人民保险公司投保水渍险，后来由于国内用户发生变更，我进口公司通知承运人货改卸广州黄埔港。在货由黄埔港装火车运往南京途中遇到山洪，致使部分货物受损，我进口公司据此向保险公司索赔但遭拒绝。保险公司拒赔有无道理？说明理由。

Answers for Reference 参考答案

1. Analysis: T.P.N.D. covers loss of or damage to the insured goods on the insured value caused by theft and/or pilferage; non-delivery or entire package. In this case, the loss of the goods resulting from detain causes by war does not belong to the above coverage, so the insurance company shall not compensate.

分析：偷窃提货不着险承保偷窃行为所致的损失和整件提货不着的损失。在本例中，由于战争引起的扣押所造成的货物损失不在上述承保范围内，所以保险公司将不予赔偿。

2. Analysis: Failure to deliver risk shall be covered. Failure to deliver risk refers to the risk, once the goods loaded on board the seagoing vessel, fail to be delivered at the destination within six months of scheduled date for arrival due to whatever cause it might be. The insurer will have to compensate for total loss. However, the insured shall handle equity-transferring procedures so as to get compensation.

分析：应投保交货不到险。因交货不到险是指从货物装上船开始，六个月内不能运到目的地，不论什么原因，保险公司要按全部损失赔偿。不过被保险人要向保险人办理权益转让手续，否则保险人不予赔偿。

3. Analysis: The insurance company is not liable unless fresh water rain damage was covered. Because W.P.A. doesn't cover the loss of goods caused by fresh and rain water damage which belongs to general extraneous risks.

分析：保险公司不予赔偿。因为水渍险不承保由于淡水雨淋这一外来风险所致货物的损失。

4. Analysis: Particular Average: Crack of the vessel and part of the cargo having undergone soaking; General Average: The vessel shipped to the nearest port and the losses thereafter.

分析：单独海损：船体撞裂和部分货物遭受浸泡。共同海损：船只驶上浅滩并由此产生的一系列损失。

5. Analysis: Particular Average: The main engine was damaged and one lot was burned down partially. General Average: The other lot was water logging.

分析：单独海损：烧坏的主引擎和被火烧毁的那批货物。共同海损：遭水浸的另一批货物。

6. Analysis: F.P.A. does not cover particular average caused by natural calamities. But in this case, accidents came after natural calamities. According to China Ocean Marine Cargo Clauses of PICC, F.P.A. covers partial loss of the insured cargo attributable to heavy weather, lightening, and/or tsunami, where the conveyance has been grounded, stranded, sunk or burnt irrespective of whether the event or events took place before or after such accidents. So the insurance company shall make compensations.

分析：平安险对自然灾害引起的单独海损不赔，但本案中在发生自然灾害之后又发生意外事故，根据中国人民保险公司的《海洋运输货物保险条款》，平安险承保在运输工具已经发生搁浅、触礁、沉没、焚毁等意外事故的情况下，货物在此前后又在海上遭受恶劣气候、雷电、海啸等自然灾害所造成的部分损失。所以，保险公司应该赔偿。

7. Analysis: It is wrong. All risks include risk of clash and breakage. So risk of clash and breakage is redundant.

分析：错误。一切险已包含碰撞险，不应再加保碰撞险。

8. Analysis: The insurance company shall disclaim compensations according to W/W clauses, If the insured cargo is unloaded from the ship but does not arrive at the warehouse of the receiver immediately, the cargo shall be transshipped from the destination not indicated in the policy, the insurance shall terminate when transshipment begins..

分析：保险公司可以拒赔。因为根据仓至仓条款，如货物卸离海船后，没有马上进入收货人仓库，被保险货物需转运至非保险单所载明的目的地时，则以该项货物开始转运时保险责任终止。

Chapter 7　Inspection of Commodity

第 7 章　国际货物贸易商品检验

Section 1　Functions and Classifications of Inspection

第 1 节　商品检验的作用与分类

1. Functions of Inspection 商品检验的作用

Commodity inspection, refers to the inspection and accreditation conducted by the authoritative specialized import and export commodities inspection authority in accordance with the provisions of laws, regulations or contracts during the process of international sales of goods, such inspection activities may involve the quality, quantity, weight, packaging, health and safety, as well as issuing of the inspection certificates.

商检即商品检验,是指在国际货物买卖过程中,由具有权威性的、专门的进出口商品检验机构依据法律、法规或合同的规定,对商品的质量、数量、重量、包装和卫生安全等方面的检验和鉴定,同时出具检验证书的活动。

It is quite often the case that export and import goods are subject to damage or shortage in transit because of rough handling in loading and unloading, and the long distance they are traveling. Besides, the quality of the goods received by the buyer may not be in conformity with the contract of sale. All these will surely lead to disputes, and it is necessary to find out who is the right party responsible for that. If the commodity has been inspected by the authoritative specialized import and export commodities inspection authority and a commodity inspection certificate issued, the certificate will serve to ascertain where the trouble lies and who is to blame. Commodity inspection is one of key steps during the sales of goods in international trade, which is the extension of the quality clause of contract and the warranty of it as well.

进出口货物需要经过长途运输,多次装卸,到货可能出现与合同不符的情况,容易引起有关方面的争议。为了避免争议的发生,以及发生争议后便于分清责任和进行处理,就需要有一个由具有权威性的、专门的进出口商品检验机构负责对货物进行检验或鉴定。检验机构检验或鉴定后出具相应的检验证书,作为买卖双方交接货物、支付货款和进行索赔、理赔的重要依据。因此,商品检验是国际贸易中买卖双方交接货物的重要环节之一,是合同中品质条款的延续和保障。

2. Classifications of Inspection 商品检验的分类

The governmental inspection authorities are committed to implementing the compulsory inspection on the important imported and exported commodities related to the national economy and the people's livelihood in accordance with the concerning laws and regulations. The commodities, which are not inspected or failed to pass the inspection, are not released by the custom.

国家检验机构根据有关的法律、法规,对关系到国计民生的重要进出口商品实施强制性检验。未经检验或检验不合格的商品,海关不予放行。

It's not all commodities that are compulsory to be inspected. In China, the specific regulations on the commodities which are compulsory to the inspection are as follows:

并不是所有的商品都必须进行法定检验,我国对必须进行法定检验的商品做了明确的规定,主要有以下几种:

① the commodities which are listed in the " Catalogue of Enter-exit Goods that shall be Inspected and Quarantined by Enter-exit Inspection and Quarantine Authorities"(hereinafter referred to as "the Catalogue");

列入"出入境检验检疫机构实施检验检疫的进出境商品目录"(简称目录)的商品;

② the exported food stuff shall be inspected for their sanitary purpose;

对出口商品的卫生检验;

③ the appraisal for the function and operation of the packing container for the exported dangerous goods;

对出口危险货物包装容器的性能鉴定和使用鉴定;

④ the inspection of the container and cabin's adaptability for the transportation of the perishable food stuff and the frozen food stuff;

对装运出口易腐烂变质食品、冷冻品的船舱、集装型等运输工具的适载检验;

⑤ the inspection on the imported and exported commodities which are required to be inspected by the inspection authorities according to the related international treaties;

对有关国际条约规定须经商检机构检验的进出口商品的检验;

⑥ the inspection of the imported and exported commodities which are required to be inspected according to other laws or administrative regulation and rules.

对其他法律、行政法规规定必须经商检机构检验的进出口商品的检验。

Section 2 Inspection Clause in Contract

第 2 节 合同中的商检条款

The inspection clauses cover the follows: time and place of inspection; inspection authority; inspection standards and methods; inspection certificate; re-inspection.

检验条款主要包括：检验时间、地点；检验机构；检验标准与方法；检验证书；商品复验。

1. Time and Place of Inspection 检验时间与地点

The inspection time and place refer to when and where to inspect the commodity, which is practically matter of whether the seller or the buyer is entitled to exercise the right of inspection, with the result as the evidence for the delivery and the acceptance of the goods. The confirmation of the inspection time and place means to confirm which party exerts the inspection right, that is to say, to confirm which party's inspection certificate is taken as the final inspection result. This problem, therefore, is often one of the main terms to be talked over and agreed upon during their business negotiation. In international trade, the following methods to stipulate time and place for commodity inspection are often employed.

何时何地检验关系到买卖双方的检验权。所谓检验权，是指买方或卖方有权对所交易的货物进行检验，其检验结果即作为交付与接收货物的依据。确定即检验的时间和地点，实际上就是确定买卖双方中的哪一方行使对货物的检验权，也就是确定检验结果以哪一方提供的检验证书为准。因此，检验的时间和地点通常都是外贸磋商过程中需要谈妥并列入合同中的重要条款之一。在国际贸易中，关于商品检验的时间和地点通常有以下几种规定方法。

(1) Inspection in Export Country 在出口国检验

① Shipping Quality and Quantity as Final 以离岸品质和数量为准

Under this provision, cargo inspection will be carried out before shipment from the port of loading by quality inspection authorities to issue quality and quantity certificates. The certificates will be the final evidence to determine the quality and quantity, and the buyer is not in a position to lodge with the seller a claim even though he finds out any discrepancy in the quality or quantity by inspection at the port of destination. Such a practice denies the buyer the right of reinsertion, and is undoubtedly beneficial to the seller. Here, to illustrate, a commodity inspection clause quoted from a sales contract is given as follows:

按此规定，货物在装运前由装运港的检验机构检验并出具品质数量检验证书，该证书将作为决定该批交货品质和数量的最后依据,即使货物在目的港的复验结果与此不符,买方也无权向卖方提出索赔。这种规定方法,实际上否定了买方的复验权,对卖方有利。合同中可规定如下:

"It is mutually agreed that the Certificate of Quality/Quantity issued by China Customs at the port of shipment shall be regarded as final and binding upon both parties."

"双方同意以装运港中国海关所签发的品质/数量检验证书作为最后依据,对双方具有约束力。"

② Manufacture's Quality as Final 以出厂品质为准

The goods are to be inspected only by the manufacture itself, which often benefits the manufacturer. Therefore, the buyer is generally reluctant to adopt this provision except some special goods.

以货物经过厂商自行检验通过的品质为准。这种规定方法对制造厂最为有利,所以除了少数特殊货物外,买方一般不愿意采用这一规定。

(2) Inspection in Import Country 在进口国检验

① Landed Quality and Quantity as Final 以到岸品质和数量为准

In this case, the quality and quantity of the commodity is to be inspected by the inspection authority at the port of destination after the goods are unloaded. The commodity inspection certificate thus issued is looked up as final. Should there be any discrepancy, which is not in conformity with the contract of sale, the seller, provided that the insurers or the carriers are supposed not to be liable for such discrepancies, is responsible for the reimbursement in case the buyer loges claims against him. Evidently, this practice denies the seller the right of insertion, and is advantageous to the buyer. Here, to illustrate, a commodity inspection clause quoted from a sales contract is given as follows:

按此规定,货物到达目的港卸货后,由目的地检验机构进行检验,其出具的商检证书就作为交货品质和数量的最后依据。如买方的检验结果与合同规定不符,除非是保险公司或承运人的责任,否则应由卖方负责赔偿。这种规定方法,实际上剥夺了卖方的检验权,对买方有利。合同中可规定如下:

"It is mutually agreed that the Certificate of Quality/Quantity issued by China Customs at the port of destination shall be regarded as final and binding upon both parties."

"双方同意以目的港中国海关所签发的品质/数量检验证书作为最后依据,对双方具有约束力。"

② Inspection of goods after the arrival of the destination as final 以货物达到目的地后的检验为准

When the buyer's place of business and commodities' selling place are located in the country's inland, in common practice, the buyer will send a notice to seller in advance to require the inspection time and place be extended to the final destination of the goods.

当买方的营业所在地点和货物的发售地点在进口国家的内陆时，按照习惯的做法，在事先通知卖方的情况下，买方可以要求将检验的时间和地点延伸到货物的最后目的地。

(3) Inspection in Export Country and Re-inspection in Import Country 出口国检验，进口国复验

Under this provision, the goods must be inspected before shipment by inspection authority at the loading port, and the inspection certificates will be presented to the bank for collecting payment. After the arrival of the goods at the port of destination, the buyer shall have the right to re-inspect, if the result does not conform to that stipulated in the contract, and prove that this discrepancy has existed before seller's delivery (i.e. before the risk is transferred from the seller to the buyer), the buyer has right to lodge claims with re-inspection certificates. This is very commonly used in foreign trade today, which acknowledges the inspection certificates provided by both parties. The following commodity inspection clause of this kind may often be found in a sales contract:

按照这样的规定，货物必须在装运前由装运港的检验机构进行检验，其检验证书将作为卖方向银行收取货款时提交的单据之一。而在货物运抵目的港卸货后，买方有复验权，如经复验发现货物不符合同规定，并证明这种不符是在卖方交货时(即货物风险由卖方转移到买方时)就已存在，买方可以凭复验证书向卖方提出异议和索赔。这种规定方法同时承认了买卖双方所提供的检验证书，被广为采用。合同中可规定如下：

"It is mutually agreed that the Inspection Certificate of Quality/Quantity (Weight) issued by China Customs at the port of shipment shall be part of the documents to be presented for negotiation under the relevant L/C. The Buyer shall have the right to reinspect the quality and quantity (weight) of the cargo. The reinspection fee shall be borne by the Buyers. Should the Quality and/or Quantity (Weight) found not in conformity with that of the contract, the Buyers are entitled to lodge with the Sellers a claim which should be supported by survey reports issued by a recognized surveyor approved by the Sellers. The claim, if any, shall be lodged within … days after arrival of the cargo at the port of destination."

"双方同意以装运港中国海关签发的品质/数量(重量)检验证书，作为信用证项下所提交单据的一部分。买方有权对货物的品质和数量(重量)进行复验。复验费用由买方负担。如发现品质和/数量(重量)与合同不符，买方有权向卖方索赔，但必须提供经卖方同意的公证机构出具的检验报告。索赔期限以货物到达目的港××天为限。"

(4) Quantity Inspection in Export Country and Quality Inspection in Import Country 出口国检验数量，进口国检验质量

It is also called "Shipping Quantity and Landed Quality as Final", which means that for the inspection of goods in large amount, in order to conciliate the conflict of the buyer and the seller on the inspection, the inspection on the quantity/weight and the quality are respectively carried out. That is to say, the inspection certificate of weight issued by the inspection authority at the loading port or place is taken as the final proof for the weight of the delivered goods, and the quality inspection certificate issued by the inspection authority at the destination port is taken as the final proof of the commodity quality.

它也被称为"以离岸数量到岸品质为准",是指在大宗商品交易的检验中,为了调和买卖双方在商品检验问题上存在的矛盾,常将商品的重量和品质检验分别进行,即以装运港或装运地验货后检验机构出具的重量检验证书,作为卖方所交货物重量的最后依据,以目的港或目的地检验机构出具的品质检验证书,作为商品品质的最后依据。

2. Inspection Authority 检验机构

(1) Official Inspection Authority 官方检验机构

The official inspection authorities generally focus on certain commodities such as food and medicines. FDA (U.S. Food and Drug Administration) is the most common one in practice. The official inspection authorities in China is China Customs.

官方的检验机构一般对特定的商品,如粮食、药品等进行检验,实务中最常见的是FDA,即美国食品药品监督管理局。我国的官方检验机构是中国海关。

(2) Private or Non-governmental Organizations(NGO)
民间私人或社团经营的非官方机构

Most of the commodity inspections are undertaken by non-governmental organizations, and these private inspection authorities have the legal status of a notary public. In common practice, the most famous of these authorities are SGS (Société Générale de Surveillance Holding S.A.), OMIC (Overseas Merchandise Inspection Co., Ltd), UL (Underwriters Laboratories), Lloyd's Surveyor, BV (Bureau Veritas) and so on.

大多数的商品检验是由民间机构承担,因而民间商检机构也具有了公证机构的法律地位。实务中常见的、比较有名的这些机构有瑞士的日内瓦通用鉴定公司(SGS)、日本海外货物检查株式会社(OMIC)、美国保险人实验室、英国劳合氏公证行(Lloyd's Surveyor)、法国船级社(BV)等。

(3) Some Testing Rooms, Laboratories owned by Enterprises or Factories
某些工厂或者企业设立的检测室、化验室等

3. Standards and Methods of Inspection 检验标准与方法

The inspection standards and methods are the measures and rules adopted for the inspected commodity and inspection process, which are the criteria to appraise and identity if the inspected commodity is complying with the related regulations and requirement. The inspection results are different for the same commodity inspected according to different standards. Therefore, it is better to specify in which way to inspect the goods in contract in order to avoid any dispute.

检验标准与方法是指检验机构从事检验工作在实体和程序方面所遵循的尺度和标准，是评定检验对象是否符合规定要求的准则。同一商品采用不同的标准可能会得出不同的结论，因此，最好在合同中明确规定用哪种方法进行检验，以免事后发生纠纷。

In the business of import and export, the inspection is made according to the following standards:

在进出口业务中，一般按以下检验标准进行：

(1) According to "Law of Inspection", all the imported and exported commodities listed in the catalogue must be inspected according to the governmental technical regulations; for the commodities which are not required by the governmental technical regulations, the inspection can be made in reference to the related standards of foreign countries, stipulated by national commodity inspection body.

根据《商检法》的规定，凡列入目录的进出口商品，按照国家技术规范的强制性要求进行检验；没有国家技术规范的强制性要求的，可以参照国家商检部门制定的国外有关标准进行检验。

(2) In the absence of the compulsory standards or other inspection standards specified in the Law and Regulations, the inspection shall be performed according to the standards agreed upon in the international trade contracts about the quality, specification, packing, and sampling inspection.

无强制性检验标准或其他法律法规制定的检验标准的，按合同中对品质、规格、包装、抽样检验的规定进行检验。

(3) In the process of inspection, if the standards specified in the Law and the Regulations are not consistent with those agreed upon by the seller and buyer in the sales contract, the inspection shall be conducted subject to the higher standard.

当法律法规制定的检验标准与合同规定的标准不一致时，按高的标准进行检验。

(4) If the inspection standards are not specified in the Law and the Regulations or the inspection standards are either not agreed upon or unclear in the contract, the inspection shall be conducted according to the standard of the manufacturing country, the import country, or the usual standard adopted internationally.

若既无法律法规制定的标准，合同中也未规定检验标准，一般按生产国标准、进口国标准，或按国际上已用标准；

4. Inspection Certificates 检验证书

Inspection statements issued by the commodity inspection authorities after the commodities have undergone inspection are called inspection certificates. Commodity inspection certificate plays the role of evidences for the transferring of goods between buyers and sellers, the settlement payment and processing of claims as well as customs clearance, tax paying and freight clearing.

检验证书是进出口商品经由商检机构检验、鉴定后出具的证明文件。商检证书起着公证证明的作用，是买卖双方交接货物、结算货款和处理索赔、理赔的主要依据，也是通关、纳税、结算运费的有效凭证。

(1) Inspection Certificate of Quality 品质检验证书

Inspection Certificate of Quality certifies the quality and specifications of commodities and is an effective document for payment settlement and imports of goods.

品质检验证书证明进出口商品的品质和规格等，是商品交货结汇和进口商品的有效凭证。

(2) Inspection Certificate of Weight or Quantity 重量或数量检验证书

Inspection Certificate of Weight or Quantity certifies the weight, quantity, length and area of commodities and is a valid document for goods delivery, payment settlement, issuing bill of lading, which is also a certificate for calculation of foreign taxation, freight and handling charges.

重量或数量检验证书证明进出口商品的重量、数量、长度、面积等，是商品交货结汇、签发提单的有效凭证，也是国外征税和计算运费、装卸货费用的证件。

(3) Sanitary Inspection Certificate 卫生证书

Sanitary Inspection Certificate is a document for animal products to prove that it is edible after quarantine. This kind of certificate is applied to those goods like sausages, canned, frozen fish, shrimps and eggs. They are valid identifications for goods delivery, customs clearance and bank's settlement.

卫生证书是证明可供人类食用的动物产品等经过卫生或检疫合格的证件。适用于肠衣、罐头、冻鱼、冻虾、蛋品等，是对外交货、银行结汇和通关验放的有效证件。

(4) Fumigation Inspection Certificate 熏蒸证书

Fumigation Inspection Certificate is to show the goods have been experienced fumigation, such as the grain, oilseeds, pulses, hides and other commodities, as well as the wooden packages and the filling materials of plant.

熏蒸证书是用于证明粮谷、油籽、豆类、皮张等商品，以及包装用的木材与植物性填充物等，已经过熏蒸灭虫的证书。

(5) Inspection Certificate on Damaged Cargo 残损证书

Inspection Certificate on Damaged Cargo is the certificate of damaged cargo. This kind of certificate applies to circumstances like imported goods' incompleteness, shortage, stain and damages. It is an effective certificate to be used by the consignee to claim the shipper, the carrier, the insurer or the other relevant responsible parties.

残损证书是证明进出口商品残损情况的证件。适用于进出口商品发生残、短、渍、毁等情况；可作为收货人向发货人、承运人或保险人等有关责任方提供的有效证件。

5. Re-inspection 复验

The re-inspection right of buyer is not compulsory, not the basic condition for the acceptance of goods, depending on the buyer's selection. The buyer must finish the re-inspection within a reasonable time if the re-inspection is needed. The reasonable time is regulated in the contract and shall be specified in the contract according to the specific property of the cargo.

买方对到货的复验权不是强制性的，也不是接收货物的前提条件，由买方自决，如进行复验，买方必须在合理的时间内完成。合理的期限由买卖双方在合同中规定。同时在合同中规定复验时间的长短，并根据货物性质的不同来规定具体时间。

Terminology 本章术语

1. discrepancy 差异、差别
2. quarantine 检疫
3. inspection certificate 检验证书
4. re-inspection 复验
5. inspection authority 检验机构
6. enforced legal inspection 法定检验
7. Law of the People's Republic of China on Import and Export Commodity Inspection 中华人民共和国进出口商品检验法

Exercises 本章练习

1. Please translate the following clause into Chinese. 请翻译以下条款。

It is mutually agreed that the Certificate of Quality and Weight (Quantity) issued by China Customs at the port/place of shipment shall be the part of documents to be presented for negotiation under the relevant L/C. The Buyer shall have the right reinspect the quality and weight (quantity) of the cargo. The reinspect fee will be borne by the buyer. Should quality and weight (quantity) be found not in conformity with that of the contract, the Buyers are entitled to lodge with the Sellers a claim which should be supported by survey reports issued by recognized surveyor approved by the Sellers. The claims, if any, shall be lodged within 30 days after arrival of cargo at the port/place of destination.

2. Why must there be the inspection clause in contracts for the international sale of goods? What does the inspection clause generally include?

外贸合同中为什么必须有商检条款？商检条款一般包括哪些内容？

3. How is it stipulated about the time and the place of inspection in the international trade?

在国际贸易中关于检验的时间和地点是怎样规定的？

Answers for Reference 参考答案

1. 双方一致同意卖方在交单议付时应该出具由中国海关在装运港(地)签发的重量和品质证书作为结汇单据之一。买方在收到货物以后也有对货物的重量(数量)和品质重新检验的权利，复验费由买方承担。如果重新检验货物的质量或(和)数量不符合合同约定，买方通过提交经过卖方确认的商检结构出具的检验报告向卖方提出索赔，索赔需要在货物达到目的港/地 30 天内提出。

2. It is quite often the case that export and import goods are subject to damage or shortage in transit because of rough handling in loading and unloading, and the long distance they are traveling. Besides, the quality of the goods received by the buyer may not be in conformity with the contract of sale. All these will surely lead to disputes, and it is necessary to find out who is the right party responsible for that. If the commodity has been inspected by the authoritative specialized import and export commodities inspection authority and a commodity inspection certificate issued, the certificate will serve to ascertain where the trouble lies and who is to blame. Commodity inspection is one of key steps during the sales of goods in international trade, which is the extension of the quality clause of contract and the warranty of it as well.

进出口货物需要经过长途运输，多次装卸，到货可能出现与合同不符的情况，容易引起有关方面的争议。为了避免争议的发生，以及发生争议后便于分清责任和进行处理，就需要有一个由具有权威性的、专门的进出口商品检验机构负责对货物进行检验或鉴定。检验机构检验或鉴定后出具相应的检验证书，作为买卖双方交接货物、支付货款和进行索赔、理赔的重要依据。因此，商品检验是国际贸易中买卖双方交接货物的重要环节之一，是合同中品质条款的延续和保障。

The inspection clauses cover the follows: time and place of inspection; inspection authority; inspection standards and methods; inspection certificate; re-inspection.

检验条款主要包括：检验时间、地点；检验机构；检验标准与方法；检验证书；商品复验。

3. In international trade, the following methods to stipulate time and place for commodity

inspection are often employed.

在国际贸易中，关于商品检验的时间和地点通常有以下几种规定方法。

(1) Inspection in Export Country 在出口国检验

① Shipping Quality and Quantity as Final 以离岸品质和数量为准

② Manufacture's Quality as Final 以出厂品质为准

(2) Inspection in Import Country 在进口国检验

① Landed Quality and Quantity as Final 以到岸品质和数量为准

② Inspection of goods after the arrival of the destination as final 以货物达到目的地后的检验为准

(3) Inspection in Export Country and Re-inspection in Import Country 出口国检验，进口国复验

(4) Quantity Inspection in Export Country and Quality Inspection in Import Country 出口国检验数量，进口国检验质量

Chapter 8　Settlement of Trade Disputes

第 8 章　贸易争议的解决

Section 1　Dispute and Claim

第 1 节　争议与索赔

For the claim concerning the international cargo trade, there are three kinds of claims, namely, the claim regarding the transaction of cargo, the claim regarding the transportation and the claim regarding the insurance. In this section, we are talking about the first type, namely, the claim about the transaction of cargo.

涉及国际货物买卖的索赔，一般有三种情况，即货物买卖索赔、运输索赔和保险索赔。本节讲述的是第一种情况，即货物买卖的索赔。

1. Dispute　争议

Disputes arise when one party thinks that the other party fails to perform all or part of the contract. The main disputes are whether the contract is established, breach of contract or not, responsibility of breaches and results, etc. In international trade, there are many reasons causing disputes which can be classified into the following three.

争议是指交易的一方认为另一方未能全部或部分履行合同规定的责任而引起的业务纠纷。争议的内容主要是关于合同是否成立、是否构成违约、违约的责任与后果等。在国际贸易中，引起争议的原因很多，大致可归纳为以下三种情况。

(1) Breach of Contract by the Seller　卖方违约

Breach of contract by the seller means non-performance or incomplete performance of the contract by the seller. A seller may breach a contract in such cases as inferior quality or discrepancy in quality, deficient or poor packing, insufficient quantity, delayed delivery or the documents presented are not in consistency with each other etc.

卖方违约是指卖方未能全部或部分履约。例如，不按合同规定的时间、品质、数量、包装交货或单证不符等。

(2) Breach of Contract by the Buyer 买方违约

A buyer may breach a contract if he fails to open or delay to open L/C, refuses to pay or fails to gain documents against payment, rejecting the goods unreasonably, does not dispatch a vessel to carry the goods on time under FOB term, etc.

买方不开或缓开信用证，不付款或不按时付款赎单，无理拒收货物，在 FOB 条件下未能及时安排货船装货等。

(3) Stipulation of the Contract are Unclear 合同规定不明确

One party or both parties may breach a contract resulting in disputes if both parties have misunderstanding or different explanation of the clauses in the contract due to some unclear clause, such as "prompt shipment" "quantity about 100 M/T" "port of destination China main ports" etc.

如"立即装运""大约 100 公吨""目的港中国主要港口"之类不明确的合同条款，致使双方理解或解释不统一，造成一方或双方违约，引起纠纷。

According to the nature of the breach of contract, there are two kinds of reasons leading to the disputes, one kind of dispute is caused by the involving party's breach of a contract on purpose; the other kind of dispute is due to neglect, fault on the business operation resulting in the breach. In addition, the neglect on the obligation of the contract also results in the breach of contract and the disputes.

从违约性质看，争议产生的原因，一是当事人一方故意行为导致违约而引起争议；二是由于当事人一方的疏忽、过失或业务生疏导致违约而引起争议。此外对合同义务的重视不足，往往也是导致违约、发生纠纷的原因在之一。

2. Claim 索赔

Claim can be defined as a demand made upon a person or persons for payment on account of a loss sustained through negligence. In international trade, if the buyer or the seller does not fulfill or wholly fulfill the contract, his act amounts to breach of the contract and the injured party can file a claim.

索赔是指买卖合同的一方当事人因另一方当事人违约致使其遭受损失而向另一方当事人提出要求损害赔偿的行为。国际贸易业务过程中，若一方未能全部或部分履约，则另一方可就其违约行为提出索赔。

3. Claim Clauses in Contract 合同中的索赔条款

There are two kinds of claim clauses in sales contract: one is the discrepancy and claim clause, the other one is penalty clause. Generally speaking, there is only the discrepancy and claim clause in most of sales contracts, but in the contracts involving a large quantity or concerning machinery equipment, there are dispute and claim clause as well as penalty clause.

进出口合同中的索赔条款有两种规定方式：一种是异议和索赔条款，另一种是罚金条款。一般在买卖合同中，多数只订立异议和索赔条款，只有在买卖大宗商品和机械设备一类商品的合同中，除订明异议和索赔条款外，再另订罚金条款。

(1) Discrepancy and Claim Clause 异议与索赔条款

The discrepancy and claim clause is generally stipulated in case the quality, quantity or packing of the goods delivered by the seller is not in conformity with the relevant contract provisions. It mainly include the claim foundation, time limitation, the ways to compensate for the loss and the compensation sum etc.. Normally, a discrepancy and claim clause in a contract goes as follows:

异议和索赔条款一般是针对卖方交货质量、数量或包装不符合规定而订立的，主要包括索赔依据、索赔期限、赔偿方法和赔偿金额等。例如：

In case of quality discrepancy, claim should be filed by the Buyers within 30 days after the arrival of the goods at the port of destination, while for quantity discrepancy, claim should be filed by the Buyers within 15 days after the arrival of the goods at port of destination. In all cases, claims must be accompanied by survey report of recognized public surveyors agreed to by the Sellers. Should the responsibility of the subject under claim be found to rest on the part of the Sellers, the Sellers shall, within 20 days after receipt of the claim, send his reply to the Buyers together with suggestion for settlement.

品质异议需于货到目的港之日起 30 天内提出，数量异议需于货到目的港之日起 15 天内提出，但均需提供经卖方同意的出证行的检验证明，如责任属于卖方，卖方于收到异议 20 天内答复买方并提出处理意见。

As this clause is closely related to the inspection clause, they can be combined as the inspection & claim clause in some contracts.

由于这一条款与检验条款有密切联系，有的合同将这两种条款结合起来订立，成为"检验与索赔条款"。

① Claim Foundation 索赔依据

Claim foundation is the proofs for lodging a claim, mainly covering the necessary proofs or certificates for claims and the relevant certificate issuing authorities. It includes legal proof and fact proof. The former refers to the trade contract and the related national laws and regulations while the latter refers to the facts and the written evidence of the breach to verify the truth of the breach.

索赔依据主要指索赔时需具备的证据及出证机构，具体包括法律依据和事实依据两个方面。前者是指贸易合同和有关的国家法律规定；后者是指违约的事实真相及其书面证明，以证实违约的真实性。

② Time Limitation 索赔期限

Time limitation is the effective period for filing a claim, which means the period in which the claimant can make a claim against the party in breach. Claims beyond the time limitation can be refused by the party in breach. Generally speaking, the time limitation shall be dependent on the nature of the commodity and the inspection time etc.. In order to avoid extra obligation undertaken by the seller, the stipulated claim period shall not be too long except for some special commodities such a mechanical equipment; and to assure the time for buyers to file a claim, the stipulated claim period shall not be too short either.

索赔期限是指索赔方向违约方提出索赔的有效期限，逾期索赔，违约方可以不予受理。一般来说，索赔期限要根据商品性质及检验所需时间多少等因素而定。除一些性能特殊的产品(如机械设备)外，索赔期限一般不宜过长，以免使卖方承担过重的责任；也不宜规定得太短，以免使买方无法行使索赔权。

③ Ways to compensate for the loss and the compensation sum 赔偿方法和赔偿金额

The ways of settling claims and the compensation sum will be stipulated in the contract in general. It is very difficult to estimate the exact compensation sum and the losses caused prior to the breach of contract, so there in no specific stipulation about the compensation sum.

赔偿方法和赔偿金额通常在合同中只做一般规定。因为违约的情况比较复杂，究竟在哪些业务环节上违约和违约的程度如何等，订约时难以预计，因此对于违约的赔偿金额也难以预知，所以在合同中不做具体规定。

Discrepancy and Claim Clause is a restriction for the seller to fulfill the contract as well as for the buyer. No matter which party is in the breach of contract, the other party suffering the losses has the right to make a claim for compensation against the party in breach.

异议和索赔条款不仅是约束卖方履行合同义务条款，同时也对买方起约束作用。不论何方违约，受害方都有权向违约方提出索赔。

(2) Penalty Clause 罚金条款

The penalty clause is applicable to the situations including the delayed delivery of goods, the deferred issuance of L/C, the delayed payment etc.. Under this clause, the party who fails to carry out the contract shall pay a certain sum of money to the other party in loss as the compensation. The penalty is also called as the fine for the breach of contract.

罚金条款适用于延期交货、拖延开立信用证、拖欠货款等情况。当一方未履约时，应向对方支付一定数额的约定金额，以补偿对方的损失。罚金亦称"违约金"或"罚则"。

In the law of Contract of our country, it is stipulated about the penalty as follows: The parties involved may agree in the contract, that one party shall pay penalty to the other party when he is in breach of contract; or the both parties agree the way of calculating the compensation sum for the losses arising from the breach. However, when the agreed penalty sum is much lower or higher than the losses resulting from the breach of contract, the party involved may ask the court or the arbitration to make a proper increase or reduction. Meanwhile, it is stipulated that, the party involved whoever pays the penalty for the delayed fulfillment of the contract shall continue to fulfill the contract after paying the penalty.

《中华人民共和国合同法》对违约金的规定：当事人可以在合同中约定，一方违约时，向对方支付违约金；也可以约定因违约产生的损失赔偿额的计算方法。但约定的违约金低于或过分高于违反合同所造成的损失，当事人可以请求法院或者仲裁机构予以增加或适当减少。我国法律还规定，当事人就延迟履行约定交纳违约金的，违约方支付违约金后，还应当履行债务。

The penalty clause aimed at delayed delivery by the seller, for example, reads as follows:
卖方延期交货的罚金条款举例如下：

Should the Sellers fail to make delivery on time as stipulated in the contract, the Buyers shall agree to postpone the delivery on the condition that the Sellers agree to pay a penalty which shall be deducted by the paying bank from the payment under negotiation, or by the Buyers direct at the time of payment. The rate of penalty is charged at 0.5% of the total value of the goods whose delivery has been delayed for every seven days, odd days less than seven days should be counted as seven days. But the total amount of penalty, however, shall not exceed 5% of the total value of the goods involved in the late delivery. In case the Sellers fail to make delivery ten weeks later than the time of shipment stipulated in the contract, the Buyers shall have the right to cancel the contract and the Sellers, in spite of the cancellation, shall still pay the aforesaid penalty to the Buyers without delay.

如卖方不能按合同规定的时间交货，在卖方同意由付款银行在议付货款中扣除罚金或由买方于支付货款时直接扣除罚金的条件下，买方应同意延期交货。罚金率按每七天收取延期交货部分总值的 0.5%。如卖方延期交货超过合同规定期限十周时，买方有权撤销合同，但卖方仍应不延迟地按上述规定向买方支付罚金。

The following is the penalty clause aimed at delayed establishment of L/C by the buyer.
买方延期开立信用证的罚金条款举例如下：

Should the Buyers for its own sake fail to open the letter of credit on time stipulated in the contract, the Buyers shall pay a penalty to the Sellers. The penalty shall be charged at the rate of … % of the amount of the Letter of Credit for every … days of delay in opening the Letter of Credit, however, the penalty shall not exceed … % of the total value of the Letter of Credit which the Buyers should have opened. Any fractional days less than … days shall be deemed to be … days for the calculation of penalty. The penalty shall be the sole compensation for the damage caused by such delay.

买方因自身原因不能按合同规定的时间开立信用证，应向卖方支付罚金。罚金按迟开证每…天收取信用证金额的…%，不足…天者按…天者计算，但罚金不超过买方应开信用证金额的…%。该罚金仅作为因迟开信用证引起的损失赔偿。

Section 2　Disputes Settlement

第2节　纠纷解决

When a trade conflict occurs, the parties involved often try to resolve it through amicable negotiations to maintain the goodwill and friendly business relations between them. In case no settlement can be reached through negotiation, the case shall then be settled through conciliation, arbitration or even litigation depending on different situations.

实际业务中，当发生争议时，为维护友好的业务关系，双方当事人一般都愿意通过友好协商达成和解的方式解决。如协商得不到解决时，则分别视情况而采取通过第三者调解、提交仲裁机构仲裁或进行司法诉等方式进行处理。

1. Amicable Negotiation 协商解决

When disputes arise in international trade, the two parties often resolve the disputes through amicable negotiations to maintain the goodwill and friendly business relations between them. In some contracts there is the clause of Settlement of Claims as follows:

买卖双方遇有争议时，一般都愿意协商解决，维护友好的业务关系。有的合同会订立索赔处理条款如下：

Settlement of claims:

In case of the Sellers are liable for the nonconformity of the goods with the contract and a claim is made by the Buyers within the period of claim or the period of quality guarantee as stipulated in Clause … and … of this Contract the Sellers shall settle the claim upon the agreement of the Buyers in the following ways:

a. Agree to the rejection of the goods and refund to the Buyers the value of the rejected goods in the same currency as contracted herein, and bear all direct losses and expenses incurred from the rejection, including interest, banking charges, freight, insurance premium, inspection charges, storage, stevedore charges and all other necessary expenses required for the custody and protection of the rejected goods.

b. Devaluate the goods according to the degree of inferiority, extent of damage and amount of losses suffered by the Buyers.

c. Replace the defective goods with new ones which conform to the specifications, quality and performance as stipulated in this contract, and bear all expenses incurred to and direct losses sustained by the Buyers. The Sellers shall, at the same time, guarantee the quality of the replaced goods for a further period of … months according to Clause … of this contract.

索赔处理：

如货物不符合本合同规定应由卖方负责，同时买方按照本合同第××条和第××条的规定在索赔期限或质量保证期限内提出索赔者，卖方在取得买方同意后，应按下列方式理赔：

(甲)同意买方退货，并将退货金额以成交原币偿还买方，并负担因退货而发生的一切直接损失和费用，包括利息、银行费用、运费、保险费、商检费、仓租、码头装卸费以及为保管退货而发生的一切其他必要费用。

(乙)按照货物的次劣程度、损坏的范围和买方所遭受的损失，将货物贬值。

(丙)调换有瑕疵的货物，换货必须全新合并符合本合同规定的规格、质量和性能，卖方并负担因此而产生的一切费用和买方遭受的一切直接损失。对换货的质量，卖方仍应按本合同第××条，保证××个月。

2. Conciliation 第三方调解解决

It's called conciliation when the parties involved seek amicable settlement through a third party or a trade authority. The disputes being so dealt with by conciliation can be settled in an amicable way, where goodwill and friendly feelings between the disputing parties are so maintained as to least affect their future business relationship. If both parties agree to solicit the help of a third party, this third party can be any impartial party or international chamber of commerce or government trade authority. A negotiation merely facilitates negotiation, no award or opinion or the merits of the disputes are given. For the conciliation to arrive at a satisfactory result, both sides involved in the conflict have to be prepared to make concessions.

由第三方出面从中调停，促进双方当事人达成和解，这种做法习惯称为调解。第三方协调解决争议气氛和善、友好，有利于双方今后业务的进一步发展。调解员可以是中立的第三方、国际商会或政府外贸部门。调解员只是促成双方协商解决，不对争议作任何评论或裁决。若寻求第三方调解解决，为了达成和解，争议双方均需做出让步。

3. Arbitration 仲裁解决

When either party is reluctant to make concessions or is in disagreement during negotiation, arbitration becomes an alternative solution to make a settlement.

如双方当事人经协商或调解，都不肯做出让步达成和解协议，则可选择仲裁的方式来解决争议。

(1) The Definition of Arbitration 仲裁的定义

The arbitration means that the two parties, before or after the disputes arise, reach a written agreement that they will submit the disputes which cannot be settled through amicable negotiations to a third party for arbitration. Arbitration provides an economic, expeditious and informal remedy for settlement of disputes. Both parties shall settle the disputes complying with the result of arbitration as the arbitration result has legally binding force. Thus, arbitration is the most suitable way to settle the disputes incurred in international trade.

所谓仲裁，又称公断，是指买卖双方在争议发生之前或发生之后，签订书面协议，自愿将争议提交双方所同意的第三者予以裁决，以解决争议的一种方式。仲裁程序费用较少，处理问题迅速、气氛好，而且仲裁裁决具有法律约束力，当事人双方必须遵照执行。正因如此，通过仲裁来解决对外贸易争议已称为当前国际贸易中普遍采用的方式。

(2) The Characteristics of Arbitration 仲裁的特点

Arbitration is different from litigation in following aspects:

仲裁与诉讼方式相比，具有以下特点：

① An arbitral body composing of dignitaries or experts in the trade field is set to settle trade disputes, neither a governmental power nor with a coercive jurisdiction. The parties involved can appoint one party's own arbitrator, and the third one will be appointed by the arbitration institution. Litigation has jurisdiction and litigation organization, the court, is official. The judges are appointed by the government.

受理争议的仲裁机构属于由贸易届的知名人士或专家组成的、为解决贸易纠纷而设立的民间组织，不是国家政权机关，不具有强制管辖权。仲裁的双方当事人有权各指定一名仲裁员，另外由仲裁机构指定一名首席仲裁员组成仲裁庭审理案件。诉讼具有管辖权，诉讼机构法院是国家机构，法官由国家任命，不能由诉讼当事人选定。

② The settlement of the case is based on the will of both parties involved. The parties involved shall sign an arbitral agreement before resorting to arbitration. The settlement of a case is in accordance with the arbitration agreement concluded by both parties, excluding the possibility of resorting to the litigation and the jurisdiction of the court for the disputes. At the same time, the arbitral body and the concerned arbitrators are granted the jurisdiction relating to the case.

仲裁是建立在双方自愿的基础上的。当事人通过仲裁解决争议时，必须先签订仲裁协议。仲裁机构或仲裁员审理案件，必须以争议双方同意的仲裁协议为依据，这就排除了争议双方去法院诉讼的可能，排除了法院对有关争议的管辖权，同时也使仲裁机构和仲裁员获得了有关争议案件的管辖权。

③ The arbitral award is final and binding upon both parties. Neither party may bring a suit before a law court or make a request to any other organization for revising the arbitral award. But if one party refuses to obey the award, the other can ask a court to enforce the implementation of the award. While settling disputes through litigation, the part not satisfied with the litigation award is allowed to lodge an appeal.

仲裁裁决一般是终局的，即裁决做出后，当事人不能上诉。如有一方拒绝执行，可要求法院强制执行。诉讼方式下，如不服，允许上诉。

④ Compared with litigation, the procedures of arbitration are simple, settling the disputes more quickly, with a low cost.

与诉讼相比，仲裁程序比较简单，处理问题比较迅速及时，费用也较为低廉。

(3) Arbitration Clause in Contract 合同中的仲裁条款

Arbitration clauses in the contract will usually include the following terms:

合同中的仲裁条款一般包括以下内容

① Arbitration Place 仲裁地点

The arbitration place is the main content and the key element of an arbitration clause since the arbitration place generally determines the arbitration rules and the relevant laws which differ in their interpretations in respect of the rights and obligations of the parties involved from country to country. The selection and arrangement of arbitration place in international practice are generally in the following ways: the country of buyer, the country of seller, the third country, the country of defendant, the country of complaint, the location of the goods, etc..

仲裁地点是仲裁条款的主要内容，是一个关键问题。在什么地点仲裁就适用哪个国家的仲裁规则或有关法律，而各国的仲裁规则或有关法律对双方当事人的权利、义务的解释会有差异。国际上对仲裁地点的选择与安排，一般有以下几种情况：在买方所在国、在卖方所在国、在第三国、在被告所在国、在原告所在国、在货物所在地等进行仲裁。

When a dispute in international trade arises, the both parties hope the arbitration is made in its own country as the arbitration is usually conducted according to the local law. However, upon the need of business, both parties usually agree to adopt the arbitration rules of the country of the defendant or the third country.

发生贸易纠纷时，买卖双方都希望采用在本国仲裁的规定，因为在本国仲裁可按本国法律处理和进行裁决；但是，根据义务需要，买卖双方往往同意采用在被告所在国或第三国仲裁的规定。

② Arbitration Body 仲裁机构

The arbitration body can be a permanent arbitration body, such as the Arbitration Court of International Chamber of Commerce (ICC), the London Court of Arbitration, and American Arbitration Association, or it may be a temporary organized body for specific arbitration and which is automatically dismissed when the arbitration is over. Under such a circumstance, the two parties should make it clear in the arbitration clause in respect of manner of arbitration, number of arbitrators, etc..

目前国际上受理贸易争议的仲裁机构一般有两种形式：一是常设仲裁机构，如国际商会仲裁院、伦敦仲裁院、美国仲裁协会等；二是临时性仲裁机构或仲裁庭。临时性仲裁机构或仲裁庭是为解决特殊的贸易争议临时组成的，案件处理完毕即自动解散。在这种情况下，双方当事人应在仲裁条款中就双方指定的仲裁员的人数、办法等作明确规定。

In our country, the China International Economic and Trade Arbitration Commission (CIETAC) in Beijing and its Sub-Commissions in Shenzhen, Shanghai, Tianjin, Chongqing, Hangzhou, Wuhan, Fuzhou, Xi'an, Nanjing, Chengdu and Jinan accept arbitration cases according to arbitration rules and regulations, and use the unified Arbitration Rules and panel of arbitrators.

我国的常设仲裁机构是中国国际经济贸易仲裁委员会(英文简称CIETAC，中文简称"贸仲委"）。贸仲委设在北京，并在深圳、上海、天津、重庆、杭州、武汉、福州、西安、南京、成都、济南分别设有分会。贸仲委及其分会是一个统一的仲裁委员会，适用相同的《仲裁规则》和《仲裁员名册》。

③ Applicable Arbitration Rules 仲裁规则的适用

The country where the arbitration is going to be made and the relevant applicable arbitration rules should be made clear in the sales contract. If Chinese arbitration rules are applicable, then the Chinese International Economic and Trade Arbitration Commission Rules shall apply. It should be noted that arbitration rules do not always go with the arbitration place. According to the usual international practice of arbitration, the arbitration rules in the arbitration place shall in principle apply, but it is legal for the parties involved to agree in their contract that the arbitration rules of the arbitration organization in other country (regional), other than the arbitration rules of the country where the arbitration is going to be made, shall apply.

在买卖合同中，应注明进行仲裁的所在国以及适用的仲裁规则。适用我国的仲裁规则，是指适用《中国国际经济贸易仲裁委员会仲裁规则》。应注意，所采用的仲裁规则与仲裁地并非绝对一致，按国际仲裁的一般做法，原则上采用仲裁所在地的仲裁规则，但有的法律也允许双方当事人在合同中约定，采用仲裁地点以外的其他国家(地区)仲裁机构的仲裁规则进行仲裁。

④ Arbitration Award 仲裁裁决

The arbitral award is usually final. But it is still important to stipulate in the contract that: "The arbitration award is final and shall have binding force upon the two parties."

仲裁裁决一般是终局的。但仍应规定：仲裁裁决是终局的，对双方有约束力。

(4) Example of Arbitration Clauses 仲裁条款实例

The following are some examples of arbitration clauses in the contract of our import and export business.

以下是我国进出口合同中仲裁条款实例。

① Arbitration in Our Country 规定在我国仲裁

Any dispute arising from or in connection with this Contract shall be submitted to China International Economic and Trade Arbitration Commission for arbitration which shall be conducted in accordance with the Commission's arbitration rules in effect at the time of applying for arbitration. The arbitration award is final and binding upon both parties.

凡因本合同引起的或与本合同有关的任何争议，均应提交中国国际经济贸易仲裁委员会，按照申请仲裁时该会现行有效的仲裁规则进行仲裁。仲裁裁决是终局的，对双方均有约束力。

② Arbitration in the Country of the Defendant 规定在被诉人所在国仲裁

All disputes arising out of the performance of, or relating to this contract, shall be settled amicably through friendly negotiation. In case no settlement can be reached through negotiation, the case shall then be submitted for arbitration. The location of arbitration shall be in the country of the domicile of the defendant. If in China, the arbitration shall be conducted by the China International Economic and Trade Arbitration Commission in accordance with its rules of arbitration. If in …, the arbitration shall be conducted by … in accordance with its rules of arbitration. The arbitral award is final and binding upon both parties.

凡因执行本合同所发生的或与本合同有关的一切争议，双方应通过友好协商解决；如果协商不能解决，应提交仲裁。仲裁在被诉人所在国进行。如在中国，则由中国国际经济贸易仲裁委员会根据该会仲裁规则进行仲裁。如在××(国家)，由××(仲裁机构)根据该机构仲裁规则进行仲裁。仲裁裁决是终局的，对双方都有约束力。

③ Arbitration in a third Country agreed by Both Parties 规定在双方同意的第三国仲裁

Any dispute, controversy or claim arising out of or relating to this contract, or the breach, termination or invalidity thereof, shall be settled amicably through negotiation. In case no settlement can be reached through negotiation, the case shall then be submitted to … for arbitration, in accordance with its Rules of Arbitration. The arbitral award is final and binding upon both parties.

由于本合同或者由于违背本合同、终止本合同或者合同无效而发生的或与此有关的任何争端、争议或要求，双方应通过友好协商解决；如果协商不能解决，应提交如在××(国)、××(地)××(仲裁机构)，根据该仲裁机构的仲裁程序规则进行仲裁。仲裁裁决是终局的，对双方都有约束力。

4. Litigation 诉讼解决

Litigation is probably the last resort with which to settle disputes because the procedures for a lawsuit are complicated and often take a long time to handle the case. In addition, high cost and expenses involved in a lawsuit, and tense and unfriendly atmosphere between the parties are other demerits of litigation. Not like arbitration where an agreement to submit to arbitration should first of all be agreed upon by both parties, the party who wishes to make a claim at a court may do so without the agreement of the opposite party. Further, unlike arbitrators, who are chosen by the plaintiff and defendant, judges are public officers, appointed by the government.

诉讼一般是解决争议的最后选择,因为通过法院诉讼所花时间一般较长,断案较难,所需费用较高,且诉讼时双方处于原告和被告的对峙位置,气氛较紧张。仲裁是以双方当事人自愿为基础的,而一方当事人向法院提出诉讼无须征得另一方当事人的同意。另外,仲裁员可以由双方当事人自选定,而法官是政府官员,由国家任命。

Section 3　Force Majeure

第3节　不可抗力

1. Definition of Force Majeure　不可抗力的含义

Force Majeure, also called Act of God, refers to an event that can neither be anticipated nor be preventable, avoidable and controllable after the conclusion of the contract. It does not result from the fault or neglect of the parties involved, leading to the failure or the delay of the fulfillment of contract; the party who fails or delays to fulfill the contract due to such event can be free from the liabilities, or to be given an option of terminating the contract or postponing the performance of the contract.

不可抗力又称人力不可抗力。它是指在买卖合同签订后,不是由于合同当事人的过失或疏忽,而是由于发生了合同当事人无法预见、无法预防、无法避免和无法控制的事件,以致不能履行合同或不能如期履行合同,发生意外事件的一方可以免除履行合同的责任或推迟履行合同。

2. Force Majeure Clause in Contract　合同中的不可抗力条款

Force majeure clause is an escape clause in a contract, and a legal principle as well. In United Nations Convention on Contracts for the International Sales of Goods of 1980, the exemption is regulated as follows: "A party is not liable for a failure to perform any of its obligation if it proves that the failure was due to an impediment beyond its control and that it could not reasonably expect to have taken the impediment into account at the time of the conclusion of the contract or have avoided or have overcome it or the consequence of it." The Convention has pointed out that the party who fails to perform the contract due to the occurrence of an impediment beyond his control, which cannot be expected, avoided or overcome, can be free from the liability.

不可抗力是合同中的一项免责条款，也是一项法律原则。1980年《联合国国际货物销售合同公约》在其免责一节中做了如下规定："如果他(指当事人)能证明此种不履行义务是由于某种非他所能控制的障碍，而且对于这种障碍没有理由预期他在订立合同时能考虑到或能避免或能克服它或它的后果。"该《公约》指明了一方当事人不能履行义务，是由于发生了他不能控制的障碍，而且这种障碍在订约时是无法预见、避免或克服的，可予以免责。

With a view to avoiding the unnecessary disputes due to a Force Majeure event, and to preventing the arbitrary explanation of the Force Majeure event, unreasonable requirement proposed by the other party, it is very necessary to make a Force Majeure clause in a contract, specifying the scope, principle, and settlement of the Force Majeure, notification and proof of Force Majeure events clearly so as to the execution of the contract.

为避免因发生不可抗力事件而引起不必要的纠纷，防止合同当事人对发生不可抗力事件的性质、范围做任意的解释，或提出不合理的要求，或无理拒绝对方的合理要求，故有必要在合同中订立不可抗力条款，明确规定不可抗力的范围、处理原则和处理办法，不可抗力发生后通知对方的期限和方法，以及出具证明文件的机构等，以利于合同的履行。

(1) Content of Force Majeure Clause 不可抗力条款的内容

① Scope of Force Majeure 不可抗力的范围

Typically, Force Majeure clauses are usually applicable to performance failures caused by natural disasters such as flood, fire, ice damage, storm, heavy snow, earthquake and social disasters such as war, strike, the governmental ban, etc.. The definitions of a Force Majeure event in different laws and rules are not explanatorily unified, nor its descriptions. In the US, Force Majeure is limited to natural disasters and social disasters are excluded. The Contingency Clause is used instead of the Force Majeure Clause in their contracts. Therefore, it is very necessary to specify the scope of Force Majeure in a contract.

导致不可抗力主要有自然原因如水灾、火灾、冰灾、暴风雨、大雪、地震和社会原因如战争、罢工、政府禁令等。不同法律、法规对不可抗力的确切含义在解释上并不统一，叫法也不一致。如在美国，习惯认为"不可抗力"事故仅指由于自然力量所引起的以外事故，而不包括由于社会力量引起的意外事故。故美国的贸易合同中往往使用"意外事故条款"，不使用"不可抗力"。因此，在合同中明确不可抗力的具体范围非常有必要。

② Settlement of Force Majeure Events 不可抗力事件的处理

There are two kinds of legal consequences arising from a force majeure event: termination of the contract and postponement of the contract fulfillment. The adoption of the settlement ways is dependent on the effect of the force majeure event.

不可抗力引起的法律后果有两种：解除合同和延期履行合同。究竟何时可不履约，何时只能延迟履约，需视不可抗力事件对履行合同的影响程度。

③ Notification and Proof of Force Majeure Events 不可抗力事件的通知和证明

In case of a force majeure event, the party seeking to use the clause of force majeure has a duty to inform the other party promptly. A force majeure event also should be verified by a certificate that attests such an event. The party who receives the notification and supporting document about the force majeure event from the other party shall reply promptly as required. For example, one party shall notify the other party by fax or email and furnish the details and the effect of the event or events within 15 days by registered airmail with the documents attesting such an event or events.

原则上，发生不可抗力事件的一方要及时通知另一方，同时出具证明文件。一方收到另一方关于不可抗力事故的通知和证明文件后，应按规定及时答复对方。例如："一方遭受不可抗力事故后，应以传真或电子邮件通知对方，并应在15天内以航空挂号信提供事故的详情及影响履行程度的证明文件。"

(2) Ways of Stipulating Force Majeure Clause 不可抗力条款的表述方法

① In a General Way 概括式

"The Sellers shall not be liable for delay in shipment or non-delivery of the goods due to Force Majeure events, which might occur during the process of manufacturing or in the course of loading or transit. The Sellers shall notify the Buyers and send by airmail a certificate of accident issued by the competent Government Authorities where the accident occurs as thereof within 14 days of the certificate. Under such circumstance, the Sellers, however, are still under the obligation to take all necessary measure to hasten the delivery of the goods. In case the accident lasts for more than 10 weeks, the Buyers shall have the right to cancel the Contract"

"凡在制造或装船运输过程中，因不可抗力事件，致使卖方推迟或不能交货时，卖方可不负责任。但发生上述事件时，卖方应立即通知买方，并在14天内，给买方航寄一份由主管政府当局颁发的事件证明书。在此情况下，卖方仍有责任采取一切必要措施加快交货，如事件延续10周以上，买方有权撤销合同。"

The above stipulation is only stating Force Majeure events in general way with words "due to Force Majeure events". In this way, the specific contents and scope of Force Majeure events are not mentioned and listed in the clause. It is hard to be taken as the proof for disputes settlement, likely being misunderstood or used on purpose by the other party; the stipulation is so ambiguous that it can be only explained by the judicial institutes according to the suggestions of the parties involved without proper standards, not beneficial to the settlement of the disputes.

上述规定只笼统地指出"由于不可抗力的原因"，至于不可抗力的具体内容和范围如何，并未予以说明，难以作为解决问题的证据，也容易被对方曲解、利用；同时由于这种规定过分空泛，缺乏确定含义，一旦发生争议而诉诸司法机构时，该机构也仅能凭当事人的意见进行解释，任意性较大，不利于问题的正确解决。

② In a Way of Listing 列举式

"If the shipment of the contracted goods prevented or delayed in whole or in part by reason of war, earthquake, flood, fire, storm, heavy snow, the Sellers shall not be liable for non-shipment or late shipment of the goods or non-performance of this contract. However, the Sellers shall notify the Buyers by cable or by telex and furnish the latter within 15 days by registered airmail with a certificate issued by the China Council for the Promotion of International Trade attesting such event or events."

"由于战争、地震、火灾、水灾、暴风雪的原因，致使卖方不能全部或部分装运或延迟装运合同货物，卖方对于这种不能装运或迟延装运本合同货物不负责任。但卖方需用电报或电传通知买方，并需在15天以内以航空挂号信向买方提交由中国国际贸易促进委员会出具的证明此类事件的证明书。"

In the above mentioned stipulation, the scope of the force majeure events is specified in details, however, it's hard to list all the possible force majeure events in the clause of the contract. In case of the occurrence of the force majeure event unlisted in the contract, the dispute will arise nevertheless.

上述规定方法，虽然对于不可抗力事件的范围做出了具体规定，但是由于不可抗力事件很多，合同中难以一览无余，一旦遇到未列明的事件时，仍有可能发生争执。

③ In a Way of Colligation 综合式

"If the shipment of the contracted goods prevented or delayed in whole or in part by reason of war, earthquake, flood, fire, storm, heavy snow or other causes of Force Majeure, the Sellers shall not be liable for non-shipment or late shipment of the goods or non-performance of this contract. However, the Sellers shall notify the Buyers by cable or by telex and furnish the latter within 15 days by registered airmail with a certificate issued by the China Council for the Promotion of International Trade attesting such event or events."

"由于战争、地震、火灾、水灾、暴风雪或其他不可抗力的原因，致使卖方不能全部或部分装运或延迟装运合同货物，卖方对于这种不能装运或迟延装运本合同货物不负责任。但卖方需用电报或电传通知买方，并需在15天以内以航空挂号信向买方提交由中国国际贸易促进委员会出具的证明此类事件的证明书。"

In the above mentioned clause, besides the various force majeure events recognized in common by both parties, the words "other causes of Force Majeure" are added too. It is helpful to identify the unlisted force majeure events by the both parties. This way of stipulation is specific, flexible and widely adopted in Chinese international trade practice.

上述规定方法，既列明了双方当事人已经取得共识的各种不可抗力事故，又加列上"其他不可抗力原因"这一句，将来如果发生合同未列明的意外事故时，便于双方当事人共同确定是否作为不可抗力事故。因此，这种规定方法既明确又具体，又有一定的灵活性，比较科学实用。在我国的业务实践中,多采用这一种。

Terminology 本章术语

1. claims 索赔
2. penalty 罚款
3. litigation 诉讼,起诉
4. negotiation 商讨,议付
5. conciliation 调解
6. arbitration 仲裁
7. arbitrator 仲裁员
8. arbitration clause 仲裁条款
9. arbitration association 仲裁协会
10. issue an award 做出裁决
11. International Chamber of Commerce 国际商会
12. China International Economic and Trade Arbitration Commission 中国国际经济贸易仲裁委员会
13. force Majeure 不可抗力

Exercises 本章练习

Case 1 案例 1

One Chinese company A and an American company B signed a contract according to FOB Dalian terms, which sold a batch of chemical raw material. The goods were loaded to the ship assigned by the company B 3 days before due. The goods shipped were well inspected and found the quality was in conformity with the stipulation of the contract.

When the goods arrived at the destination port, the company B found the goods partly lumped or massed through inspection; the quality changed. With investigation, they confirmed that the reason for the granular materials turning into lump ones was the insufficient packing, which caused the granular materials absorb water in transit. Therefore, the company B filed a claim to company A.

However, the company A argued that the goods were qualified by inspection before shipment, and the quality changed in transit. According to international trade practices, the buyers should be liable to make compensation. Therefore, the company A refused to compensate.

Were the arguments put forward by the company A reasonable? How should the dispute be handled? Please give your reasons.

中国某公司 A 与美国某公司 B 按照 FOB 大连签订了一笔化工原料的合同。A 公司在规定的装运期届满前三天将货装上 B 公司指定的海轮上,且装船前检验时货物品质良好,符合合同规定。

货到目的港后,B 公司提货后经目的港商检机构检验发现部分货物结块,品质发生变化。经调查确认原因是货物包装不良,在运输途中吸收空气中的水分导致原颗粒状的原料结成硬块。于是,B 公司向 A 公司提起索赔。

但 A 公司认为,货物装船前经检验是合格的,品质变化是在运输途中发生的,按照国际贸易惯例,其后果应由买方承担,因此,A 公司拒绝赔偿。

问题:A 公司的申辩是否有理?此争议应如何处理?并说明理由。

Case 2 案例 2

A Chinese importer had concluded a contract with a foreign company to import chemical products, however the foreign seller found he would be at a loss as the price of the products in the international market was rising. So he required to cancel the contract due to Force Majeure. Then as the Chinese importer, how to deal with the situation?

我国某外贸公司与外商签订一份化工产品进口合同,订约后由于该产品的国际市场行情上扬,外商亏本。于是他以不可抗力为由要求撤销合同。进口商应如何对待此问题?

Case 3 案例 3

A British exporter made an offer of raw materials in 20,000 tons in term of CIF SHANGHAI to a Chinese importer. The applicable law for the contract is the law of UK. Before the delivery, the Gulf War broke out, the UK seller had to ship the goods to China port via Cape of Good Hope of South Africa due to failing to go through Suez Canal, thus the exporter asked for the Chinese buyer to raise the price or remove the contract. What shall the Chinese buyer do?

某英国商人向中国出口原料 2 万吨,价格条件为 CIF 上海。合同适用的法律为英国法。交货前,海湾战争爆发,英国商人如交货就要通过南非好望角航行,不能走苏伊士运河,故要求中方或提高价格或解除合同。问中方应如何处理?

Case 4 案例 4

20,000 tons of soybean cakes were going to be imported from Argentina to China, with the scheduled delivery time by the end of Aug. and resold in Europe. However, the scheduled purchase place was attacked by flood leading to the purchase plan's failure. The Argentina seller required for the exemption from the contract fulfillment according to Force Majeure. As the Chinese buyer, how to settle the matter?

我国某公司从阿根廷进口普通豆饼 2 万吨，交货期为 8 月底，拟转售欧洲。然而，4月阿根廷原定的收购地点发生洪水，收购计划落空。阿商要求按不可抗力处理免除交货责任，问该进口公司怎么办？

Case 5 案例 5

Guangzhou umbrella factory signed an umbrella contract with a client of Italy. The L/C opened by the buyer stipulated goods delivery in August. But the warehouse caught fire in early July. All products and semi-finished products were destroyed, made the seller unable to delivery. Can the seller cite Force Majeure Clause to cancel delivery?

广州伞厂与意大利一个客户签订了雨伞出口合同。买方开来的信用证规定，8 月装运交货，不料 7 月初，该伞厂仓库失火，成品、半成品全部烧毁，以致无法交货。卖方可否援引不可抗力条款要求免交货物？

Answers for Reference 参考答案

Case 1 案例 1

In this case, the seller was responsible for the claim. Although the quality was changed in transit which means that the risk had transferred to the buyer, the loss was due to insufficient packing which was happened before shipment. Therefore, it was the seller's fault when acting up to the contract, and the seller made a breach of contract. As to the risk transfer on FOB terms, the international trade practices explain that if damages suddenly occurred in transit, the buyer shall be liable to make compensation. Obviously, this case is not in the scope of the practices, so it is unreasonable for the seller, Company A to refuse compensation.

本案中卖方应承担赔偿责任。虽然货物品质发生变化是在运输途中，但损失是由于包装不良造成的，说明致损原因是在装船前已经存在了。这属于卖方履约中的过失，应构成违约。而根据国际贸易惯例对 FOB 的风险转移的解释，如果运输途中由于突然发生的意外事件导致货物的损失由买方承担。本案的情况显然不属于惯例规定的范围，所以卖方 A 公司拒赔是没有道理的。

Case 2 案例 2

The seller's requirement is not valid. The price rise is a kind of commercial risk instead of a Force Majeure. The buyer shall refuse the seller's requirement and urge the seller to make delivery promptly.

外商的撤约要求不能成立。因为合同货物市价上扬属商业风险，不构成不可抗力事故。故我方应拒绝外商撤约要求，催促其按时发货。

Case 3 案例 3

(1) No specific route is mentioned in the contract, so it is acceptable to ship goods via Cape of Good Hope; (2) There has cases in UK, taking the failure of delivery as the breach of contract; (3) So the Chinese buyer shall insist on the delivery without raising price, and claim for the compensation in case that the seller refuses to make delivery.

(1) 合同未规定运输走什么航线，走好望角也属可行的航线；(2) 英国已有判例，认为在此情况下卖方如不交货应负违约责任；(3) 故中方应坚持卖方交货，不同意提价，如卖方拒不交货，可要求卖方赔偿损失。

Case 4 案例 4

(1) The convention is applicable to the contract unless special agreement is made between both sides; (2) In accordance with the convention, the event in Argentina is not a Force Majeure as the result of the event can be overcome. The bean cake is a kind of substitutable product which can be purchased in other countries or regions as no specific origin was stipulated in the contract. Moreover, there were still four months left for delivery from the attack of flood; (3) The Chinese buyer may import the bean cakes from other suppliers and claim against the Argentina seller for the price difference or compensation.

(1) 合同如无特殊约定，本合同适用《联合国国际货物销售合同公约》；(2) 依《公约》有关规定，阿商发生的事件不构成不可抗力，因为事件的后果不是不可克服的。豆饼属种类货，可以替代，合同不要求特定的产地，阿商应从其他地区或国家购买货物交货，尤其是从发生洪水到交货尚有 4 个月时间可供阿商购货；(3) 阿商如拒不履约，我国进口商可从国际市场上补进，然后向阿商索取差价和损害赔偿金。

Case 5 案例 5

Firstly, we should identify whether the umbrella factory fire is Force Majeure (unforeseeable, unpreventable, unavoidable and uncontrollable). If it is Force Majeure, according to the United Nations Convention on Contract for the International Sales of Goods, the factory can be exempted from an obligation by providing relative certificate documents of the Promotion of International Trade of China.

首先应认定该伞厂的火灾是否属于不可抗力事件(无法预见、无法预防、无法避免、无法控制)。如实为不可抗力，应由中国国际贸易促进委员会出具相关证明文件，根据《联合国国际货物销售合同公约》可免除责任。

Chapter 9 Other Modes of International Business

第9章 一般贸易外的其他贸易方式

Section 1 Exclusive Sales

第1节 包 销

1. Definition of Exclusive Sales 包销的含义

Exclusive sales, also known as sole distribution, refers to the way in which an exporter grants the right of operation of a certain or a certain kind of goods to a certain foreign customer in a certain region and within a certain period of time through an exclusive sales agreement.Exclusive sales are also selling, they are different from the usual one-sided export one by one,in addition to sales contracts, both parties must also sign an exclusive sales agreement in advance.

包销，亦称独家经销，指出口商通过包销协议，把某种或某类商品在某一地区和期限内的经营权单独给予国外某个客户的做法。包销也是售定，但包销跟通常的单边逐笔出口不同，它除了当事人双方签有买卖合同外，还须在事先签有包销协议。

2. Exclusive Sales Agreement 包销协议

By using exclusive sales method, the rights and obligations of the buyer and the seller are determined by the exclusive sales agreement. The sales contract signed by the two must also comply with the provisions of the exclusive sales agreement. The exclusive sales agreement includes the following main contents:

采用包销方式，买卖双方的权利与义务由包销协议确定，两者签订的买卖合同也必须符合包销协议的规定，包销协议包括下列主要内容：

(1) Name of the exclusive sales agreement, date and place of signing

包销协议的名称、签约日期与地点

(2) The foregoing article of the exclusive sales agreement 包销协议的前文

It is clearly clarified that the relationship between the exclusive distributor and the exporter is a kind of principle to principle, which is a relation of buyer and seller.

明确包销商与出口商之间的关系是本人与本人的关系,既买卖关系。

(3) Scope of exclusive sales goods 包销商品的范围

(4) Exclusive sales area 包销地区

(5) Exclusive sales period 包销期限

(6) The right of exclusive sales 专营权

Usually it refers to the right of exclusive sales in the specified area and time limit given by the exporter to the exclusive distributor.

通常指出口商将指定商品在规定地区和期限内给予包销商独家销售的权利。

(7) Exclusive sales quantity or amount 包销数量或金额

It is usually stated in the exclusive sales agreement that the exclusive distributor must bear the obligation to purchase the prescribed quantity and amount from the exporter, and the exporter must bear the obligation to export the above amount and amount to the the other party.

通常在包销协议中规定包销商必须承担向出口商购买规定数量和金额的义务,出口商必须承担向包销商出口上述数量和金额的义务。

(8) Pricing 作价方法

One approach is to make prices in batches within the prescribed period of exclusive sales. Due to possible changes of commodity prices in the international market, it is more common to use batches for pricing. Of course, another method can be adopted, that is, just one price is made within the prescribed time limit, regardless of the fluctuation in the market,subject to the sole price stipulated in the agreement

一种做法是在规定的包销期限内分批作价,由于国际市场商品价格变化,因此采用分批作价较为普遍,当然也可采取另外一种做法,即,在规定的期限内一次作价,无论协议内包销商品市场价格上涨下落,以协议规定的价格为准。

(9) Advertising, publicity, market reporting and trademark protection
广告、宣传、市场报道和商标保护

The two parties in the exclusive sales agreement are trading relationships, so the exporter does not actually engage in the sales business in the exclusive sales area, but some exporters are very concerned about exploration and development of overseas markets,in order to promote their products and brands, they often request the exclusive distributor to be responsible for advertising and visiting prospective customers regularly, etc.

包销协议的双方当事人是买卖关系,因此出口商一般不实际涉足包销地区的销售业务,但有的出口商十分关心开拓海外市场,为宣传其产品和品牌,常常要求包销商负责为其刊登广告以及定期访问有希望达成交易的客户等等。

3. Advantages and Disadvantages of Exclusive Sales 包销的优缺点

The exclusive sales agreement is essentially a sales contract, because the foreign distributor buys the goods in his own name and is responsible for the profits and losses. When he resells the goods in his area, the third party and the exporter do not have any contractual relationship, and the exclusive distributor has the right of exclusive sales in the exclusive sales area, the exporter has the obligation not to sell directly to customers in the area. Therefore,through offering the privilege of franchising,the exporter mobilizes the enthusiasm of the exlusive distributor, consolidates and expands the market, and reduces self-competition from multi-channel operations. On the other hand, if the exporter improperly uses the exclusive sales method, it may restrict the export, and there is a risk that the goods will not be sold or the exclusive distributor's dependence on the exporter will cause the export to be blocked. When the exclusive distributor is too capable,he possibly uses monopoly positions, manipulates prices, and controls the market.

包销协议实质上完全是一个买卖合同，因为国外经销商是用自己的名义买货，自负盈亏，他在他的地区转售商品时，第三者和出口商不发生任何契约关系，同时包销商在包销地区享有专营权，出口商负有不向该地区的客户直接售货的义务，因此包销具有通过专营权的给予，调动包销商经营的积极性，巩固和扩大市场，减少多头经营产生的自相竞争的优点。但另一方面，如果出口商不适当的运用包销方式，可能使出口经营活动受到约束，存在包而不销或者包销商对出口商的依赖而招致出口受阻的风险，包销商能力过强时，可能利用垄断地位，操纵价格，控制市场。

4. Problems to be aware of when using the exclusive sales method
采用包销方式时应注意的问题

(1) Correctly choose the exclusive distributor 正确选择包销商

When choosing an exclusive distributorr, the main consideration is his credit status, operational capabilities and commercial status in the area.

选择包销商时，主要考虑其资信状况、经营能力以及在该地区的商业地位。

(2) Appropriately specify the scope, area, quantity or amount of the goods
适当规定包销商品范围、地区、数量或金额

Determine the range of the goods, the size of the area, mainly consider the credit status of the distributor and the business intention of the exporter. The quantity or amount of the exclusive sales will be specified, taking into account the exporter's business intentions, source of supply, and market capacity. In order to promote a certain type of goods, the distributor may also be allowed to over-subscribe, and acquire a certain percentage of rewards for the excess completion.

确定商品范围、地区的大小，主要考虑包销商的资信状况和出口商的经营意图。规定包销数量或金额的大小，应考虑出口商的经营意图、货源，以及市场容量。为了推销某类商品，还可允许包销商超额承购，对超额完成部分及以一定比例的奖励。

(3) Specify provision of termination and claim clause 规定终止和索赔条款

In order to prevent the exclusive distributor from monopolizing the market or operating in a poor manner, the goods are not sold or sold less, the termination clause or the claim clause shall be specified in the exclusive sales agreement.

为了防止包销商垄断市场或经营不力，包而不销或包而少销等情况，应在包销协议中规定终止条款或索赔条款。

Section 2 Agency

第2节 代　理

1. Definition of Agency 代理的含义

Agency means that the agent, in accordance with the authorization of the principal, concludes a contract with the third party on behalf of the principal or performs other legal acts, and the resulting rights and obligations directly affect the principal.

代理是指代理人按照委托人的授权，代表委托人同第三者订立合同或做其他法律行为，由此产生的权利与义务直接对委托人发生效力。

2. Features of Agency 代理的特点

Compared with exclusive sales, agency has the following basic features.
代理与包销相比较，具有以下基本特点。

(1) The relationship between the agent and the principal belongs to principal-agent relationship, the agent only acts on behalf of the principal in the agency business, such as soliciting customers, soliciting orders, signing sales contracts on behalf of the principal, processing the goods of the principal, and accepting payment for the goods, he does not participate in the transaction as a party of the contract.

代理人与委托人之间的关系属于委托代理关系，代理人在代理业务中只是代表委托人行为，例如招揽客户、招揽订单、代表委托人签订买卖合同、处理委托人的货物、收受货款等，他本身并不作为合同的一方参与交易。

(2) The agent usually uses the funds of the principal to carry out business activities.
代理人通常运用委托人的资金开展业务活动。

(3) An agent generally does not sign a contract with a third party in his own name.

代理人一般不以自己的名义与第三者签订合同。

(4) The reward earned by the agent is a commission.

代理人赚取的报酬是佣金。

3. Types of Agent 代理的种类

There are usually the following types of agents.

通常有下列几种代理。

(1) General agent 总代理

The general agent is the plenipotentiary representative of the principal in the designated area. In addition to the right to sign the sales contract on behalf of the principal, and to handle commercial activities, he can also carry out some non-commercial activities. He has the right to assign sub-agents and share sub-agent commission.

总代理是在指定地区委托人的全权代表，他除了有权代表委托人签订买卖合同，处理货物等商务活动外，也可进行一些非商业性的活动，他有权指派分代理，并可分享分代理的佣金。

(2) Exclusive agent/Sole agent 独家代理

An exclusive agent is an agent who acts on behalf of the principal in a designated area. The principal may not entrust another second agent in the designated area. Therefore, the exclusive agent is used in the export business, and the principal gives the agent the franchise to sell the designated goods in a specific area and within a certain period of time.

However, the franchise enjoyed by the exclusive agent is not exactly the same as the franchise enjoyed by the exclusive sales. Usually, unless otherwise stipulated in the agreement, the principal may also be allowed to directly deal with the buyer of the designated agent area, in order not to harm the interests of the exclusive agent, some agreements stipulate that where the principal directly concludes a transaction with the buyer of the designated agency area, the commission is still paid to the exclusive agent.

独家代理是在指定地区内，由他单独代表委托人行为的代理人。委托人在该指定区域内，不得委托其他第二个代理人，因此在出口业务中采用独家代理的方式，委托人给予代理人在特定地区和一定期限内享有代销指定商品的专营权。

但是独家代理享有的专营权与包销所享有的专营权并不完全一样，通常除非协议另有规定，一般也可允许委托人直接向指定的代理地区的买主进行交易，为了不损害独家代理的利益，有些协议规定，凡是委托人直接与指定代理地区的买主达成交易的，仍然向独家代理计付佣金。

(3) Commission agent 佣金代理

Commission agent, also known as agent, refers to a few agents act on behalf of the principal in the same agency area and time limit. The commission agent counts the principal according to the actual amount of the goods promoted or the method or percentage specified in the agreement. The principal can directly deal with the actual buyer in the agency area without giving the agents commission.

佣金代理又称一般代理，是指在同一代理地区、时间期限内，有几个代表委托人行为的代理人，佣金代理根据推销商品的实际金额或根据协议规定的办法或百分率向委托人计收佣金，委托人可以直接与该地区的实际买主成交，而无须给代理佣金。

4. Agency Agreement 代理协议

(1) Both parties to the agreement 协议双方

Usually, the parties in the agency agreement are the principal and the agent. The agent engages in the business activities in the name of the principal and uses funds of the principal. The parties in the agreement are independent legal persons or natural persons. The agreement should specify the full name, address, and legal status, type of business, date and place of registration, etc.

In the preamble of the agency agreement, the legal relationship between the principal and the agent, the scope of authorization and the scope of the agent's authority are generally clarified.

通常代理协议的双方为委托人及代理人，代理人以委托人的名义和资金从事业务活动，协议的双方是互为独立的法人或自然人。协议应明确每一方的全称、地址、法律地位、业务种类以及注册日期和地点等。

代理协议的序言中，一般明确委托人与代理人之间的法律关系、授权范围和代理人的职权范围等。

(2) Designated agent goods 指定的代理商品

(3) Designated agency area 指定的代理地区

(4) The right to grant an agent 授予代理的权利

It varies depending on the type of agent.

因代理种类的不同而不同。

(5) Validity and termination clause 有效期及终止条款

The agency agreement should generally indicate the period of validity, in addition, the termination clause may be added. If one party fails to perform the agreement, the other party has the right to terminate the agreement.

代理协议一般应注明有效期，另外，还可加注终止条款，一方不履行协议情况下，另一方有权终止协议。

(6) Commission clause 佣金条款

The commission clause is one of the important clausess of the agency agreement and should generally include the following.

佣金条款是代理协议的重要条款之一，一般应包括下列内容。

① The time when the agent has the right to request commission 代理人有权索取佣金的时间

It should be clearly specified that the agent collects the commission from the principal when completing a certain agency business activity. As a general rule, as long as the agent acts on behalf of the principal, he is entitled to receive a commission, and even if the agent fails to perform an act for the reason of the principal, the agent still has the right to request the commission from the principal.

明确代理人在完成何种代理业务活动时，向委托人收取佣金。一般做法是，只要代理人代表委托人行为，就有权收取佣金，甚至在属于委托人的原因而未能履行某一行为时，代理人仍有权向委托人索取佣金。

② Commission rate 佣金率

The proportion of the commission is directly related to the interests of both parties in the agreement. The commission rate must be clearly agreed in the agreement.

佣金比例的高低，直接关系协议双方的利益，在协议中必须明确约定佣金率。

③ The basis of commission calculating 计算佣金的基础

The calculation basis of the commission can be based on different methods, some subject to the actual export amount, and some based on the actual payment received. It can be valued by FOB or by CIF or other trade terms.

佣金的计算基础可以按不同的方法，有的以实际出口的金额为准，有的则以实际收到的货款为准。可按 FOB，也可按 CIF 或其他贸易术语计值。

④ Ways to pay commissions 偿付佣金的方法

It can be paid at regular intervals or once in accordance with the agreed time limit.

可按照一定时间间隔支付，也可按照协商的期限一次总付。

⑤ How to pay the commission for the excess sales part 超额销售部分的佣金的支付方式

The commission paid to the agent's over-sales portion is generally not paid on a case-by-case basis, but is aggregated over a certain period of time, based on the amount of excess sales and the corresponding commission rate.

Progressive commission calculation and payment can be divided into two types: full progressive commission and excess cumulative commission.

Full Progressive Commission: Calculates the full commission based on the commission rate level reached by the amount of overselling over a certain period of time.

Excessive Progressive Commission: Excessive sales of each level, each calculated according to the commission rate of the applicable level, and then accumulating the calculation results,it is the total amount of excess progressive commission.

支付给代理商的超额销售部分的佣金一般不是逐笔支付,而是在一定时期内汇总支付,根据超额销售的金额和相应的佣金率。

累进佣金计算支付可以分为全额累进佣金和超额累计佣金两种方式。

全额累进佣金:按照一定时期内超额推销的金额所达到的佣金率等级计算全额佣金。

超额累进佣金:各个等级的超额推销部分,各自按照适用等级的佣金率计算,再把计算结果累计起来,就是超额累进佣金总额。

(7) Minimum turnover terms 最低成交额条款

The agent should undertake to sign a sales contract not lower than the prescribed amount (minimum turnover). If the minimum turnover is not met or exceeded, the reward for the agent may be adjusted accordingly.

代理人要承担签订不低于规定数额(最低成交额)的买卖合同,如果未能达到或超过最低成交额时,对代理人的报酬可相应调整。

(8) Non-competition clause 非竞争条款

The agent has no right to provide or purchase goods that compete with the principal's goods during the validity period of the agreement, and does not have the right to advertise the competing goods or to represent other competing companies in the agreement area.

代理人在协议有效期内无权提供、购买与委托人的商品相竞争的商品,无权为该种商品打广告,也无权代表协议地区内的其他相竞争的公司。

(9) Provisions on market intelligence, advertising and protection of trademarks, etc. provided by the agent for the principal

代理人向委托人提供市场情报,广告宣传和保护商标等的条款

During the validity period of the agency agreement, the agent is obliged to provide the principal with information on market trends, foreign exchange, customs regulations and the relevant import regulations in the country on a regular basis,he should also organize advertising and publicity under the instructions of the principal and consult with the principal contents and form of advertisement. Generally, the principal should clarify in the agency agreement that the owner of the goods retains the trademark registration right for the goods sold through the agent.

代理人在代理协议有效期内,有义务定期向委托人提供市场趋势、外汇、海关规定以及本国有关进口的规定的资料,还应在委托人的指令下组织广告和宣传,与委托人磋商广告内容及广告形式。一般,委托人在代理协议中要明确货主保留对通过代理人销售的商品的商标注册权。

Section 3　Consignment

第3节　寄　　售

1. Definition of Consignment　寄售的概念

Consignment is different from the usual agent. It means that the consignor (principal) delivers the goods to the consignment place, and the consignee (trustee) sells the consigned goods instead of the consignor according to the conditions stipulated in the consignment agreement. After the goods are sold, the consignee settles the payment to the consignor.

寄售有别于通常的代理，指寄售人(委托人)将货物运往寄售地，委托代销人(受托人)按照寄售协议规定的条件，由代销人代替寄售人进行销售，货物出售后，由代销人向寄售人结算货款。

2. The Main Difference between The Consignee and The Agent 代销人与代理人的主要区别

(1) The consignee has the right to sign a contract with the local purchaser in his own name, and the agent signs the contract with the local purchaser on behalf of the client.

代销人有权以自己的名义与当地购货人签订合同，而代理人则代表委托人与当地的购货人签订合同。

(2) The consignee has the right to sue the local purchaser in his own name when the other party fails to perform the contract, and the agent usually does not have this right.

代销人在当地购货人不履行合同时，有权以自己的名义起诉对方，而代理人通常无此权利。

(3) When the consignor does not execute the consignment agreement, the consignee may exercise the lien on the consignor's goods or the consignment goods as a guarantee and mortgage. Therefore, the consignee in consignment mode often has more authority than the agent in the agency mode legally.

代销人在寄售人不执行寄售协议时，可以对寄售人的货物行使留置权或将寄售的货物作为担保和抵押，因此在法律上寄售方式中的代销人的权限往往大于代理方式中的代理人。

3. Features of Consignment　寄售的特点

Consignment has the following features compared with normal selling.

与正常的卖断相比，寄售有下列特点。

(1) The consignee is entrusted by the consignor to sell, not to buy or sell. The consignee can

only dispose of the goods according to the instructions of the consignor. The consignor remains the ownership of the goods until the consignment is sold.

寄售人与代销人之间是委托代售关系，而非买卖关系，代销人只能根据寄售人的指示处置货物，货物的所有权在寄售地出售之前仍属寄售人。

(2) All costs and risks of consignment goods before they are sold, including during transit and after arrival at the consignment place, are borne by the consignor.

寄售货物在售出之前，包括运输途中和到达寄售地后的一切费用和风险，均由寄售人承担。

(3) The consignor delivers the goods to the destination market first, that is, the consignment place, and then the consignee sells them to the local buyer at the consignment place, therefore, it is a typical physical market trading.

寄售人先将货物运至目的地市场，即寄售地，然后经代销人在寄售地向当地买主销售，因此它是典型的凭实物进行的现货市场买卖。

4. Advantages and Disadvantages of Consignment 寄售的优缺点

(1) Advantages 优点

① Before the sale of consignment goods, the consignor owns the ownership of the goods. Although the consignor has shipped the goods to the consignment place, the sales of the goods and the determination of the price are still in the hands of the consignor, which is favorable to fluctuate in line with market changes.

寄售货物出售前，寄售人拥有货物的所有权，尽管寄售人已将货物运往寄售地，但对货物的销售处理和价格确定等大权，仍操在寄售人手中，有利于随行就市。

② The consignment is based on physical purchase, the buyer could see the goods directly, it facilitates the transaction.

寄售方式是凭实物买卖，买主与货物直接见面，促进成交。

③ The consignee does not bear the risks and expenses, generally, the consignor pays the capital and does not occupy the funds of the consignee, which can stimulate the enthusiasm of the consignee's operation.

代销人不负担风险与费用，一般寄售人垫资，不占用代销人的资金，可以促进其经营的积极性。

(2) Disadvantages 缺点

① The exporter as the principal bears a higher risk and costs, and it increases the financial burden of the exporter, which is not favorable to capital turnover.

出口商作为委托人承担的风险较大，费用较多，而且增加出口商的资金负担，不利于资金周转。

② Payment for consignment goods are collected slowly. Once the consignee fails to abide by the agreement, the consignor may lose both the goods and money.Therefore, the selection of the consignee, the place of consignment and the formulation of the consignment agreement must be cautious.

寄售货物收款较慢，一旦代销人不守协议，寄售人可能货款两空，因此，对代销人、寄售地的选择和对寄售协议的制订必须谨慎。

5. Consignment Agreement 寄售协议

The consignment agreement generally includes the following terms.
寄售协议一般包括下列条款。

(1) Terms of the relationship between the parties 协议双方关系的条款

In the consignment agreement, it is necessary to clarify that the relationship between the principal and the consignee is consigned; the consignment goods are still owned by the principal before the sale; the consignee sells the merchandise, collects the payment from the buyer in his own name, and handles the dispute,even for prosecution, etc., the expenses required shall be borne by the principal; the principal has the right to supervise the consignee to carry out the conditions in the consignment agreement.

寄售协议中要明确，委托人与代销人之间是委托代销的关系；寄售商品在未出售前，所有权仍属委托人；代销人出售商品后，以自己的名义向买主收取货款，处理争议，甚至进行起诉等，所需费用应由委托人承担；委托人有权监督代销人执行寄售协议中的各项条件。

(2) Price terms for consignment goods 寄售商品的价格条款

The price clause mainly stipulates the pricing method of consignment goods, usually in the following three types.

价格条款主要规定寄售商品的作价办法，通常有下列三种。

① Minimum price. The principal specifies the minimum price in the consignment agreement and authorizes the consignee to sell the goods only at or above that price.

最低售价。委托人在寄售协议中明确规定最低价格，授权代销人只能按照该价格或高于该价格出售货物。

② Unlimited price. The principal does not impose restrictions on the price. The consignee can freely replace the principal to sell the goods, but the minimum price should be equal to or above the local market price, and the consignee has no right to sell the consignment goods below the market price.

不限价。委托人在价格上不做限制，代销人可以自由代替委托人出售货物，但不限价的最低限度应当等于当地市场价，代销人无权以低于市场价出售寄售货物。

③ The specific quotation is made by the principle before the sale, which is flexible.

销售前才由委托人具体报价，这种做法富于弹性。

(3) Commission terms 佣金条款

The payment term of the consignee's commission in the consignment agreement is similar to that of agency agreement.

寄售协议中支付代销人佣金的规定与代理协议相似。

(4) Obligations of the parties to the agreement 协议双方当事人的义务条款

① Consignee's obligation 代销人的义务

A. Provide a warehouse for storing consignment goods, hire staff, and obtain a license for imported goods.

提供储存寄售商品的仓库，雇用工作人员，取得进口商品的许可证。

B. Ensure that the goods are as intact as possible during the storage of the warehouse. If the goods are damaged or lost, the trustee shall be liable for compensation.

保证货物在仓库存放期间尽量完好无损，如发生货物损失、灭失等，受托人应负赔偿责任。

C. Advance all expenses incurred in the operation and storage area of the consignment goods.

代垫寄售商品在经营、仓储区内所产生的一切费用。

D. Insurance for consignment goods.

对寄售商品办理保险。

E. Advertise, display products and provide after-sales service.

广告宣传，展示商品，提供售后服务。

F. Report the market situation to the principal timely.

及时向委托人报告市场情况。

② The obligations of the consignor 寄售人的义务

A. Provide consignment goods as agreed quality, quantity and schedule, and maintain a certain level.

按质、按量、按期提供寄售商品，并保持一定的水准。

B. Reimbursement of all expenses incurred by the consignee in the consignment process.

偿付代销人在寄售过程中所产生的一切费用。

6. Problems to be paid attention to when using consignment
采用寄售方式应注意的问题

(1) Strictly choose the consignee.

严格选择代销人

(2) Carefully choose the pricing method.

慎重选择作价方法

(3) Investigate the market dynamics, supply and demand, business habits, etc. of the consignment place before signing theconsignment agreement.

在签订寄售协议前，调查寄售地的市场动态、供求情况、商业习惯等

(4) 为 In order to reduce the risk, request the consignee to provide a bank guarantee. If the consignee fails to perform the obligations stipulated in the agreement, the bank shall bear the payment responsibility.

减少风险，最好要求代销人提供银行保函，如代销人不履行协议规定义务时，由银行承担支付责任。

Section 4　Auction

第4节　拍　　卖

1. Definition of Auction　拍卖的含义

Auction means that the auction house,which specializes in the auction business, accepts the entrustment of the owner of the goods, takes the way of open bidding, sells the goods to the buyer with the highest bid, at a certain time and place, according to certain rules and regulations, it is a mode of spot trading.

拍卖是指由专营拍卖业务的拍卖行接受货主的委托，在一定时间和地点按照一定的章程和规则，以公开叫价竞购的方法，把货物卖给出价最高的买主的一种现货交易方式。

2. Features of Auction　拍卖的特点

(1) The auction is a spot transaction for open bidding　拍卖是公开竞买的现货交易

Before the auction starts, the buyer can check the goods, after the auction starts, the buyer open bids on the spot, and the auction host chooses the transaction object on behalf of the owner of the goods. After the conclusion of transaction, the buyer can pay for and take the goods.

拍卖开始前，买主可以查看货物，拍卖开始后，买主当场出价、公开竞买、拍卖主持人代表货主选择交易对象，成交后，买主即可付款提货。

(2) The auction is organized in a certain organization　拍卖是在一定的机构内有组织的进行的

Auctions are generally organized regularly by the auction house, buying and selling a certain commodity at a certain time and place, there is as well an auction organized temporarily by the owner of the goods.

拍卖一般都是由拍卖行定期组织，集中在一定时间和地点买卖某种特定商品，也有由货主临时组织的拍卖会。

(3) Auctions have their own unique regulations 拍卖具有自己独特的规章

Auctions are different from general import and export transactions, there are special regulations on the procedures and methods of transaction negotiation, the establishment and performance of contracts, and different auction houses also have different rules and regulations.

拍卖不同于一般的进出口交易，在交易磋商的程序和方式，合同的成立和履行等问题上都有其特殊的规定，拍卖行也有各自不同的章程和规则。

3. General Procedure of Auction 拍卖的一般程序

(1) Preparation 准备

The owner of the goods delivers the goods to the auction site, commissions the auction house to select and batch, print the catalogue and solicit the buyer. The participating buyers can check the goods at the warehouse within the specified time.

参加拍卖的货主把货物运到拍卖地点，委托拍卖行进行挑选和分批，编印目录并招揽买主。参拍的买主可以在规定的时间内到仓库查看货物。

(2) Auction 正式拍卖

Formal auctions are made one by one through open bidding at the specified time and place, in accordance with the order specified in the auction catalogue.

正式拍卖是在规定的时间和地点，按照拍卖目录规定的次序，逐笔喊价成交。

(3) Transaction conclusion and delivery 成交与交货

After the auction is completed, the buyer signs the confirmation of the transaction, makes the payment by cash, and picks up the goods on ex warehouse basis within the specified time limit.

拍卖成交后，买主即在成交确认书上签字，以现汇支付货款，在规定的期限内，按仓库交货条件到指定仓库提货。

4. Bidding Methods of Auction 拍卖的出价方法

(1) Price increase auction 增价拍卖

It is the most common auction method. The auctioneer announces the predetermined bid price of the goods according to the order specified in the auction catalogue, and the bidder competes to increase the price according to the prescribed price increase. When the auctioneer thinks that no one can bid a higher price, the auctioneer announces the transaction by striking the gavel to sell the goods to the buyer at the highest price.

增价拍卖是最常见的拍卖方式。拍卖人按照拍卖目录规定的顺序，宣布预定的货物起叫价，由竞买者按规定的增价额度竞相加价，当主持人认为无人再出更高价格时，即以击槌方式宣布成交，将货物卖给出价最高的买主。

(2) Price decrease auction 减价拍卖

Also known as the Dutch auction, the auctioneer first announces the highest price, and if no one accepts, the bidding price is gradually lowered until a bidder believes that the price has been lowered to an acceptable price and accepts in a prescribed manner.

减价拍卖又称荷兰式拍卖，是由拍卖人先宣布最高价，无人接受就逐渐降低叫价，直到有竞买者认为已降到可以接受的价格，并以规定的方式表示接受时为止。

Both of the above two methods are open bidding and deal on the spot.

以上两种方法都是公开竞买并当场成交。

(3) Sealed bidding auctin 密封递价拍卖

Also known as bidding auction, the specific method is that the auctioneer announces the specific situations and auction conditions of each batch of goods, and then the buyer submits his bid to the auctioneer within the specified time, and then the auctioneer selects the most suitable condition to conclude the transaction. This way has lost the nature of open bidding,in this way, the auctioneer possibly does not accept the highest bid, he also takes other factors into consideration.

密封递价拍卖又称招标式拍卖，具体做法是由拍卖人公布每批商品的具体情况和拍卖条件，然后由买主在规定的时间内将自己的出价递交拍卖人，再由拍卖人选择条件最合适的达成交易。这种方式已失去了公开竞买的性质，采用这一方式，拍卖人不一定接受最高的递价，还要考虑其他因素。

During the auction process, each bid price of the buyer at the time of the official auction is an offer, and the auction house will reach the transaction once it accepts the transaction.

拍卖过程中买主在正式拍卖时的每一次叫价都是一项要约，拍卖行一旦接受交易即告达成。

Section 5　Tendering/ Bidding

第 5 节　招 标 投 标

Tendering/Bidding is a traditional method of trade, often used for the procurement of bulk materials and international engineering contracting. This section only describes tendering/

bidding in bulk commodity procurement.

招标投标是一种传统的贸易方式，经常用于大宗物资的采购业务和国际工程承包。本节仅介绍大宗商品采购中的招标投标。

1. Definition of Tendering/Bidding 招/投标的含义

Invitation to tender/bid and submission of tender/bid are two aspects of a trade approach.

Invitation to tender/bid means that the tenderee (buyer) issues a notice of tender, indicating the name, specification, quantity and other conditions of the commodity to be purchased, and invites the tenderer/bidder (seller) to conduct the tendering/bidding at a specified time and place according to certain procedures.Submission of tender/bid means that the tenderer/bidder (seller) at the invitation of the tenderee, submits the price to the tenderee within the prescribed time limit in accordance with the requirements and conditions of the tender/bid, and strive for the winning of the tender/bid.

招标和投标是一种贸易方式的两个方面。招标是指招标人(买方)发出招标通知，说明拟采购的商品名称、规格、数量及其他条件，邀请投标人(卖方)在规定的时间、地点，按照一定的程序，进行投标的行为。投标是指投标人(卖方)应招标人的邀请，按照招标的要求和条件，在规定的时间内向招标人递价，争取中标的行为。

2. Features of Tendering/Bidding 招/投标的特点

Compared with other trade modes, tendering/bidding has obvious characteristics: (1) Under the this mode, the tender/bidder makes a one-off offer according to the time, place and conditions stipulated by the tenderee. Such offer is legally binding on the tender/bidder, once the tender/bidder defaults, the tenderee may request compensation. (2) Tendering/bidding is a kind of competitive selling, one buyer faces multiple sellers, the competition between the sellers makes the buyer have more comparisons and choices in terms of price and other conditions, thus ensuring the best purchase of goods to a certain extent of quality.

与其他贸易方式相比，招/投标具有明显的特点：(1) 该方式下，投标人是按照招标人规定的时间地点和条件进行一次性报盘，这种报盘是对投标人有约束力的法律行为，一旦投标人违约，招标人可要求补偿。(2) 招/投标属于竞卖方式，一个买方面对多个卖方，卖方之间的竞争使买方在价格及其他条件上有较多的比较和选择，从而在一定程度上保证了采购商品的最佳质量。

3. General Procedure of Tendering/Bidding 招/投标的基本程序

The tendering/bidding business in commodity procurement generally consists of four steps, namely, invitation to tender/bid, submission of tender/bid, tender/bid opening and contract signing.

商品采购中的招标投标业务一般包括了四个步骤,即招标、投标、开标和签约。

(1) Invitation to tender/bid 招标

It is legally an invitation to offer.

There are two types: open tendering/bidding and non-public tendering/bidding.

Open tendering/bidding means that the tenderee issues a tender notice on domestic and foreign newspapers and magazines, so that all legitimate tenderers/bidders have the opportunity to participate in the competition. This practice is also called unlimited competitive tendering/bidding. Open tendering/bidding usually requires tenderers/bidders to be qualified.

Non-public tendering/bidding, also known as selected tendering/bidding, means that the tenderee does not publicly issue the tender notice, but only issues a tender notice to a small number of customers based on past business relationships and intelligence materials or the situation of the tenderer/bidder provided by the consulting company, it is also called limited competitive tendering/bidding.

招标在法律上是一项邀请发盘。

国际招标有公开招标和非公开招标两种。

公开招标,是指招标人在国内外报刊上发布招标通告,使所有合法的投标人都有机会参与竞争,这种做法又称为无限竞争性招标,公开招标,通常要对投标人进行资格预审。

非公开招标又称选择性招标,是指招标人不公开发布招标通告,只是根据以往的业务关系和情报资料或者由咨询公司提供投标人的情况,向少数客户发出招标通知,这种做法也称为有限竞争性招标。

(2) Submission of tender/bid 投标

The tenderer/bidder must first obtain the tendering/bidding documents, and carefully prepare the tender/bid after the analysis. The tender/bid is essentially an offer that is valid until the date of the tender/bid opening. The content must be very clear, the important contents, to be included in the contract with the tenderee after winning the tender/bid, should be all included, the tender/bid should be delivered to the tenderee or its designated recipient before the deadline for submission of the tender/bid, and the delay of sending means invalidity. In accordance with usual practice, the tenderer/bidder may ask for amendments to the tender/bid or withdraw it in writing before the deadline of submission of tender/bid.

投标人首先要取得招标文件,认真分析研究之后编制投标书,投标书实质上是一项有效期至规定开标日期的发盘,内容必须十分明确,中标后与招标人签订合同所要包含的重要内容应全部列入,投标书应在投标截止日期之前送达招标人或者其指定的收件人,逾期无效。按照一般的惯例,投标人在投标截止日期之前可以书面提出修改或者撤回。

(3) Opening the tender/bid 开标

The opening of tender/bid has two methods: public tender/bid opening and non-public tender/bid opening. The tenderee should stipulate the tender/bid opening method in the tendering/bidding notice.

The public opening of the tender/bid means that the tenderee opens the tender/bid in public at the specified time and place and reads the contents. Tenderers/bidders can participate and monitor the tender/bid opening.

If the tender/bid is not open, the tenderee will open the tender/bid by himself and evaluate the bid, and deside which tenderer/bidder is selected. Tenderers/bidders will not participate. This is non-public tender/bid opening.

After the tender/bid opening, the tenderee will weigh the pros and cons, that is, tender/bid evaluation, to select the most favorable person as the winning tenderer/bidder. If the tenderee thinks that all tenders/bids are not satisfactory, the tendering/bidding may be declared unsuccessful.

开标有公开开标和不公开开标两种方式，招标人应在招标通告中对开标方式作出规定。

公开开标，是指招标人在规定的时间和地点当众启封投标书，宣读内容。投标人都可参加，监视开标。

不公开开标则是由招标人自行开标和评标，选定中标人，投标人不参加。

开标后，招标人进行权衡比较，即评标，以选择最有利者为中标人，如果招标人认为所有的投标均不理想，可宣布招标失败。

(4) Contract signing 签约

After the tenderee selects the winning tenderer/bidder, he should issue a notice of winning the tender/bid to the winning tenderer/bidder the time and place of signing the contract. The tenderer/bidder submits a performance deposit when signing the contract to guarantee that he will perform the obligation in accordance with the contract.

招标人选中中标人之后，要向其发出中标通知书，约定双方签约的时间和地点，中标人签约时要提交履约保证金，用以担保中标人将遵照合同履行义务。

Section 6 Counter Trade

第 6 节 对 销 贸 易

1. Definition of Counter Trade 对消贸易的含义

Counter trade means that under the premise of reciprocity, two or more trade parties reach an agreement that one party's import products can be partially or fully paid by relative export products.

对销贸易是指在互惠的前提下,有两个或两个以上的贸易方达成协议,规定一方的进口产品可以部分或者全部以相对的出口产品来支付。

2. Features of Counter Trade 对销贸易的特点

Counter-trading trade is different from unilateral import and export, it is essentially a combination of import and export, the export of commodity or service of one party must be based on import, which reflects the characteristics of reciprocity, that is, mutual export opportunities, but this method of taking the import to make up for the export is not a simple repetition of barter, it is often accompanied by the movement of loan capital or even commodity capitalization.

对销贸易不同于单边进出口,实质上是进口和出口相结合的方式,一方商品或劳务的出口必须以进口为条件,体现了互惠的特点,即相互提供出口机会,但这种以进口弥补出口的贸易方式又不是易货的简单重复,它常常伴随着借贷资本甚至商品资本化的运动。

3. Types of Counter Trade 对销贸易的种类

There are many forms of counter trade, and there are basically four types, namely barter trade, counter purchase or mutual purchase, compensation trade and switch trade.

对销贸易有多种形式,归纳起来基本有四种,即易货贸易、反购或互购、补偿贸易和转手贸易。

(1) Barter trade 易货贸易

Barter has a narrow barter and a broad barter. The narrow barter is purely in exchange for goods, without money payment. Modern barter trade is called the broad barter, which is a more flexible way. The two parties will record the value of the goods, offset each other, or settle the payment by means of reciprocal letter of credit. It should be noted that this practice is still a replacement for goods, not a spot trading.

易货有狭义的易货和广义的易货之分,狭义的易货是纯粹的以货换货方式,不用货币支付,现代的易货贸易即所谓广义的易货,是采用比较灵活的方式,双方将货值记账,相互抵冲,或通过对开信用证来结算货款,需要说明的是,这种做法仍是以货换货,而非现汇交易。

(2) Counter purchase or mutual purchase 反购或互购

Counter purchase or mutual purchase means that the exporter promises to purchase a certain quantity or amount of goods from the importer within the prescribed time limit when selling the goods to the importer. It involves two separate and mutually related contracts, each contract is paid in currency and the amount is not required to be equivalent.

反购或互购是指出口商在出售货物给进口商时，承诺在规定的期限内向进口商购买一定数量或金额的商品，反购贸易涉及两个既独立又相互联系的合同，每个合同都以货币支付，金额不要求等值。

(3) Compensation trade 补偿贸易

Compensation trade is a mode of trade in which machinery or equipment or technology is imported on one's credits, and the one does not need to pay by cash, but repays the equipment in full or in part of his products or services.

The fundamental characteristics of compensation trade differs from other modes of trade are:

补偿贸易是在信贷的基础上，一方进口机器设备或技术，不用现汇支付，而以产品或劳务分期全额或部分偿还设备价款的一种贸易方式。

补偿贸易区别于其他贸易方式的根本特点是：

① Compensation trade must be carried out on the basis of credit;

补偿贸易必须在信贷的基础上进行；

② The equipment supplier must undertake to buy back products or services.

设备供应方必须承担回购产品或者劳务的义务。

Compensation trade is a trading method that makes use of foreign capitals through commodity trading.

补偿贸易是一种通过商品交易起到利用外资作用的交易方式。

(4) Switch trade 转手贸易

Switch trade can be said to be a product of account trade, which converts non-convertible currencies under account trade into hard currency. The simple switch trade uses the goods purchased under the account trade to be directly transferred to the international market for sale and to obtain free foreign exchange. Complex switch trade is often shown as the transfer of purchase rights at low price in exchange for goods or equipments that would otherwise be available in free foreign exchange,those who obtain the right of purchase then purchase goods in the corresponding deficit countries and transfer hands in the international market to recover the funds.

转手贸易可以说是记账贸易的产物，它把记账贸易项下的不可兑换的货币转换成为硬通货。简单的转手贸易使用记账贸易项下购进的货物直接转运到国际市场上售出，取得自由外汇。复杂的转手贸易往往表现为低价转让购买权，以换取本来要用自由外汇才能获得的商品或设备，获得购买权的人再在相应的逆差国选购商品，并在国际市场上转手，收回资金。

Section 7 Processing Trade

第 7 节 加 工 贸 易

1. Definition of Processing Trade 加工贸易的含义

Processing trade refers to the trade mode in which a country's enterprises use their own equipment and production capacity to process or manufacture raw materials, parts, or components from abroad, and then ship the products to foreign countries for sale.

加工贸易是指一国的企业利用自己的设备和生产能力,对来自国外的原材料、零部件或元器件进行加工制造或装配,然后再将产品运往国外销售的贸易方式。

2. Types of Processing Trade 加工贸易的种类

Processing trade is generally divided into two types: processing with imported materials and processing with customer's free materials. The commonality between the two is "two heads outside", that is, raw materials come from abroad and finished products are sold abroad.

加工贸易一般分为进料加工和来料加工两种,两者的共同点是"两头在外",即原料来自国外,成品又销往国外。

(1) Processing with imported materials 进料加工

Processing with imported materials, generally speaking, refers to the raw materials are purchased from abroad, and the products are processed and produced and sold abroad. Since the purpose of importing raw materials is to support the export, it can be called "raise the export with the import".

进料加工一般指从国外购进原料,加工生产出产品再销往国外,由于进口原料的目的是为了扶植出口,所以又可称为"以进养出"。

(2) Processing with customer's free material 来料加工

Processing with customer's free material, in China, it is also called the outward processing and assembly business. It means that certain raw materials, parts and components are supplied by foreign companies, we process and assemble according to the requirements of the other party, the products are disposed of by the other party, we charge the other party processing fees as remuneration.

来料加工,在我国又称为对外加工装配业务,是指由外商提供一定的原材料、零部件、元器件,由我方按对方的要求进行加工、装配,产品交由对方处置,我方按照约定收取加工费作为报酬。

The business of processing with customer's free materials is not a sale of goods, because the ownership of raw materials and products belongs to the entrusting party, and no transfer occurs.,we only provide labor services and collect the agreed processing fees,therefore, it can be said that processing with customer's free materials belongs to the scope of labor service trade, it is the export of labor service with goods as carrier.

来料加工业务不属于货物买卖,因为原料和产品的所有权都属于委托方,并未发生转移,我方只提供劳务并收取约定的加工费,因此可以说来料加工属于劳务贸易的范畴,是以商品为载体的劳务出口。

Both of above mentioned two types are processing trade methods with "two heads outside", but there are obvious differences between the two.First, there is no transfer of ownership in the business of processing with customer's materials, belonging to the same business,the raw materials are transported in and the finished products are shipped out, the supplier of raw material is the recipient of the recipient of the finished products, while in the business of processing with imported materials, the import of raw materials and the export of products are two different transactions, both of which have a transfer of ownership, and there is no certain connection between the raw material supplier and the finished product purchaser. Second, in the business of processing with customer's materials, we do not bear the risk of sales, do not bear the profits and losses, only charge processing fees, while in the business of processing with imported materials, we earn the added value from raw materials to finished products, we have to do self-financing, self-marketing, self-assumption of risks and be responsible for our own's profits and losses by ourselves.

来料加工与进料加工方式都是"两头在外"的加工贸易方式,但两者又有明显的不同,第一,来料加工在加工过程中均未发生所有权的转移,原料运进和成品运出,属于同一笔贸易,原料供应者是成品接收人,而在进料加工中,原料进口和产品出口是两笔不同的交易,均发生所有权的转移,原料供应者和成品购买人之间也没有必然的联系。第二,在来料加工中,我方不承担销售风险,不负盈亏,只收取加工费,而在进料加工中,我方是赚取从原料到成品的附加价值,要自筹资金、自寻销路、自担风险、自负盈亏。

Section 8　Futures

第8节　商品期货交易

1. Definition of Futures　商品期货交易的含义

Futures trading, also known as futures contract trading, is developed on the basis of the early physical trading of commodity exchanges. Futures contract transactions are only the trading of futures contracts themselves. The result of the transaction is the delivery or acquisition of the price difference between buying and selling the same number of futures contracts.

期货交易又称期货合同交易，是在商品交易所早期的实物交易的基础上发展起来的，期货合同交易只是期货合同本身的买卖，交易结果是交付或取得，买进或卖出同等数量的期货合同的价格差额。

2. Features of Futures 商品期货交易的特点

There is a clear difference between futures trading and spot trading. Whether spot trading is prompt delivery or forward delivery, both parties must deliver the actual goods and transfer the ownership of the goods. While in futures trading, trading subject is a standard futures contract, it must be done in the commodity exchange, generally does not involve the actual delivery of goods, only need to close the position before the expiration of the futures contract, the so-called position closing/liquidation or hedging, refers to that the trader does another business of futures on the reverse direction, at the same delivery time and with the same amount before the expiration of the futures contract, thereby his obligation of physical delivery is discharged.

期货交易与现货交易有明显的区别，现货交易无论是即期交货还是远期交货，交易双方都必须交付实际货物，转移货物所有权，而期货交易，买卖的是标准期货合同，必须在商品交易所内进行，一般不涉及货物的实际交割，只须在期货合同到期前平仓，所谓平仓，清算或称对冲，是指在期货合同到期前，交易者做一笔方向相反、交割月份和数量相同的期货交易，从而解除其实物交割的义务。

The features of futures trading can be summarized as:
期货交易的特点可以概括为：

(1) Standard futures contract as the subject of the transaction
以标准期货合同作为交易的标的

The standard contract is formulated by each commodity exchange, the quality, specifications, quantity and other trading conditions of the goods are uniformly formulated, the buyers and sellers only need to negotiate the price, delivery date and number of contracts.

标准合同是由各商品交易所制定的，商品的品质、规格、数量以及其他交易条件都是统一拟定的，买卖双方只需洽谈价格、交货期和合同数目。

(2) Special liquidation system 特殊的清算制度

Futures contracts for sale and purchase in commodity exchanges are uniformly delivered, hedged and settled by the clearing house. The clearing house is the buyer of all futures contracts and the seller of all futures contracts as well. The two parties of buyer and seller establish a legal relationship with the clearing house respectively.

商品交易所内买卖的期货合同由清算所进行统一交割、对冲和结算。清算所既是所有期货合同的买方,也是所有期货合同的卖方。交易双方分别与清算所建立法律关系。

(3) Strickt deposit system 严格的保证金制度

The clearing house requires each member to open a deposit account. When starting to establish futures trading, the initial deposit is paid according to a certain percentage of the transaction amount, after the daily trading, the clearing house will calculate the profit and loss according to the settlement price of the day, if the loss exceeds the specified percentage, the clearing house requires an increase of deposit,the member must pay before the opening of the next day's trading, otherwise the clearing house will stop the member's transaction.

清算所要求每个会员必须开立一个保证金账户,在开始建立期货交易时,按交易金额的一定百分比缴纳初始保证金,以后每天交易结束后,清算所都按当日结算价格,核算盈亏,如果亏损超过规定的百分比,清算所即要求追加保证金,该会员须在次日交易开盘前交纳追加保证金,否则清算所有权停止该会员的交易。

3. Types of Futures 商品期货交易的种类

According to the trader's purpose, there are two different types of futures trading, one is hedging and the other is speculative trading.

根据交易者的目的,期货交易有两个不同的种类,一种是套期保值,另外一种是投机交易。

(1) Hedging 套期保值

The usual practice of hedging is to buy or sell the same amount of futures in the futures market while selling or buying the actual goods. Hedger is generally the dealer and producer of physical goods. The reason why the hedging can transfer the risk of spot price fluctuation is because the trend of the physical price of the same commodity and the futures price change is basically the same. When the spot is purchased, the futures are sold, the opposite transactions with the same amount in the spot market and the futures market will inevitably lead to a loss-and-profit situation, and the hedger hopes to make up for the loss with the profit.

Hedging basically has two ways, one is called selling hedge, usually the trader buys a batch of physical objects, in order to avoid losses due to prices falling, and presell the same number of futures contracts in the exchange, to preserve the value.The other way of hedging, called buying hedge,the trader sells a physical product that is delivered in the future in order to avoid the price increase of the commodity at the time of delivery, the futures are bought at the exchange to make up for the loss.

套期保值的通常做法是在卖出或买入实际货物的同时,在期货市场上买入或者卖出同等数量的期货。套期保值者,一般是从事实物交易的经营者和生产者。套期保值之所以能转移现货价格波动的风险,是因为同一商品的实物价格与期货价格变化的趋势是基本一致的,在购入现货的同时出售期货,这样在现货市场和期货市场上做等量相反的交易,必然会出现一亏一盈的情况,套期保值者正是希望这样以盈补亏。

套期保值基本上有两种方式,一种称为卖期保值,通常是经营者买进一批实物,为避免因价格下跌遭受损失,而在交易所预售同等数量的期货合同,进行保值。另一种保值方法,称为买期保值,经营者卖出一笔日后交货的实物,为避免交货时该商品价格上涨,在交易所买入期货来弥补损失。

(2) Speculative trading 投机交易

Speculators use the "paper contract" as a bargaining chip to obtain the difference profit from the fluctuation of the price by means of buying and selling. According to his own forecast of the futures market price trend, he buys futures contracts when the price is expected to rise, this is so-called buying long or long position,when the price is estimated to fall, he throws out futures contracts, this is so-called selling short or short position,at the time of expectations coming true,he seizes the opportunity to hedge and get the

difference between the two transactions. Speculators usually have to bear a lot of risks in such buying low and selling high.

投机者利用"纸合同"作为筹码,通过买进卖出的手段,从价格的涨落中取得差额利润。他根据自己对期货市场价格走势的预测,在预计价格上涨时买进期货合同,即所谓买空或多头,在估计价格下跌时,抛出期货合同,即所谓卖空或空头,等到价格与预期变化方向一致时,便抓住时机对冲,获取两次交易的差额。投资者在这样的贱买贵卖中通常要承担很大的风险。

Terminology 本章术语

1. exclusive sales 包销
2. agency 代理
3. principal and agent 委托人与代理人
4. general agent 总代理
5. exclusive agent/sole agent 独家代理
6. commission agent 佣金代理
7. consignment 寄售
8. consignor/principal and consignee/trustee 寄售人/委托人与代销人/受托人
9. auction 拍卖
10. tendering/bidding 招标投标

11. invitation to tender/bid 招标
12. submission of tender/bid 投标
13. open tendering/bidding and non-public tendering/bidding 公开招标和非公开招标
14. counter trade 对销贸易
15. barter trade 易货贸易
16. counter purchase or mutual purchase 反购或互购
17. compensation trade 补偿贸易
18. switch trade 转手贸易
19. processing trade 加工贸易
20. processing with imported materials 进料加工
21. processing with customer's free material 来料加工
22. futures 商品期货交易
23. hedging 套期保值
24. speculative trading 投机交易

Exercises 本章练习

1. What are the characteristics of agency compared with exclusive sales?
代理较之于包销的特点是什么？
2. What are the main difference between the consignee and the agent?
代销人与代理人的主要区别是什么？
3. What is the difference between auction and tender?
拍卖和招投标的区别是什么？

Answers for Reference 参考答案

1. Compared with exclusive sales, agency has the following basic features.
代理与包销相比较，具有以下基本特点：

(1) The relationship between the agent and the principal belongs to principal-agent relationship, the agent only acts on behalf of the principal in the agency business, such as soliciting customers, soliciting orders, signing sales contracts on behalf of the principal, processing the goods of the principal, and accepting payment for the goods, he does not participate in the transaction as a party of the contract.

代理人与委托人之间的关系属于委托代理关系，代理人在代理业务中只是代表委托人行为，例如招揽客户、招揽订单、代表委托人签订买卖合同、处理委托人的货物、收受货款等，他本身并不作为合同的一方参与交易。

(2) The agent usually uses the funds of the principal to carry out business activities.

代理人通常运用委托人的资金开展业务活动。

(3) An agent generally does not sign a contract with a third party in his own name.

代理人一般不以自己的名义与第三者签订合同。

(4) The reward earned by the agent is a commission.

代理人赚取的报酬是佣金。

2. The main difference between the consignee and the agent 代销人与代理人的主要区别

(1) The consignee has the right to sign a contract with the local purchaser in his own name, and the agent signs the contract with the local purchaser on behalf of the client.

代销人有权以自己的名义与当地购货人签订合同，而代理人则代表委托人与当地的购货人签订合同。

(2) The consignee has the right to sue the local purchaser in his own name when the other party fails to perform the contract, and the agent usually does not have this right.

代销人在当地购货人不履行合同时，有权以自己的名义起诉对方，而代理人通常无此权利。

(3) When the consignor does not execute the consignment agreement, the consignee may exercise the lien on the consignor's goods or the consignment goods as a guarantee and mortgage. Therefore, the consignee in consignment mode often has more authority than the agent in the agency mode legally.

代销人在寄售人不执行寄售协议时，可以对寄售人的货物行使留置权或将寄售的货物作为担保和抵押，因此在法律上寄售方式中的代销人的权限往往大于代理方式中的代理人。

3. Auction is a kind of competitive buying, several buyers compete for buying the thing from a seller. Tender is a kind of competitive selling, several sellers compete for selling the thing or service to a buyer.

拍卖是一种竞争性购买，几个买家竞相从一个卖家那里买东西。招投标是一种竞争性销售，多个卖方为了向买方出售货物或服务而竞争。

Chapter 10　Case on Procedures of International Business

第 10 章　国际货物贸易流程案例

Procedure 1　Establishment of Business Relation

流程 1　建立业务关系

On June 1, 2006, Wang Ming, a salesman of Yunnan Electronics Import and Export Corporation, the exporter, drew up an email to establish a business relationship, and sent product catalog by another post, to express his desire to establish a long-term business relationship with the other party.

2006 年 6 月 1 日出口方云南电子进出口公司的业务员王明拟写了一封建立业务关系的电子邮件，并另寄产品目录，表达与对方建立长期业务关系的热切愿望。

YUNNAN ELECTRONICS I/E CORP.
Add: 211 RENMIN Road, Kunming, Yunnan, China　Post Code: 530000
Tel: 86-871-3556789 FAX: 86-871-3556788 E-mail:wm@yniec.com

June 1, 2006

U.S GLOBAL ELECTRONICS CO., LTD.
308 SEASHORE ROAD NEWYORK,
PA 19446 U.S.A FAX: 215-393-3921

Dear Sirs,

Through the courtesy of China Light Industry Products I/E Corp., we got your name and address. We are glad to learn that you are seeking for Chinese microwave. Our Company was founded in 1980 and has grown to be one of the leading imp. & exp. companies in China, specialized in electronics. As the commodities we supply are of good quality and reasonable price, we have won a very good reputation from our clients all over the world.

We take the liberty of writing to you with a view to establishing business relations with you and are sending you by separate post our illustrated catalogs for your reference.

We are looking forward to your early reply and trust that through our cooperation we shall be able to conclude some transactions with you in the near future.

Yours faithfully,
Wang Ming

Procedure 2　Inquiry

流程2　询盘

On June 5, 2006, the importer, U.S. Global Electronics Co., Ltd., sent the following feedback letter (inquiry letter) after receiving the letter of establishing business relationship from the exporter, Yunnan electronics import and export company:

2006年6月5日进口方美国全球电子有限公司收到出口方云南电子进出口公司的建立业务联系信函之后发来如下反馈信函(询盘函)：

U.S GLOBAL ELECTRONICS CO., LTD.
308 SEASHORE ROAD, NEWYORK
PA19446 U.S.A　　FAX: 215-393-3921

June 5，2006

YUNNAN ELECTRONICS I/E CORP.
211 RENMIN ROAD KUNMING
YUNNAN, CHINA

Dear Mr. Wang,

We have received your letter together with your catalogs. Having thoroughly studied the catalogs, we find that Art. No. TRM-12 is quite suitable for our market. We may need one 20' FCL for August, 2006 delivery. Please kindly inform us if you are able to supply and quote us your most favorable price for the above goods on the basis of CIFC3 NEWYORK with details, including packing, shipment, insurance and payment.

Looking forward to your early reply.

Yours faithfully,
Smith

Procedure 3　Offer

流程 3　发盘

On June 10, 2006, Wang Ming wrote an offer letter according to the feedback letter from the importer and the calculation results of the offer, answering the questions raised by the customer in detail, informing the other party of the basic terms of the transaction, and urging the other party to make a decision as soon as possible.

The basic terms of the transaction are as follows:

1. Cover all risks at 110% of the invoice value.
2. The payment method is sight letter of credit.
3. Shipment at the end of August.
4. The validity period is seven days.

根据进口方反馈回函及报价核算结果，2006 年 6 月 10 日王明写了一封发盘函，详细地回答客户提出的问题，告知对方交易的基本条款，并敦促对方尽快做出决定。

交易的基本条款如下：

1. 按发票金额加成 10%投保一切险。
2. 付款方式是即期信用证。
3. 8 月底装运。
4. 有效期 7 天。

YUNNAN ELECTRONICS I/E CORP.

Add: 211 RENMIN Road Kunming China　Post Code: 530000

Tel: 86-871-3556189 FAX: 86-871-3556788 E-mail: wm@yniec.com

June 10，2006

U.S GLOBAL ELECTRONICS CO., LTD.
306 SEASHORE ROAD NEWYORK,
PA 19446 U.S.A

Dear Mr. Smith,

Thank you for your inquiry of June 5, 2006. We are very glad to learn that you are interested in our products. Recently we have received a large number of orders from our clients and it seems that the demand is still increasing. We hope the same thing will happen in your market and are very glad to quote as follows:

Commodity: ART. NO. TRM-12 USD 132.60/set CIFC3 NEWYORK

Packing: ART. NO. TRM-12 to be packed in cartons of 1 set each 500 cartons in one 20' FCL

Shipment: Shipment is to be effected within 30 days of the receipt of the relevant L/C, but not later than August 31th, 2006.

Insurance: To be covered by the seller for 110% of total invoice value against all risks.

Payment: By irrevocable sight letter of credit for full amount of the invoice value.

This offer is valid for 7 days and we are looking forward to receiving you order.

Yours faithfully,
Wang Ming

Procedure 4　Counter Offer

流程4　还盘

After receiving the offer letter from Yunnan Electronics Import and Export Corporation, U.S. Global Electronics Co., Ltd. sent a counter-offer letter on June 15, 2006, making the following counter-offer:

美国全球电子有限公司收到云南电子进出口公司的发盘函之后，2006年6月15日发来还盘函，作出如下还价：

U.S GLOBAL ELECTRONICS CO., LTD.
308 SEASHORE ROAD, NEWYORK
PA19446 U.S.A　　FAX: 215-393-3921

June 15，2006

YUNNAN ELECTRONICS I/E CORP.

211 RENMIN ROAD KUNMING
YUNNAN, CHINA

Dear Mr. Wang,

We write to thank you for your offer of June 10th, 2006. However after a careful study of your quotation, we find that your price seems to be on the high side. It will leave us with almost no profit to accept your price.

We appreciate the quality of your products and are glad to have the opportunity to do business with you. We suggest that you make some allowance on your price. For your reference, the highest prices we can accept are as follows:

ART.NO.TRM-12 USD 120 /set CIFC3 NEWYORK

Please take it into serious consideration and your early reply will be appreciated.

Yours faithfully,
Smith

Procedure 5　Acceptance

流程5　接受

According to the counter offer made by Global Electronics Co., Ltd.,and the counter offer calculation, Wang Ming again wrote an offer letter on June 20, 2006, conveying the following information:

1. We regret the other party's failure to accept our offer.

2. Competition should be won by quality, not by low price. Our products are of high quality, reasonable price, novel design, complete functions and very marketable.

3. The counter-offer of the other party is unacceptable, but for the consideration of market development, the first transaction is given a very favorable offer to enhance the competitiveness of the goods.

4. The offer is valid for eight days.

根据美国全球电子有限公司的还盘以及所作的还价核算，2006年6月20日王明再次拟写发盘函，传达如下信息：

1. 遗憾对方未能接受我方报价。

2. 竞争应以质取胜，而非低价竞销。我方产品质量上乘，价格合理，设计新颖，功能齐全,非常适销。

    3. 对方的还盘无法接受,但出于开拓市场的考虑,首笔交易给予极优惠的报价,以增强商品的竞争能力。

    4. 该盘有效期 8 天。

YUNNAN ELECTRONICS I/E CORP.

Add: 211 RENMIN Road Kunming China   Post Code: 530000
Tel: 86-871-3556189 FAX: 86-871-3556788 E-mail: wm@yniec.com

June 20, 2006

U.S GLOBAL ELECTRONICS CO., LTD.
308 SEASHORE ROAD NEWYORK,
PA 19446 U.S.A.

Dear Mr. Smith,

Thank you for your letter of June 15th, 2006. We have discussed the matter with our manufacturers and brought them to see eye to eye with the idea of lowering our price, but still your counter-offer seems too low to be accepted. Since this is the first business between us, we try our best to quote as follows:
ART.NO.TRM-12 USD 123.52/set CIFC3 NEW YORK
This quotation is valid for only 8 days. Please take advantage of this chance and send your acceptance to us as soon as possible.

Yours faithfully,
Wang Ming

    After receiving the second offer letter from Yunnan Electronic Import and Export Corporation, Global Electronics Co., Ltd. accepted the re offer on June 25, 2006 and sent back the transaction confirmation letter as follows:
    美国全球电子有限公司收到云南电子进出口公司的第二次发盘函之后,2006 年 6 月 25 日接受了其再次报价并发回成交确认函如下:

U.S GLOBAL ELECTRONICS CO., LTD.
308 SEASHORE ROAD, NEWYORK
PA19446 U.S.A   FAX: 215-393-3921

June 25, 2006

YUNNAN ELECTRONICS I/E CORP.
211 RENMIN ROAD KUNMING
YUNNAN, CHINA

Dear Mr. Wang,

Your quotation of June 20th, 2006 has been accepted and we are glad to place our order ART NO.TRM-12 as follows:
ART.NO.TRM-12 USD 123.52/set CIFC3 NEWYORK
Other terms and conditions are the same as we agreed before.
As this is the very first transaction we have concluded, your cooperation would be very much appreciated. Please send us your sales confirmation in duplicate for counter-signing.

Yours faithfully,
Smith

Procedure 6   Contracting

流程6   签约

Wang Ming made the sales confirmation according to the requirements of the basic terms of the export contract and the conditions determined by both parties in the letter, date: July 5, 2006, No.: CX-TRMSQ06.

王明根据出口合同基本条款的要求和双方在信中确定的条件制作售货确认书，日期：2006年7月5日，号码：CX-TRMSQ06。

售货确认书
SALES CONFIRMATION

编号 No. CX-TRMSQ06   日期 Date: July 5th, 2006

the sellers:

云南电子进出口公司

YUNNAN ELECTRONICS I/E CORP.

Add: 211 RENMIN Road Kunming, Yunnan, China   Post Code:530000

the buyers:

U.S GLOBAL ELECTRONICS CO., LTD.

ADD: 308 SEASHORE Road NEWYORK, PA 19446 U.S.A.

TEL: FAX: 215-393-3921

兹确认售予你方下列货品，其成交条款如下：

We hereby confirm having sold to you the following goods on the terms and conditions as specified below:

(1)货物名称及规格 Name of Commodity and Specifications	(2)数量 Quantity	(3)单价 Unit price(US$)	(4)总值 Total Amount(US$)
Microwave article no. TRM-12	**500SETS**	**CIFC3 NEWYORK** 123.52	61760

(5) 包装

　　Packing: ART. NO.TRM-12 to be packed in cartons of 1 set each

　　　　500 cartons in one 20' FCL

(6) 装运唛头

　　Shipping Mark: U.S GLOBAL ELECTON CO., LTD.

　　　　　　　　NEWYORK, U.S.A

　　　　　　　　CX-TRMSQ06   NO.1-500

(7) 装运期限：收到可以转船及分批装运之信用证后 30 天内装出。

　　Time of Shipment: within 30 days after receipt of L/C but not later than August 31th, 2006, allowing transshipment and partial shipment.

(8) 装运口岸：广州   目的地：纽约

　　Port of Shipment: GUANGZHOU   destination: NEWYORK

(9)付款条件：买方开给售方 100%不可撤回即期付款及可转让可分割并无追索权之信用证，并须注明可在上述装运日期后十五天内在中国议付有效。

Terms of payment: By 100% Confirmed, Irrevocable , Transferable, Divisible and without Recourse Letter of Credit to be available by sight draft and to remain valid for negotiation in China until the 15th day after the aforesaid time of shipment.

(10)保险：由卖方按发票金额的110%，按照中国人民保险公司海洋运输货物保险条款(1981年1月1日)投保一切险和战争险。

Insurance: to be covered by the seller for 110% of total invoice value against all risks and war risk as per the ocean marine cargo clauses of the people's insurance company of china, dated Jan 1st, 1981.

(11)买方须于2006年8月01日前开出本批交易的信用证(或通知售方进口许可证号码)。否则，售方有权：不经通知取消本确认书，或接受买方对本售货确认未执行的全部或部分，或对遭受的损失提出索赔。

The Buyer shall establish the covering Letter of Credit(or notify the Import License Number) before August 1st, 2006 failing which the Seller reserves the right to rescind without further notice, or to accept Whole or any part of this Sales confirmation unfulfilled by the Buyer, or to lodge a claim for direct losses sustained if any.

(12)凡以CIF条件成效的业务，保额为发票价的110%，投保险别以本售货确认书中所开列的为限，买方如要求增加保额或保险范围应于装船前经售方同意，因此而增长率加的保险费由买方负责。

For transactions concluded on C.I.F basis it is understood that the insurance amount will be for 110% of the invoice value against the risks specified in the Sales Confirmation, If additional insurance amount or coverage is required, the Buyer must have the consent of the Seller before shipment, and the additional premium is to be borne by the Buyer.

(13)品质/数量异议：如买方提出索赔，凡属品质异议须于货到目的口岸之日起2个月内提出。凡属数量异议须于货到目的口岸之日起15天内提出，对所装货物所提任何异议属于保险公司，轮船公司及期货有关运输机构所负责者，售方不负任何责任。

QUALITY/QUANTITY DISCREPANCY：In case of quality discrepancy, clam should be filed by the Buyer within 2 months after the arrival of the goods at the port of destination while for quantity discrepancy claim should be filed by the Buyer within 15 days after the arrival of the goods at the port of destination. It is understood that Seller shall not be liable for any discrepancy of the goods shipped due to causes for which the Insurance Company Shipping Company other transportation organization/or Post Office are liable.

(14)本确认书内所述全部或部分商品，如因人力不可抗拒的原因，以致不能履约或延迟交货，售方概不负责。

The Seller shall not be held liable for failure or delay in delivery of the entire lot or Portion of the good s under this Sales Confirmation in consequence of any Force Majeure incidents.

确认签署 Confirmed by

_____   _____
买方(the buyers)   卖方(the sellers)

While sending the sales confirmation, Wang Ming attached the following letter for counter signature.

在寄送售货确认书的同时，王明随附了如下签约函。

YUNNAN ELECTRONICS I/E CORP.

Add: 211 RENMIN Road, Kunming, Yunnan, China   Post Code: 530000
Tel: 86-871-3556789 FAX: 86-871-3556788 E-mail:wm@yniec.com

July 5，2006

U.S GLOBAL ELECTRONICS CO., LTD.
308 SEASHORE ROAD NEWYORK,
PA 19446 U.S.A

Dear Mr. Smith,

Thank you for your order of June 25th 2006. We are pleased to do business with you and are sending you our signed Sales Confirmation No.CX-TRMSQ06 in duplicate. Please return one copy with your counter-signature for our file.

You can be assured that we will try our best to execute the order, and that the good quality of our commodities will meet your request. As the shipment date is approaching, please open the relevant L/C to reach us before August 1st so that we can effect shipment on time.

Yours faithfully,
Wang Ming

    On July 25, 2006, the US Global Electronics Co., Ltd. sent a letter to inform Yunnan Electronics Import and Export Corporation that they had countersigned the contract and sent one copy back. At the same time, they informed Yunnan Electronic Import and Export Corporation that the L / C has been opened, requested to arrange the shipment in time so that the contract can be completed smoothly.

    2006年7月25日，美国全球电子有限公司发来函电，告知云南电子进出口公司已经会签了合同并将其中一份寄回。同时通知云南电子进出口公司信用证已经开出，请及时安排装运事宜，使合同顺利完成。

U.S GLOBAL ELECTRONICS CO., LTD.
308 SEASHORE ROAD, NEWYORK
PA19446 U.S.A   FAX: 215-393-3921

July 25, 2006

YUNNAN ELECTRONICS I/E CORP.
211 RENMIN ROAD KUNMING
YUNNAN, CHINA

Dear Mr. Wang,

We have duly received and signed your Sales Confirmation NO.CX-TRMSQ06 and are sending back one copy for your file as requested.

Meanwhile the relevant L/C has been opened through Industry Bank New York and we are certain that it will reach you in a few days. Please arrange shipment upon receipt of it. We hope the first transaction between us will turn out to be successful.

Yours faithfully,
Smith

Procedure 7   L/C Notifying, Examination and Amendment

流程7   信用证通知、审核和修改

On July 29, 2006, the L/C was notified to Yunnan Electronic Import and Export Corporation by Yunnan Branch of Bank of China.

2006年7月29日信用证由中国银行云南省分行通知云南电子进出口公司。

中国银行云南省分行
BANK OF CHINA YUNNAN BRANCH
信用证通知书
Notification of Documentary Credit

ADDRESS: 100 DONGFENG ROAD.
CABLE: CHUNGKUO
TELEX: 3062 BOCSH ECN
SWIFT: BKCHCMBJ30

To: 致: YUNNAN ELECTRON I/E CORP. 211 RENMIN ROAD KUNMING YUNNAN CHINA	WHEN CORRESPONDING PLEASE QUOTE OUR REF.NO.:
ISSUING BANK INDUSTRY BANK NEWYORK 55 WATER STREET, ROOM 1000, NEWYORK U.S.A	Transmitted to us through 转递行
L/C NO. 信用证号 ETN-CXLC06	**Amount** 金额
DATED 开证日期 July 25th 2006	US$61760

Dear sirs, 敬启者
We have pleasure in advising you that we have received from the a/m bank a(n)
兹通知贵司，我行收自上述银行

( ) pre-advising of	预先通知	( ) mail confirmation of	证实书
( ) telex issuing	电传开立	( ) ineffective	未生效
( ) original	正本	( ) duplicate	副本

letter of credit, contents of which are as per attached sheet(s).
This advice and the attached sheet(s) must accompany the relative documents when presented for negotiation.
信用证一份，现随附通知。贵司交单时，请将本通知书及信用证一并提示。

( )Please note that this advice does not constitute our confirmation of the above L/C nor does it convey any engagement or obligation on our part.
本通知书不构成我行对此信用证之保兑及其他任何责任。

( )Please note that we have added our confirmation to the above L/C, negotiation is restricted to ourselves only.
上述信用证已由我行加具保兑，并限向我行交单。

This L/C consists of __two__ sheet(s), including the covering letter and attachment(s).
本信用证连同面函及附件共 2 纸。

| If you find any terms and conditions in the L/C which you are unable to comply with and or any error(s), it is suggested that you contact applicant directly for necessary amendment(s) as to avoid any difficulties which may arise when documents are presented.
如本信用证中有无法办到的条款及/或错误，请径与开证申请人联系进行必要的修改，以排除交单时可能发生的问题。 | FOR **BANK OF CHINA YUNNAN BRANCH**
中国银行
云南省分行
信用证
通知章

日期 Date: |

Letter of Credit

信用证

34127 B BOCSH CN

6229

1705 03/25 04803089 TCH0063

0325004658

ZCZC

FROM: INDUSTRY BANK NEWYORK

OUR REF: NY980520004658001T01

TO : BANK OF CHINA YUNNAN BRANCH

    100 DONGFENG ROAD, KUNMING PEOPLE'S REPUBLIC OF CHINA

TEST: FOR USD61760 ON DATE25/07/2006

PLEASE ADVICE BENEFICIARY OF THE FOLLOWING IRREVOCABLE LETTER OF CREDIT ISSUED BY US IN THEIR FAVOR SUBJECT TO UCP 500:

DOCUMENTARY CREDIT NUMBER: ETN-CXLC06

DATE AND PLACE OF EXPIRY: September 8th 2006 , IN AMERICA

APPLICANT:U.S GLOBAL ELECTRONICS CO., LTD.，308 SEASHORE Road NEWYORK, PA 19446 UNITED STATES

BENEFICIARY: YUNNAN ELECTRONICS CORP. No.211 RENMING Road KLINMING China

AMOUNT: USD61760

SAY UNITED STATES DOLLARS SIXTY ONE THOUSAND SEVEN HUNDRED AND SIXTY ONLY.

AVALIABLE WITH : ANY BANK

BY: NEGOTIATIN OF BENEFICIARY'S DRAFT(S) AT 30 DAYS' SIGHT DRAWN ON INDUSTRY BANK NEWYORK, ACCOMPANIED BY THE DOCUMENTS INDICATED HEREIN.

COVERING SHIPMENT OF :

COMMODITY ART.NO. QUANTITY

microwave: ART.NO.TRM-1002 1000 sets

SHIPPING TERMS: CIF NEWYORK

SHIPPING MARK: U.S GLOBAL ELECTRONICS CO., LTD

NEWYORK U.S.A

CX-TRMSQ06

NO.1-500

DOCUMENTS REQUIRED:

- 3 COPIES OF COMMERCIAL INVOICE SHOWING VALUE IN U.S. DOLLARS AND INDICATING L/C NO. AND CONTRACT NO..

- 2COPIES OF PACKING LIST SHOWING GROSS/NET WEIGHT AND MEASUREMENT OF EACH CARTON.

- CERTIFICATE OF ORIGIN IN TRIPLICATE ISSUED BY CHINA CHAMBER OF INTERNATIONAL COMMERCE.

- 2 COPIES OF INSURANCE POLICY OR CERTIFICATE ENDORSED IN BLANK FOR THE INVOICE VALUE OF THE GOODS PLUS 110% COVERING ALL RISKS AS PER AND SUBJECT TO OCEAN MARINE CARGO CLAUSES OF THE PEOPLE'S INSURANCE COMPANY OF CHINA DATED 1/1/1981.

- FULL SET AND ONE COPY OF CLEAN ON BOARD OCEAN BILLS OF LADING MADE OUT TO ORDER AND BLANK ENDORSED MARKED FREIGHT PREPAID AND NOTIFY APPLICANT.

PARTIAL SHIPMENTS: PERMITTED
TRANSSHIPMENTS: PERMITTED
SHIPMENT FROM :   GUANGZHOU, CHINA   TO: NEWYORK
NOT LATER THAN :   AUGUST 31ST, 2006

DOCUMENTS MUST BE PRESENTED WITHIN 15DAYS AFTER SHIPMENT, BUT WITHIN VALIDITY OF THE LETTER OF CREDIT.

INSTRUCTIONS TO THE PAYING/ACCEPTING /NEGOTIATING BANK
NEGOTIATING BANK IS TO FORWARD ALL DOCUMENTS IN ONE AIRMAIL TO INDUSTRY BANK NEWYORK, 55 WATER STREET, ROOM 1000 , NEWYORK, U.S.A. ATTN: LETTER OF CREDIT DEPARTMENT

END OF MESSAGE
NN/
62814 CBC VW
(WRU)
34127 8B BOCSH CN
NNNN

Examination and Amendment of L/C

信用证的审核与修改

According to the sales confirmation signed by both parties, Wang Ming carefully examined the received L/C, listed the existing problems of the L/C and stated the reasons for the amendment to the L/C.

根据双方签订的销售合同，王明对收到信用证进行了认真细致的审核，列明信用证存在的问题并陈述要求改证的理由。

云南电子进出口公司

地址：中国云南省昆明市人民路 211 号　邮编：530000
电话：(0871)3556189　传真：(0871)3556188　电子邮件：wm@yniec.com

审核意见：

信用证存在的问题：	需要修改的理由：
1. 信用证到期日提前	易产生逾期交单
2. 国外到期	易产生逾期交单
3. 受益人公司名称有误	易出现单、证不符
4. 付款期限不妥	超出合同规定期限
5. 交易货物货号有误	与实际出运货号不符
6. 交易货物数量有误	少于合同规定数量
7. 投保加成错误	增加保费支出

审核人：王明

According to the results of the examination, Wang Ming wrote a letter of amendment to the letter of credit on July 30, 2006, and sent it to Global Electronics Co., Ltd. of the United States, in which he listed the discrepancies of the letter of credit and clearly informed how to modify it.

根据审证结果，2006 年 7 月 30 日王明拟写了一封改证函发给美国全球电子有限公司，在其中列明了信用证的不符点，并清晰地告知对方如何进行修改。

YUNNAN ELECTRONICS I/E CORP.
Add: 211 RENMIN Road, Kunming, Yunnan, China　Post Code: 530000
Tel: 86-871-3556789　FAX: 86-871-3556788　E-mail:wm@yniec.com

July 30, 2006

U.S GLOBAL ELECTRONICS CO., LTD.
308 SEASHORE ROAD NEWYORK,
PA 19446 U.S.A

Dear Mr. Smith,

We are very glad to receive your L/C No.ETN-CXLC06, but we are quite sorry to find that it contains some discrepancies with the S/C No.CX-TRMSQ06. Please instruct your bank to amend the L/C as quickly as possible.

The L/C is to be amended as follows:

-The date of expiry should be September 15th, 2006 instead of 'September 8th, 2006'.
-The place of expiry should be In China, instead of 'In America'.
-The beneficiary should be YUNNAN ELECTRONICS I/E CORP., instead of 'YUNNAN ELECTRONICS CORP.'.
-The draft(s) should be sight draft(s) instead of 'at 30 days' sight'.
-The Article number of the goods is ART.NO.TRM-12 instead of 'ART.NO.TRM-1002'.
-The quantity of the goods should be 500 sets instead of '1000 sets'.
-The insurance value should be total invoice value plus 10% instead 'plus 110%'.

Yours faithfully,
Wang Ming

After receiving the letter for amendment, the U.S. Global Electronics Co., Ltd. requested the issuing bank, Industry Bank New York, to amend the letter of credit in response to the discrepancies proposed by Yunnan Electronic Import and Export Corporation. The following is the letter of credit amendment notice of Yunnan Branch of Bank of China.

美国全球电子有限公司收到改证函之后,针对云南电子进出口公司提出的不符点要求开证行纽约工业银行对信用证进行了修改。以下是中国银行云南省分行的信用证修改通知书。

中国银行云南省分行
BANK OF CHINA YUNNAN BRANCH
ADDRESS: 100 DONGFENG ROAD
CABLE: CHUNGKUO
TELEX: 33062 BOCSH E CN
SWIFT: BKCHCMBJ300
FAX: 0871-5323207

信 用 证 修 改 通 知 书
Notification of Amendment to Documentary Credit

YEAR/MONTH/DAY   2006/08/04

ISSUING BANK INDUSTEY BANK NEWYORK 55 Water Street, Room 1000, NEWYORK, U.S.A	DATE OF THE AMENDMENT August 03, 2006
BENEFICIARY YUNNAN ELECTRON I/E CORP. NO. 211RENMIN ROAD KUMING, YUNNAN CHINA	APPLICANT GLOBAL ELECTRON CO.,LTD. 308 SEASHORE ROAD NEWYORK PA 30997 U.S.A

L/C NO. ETN-CXLC06	DATED JULY 25TH 2006	THIS AMENDMENT IS TO BE CONSIDERED AS PART OF THE ABOVE MENTIONED CREDIT AND MUST BE ATTACHED THERETO.

Dear sirs,
We have pleasure in advising you that we have received from the above mentioned bank an amendment to Documentary Credit No. ETN-CXLC06 contents of which are as follows:

-The date of the expiry should be "September 15, 2006" instead of "September 8, 2006"
-The place of expiry: "In China" instead of "In NEWYORK"
-The beneficiary should be YUNNAN ELECTRONICS I/E CORP., instead of YUNNAN ELECTRONICS CORP.
-The draft(s) should be "sight draft(s)" instead "at 30 days sight"
-The Article number of the goods is "ART.NO.TRM-12" instead of "ART.NO.TRM-1002"
-The quantity should be "500 sets" instead of "1000 sets"
-The insurance value should be total invoice value "plus 10%" instead of "plus 110%"

ALL OTHER TERMS AND CONDITIONS REMAIN UNCHANGED.
THE ABOVE MENTIONED DOCUMENTARY CREDIT IS SUBJECT TO THE UNIFORM CUSTOMS AND PRACTICE FOR DOCUMENTARY CREDITS (1993 REVISION, INTERNATIONAL CHAMBER OF COMMERCE, PUBLICATION NO. 500)

THE BENEFICIARY:	ADVISING BANK'S NOTIFICATIONS:
YUNNAN ELECTRONICS I/E CORP.	CHUNGKUO

Procedure 8 Shipping Space Booking

流程 8 订舱托运

Upon receipt of the letter of credit amendment notice from the advising bank, Wang Ming began to arrange the shipment of the export goods after checking that there were no discrepancies. Wang Ming filled in the shipping space booking note for export goods by sea, together with the commercial invoice, packing list and other necessary documents, and entrusted Guangzhou Yuxiang International Freight Forwarding Company to handle the shipment. The date of booking document is August 15, 2006.

收到通知行发来的信用证修改通知书，经审核无不符点之后，王明开始安排出口货物的装运事宜。王明填制海运出口货物订舱委托书，并随附商业发票、装箱单等必要单据，委托广州宇翔国际货运代理公司办理托运。订舱单据的日期为2006年8月15日。

出口货物订舱委托书

Shipping Space Booking Note for Export Eoods

公司编号：CM01LD　　　　　　　　　　　　　　　　日期：15-Aug-06

1)发货人 YUNNAN ELECTRONICS I/E CORP. 211 RENMIN ROAD KUNMING, YUNNAN CHINA		4)信用证号码　ETN-CXLC06					
		5)开证银行　IDUSTRY BANK NEWYORK					
		6)合同号码 CX-TRMSQ06		7)成交金额 US$61760.00			
		8)装运口 GUANGZHOU		9)目的港　　NEWYORK			
2)收货人 TO ORDER		10)转船运输 PERMITTED		11)分批装运 PERMITTED			
		12)信用证效期 15-Sep-06		13)装船期限 31-Aug-06			
		14)运费　PREPAID		15)成交条 CIFC3 NEWYORK			
		16)公司联系人 Wang Ming		17)电话/传真 (0871)3556788			
3)通知人 U.S GLOBAL ELECTRONICS CO., LTD. 308 SEASHORE ROAD NEWYORK, PA 19446 U.S.A		18)公司开户行 BANK OF CHINA YUNNAN BRANCH		19)银行账号　1478523690			
		20)特别要求					
21) 标记唛码	22) 货号规格	23) 包装件数	24) 毛重	25) 净重	26) 数量	27) 单价	28) 总价
							CIFC3 NEWYORK
U.S GLOBAL ELECTRONICS CO.,LTD. NEWYORK, U.S.A. CX-TRMSQ06 NO.1-500	MICROWAVE TRM-12	500 CTNS	7700 KGS	7500 KGS	500 SETS	USD 123.52	USD 61760
		29) 总件数	30) 总毛重	31) 总净重	32) 总尺码	33) 总金额	
		500 CTNS	7700 KGS	7500 KGS	25M3	US$61760	
34)备注							

商业发票

COMMERCIAL INVOICE

1) SELLER YUNNAN ELECTRONICS I/E CORP. Address: 211 RENMIN ROAD KUNMING, YUNNAN, CHINA 2) BUYER U.S GLOBAL ELECTRONICS CO., LTD. Address: 308 SEASHORE ROAD NEWTORK, PA 19446 U.S.A	3) INVOICE NO. BK-UMQINV11	4) INVOICE DATE 15-Aug-06
	5) L/C NO. ETN-CXLC06	6) DATE 25-July-06
	7) ISSUED BY INDUSTRY BANK NEWYORK	
	8) CONTRACT NO. CX-TRMSQ06	9) DATE 5-July-06
	10) FROM GUANGZHOU	11) TO NEWYORK
	12) SHIPPED BY	13) PRICE TERM CIFC3 NEWYORK

14) MARKS	15) DESCRIPTION OF GOODS	16) QTY.	17) UNIT PRICE	18) AMOUNT
US.GLOBALELECTRONICS CO.,LTD. NEWYORK,U.S.A. CX-TRMSQ06 NO.1-500	MICROWAVE ART. NO. TRM-12	500 SETS	CIFC3 NEWYORK USD123.52 TOTAL:	USD61760.00 USD61760.00
	TOTAL NUMBER OF PACKING: 500CTNS			
	TOTAL GROSS WEIGHT: 7700KGS			
	19) TOTAL VALUE(IN WORDS) SAY UNITED STATES DOLLARS SIXTY ONE THOUSAND SEVEN HUNDRED AND SIXTY ONLY			
			20) ISSUED BY YUNNAN ELECTRONICS I/E CORP. 21) SIGNATURE Wang Ming	

装箱单

PACKING LIST

1) SELLER YUNNAN ELECTRONICS I/E CORP. Address: 211 RENMIN ROAD KUNMING YUNNAN CHINA		3) INVOICE NO. BK-UMQINV11	4) INVOICE DATE 2006-8-15	
		5) FROM GUANGZHOU	6) TO NEWYORK	
		7) TOTAL PACKAGES(IN WORDS) SAY FIVE HUNDRED CARTONS ONLY			
2) BUYER U.S GLOBAL ELECTRONICS CO., LTD. Address: 308 SEASHORE STREET NEWYORK, PA 19446 U.S.A		8) MARKS & NOS. US. GLOBAL ELECTRONICS CO., LTD. NEWYORK, U.S.A. CX-TRMSQ06 NO.1-500			
9) C/NOS.	10) NOS. & KINDS OF PKGS.	11) ITEM	12)QTY. (sets)	13)G.W. (kg)	14)N.W. (kg)	15)MEAS (m³)
NO.1-500	500 CTNS	MICROWAVE TRM-12	500	7700	7500	25
TOTAL:	500 CTNS		500	7700	7500	25
SHIPPING MARKS || WEIGHT AND MEAS. PER EXPORT CARTON:				
US.GLOBAL ELECTRONICS CO., LTD. NEWYORK, U.S.A. CX-TRMSQ06 NO.1-500		ART. NO.	G.W. (KGS.)		N.W. (KGS.)	MEAS. (M³)
		TRM-12	15.4		15	0.05
|| 16) ISSUED BY YUNNAN ELECTRONICS I/E CORP.				
|| 17) SIGNATURE Wang Ming				

The following is shipping order returned on August 17 from the shipping company, COSCO Guangzhou Shipping Co., Ltd., after accepting the booking, 2006, to Guangzhou Yuxiang International Freight Forwarding Company to transfer to the exporter. The shipping order is a necessary document for customs declaration procedures. The customs inspects, If it approves the export, the release seal shall be stamped on the shipping order, the freight forwarder shall require the master to load the cargo with the shipping order signed by the shipping company and sealed by the customs.

以下是船公司中远广州公司在接受订舱后，2006年8月17日，退还给广州宇翔国际货运代理公司转给出口商的装货单。装货单是向海关办理出口报关手续的必要文件，海关进行查验，如同意出口，则在装货单上盖放行章，货运代理持海关盖章并由船公司签署的装货单要求船长装货。

装货单

Shipping Order

Shipper (发货人) YUNNAN ELECTRONICS I/E CORP. 211 RENMING ROAD KUNMING YUNNAN CHINA				S/O No.(编号) LD-DRGBL01		
Consignee (收货人) TO ORDER				装货单		
Notify Party (通知人) U.S GLOBAL ELECTRONICS CO., LTD. 308 SEASHORE STREET NEWYORK, PA 19446 U.S.A.						
Pre-carriage by(前程运输)				Place of Receipt (收货地点) GUANGZHOU CY		
Vessel(船名) DONG FENG		Voy. No(航次) V208	Port of Loading(装货港) GUANZHOU		
Port of Discharge (卸货港) NEW YORK				Place of Delivery(交货地点) NEWYORK CY		Final Destination for the Merchant's Reference (目的地)
Container No. (集装箱号)	Marks & Nos. (标志与号码)		Nos. Kinds of Packages (包装件数与种类)	Description of Goods (货名)	G.W.(KG) 毛重(公斤)	MEAS(M³) 尺码(立方米)
TEXU67233331	U.S GLOBAL ELECTRONICS CO., LTD. NEWYORK U.S.A CX-TRMSQ06 NO.1-500		1 CONTAINER 500 CTNS	MICROWAVE	7700	25
Total Number of Containers or Packages(In Words) 集装箱数或件数合计(大写)				SAY FIVE HUNDRED CARTONS ONLY		
Freight & Charges (运费与附加费)		Revenue Tons (运费吨)	RATE (运费率)	Prepaid (运费预付)	Collect (到付)	
Ex. Rate: (兑换率) USD1=RMB8.00		Prepaid at (预付地点) GUANGZHOU	Payable at (到付地点)	Place of Issue (签发地点) GUANGZHOU	
^		Total Prepaid (预付总额) USD1500	No. of Original B(s)/L (正本提单份数) THREE		
Service Type on Receiving CY			Service Type on Delivery CY	提单签发： SIGENATURE	
可否转船: PERMITTED			可否分批: PERMITTED			
装期: 31-AUGUST-06			效期: 15-SEPTEMBER-06	中华人民共和国海关 验讫放行	
金额: US$2500						
制单日期: 17-AUGUST-06						

Procedure 9　Inspection and Customs Clearance

流程9　商检和通关

According to the customs clearance mode of applying for inspection before customs declaration, on August 19, 2006, Wang Ming filled out an inspection application form for export goods, which was attached with the contract, letter of credit, invoice, packing list, etc., and submitted to Yunnan Commodity Inspection Bureau of the people's Republic of China for inspection. The following is the inspection application form for export goods prepared by Wang Ming:

The inspection registration no. of Yunnan Electronic Import and Export Corporation is 03781

Registration No. of the manufacturer, Kunming Jinxin Electronics Factory, in the inspection and quarantine institution is ST-HZS3781

根据我国先报验后报关的通关模式，2006年8月19日王明填制了一份《出境货物报验单》，随附合同、信用证、发票、装箱单等，向中华人民共和国云南商检局报检。以下为王明所填制的《出境货物报验单》：

云南电子进出口公司的报验登记号为：03781

生产单位昆明金鑫电子厂在检验检疫机构的注册号：ST-HZS3781

中华人民共和国出入境检验检疫出境货物报验单

报验单位(加盖公章)：云南电子进出口公司　　　　　　编　号：_____

报验单位登记号：03781　联系人：王明　电话：0871-3556789　报验日期：2006年8月19日

发货人	(中文)：云南电子进出口公司					
	(外文)：YUNNAN ELECTRONICS I/E CORP.					
收货人	(中文)：美国全球电子有限公司					
	(外文)：U.S GLOBAL ELECTRONICS CO., LTD					
货物名称(中/外文)	H. S. 编码	产地	数/重量	货物总值	包装种类及数量
微波炉 MICROWAVE	85165000	中国云南省昆明市人民路	500SETS	USD61760	500CARTONS
运输工具名称号码	DONGFENG V208	贸易方式	一般	货物存放地点	工厂

合同号	CX-TRMSQ06		信用证号	ETN-CXLC06	用途	销售
发货日期	2006/08/31	输往国家(地区)	U.S.A	许可证/审批号		
启运地	GUANZHOU	到达口岸	NEWYORK	生产单位注册号		ST-HZS3781
集装箱规格、数量及号码	1个20′集装箱 TEXU67233331					
合同、信用证订立的检验检疫条款或特殊要求	标记及号码		随附单据(划"√"或补填)			
	U.S GLOBAL ELECTRONICS CO., LTD NEWYORK U.S.A CX-TRSQ06 NO.1-500		☑合同 ☑信用证 ☑发票 ☐换证凭单 ☑装箱单 ☑厂检单	☐包装性能结果单 ☐许可/审批文件 ☐ ☐ ☐ ☐		

需要证单名称(划"√"或补填)				*检验检疫费	
☑品质证书	2 正 __副	☐植物检疫证书	__正__副	总金额(人民币元)	
☐重量证书	__正__副	☐熏蒸/消毒证书	__正__副	计费人	
☑数量证书	2 正 __副	☐出境货物换证凭单			
☐兽医卫生证书	__正__副	☐		收费人	
☐健康证书	__正__副	☐			
☐卫生证书	__正__副	☐			
☐动物卫生证书	__正__副	☐			

报验人郑重声明: 1. 本人被授权报验 2. 上列填写内容正确属实,货物无伪造或冒用他人的厂名、标志、认证标志,并承担货物质量责任。 签名:王明	领取证单	
	日期	
	签名	

注:"*"号栏由出入境检验检疫机关填写　　　　国家出入境检验检疫局制

The following is the inspection certificate issued by Yunnan Commodity Inspection Bureau on August 22, 2006

以下为云南商检局在对货物验迄合格2006年8月22日签发的检验证书:

中华人民共和国云南进出口商品检验局
YUNNAN IMPORT & EXPORT COMMODITY INSPECTION BUREAU OF THE PEOPLE'S REPUBLIC OF CHINA

检 验 证 书
INSPECTION CERTIFICATE OF QUALITY

正 本
ORIGINAL
编 号 No.
S0010512337

地址：云南省昆明市滇池路8号
Address: 8. Dianchi Road Kunming, Yunnan.
电话 Tel: 63211285

发 货 人： **Consignor**	云南电子进出口公司 YUNNAN ELECTRONICS I/E CORP.		
收 货 人： **Consignee**	*********		
品 名： **Description of Goods**	MICROWAVE	标记及号码： **Marks & No.**	
报验数量/重量： **Quantity/Weight Delared**	500SETS	U.S GLOBAL ELECTRONICS CO., LTD NEWYORK U.S.A	
包装种类及数量 **Number and Type of Packages**	500CARTONS	CX-TRMSQ06 NO.1-500	
运输工具 **Means of Conveyance**	BY SEA		

检 验 结 果：
RESULTS OF INSPECTION:

We hereby certify that the goods are of the above-mentioned quantity and of sound quality.

印章 **Official Stamp**	签证地点： **Place of Issue**	KUNMING	签证日期： **Date of Issue**	AUG.22, 2006
	授权签字人： **Authorized Officer**	MA BIN	签名： **Signature**	LI HUI

On August 19, 2006, Wang Ming also filled in an application for a certificate of origin, accompanied by a commercial invoice and an original and three copies of the certificate of origin, which were submitted to Yunnan Commodity Inspection Bureau for confirmation and signature. The following is the application completed by Wang Ming and the certificate of origin confirmed and signed by the Commodity Inspection Bureau on August 22, 2006: (Note: Registration No. for C/O is ST-HZS3721 of Yunnan Electronics Import and Export Corporation in the inspection and quarantine institution)

2006年8月19日王明还填写了一份一般原产地证书申请书，同时还随附商业发票一份，以及一般原产地证书一份正本三份副本交云南商检局确认签署。以下为王明所填制的申请书，及2006年8月22日得到商检局确认签署的一般原产地证明书：（注：云南电子进出口公司在检验检疫机构申领一般原产地证的注册号为ST-HZS3721）

一般原产地证书/加工装配证明书申请书

申请单位注册号：ST-HZS3721　　　　　　　　　　　　证书号：

申请人郑重声明：
本人被正式授权代表本企业办理和签署本申请书。
本申请书及一般原产地证明书、加工装配证明书所列内容正确无误，如发现弄虚作假，冒充证书所列货物，擅改证书，自愿接受签证机关的处罚并负法律责任，现将有关情况申报如下：

企业名称	云南电子进出口公司		发票号		BK-UMQINV11	
商品名称	微波炉		H.S.编码		85165000	
商品(FOB)总值美元	51584.1125		最终目的国/地区		美国纽约	
拟出运日期	2006/08/31		转出国(地区)			
贸易方式和企业性质(请在适处画"√")						
一般贸易		三来一补		其他贸易方式		
中资企业	外资企业	中资企业	外资企业	中资企业	外资企业	
√						
包装数量或毛重或其他数量	500 箱					
证书种类(画"√")	√一般原产地证明书			加工装配证明书		

现提交中国出口货物商业发票 1 份，一般原产地证明书/加工装配证明书 1 正 3 副，以及其他附件 _____ 份，请予审核签证。

申请单位：云南电子进出口公司　　　　申领人(签名)：王明
　　　　　　　　　　　　　　　　　　电话：0871-3556789

　　　　　　　　　　　　　　　　　　日期：2006 年 8 月 19 日

一 般 原 产 地 证 书

Certificate of Origin

ORIGINAL

1. Exporter (full name and address) YUNNAN ELECTRONICS I/E CORP. 211 RENMING ROAD KUNMING YUNNAN CHINA		Certificate No. JH-FLSFMA06	
2. Consignee (full name, address, country) U.S GLOBAL ELECTRONICS CO., LTD. 308 SEASHORE ROAD NEWYORK, PA 19446 U.S.A		CERTIFICATE OF ORIGIN OF THE PEOPLE'S REPUBLIC OF CHINA	
3. Means of transport and route FROM GUANGZHOU CHINA TO NEWYOURK U.S.A BY SEA		5. For certifying authority use only	
4. Destination port NEWYOURK U.S.A			
6.Marks and Numbers of package	7.Description of goods: number and kind of package	8. H.S. Code	9.Quantity or weight	10.Number and date of invoices
U.S GLOBAL ELECTRON CO., LTD NEWYORK U.S.A CX-TRMSQ06 NO.1-500	500 CARTONS (SAY FIVE HUNDRED ONLY) MICROWAVE	85165000	500SETS	BK-UMQINV11 AUGUST15,2006
11. Declaration by the exporter The undersigned hereby declares that the above details and statements are correct; that all the goods were produced in China and that they comply with the Rules of Origin of the People's Republic of China.		12. Certification It is hereby certified that the declaration by the exporter is correct.	
YUNNAN ELECTRON I/E CORP. WANG MING KUNMING AUGUST 19，2006 Place and date. Signature and stamp of certifying authority		GAO HONG KUNMING AUGUST 22，2006 Place and date. Signature and stamp of certifying authority	

On August 30, 2006, Yunnan Electronics Import & Export Corporation handled the export declaration procedures of the goods to Guangzhou Customs.

2006年8月30日云南电子进出口公司向广州海关办理货物的出口报关手续。

中华人民共和国海关出口货物报关单

预录入编号:　　　　　　　　　　　　　　　海关编号:

出口口岸 广州小虎码头 5146	备案号		出口日期 20060831	申报日期 20060830
经营单位　云南电子进出口公司 3102911013	运输方式 江海	运输工具名称 DONG FENG V.208		提运单号 LD-DRGBL01
发货单位 昆明金鑫电器厂	贸易方式 一般贸易		征免性质 一般征税	结汇方式 信用证
许可证号	运抵国(地区) 美国		指运港 纽约	境内货源地 云南昆明
批准文号	成交方式 CIF	运费 502/2500/1	保费 142/4892/1	杂费 502/1853/1
合同协议号 CX-TRMSQ06	件数 500	包装种类 120	毛重(公斤) 7700	净重(公斤) 7500
集装箱号 TEXU67233331*1(1)	随附单据		生产厂家 昆明金鑫电器厂	
标记唛码及备注　　U.S GLOBAL ELETRON CO., LTD. /NEWYORK U.S.A/ CX-TRMSQ06/NO.1-500				

项号	商品编号	商品名称、规格型号	数量及单位	最终目的国(地区)	单价	总价	币制	征免
01	85165000	微波炉 TRM-12	500 台	美国	123.52	61760.00	美元	照章征税

录入员　　录入单位	兹声明以上申报无讹并承担法律责任	海关审单批注及放行日期(签章)	
报关员 王明	申报单位(签章)	审单	审价
单位地址	云南电子进出口公司	征税	统计
云南省昆明市人民路 211 号 邮编 650000 电话(0871)3556789 填制日期 2006.08.30		查验	放行

　　Note: the above is the vertical declaration form, and the General Administration of Customs started the use of the horizontal declaration form on August 1, 2018.

　　备注：以上为竖版报关单，2018 年 8 月 1 日海关总署启用横版报关单。

Procedure 10　Insurance

流程 10　保险

After receiving the shipping company's cabin allocation receipt, Wang Ming filled in a "Marine Export Cargo Insurance Application Form" on August 30, 2006, and sent it to the insurance company for insurance, the completed application form is as follows:

收到船公司的配舱回单后,在向海关申报出口的同时,2006 年 8 月 30 日王明填制了一份"海运出口货物投保单",送保险公司投保,所填投保单如下。

海 运 出 口 货 物 投 保 单

Marine Export Cargo Insurance Application Form

1)保险人：中国人民保险公司云南省分公司 THE PEOPLE'S INSURANCE COMPANY OF CHINA YUNNAN BRANCH		2)被保险人：云南电子进出口公司 YUNNAN ELECTRONICS I/E CORP	
3)标记	4)包装及数量	5)保险货物项目	6)保险金额
AS PER INVOICE NO. BK-UMQINV11	500 CTNS	MICROWAVE	USD67936.00
7)总保险金额(大写)： SAY CHINESE YUAN FIVE HUNDRED AND FOUTY THREE THOUSAND FOUR HUANDRED AND EIGHTY EIGHT ONLY			
8)运输工具：DONGFENG(船名)V208(航次)			
9)装运港：GUANGZHOU		10)目的港：NEWYORK	
11)货物起运日期：31－AUGUST－06			
12)投保险别：COVERING FOR TORAL INVOICE VALUE PLUS 10% AGAINST ALL RISKS AS PER CIC DATED 01/01/1981			
13)赔款地点：NEWYORK			
14)保险代理：		15)保单号次：	
16)投保人盖章及日期 YUNNAN ELECTRONICS I/E CORP. WANGMING 2006 年 8 月 30 日			

The insurance policy issued by Yunnan Branch of the People's Insurance Company of China is as follows.

中国人民保险公司云南公司分公司出具的保险单如下。

中国人民保险公司云南分公司
THE PEOPLE'S INSURANCE COMPANY OF CHINA
YUNNAN BRANCH

总公司设于北京　　　　一九四九年创立
Head office: BEIJING　　Established in 1949

货物运输保险单　　ORIGINAL
CARGO TRANSPORTATION INSURANCE POLICY

发票号(INVOICE NO.) BK-UMQINV11
合同号(CONTRACT NO.) CX-TRMSQ06　　　　保险单号次(POLICY NO.): ZC32/20061865
信用证号(L/C NO.) ETN-CXLC06
被保险人：云南电子进出口公司
INSURED：YUNNAN ELECTRONICS I/E CORP.

中国人民保险公司云南分公司（以下简称本公司）根据被保险人的要求，由被保险人向本公司缴付约定的保险费，按照本保险单承保险别和背面所载条款与下列特款承保下述货物运输保险，特立本保险单。

THIS POLICY OF INSURANCE WITNESSES THAT THE PEOPLE'S INSURANCE COMPANY OF CHINA YUNNAN BRAMCH (HEREINAFTER CALLED "THE COMPANY") AT THE REQUEST OF THE INSURED AND IN CONSIDERATION OF THE AGREED PREMIUM PAID TO THE COMPANY BY THE INSURED, UNDERTAKES TO INSURE THE UNDERMENTIONEDGOODS IN TRANSPORTATION SUBJECT TO THE CONDITIONS OF THIS POLICY AS PER THE CLAUSES PRINTED OVERLEAF AND OTHER SPECIAL CLAUSES ATTACHED HEREON.

标记 MARKS & NOS.	包装及数量 QUANTITY	保险货物项目 DESCRIPTION OF GOODS	保险金额 AMOUNT INSURED
AS PER INVOICE NO. BK-UMQINV11	500 CTNS	MICROWAVE	USD67936.00

总保险金额：　　　　　　　SAY US DOLLARS SIXTY SEVEN THOUSAND AND NINE
TOTAL AMOUNT INSURED　　HUNDRED THIRY SIX ONLY

| 保费 AS
PREMIUM ARRANGED | 费率 AS
RATE ARRANGED | 装载运输具
PER CONVEYANCE S.S. | DONGFENG V. 208 |
| 开航日期
SLG. ON OR ABT. | AS PER BILL OF LADING | 自 FROM GUANGZHOU | 至 NEWYORK TO |

承保险别：COVERING ALL RISKS AS PER AND SUBJECT TO OCEAN MARINE CARGO CLAUSES OF
CONDITIONS　PICC DATED 1/1/1981

所保货物，如发生本保险单项下可能引起赔偿的损失或损坏，应立即通知本公司下属代理人查勘。如有索赔，应向本公司提交保险单正本(本保险单共有正本 3 份)及有关文件。如一份正本已用于索赔，其余正本自动失效。

IN THE EVENT OF LOSS OR DAMAGE WHICH MAY RESULT IN A CLAIM UNDER THIS POLICY, IMMEDIATE NOTICE MUST BE GIVEN TO THE COMPANY'S AGENT AS MENTIONED HEREUNDER. IN THE EVENT OF CLAIMS, IF ANY ONE OF THE ORIGINAL POLICY WHICH HAS BEEN ISSUED IN 3 ORIGINAL(S) TOGETHER WITH THE RELEVANT DOCUMENTS SHALL BE SURRENDERED TO THE COMPANY, IF ONE OF THE ORIGINAL POLICY HAS BEEN ACCOMPLISHED, THE OTHERS SHALL BE VOID.

GODWIN INSURANCE COMPANY　　　　　　中国人民保险公司云南分公司
P.O.BOX 17764　　　　　　　　　　　　　THE PEOPLE'S INSURANCE COMPANY OF CHINA
NEWYORK U.S.A　　　　　　　　　　　　　YUNNAN BRANCH
FAX: 215-393-4152
赔款偿付地点
CLAIM PAYABLE　　NEW YORK IN USD
AT/IN　　　　　　　　　　　　　　　　　　LIUXIANG
出单日期　　　　　　　　　　　　　　　　General Manager
ISSUING DATE　　AUGUST 30TH, 2006

地址：中国云南省昆明市东风路 100 号　　　经办：jb　　电话(TEL)：6324343
Address: 100 DONGFEN ROAD KUNMING YUNNAN, CHINA　　复核：zbc　　传真(FAX)：
邮编(POST CODE)：532100　　　　　　　　　　　　　　　　　　86-871-6324333

Procedure 11 Delivery

流程 11 装运

The exporter completed the customs clearance procedures and submitted the relevant documents to the freight forwarder for shipment. The freight forwarder required the master of the ship to load the cargo with the shipping order stamped by the customs and signed by the shipping company. The following is the on board B/L that the freight forwarder exchanged with the shipping company based on the dock receipt signed by the chief mate after the cargo was loaded, the bill of lading was issued on August 31, 2006.

出口商办完通关手续，将相关单据交货运代理办理货物装运事宜。货运代理持海关盖章并由船公司签署的装货单要求船长装货。以下是货物装船后货运代理凭大副签署的场站收据向船公司换取的已装船提单，提单签发日为 2006 年 8 月 31 日。

海 运 提 单

BILL OF LADING

SHIPPER YUNNAN ELECTRONICS I/E CORP. 211 RENMING ROAD KUNMING YUNNAN CHINA		10)B/L NO.　LD-DRGBL01 C O S C O GUANGZHOU CO.,LTD 中远广州有限责任公司	
CONSIGNE TO ORDER			
NOTIFY PARTY U.S GLOBAL ELECTRONICS CO., LTD. 308 SEASHORE ROAD NEWYORK, PA 19446 U.S.A			*ORIGINAL*
PLACE OF RECEIPT GUANGZHOU CY	OCEAN VESSEL DONGFENG	**Combined Transport BILL OF LADING**	
VOYAGE NO. V.208	PORT OF LOADING GUANGZHOU		
PORT OF DISCHARGE NEWYORK	PLACE OF DELIVERY		
MARKS	NOS. & KINDS OF PKGS.	DESCRIPTION OF GOODS　G.W.(kg)　MEAS(m³)	
U.S GLOBAL ELECTRONICS CO., LTD NEWYORK U.S.A CX-TRMSQ06 NO.1-500 FREIGHT PREPAID L/C NO. ETN-CXLC06	500CARTONS	MICROWAV　　　　　　　　　　　25	
16)TOTAL NUMBER OF CONTAINERS OR PACKAGES (IN WORDS)		SAY FIVE HUNDRED CARTONS ONLY	
FREIGHT & CHARGES	REVENUE TONS　　RATE	PER　　PREPAID	COLLECT
EX. RATE	PREPAID AT	PAYABLE AT	PLACE AND DATE OF ISSUE GUANGZHOU　　　　AUGUST 31,2006
	TOTAL PREPAID	NUMBER OF ORIGINAL B(S)L THREE	
LOADING ON BOARD THE VESSEL		李立 COSCO GUANGZHOU OCEAN SHIPPING CO.,LTD.	
DATE　AUGUST 31,2006	BY　李立 　　COSCO　GUANGZHOU　OCEAN 　　SHIPPING CO.,LTD.		

After Wang Ming obtained the on board bill of lading, he sent the following shipping advice to the importer on August 31, 2006:

王明取得已装船海运提单之后，2006年8月31日给进口方发去如下装运通知：

YUNNAN ELECTRONICS I/E CORP.
Add: 211 RENMIN Road, Kunming, Yunnan, China   Post Code: 530000
Tel: 86-0871-3556789 FAX: 86-0871-3556788 E-mail:wm@yniec.com

August 31,2006

U.S GLOBAL ELECTRONICS CO., LTD.
308 SEASHORE ROAD NEWYORK,
PA 19446 U.S.A

Dear Mr. Smith,

We are very pleased to inform you that the goods (one container of microwave) under S/C No.CX-TRMSQ06 has been dispatched by s.s. DONGFENG V.208 on AUGUST 31th 2006. The B/L number is LD-DRGBL01 and the total invoice value is US$ 61760.
We trust that the goods will reach you safely and meet your requirements.

Yours faithfully,
Wang Ming

Procedure 12   Documents Preparation for Bank Negotiation

流程12   制单议付

Wang Ming prepared all kinds of documents in time after the shipment of the goods and submitted them to the bank for negotiation within the validity of the L / C. The documents Wang Ming provided to the bank include: commercial invoice, bill of lading, insurance policy, bill of exchange, general certificate of origin, inspection certificate and packing list. The following is the bill of exchange drawn by Wang Ming after the shipment of the goods (date: September 1, 2006).

王明在货物装运后及时准备了各种单据，在信用证有效期内提交银行议付。王明向银行所提供的单据包括：商业发票、提单、保险单、汇票、一般原产地证明、检验证书和装箱单。以下是王明在货物装运后所缮制的汇票(日期：2006 年 9 月 1 日)。

BILL OF EXCHANGE

NO. BK- UMQINV11

FOR US$61,760.00   YUNNAN   SEPTEMBER 01,2006

(AMOUT IN FIGURE)   (PLACE AND DATE OF ISSUE)

AT   XXXXXX   SIGHT OF THIS FIRST BILL OF EXCHANGE (SECOOND BEING UNPAID)

PAY TO BANK OF CHINA,YUNNAN BRANCH   OR ORDER THE SUM OF

SAY UNITED STATES DOLLARS SIXTY ONE THOUSAND SEVEN HUNDRED AND SIXTY ONLY

(AMOUNT IN WORDS)

VALUE RECEIVED FOR 500SETS **OF** MICROWAVE

         (QUANTITY)   (NAME OF COMMODITY)

DRAWN UNDER INDUSTRY BANK NEW YORK

L/C NO. ETN-CXLC06   **DATED** JULY 25,2006

TO: **FOR AND ON BEHALF OF**

INDUSTRY BANK NEW YORK   YUNNAN ELECTRONICS I/E CORP.

 55 WATER STREET, ROOM 1000   WANG MING

NEW YORK, U.S.A.   (SIGNATURE)

Chapter 11　Cases on Different Subjects of International Business

第11章　国际货物贸易专题案例及解析

Section 1　Cases on Trade Terms

第1节　贸易术语案例

Case 1 Is DDP Kuming feasible and workable?

案例1 DDP 昆明行得通、可操作吗？

Description of the case:

A dealer of jewelry in Kunming,Yunnan,China wants to import raw materials of emerald from Myitkyina,Myanmar,he negotiates with a Burmese exporter requesting to quote on DDP Kunming and saying if the price is competitive a substantial order is going to be placed and repeat orders will follow.

Burmese exporter is uncertain if DDP Kunming is feasible and workable,and asks the Chinese importer to make sure.

案例描述：

一个中国云南昆明的珠宝商，想从缅甸密支那进口翡翠原料，跟缅甸出口商磋商，让对方报 DDP 昆明价，并说明如果价格有竞争力，将有一个大订单，随后还持续订货，缅甸出口商不确定 DDP 昆明是否行得通、可操作，请中国进口商落实。

Analysis of the case:

The burmese exporter's conduct is worth commendation.

According to DDP Kunming,the Burmese exporter should be responsible for the delivery to Kunming and clears customs in China and pays relevant taxes for the import. If the exporter is uncertain relevant rules and regulations of importing country, he would better commission the importer to make sure, then go on accordingly.

In fact, according to current regulations of China customs, two parties are allowed to clear customs in China, the first is the owner of the cargo of import and export, the second is the customs broker company or international cargo forwarding company under the commission of the first party, both parties should be registered for business administration in principal and recorded or approved by China customs, the Burmese exporter does not comply with these regulations, he is unable to clear customs in China in the name of himself, he would better consult with the Chinese importer to make a change from DDP to other trade terms.

案例解析：

缅甸出口商的做法值得赞赏。

如果按照DDP昆明成交，缅甸出口商将负责将货从缅甸运到中国昆明，并且负责货物在中国的进口清关并缴纳相关的进口税费，在出口商自己不清楚进口国相关进口清关及税费缴纳规定的情况下，委托进口商落实后再行事。事实上，按照中国海关现行规定，可以向中国海关申报货物进出口，办理相关清关手续的报关单位有两类，第一是进出口货物的收发货人，第二是接受进出口货物收发货人委托代理清关的报关行或国际货物运输代理公司，两类报关单位原则上都须是中国境内经工商登记注册，并且已经向中国海关备案或注册许可登记，缅甸出口商不符合条件，不能以自己的名义完成中国进口清关和进口税费缴纳，所以缅甸出口商最好与中国进口商协商采用DDP昆明之外的其他贸易术语。

Case 2 Choice of Trade Terms for Export Business of Companies Located in Inland Area

案例2 内陆地区企业出口业务贸易术语选择

Description of the case:

An exporter located in Dali, Yunnan, China concludes a contract with a Japanese importer on CIF Nagoya basis, stipulating delivery from China to Nagoya Japan. The exporter wants to deliver the carto from Dali to Shanghai by truck and then ship it to Nagoya on sea. During the transit from Dali to Shanghai, the cargo is partially damaged because of a traffic accident of the carrying vehicle, according to traffic law and facts of the accident, the driver of the truck is sentenced to bear the whole of responsibilities in the traffic accident, although the transport company, the owner of the truck, which is in charge of the transit from Dali to Shanghai, is willing to compensate for the damage of the cargo according to the transport agreement, the exporter is unable to fulfill delivery in Shanghai as scheduled time, he has to reproduce to make up for the damaged goods and consult with Japanese importer for the delay.

案例描述：

一个地处中国云南大理的出口商与日本进口商按CIF名古屋签约成交，规定货从中国发往日本名古屋。出口商准备将货物从大理卡车运往上海，再从上海装船海运日本名古屋。货物在大理至上海途中因载货汽车发生交通事故而部分受损，根据交通事故事实和交通法，交通事故由货车司机负全责，尽管载货汽车所属的运输公司愿意按照运输合同赔偿出口商，但是出口商只得重新生产，补齐破损部分，已不能按原定时间在上海完成装船，不得不跟日本进口商为迟装船进行磋商。

Analysis of the case:

CIF is a trade term suitable for sea transport or inland waterway transport only, under CIF, the seller must pay the costs, freight and insurance premium necessary to bring the goods to the named destination, the risk of the loss of or damage to the goods is transferred from the seller to the buyer, when the goods are on board the ship at the port of shipment.In this case, when the Chinese exporter puts the goods on board the ship at the port of Shanghai, the risk of the loss of or damage to the goods is transferred from him to the Japanese importer, so he has to bear the damage to the goods during the inland transport from Dali to Shanghai.

Actually this delivery from Dali to Nagoya via Shanghai is a kind of sea-land combined/multimodal transport, nowadays carriers of combined/multimodal transport are available, they are responsible for the entire transport from Dali to Nagoya via Shanghai, the Chinese exporter may have a try to negotiate with the Japanese importer to adopt CIP Nagoya instead of CIF Nagoya, CIP is suitable for any modes of transport, under CIP, if only the cargo is under the control of the carrier at the named place of delivery, the risk of the loss of or damage to the goods is transferred from the exporter to the importer, and the exporter is able to get transport document from the carrier to negotiate payment in time.

案例解析：

CIF术语只适用于海运或内陆水运，CIF项下，出口商必须自付货物成本、运费、保险费将货物运输到指定目的港，在装运港装船之后的货损风险，由卖方转移给买方。本案例中出口商只有在上海港将货物装船之后，货损的风险才从中国出口商转移日本进口商，中国出口商须承担从大理至上海内陆运输的货损风险。实际上本案例从大理经上海至名古屋是陆海联运，现如今已有负责全程运输的多式联运承运人，中国出口商可尝试与日本进口商协商，用CIP术语替代CIF术语，CIP术语适用于任何运输方式，CIP项下，只要出口商在指定交货地将货物交由承运人控制，货损的风险即由出口商转移至进口商，出口商可从承运人处取得运输单据及时议付货款。

Section 2 Cases on Quality

第 2 节 货物质量案例

Case 1 Export of Indigo Blue Tie-Dyed Products
案例 1 靛蓝扎染产品出口

Description of the case:

Indigo blue tie-dyed products are traditional and representational products in Dali prefecture, Yunnan province, China, they are very popular with tourists at home and abroad, and also largely exported to foreign countries. The use of natural indigo blue dye stuff and dying by hand are 2 distinguishing features of these products, because of them, indigo blue tie-dyed products enjoy much popularity, however, these 2 features may result in color difference between one and another product, some foreign customers, especially some selective Japanese clients, are intolerant of too much color difference. Is there a solution to solve this problem?

案例描述：

靛蓝扎染产品是中国云南大理传统的代表性产品，广受海内外游客喜爱，也大量出口。使用纯天然靛蓝染料和纯手工染色是这类产品的两个典型特征，也是广受欢迎的原因，但是也会导致产品的色差。一些外商尤其相对挑剔的日本客户很难容忍太大的色差，怎么解决这个难题？

Analysis of the case:

Obviously indigo blue tie-dyed products are not standardized products, there are possibly too many shades of indigo blue color, sales of these products should be done by samples, color samples/color cuts should be made corresponding to specific blue colors in advance, anyway, because of the above mentioned 2 distinguishing features, in bulk production, color difference is still unavoidable between product and color sample, and between one and another product. A balanced solution could be taken into consideration by both parties of buyer and seller, it is to define a name or a code for a specific shade of indigo blue color accompanied by a bit lighter blue and a bit darker blue, these 3 blue colors make up of a color range, both parties of buyer and seller agree upon that this color range is one color, it is so called quality tolerance, accordingly the seller makes color samples/color cuts, they are shared and kept by both parties, delivered goods should be in completely conformity with color samples/color cuts in this range.

案例解析：

很显然靛蓝扎染产品不是标准化产品，可能存在太多深浅程度的靛蓝色，这类产品得按样成交，得提前制备色样/色卡，以对应具体的颜色。但是因为这类产品的上述两个特征，大货产品和色样之间、产品和产品之间的色差仍难避免。一个平衡的解决方案，可提供买卖双方考虑，给一个具体深浅程度的的蓝色一个专门的名称或代码，配套相应稍深和稍浅的两个蓝色，构成一个具体蓝色的颜色范围，买卖双方同意这个颜色范围为一个色，这就是所谓的品质机动幅度，卖方相应制作色样色卡供双方分享保存，装运的货物的颜色必须完全与该颜色范围相符。

Case 2　Shipping Quality or Landed Quality?

案例2　离岸品质还是到岸品质？

Description of the case:

A Chinese exporter signs a contract with the a foreign importer stipulating that taking shipping quality and quantity as final, inspection certificate issued by CCIQ is taken as the basis for negotiating payment. The Chinese prepares the goods, applies for inspection, gets qualified inspection cetificate from CCIQ and makes shipment as the contract, however, upon arrival of the goods the foreigner finds that the quality of the goods is not in conformity with the stipulation of the contract and files a claim against the Chinese immediately. Sould the Chinese exporter settle the claim?

案例描述：

中国出口商和外国进口商签订合同，规定以离岸品质、数量为准，中国进出境检验检疫局出具的检验证书为议付的依据。中国出口商按合同规定备货、报检、取得合规的检验证书并装船出口，货物一到目的港，外国进口商验货，发现到货的品质与合同规定不符，该外国进口商马上向中国出口商索赔，中国出口商是否应该理赔？

Analysis of the case:

The Chinese exporter should not settle the claim, it's just because as stipulated in the contract shipping quality and quantity as final. Shipping quality means the quality when the goods are delivered at the port of departure other than the quality when the goods are landed at the port of destination, the latter is called landed quality. In this case, the Chinese exporter has already got inspection certificate from CCIQ as the contract, it is the evidence the quality of the goods is qualified when the goods are delivered at the port of departue, the Chinese exporter is free from then on, unless the foreign importer could prove there have been inner flaws in the goods before shipment.

Anyway, in international business importer and exporter are usually separated by thousands miles, at the time of shipping the importer does not see the goods yet, making inspection before shipment and taking shipping quality and quantity as final are favorable for the exporter and unfavorable for the importer, it is better taking shipping quality and quantity with qualified inspection certificate issued by recognized surveyor as the basis for negotiating payment and taking landed quality and quantity with qualified reinspection certificate issued by designated surveyor as the ground for filing a claim.

案例解析：

中国出口商不应理赔。

因为合同规定以离岸品质为准，离岸品质指货物在装运港装船时的品质，而不是货物到达目的港卸货时的品质，后者叫做到岸品质。本案例中，中国出口商按合同规定在装运港装船时已取得中国出入境检验检疫局的合格检验证书，之后中国出口商即对货物品质免责，除非外国进口商能证明装船前货物存在内在瑕疵。

话又说回来，国际贸易当中，进出口双方一般相距遥远，出口商在装运港装船时，进口商看不到货物，以离岸品质、数量为准，对出口商有利，而对进口商不利，如果以认可的检验机构出具的合格检验证书代表的离岸品质、数量作为卖方议付货款的依据，以指定的检验机构出具的合格复检证书代表的到岸品质、数量作为买方索赔的依据，更为适宜。

Section 3　Cases on Quantity

第3节　货物数量案例

Case 1　More or Less in Assorted Quantity

案例1　分类数量溢短短装

Description of the case:

A foreign importer places an order for 5000 pieces of men's cotton shirts with a Chinese garments exporter, the order is an assortment of 5 different colors, black, white, grey, navy and Khaki, each color 1000 pieces. The contract allows 5% more or less in quantity and amount.

The Chinese exporter accepts this order and signs on the contract. He delivers the goods as follows, black 1050 pieces, white 950 pieces, grey 1000 pieces, navy 1100 pieces, khaki 900 pieces, 5000 pieces in total, and draws a draft to collect payment for the goods, but it is dishonored by the importer.

案例描述：

外国进口商向中国某服装出口商订购男士棉衬衫5000件，有黑、白、灰、海军蓝、卡其5个颜色搭配，每个颜色1000件，合同允许数量和金额增减5%。中国出口商接受了该订单，并在合同上签字，然后，交货黑色 1050 件、白色 950 件、灰色 1000 件、海军蓝 1100 件、卡其色 900 件，总数 5000 件，出具汇票，向外国进口商托收货款，但遭拒付。

Analysis of the case:

The importer has the right of refusal.

More or less clause is commonly explained according to international business practice:"It binds not only the total quantity but also each assorted quantity". In principle the exporter would better deliver each assorted item more or less at the same ratio and along the same direction.

In this case, although the total quantity delivered is in accordance with the contract, the ratio and direction of more or less for 5 colors are different, they are +5%, -5%, 0, +10%, -10% respectively, and the latitude of navy and khaki has been 10% over stipulated 5%, obviously, it is against the above mentioned explanation for more or less class, the Chinese exporter has broken the contract.

案例解析：

进口商有权拒付。

按国际贸易惯例，通常溢短装条款解释为"不仅总数量受约束，每个具体规格的数量也受其约束"。原则上出口商最好掌握多交或者少交，以同一比例按同一方向进行。

本案例中，中国出口商交货的总数量符合合同规定，但 5 个颜色的增减比例、方向分别为+5%, -5%, 0, +10%, -10%，而且海军蓝和卡其色的增减幅度已达到 10%，明显超过规定的 5%，显然与上述溢短装条款的解释相悖，已违反合同。

Case 2　The Word "About" Used in Describing Quantity
案例 2　"约"用于描述货物数量

Description of the case:

A Chinese exporter concludes a contract of 200 metric tons of dyeing stuff with a foreign importer, USD200.00 per metric ton on CIF basis, allowing quantity and amount 10% more or less. The importer opens L/C, it states "This credit is subject to UCP 600" and "About 200 metric tons", but does not remark "about" in front of the amount USD40,000.00. Chinese exporter delivers actually 220 metric ton valued USD44,000.00, and comes to an agreement with the importer that the importer will not amend the L/C, in order to make ducuments consistent with L/C, the exporter will issue invoice and draft totally in accordance with stipulated quantity and amount in the L/C to negotiate payment under L/C mentioning in the invoice actual 220 metric ton delivered, and draws a clean draft to collect payment for the excess of 20 metric ton USD4,000.00. Is it appropriate doing like this?

案例描述：

中国出口商与外国进口商按 CIF 签约成交染料 200 公吨，每公吨单价 200 美元，总值 40 000 美元，合同规定数量、金额允许增减 10%。外国进口商开来信用证，该证声明"本信用证按 UCP 600 开立"，证上数量描述为"约 200 公吨"，但是，总金额 USD 40 000.00 前未加注"约"字。中国出口商实际装运 220 公吨，货值 44 000 美元，并与外国进口商协商，不再修改信用证，为了单证相符，在信用证项下按照 200 公吨 40 000 美元缮制发票汇票议付货款，并在发票上注明实际装运 220 公吨，多装运的 20 公吨 4 000 美元，另外出具一张光票交银行托收。这样操作是否得当？

Analysis of the case:

In this case, there is a word of "about" in front of the quantity stipulated in the L/C, according to relevant stipulations in UCP600:The words "about" or "approximately" used in connection with the amount of the credit or the quantity or the unit price stated in the credit are to be construed as allowing a tolerance not to exceed 10% more or 10% less than the amount, the quantity or the unit price to which they refer, it should be allowed that Chinese exporter delivers 10% more, but the word of "about" is not added to the stipulated amount USD40,000.00 in the L/C, under common circumstance, it is appropriate that in order to make ducuments consistent with L/C, the exporter issues invoice and draft totally in accordance with stipulated quantity and amount in the L/C to negotiate payment under L/C mentioning in the invoice actual 220 metric ton delivered, and draws a clean draft to collect payment for the excess of 20 metric ton USD4,000.00 anyway, if the importer's country controls foreign exchange strictly, the excess amount is limited or prohibited, the exporter would better ask the importer to amend L/C or delivers the goods strictly in conformity with the L/C.

案例解析：

根据 UCP600 规定："约"或者"大约"用于信用证金额或者信用证规定的数量或者单价时，应解释为允许有关金额或者数量或者单价有不超过 10%的增减幅度，本案例中信用证的数量之前列有"约"字，中国出口商多装 10%是允许的，但是，信用证内总金额 40 000 美元前没有注明"约"，那么，中国出口商开具的发票和汇票均不能超过信用证规定的总金额 40 000 美元，为了使信用证项下单证相符，中国出口商将多装运的 20 公吨价值 4 000 美元的货，另外出具光票交银行托收，一般情况下是可以的，而如果对方国家外汇管制较严，限制或者禁止超出信用证金额的光票托收，那最好还是，要么要求进口商严格按照合同修改信用证或者出口商严格按照信用证规定的数量金额装运货物。

Section 4　Cases on Packing and Marks

第 4 节　货物包装与标志案例

Case 1　Shipping Mark
案例 1　运输标志

Description of the case:

A Chinese seller signs a sales contract with a foreign buyer, stipulating shipping mark is decided by the seller including design and stenciling. When the covering credit reaches the seller, the seller finds that the inconformity between the stipulation of the credit and that of the contract about shipping mark, however according to the contract the seller has already finished shipping mark stenciling. What should the seller do right now?

案例描述：

中国卖家与某外国买家就某商品签订销售合同，规定运输标志(唛头)由卖方决定，设计并印刷，但在收到对方开来的信用证时，买方发现，证内又规定了运输标志，而且与合同规定的运输标志不符，因合同规定运输标志由卖方决定，卖方早已按合同刷妥，现信用证规定与合同规定不符，卖方该怎么办？

Analysis of the case:

Chinese seller may ask for an amendment to the credit according to the contract, or, consult with the buyer to pay the fees for modifying stenciled shipping mark as the credit.

If it is stipulated in the contract shipping mark is decided by the seller, both parties of the buyer and the seller should follow this stipulation. The seller should open the credit according to the contract. If there is not a stipulation in the contract for the decision of shipping mark, according to international business practice, it is usually decided by the seller. This case belongs to the former, but the buyer does not open the credit as contract. The credit is closely connected with the contract, they are also separate and independent, opening bank does not care about the contract. If only documents presented by the beneficiary are in full conformity with the stipulation of the credit, opening bank should pay. In this case, the Chinese seller is going to be paid by the credit, he has to present documents consistent with the credit, otherwise the opening bank may refuse to pay.

So Chinese seller would better ask for an amendment to the credit according to the contract, or, be flexible to consult with the buyer to pay the fees for modifying stenciled shipping mark as the credit.

案例解析：

中国卖家可以按合同规定要求外国买家修改信用证，也可与外国买家协商，由中国卖家参照信用证改运输标志重新刷唛，并由外国买家支付改唛的费用。

如果合同已规定运输标志由卖方决定则买卖双方均应遵守，买方有义务按照合同规定的运输标志开立信用证。如果合同未规定运输标志由哪一方决定，按照国际贸易惯例，通常由卖方决定。本案例的情况属于前者，但是买方未按合同规定的运输标志开立信用证。合同与信用证既有密切联系，又是相互独立的两个文件，信用证需按合同开立，但信用证又独立于合同，开证行对销售合同并不过问，只要受益人完全履行了信用证各项规定后开证须保证付款。本案例中，中国卖家是凭信用证出口收款，则提交的一切单据须与信用证完全相符，否则开证行可以拒付，为此中国卖家最好是按照合同规定要求外国买家修改信用证，当然也可考虑做些变通，与买家协商，不修改信用证，而照信用证的规定修改已经刷妥的运输标志，由买家支付修改运输标志的费用。

Case 2　Wooden Case for Garments Packing

案例2　木箱装服装

Description of the case:

A letter of request for garments packing from the buyer to seller as follows, what will the seller do?

Our Order for 1000 doz. Gent's Shirts

We dispatched to you this order as per yesterday's cable:

"1000DOZ MENSSHIRTS HAIDABRAND MAYSHIPMENT DIRECT STEAMER PLSCONFIRM"

Particular care should be taken about the quality and the packing of the goods to be delivered in this first order. It is the usual practice here that 10 shirts are packed to a carton and 10 cartons to a strong seaworthy wooden case. There will be a flow of orders if this initial order proves to be satisfactory.

We are enclosing our Confirmation of Purchase in duplicate. Please sign one copy and return it to us for our records. As soon as we receive your confirmation, a letter of credit will be opened through Barclay's Bank of London.

We trust this order will be the first of a series of deals between us.

案例描述：

一封来自买家的关于服装包装要求的信件如下，卖家怎么办？

关于我方1 000打男士衬衫订单

我方昨天电报订货如下：

"1 000打男士海达牌衬衫，5月直航船交货，请确认。"

这第 1 个订单货物的质量和包装须特别注意。按我们这儿的惯例，10 件衬衫装入一个纸箱，10 个纸箱装入一个适宜海运的结实的木箱。如果第 1 次订货满意的话，随后将会有一波订单跟进。

随附我方的购货合同一式两份，请签署并返回其中一份。收到贵方确认，我方将立即通过伦敦巴克莱银行开立信用证。

我方相信此订单将会是贵我对方之间一系列贸易合作的开端。

Analysis of the case:

It is likely ponderous overkill for limited needs, in internationsl business cartons are commonly used as outer packing for garments, lined with shockproof corrugated cardboard and wrapped up with damp proof polythene sheets, they are as seaworthy as wooden cases and can stand rough handling on the docks, besides, cartons are less expensive, lighter to carry and cost lower freight, so nowadays more and more clients prefer carton to wooden case, anyway, if your counter part insists on using wooden cases, you may also meet his demand and ask him to pay extra charges.

案例解析：

用木箱装衬衫，有点儿夸张。国际贸易中，一般用防震的瓦楞纸箱做服装的外包装，纸箱内部衬上塑料薄膜防潮，已经能够替代木箱满足海上运输的需求，而且纸箱更便宜更轻便运费也更低，现在也来也多的客户更多选择纸箱而非木箱，当然，如果买家坚持要使用木箱包装，卖家也可满足其要求，让其付额外的费用。

Section 5　Cases on Pricing

第 5 节　定价案例

Case 1　Commission Calculation
案例 1　佣金计算

Description of the case:

Chinese exporter makes quotation for his product Euro100.00 per set CIFC5 Marseilles, he is actually able to get payment of Euro 95.00 for each set.If he wants to get actual payment for each set Euro100.00, his foreign counterpart wants to get 5% commission, should this Chinese exporter quote Euro 105.00 per set CIFC5 Marseilles?

案例描述：

按 CIFC5 马赛报价 100 欧元，中国出口商实际收汇为 95 欧元，如果打算实际收汇 100 欧元，对方要求给付佣金 5%，中国出口商是否应以 CIFC5105 欧元报价？

Analysis of the case:

The correct answer is CIFC5105.26 In international business there are various ways of calculating commission, the amount of commission could be figured out according to agreed price including commission multiplied by the rate of commission, it could also be figured out according to agreed net price multiplied by that percentage, in case price agreed upon by both parties of importer and exporter on the basis of other delivery terms, for example, on CIF basis, we may deduct firstly freight and premium, change CIF into FOB, and then figure out the amount of commission on FOB basis. There are not general rules, both parties of importer and exporter may consult with each other to decide.

In this case, Chinese exporter makes quotation for his product Euro100.00 per set CIFC5 Marseilles, he is actually able to get payment of Euro 95.00 for each set, it tells the amount of commission Euro 5.00 is figured out according to the price including commission Euro 100.00 multiplied by the rate of commission 5%, if he wants to get actual payment for each set Euro100.00, ie. Euro 100.00 per set CIF Marseilles net, price including commission on CIFC5 Marseilles could be figured out according to the following formula, CIFC5=CIF net/(1-rate of commission)=100/(1-5%)=105.26

案例解析：

正确答案是CIFC5105.26 在国际贸易中，佣金的计算方式多种多样，有的按照成交含佣价乘以一定百分比的佣金率计算；有的按照成交净价的百分比计算；有的先把成交价，如CIF价，减去运费和保险费，转换为FOB价之后，再计算佣金额。没有统一规定，交易双方可自行协商确定。

本案例，按CIFC5马赛报价100欧元，中国出口商实际收汇为95欧元，说明佣金额5欧元是按CIFC5含佣价100欧元乘以佣金率5%计算得来，如果打算实际收汇100欧元，即，CIF净价为100欧元，佣金率仍用5%，则新的CIFC5含佣价按如下公式计算，CIFC5=CIF净价÷(1-佣金率)=100÷(1-5%)=105.26。

Case 2 How much is it and its answer

案例2 多少钱和它的答案

Description of the case:

A very young foreign sales person of a Chinese international business company is sent by the company to attend Canton Fair as an exhibitor and negotiator. At he beginning of Canton Fair, he receives foreign visitors and gives answers to their simple question How Much Is It by a simple figure such as US DOLLAR 18, after instructed by an experienced colleague, he realizes the answer to such simple question is not simple, then he makes adjustment promptly.

案例描述：

中国某外贸公司的一个非常年轻的外销员被公司派往广交会参加展洽，广交会刚开始，他在接待外商答复对方的简单提问"How much is it？"时，均用简单的一个价格数字回答，如 US DOLLAR 18，后来经同行的经验丰富的外销员指点提醒，他意识到简单问题答案却不简单，迅速进行了调整。

Analysis of the case:

How much is it? It is indeed a simple question, but the answer is not simple.

First of all, under no circumstances can a buyer get a quotation without trade terms in international business, trade terms are short terms and abbreviations which are used to explain the price composition, to define the delivery of the goods, to indicate which party bears the freight, insurance and other relevant charges, and assume the liability in case damage to or loss of the goods occurs, trade terms ensure both importer and exporter know their own responsibilities. The cost of a certain product is the same in the seller's factory, however, the prices quoted by the seller will vary with the place of delivery and possible relevant charges, for example, in the case of a contract based on CIF term as "CIF New York", that means the seller bears all the cost freight and insurance up to the named port of destination New York.

Moreover, there are various factors on pricing including needs, cost, quantity, delivery, payment rate of exchange, and so on. The seller would better take them into consideration as much as possible. It's not wise to give a simple answer of figure hastily.

案例解析：

How much is it?问题简单，答案却不简单。

首先，进出口业务的报价少不了贸易术语。贸易术语是用简单的概念或缩写来表明价格构成，规定货物的交付方法，指明由哪一方负担运费、保险费和其他相关费用、由哪一方承担货物损坏或灭失的责任。贸易术语使进出口双方明确各自的责任。某种商品出厂价格一样，交货地点不同、费用不同，卖方就应报不同的价格，例如 CIF 纽约，意味着卖方承担所有的成本、运费和保险费，交付货物直至指定的目的港纽约。

另外，影响定价的因素多样，包括市场需求、商品成本、订购数量、交货条件、支付条件、汇率风险等，应尽可能地加以考虑，不宜简单草率地给出一个价格数字了事。

Section 6　Cases on Delivery

第6节　货物装运案例

Case 1　Freight prepaid or collect?

案例1　运费预付还是运费到付？

Description of the case:

An exporter in Yunnan province contracts on FCA Singapore basis with an importer from Singapore for Puer Tea at Kunming Trade Fair, both parties agree upon delivery is made by air from Kunming to Singapore, airfreight is paid immediately by cash from buyer to seller on the spot, the seller is responsible for contracting with airlines and paying freight to deliver goods from Kunming to Singapore when the goods are ready, the amount of goods is paid by credit. Credit reaches the seller later on, without special statement for air freight. The seller makes delivery and acquires airway bill remaking"Freight prepaid" from airlines, the seller presents airway bill together with other necessary documents for negotiation, payment is refused by opening bank because of inconsistence between documents and credit.

案例描述：

云南某茶叶出口商与新加坡进口商在昆交会上按FCA新加坡签约成交一批普洱茶，双方约定货物以空运方式从昆明运至新加坡，并由买方将空运费当场以现钞交卖方，货物备妥由卖方在昆明向航空公司托运并付运费，货款以信用证方式结算。随后买方通过开证行开来信用证，信用证对运费支付问题未作特殊规定。卖方按照信用证办理装运并取得"运费预付"空运单，随同其他单据交议付行转开证行，开证行以单证不符为由拒付。

Analysis of the case:

Decision of refusal made by opening bank is correct.

Because the credit has already stated clearly "FCA" and there is no other special stipulation for the payment of freight charge. It is known to all that "Freight collect" corresponds to FCA, "Freight prepaid" remarked on airway bill, which is presented by beneficiary, is inconsistent with FCA, it is also inconsistent with the stipulation of credit, there should be a discrepancy in airway bill and credit.

In order to make airway bill consistent with credit, the seller should ask the buyer to add following words to the credit, "Freight prepaid by the beneficiary on behalf of the applicant". There is another solution of avoiding discrepancy, the seller does not charge the buyer airfreight in advance, makes delivery by air on FCA and "Freight collect", airlines charges airfreight from the buyer at destination.

案例解析：

开证行所做的拒付决定是正确的。

因为信用证载明贸易术语为 FCA，对运费支付又无特别规定，与 FCA 对应的运费支付方式应该是"运费到付"，受益人提交的空运单却载明"运费预付"，显然与 FCA 相抵触，也即，跟信用证规定相抵触，属单(空运单)证(信用证)不符。

为求得单证一致，卖方应要求买方申请开立信用证时，在信用证上规定"运费由托运人代表申请人预付"。卖方也可不提前收取买方的运费，而在向航空公司办理托运时，声明"运费到付"，运费由航空公司在货到目的地时向买方收取，而卖方取得航空公出具的载明"运费到付"的空运单，提交银行收货款，避免单证不符。

Case 2　Straight B/L

案例2　记名提单

Description of the case:

A Chinese exporter contracts with a foreign importer agreeing upon shipment by sea, payment by D/P at sight against straight B/L. The Chinese prepares goods, makes delivery, and hands full set of original of straight B/L together with other necessary documents to bank for sight D/P collection. Although collecting bank urges over and again, the buyer does not pay in exchange for documents, the seller gets to know later on, the buyer has already taken delivery of the goods at destination by surrender of a copy of B/L. The seller withdraws relevant documents immediately from bank and lodges claim against shipping company for compensation, but it is rejected by shipping company on the grounds that the B/L is a straight bill of lading, in accordance with local practice, the consignee may pick up the goods without the original B/L, the Chinese exporter loses both the goods and payment.

案例描述：

中国出口商与某外国进口商成交一笔货物。双方约定，运输方式为海运，卖方凭记名提单向买方 sight D/P 托收货款。货物备妥，卖方装船取得记名提单，通过银行向买方托收货款，可是代收行多次催促后，买方仍不付款赎单，卖方随后得知货物已被买方在目的港凭提单副本提取，卖方随即要求银行退单，并凭借提单正本向船公司交涉要求赔偿，遭船公司拒绝，理由为，该提单为记名提单，按当地惯例收货人可不凭正本提单提货，中国出口商款货两空。

Analysis of the case:

The reason why the shipping company refuses to compensate may not be terable.

According to "United Nations Convention on the Carriage of Goods by Sea 1978" (Hamburger Rules), bill of lading means a document which evidence a contract of carriage by sea and the taking over or loading of the goods by the carrier and by which the carrier undertakes to deliver the goods against surrender of the documents. A provision in the document that the goods are to be delivered to the order of a named person or to order or to bearer, constitutes such an undertaking. We can see that bill of lading fulfills at least 3 important functions:1. It serves as a receipt for goods signed by the shipping company and given to the shipper. 2.It is also the evidence of a contract of carriage between the shipping company and the shipper.3. It conveys a document of title because the legal owner of the bill of lading is the owner of the goods it covers. According to whether the bill of lading is transferable, it is divided into 3 kinds straight B/L, order B/L and blank B/L, a straight B/L is made out so that only the named consignee at the destination is entitled to take delivery of the goods under the bill, the consignee is designated by the shipper, the shipping company has to hand over the cargo to the named consignee not to any 3rd party in possession of the bill, this kind of B/L is not transferable by endorsement, of course, straight B/L has above mentioned 3 functions, especially the function of document of title. According to Hamburg Rules and international cargo transport practice, shipping company undertakes to deliver the goods against surrender of the original of bill of lading, If this straight B/L is issued according to Hamburg Rules, the shipper may argues with shipping company and lodges a claim for compensation.

Moreover, Chinese exporter may consider a change of payment mode from collection (commercial credit) to L/C(bank's credit)to reduce risk of payment, especially when the buyer's credit status is not pretty good or Chinese exporter does not know pretty much buyer's credit status, this change is much more meaningful.

案例解析：

船公司拒绝赔偿的理由未必站得住脚。

根据1978年《联合国海上货物运输公约》(汉堡规则)，海运提单是指一种用以证明海上运输合同和货物由承运人接管或装船，以及承运人据以保证交付货物的单证，单证中关于货物应交付指定收货人或按指示交付，或交付提单持有人的规定，即构成了这一保证。由此可见，海运提单具备三个功能，第一是船公司与托运人之间的货物运输合同的证明，第二是运输公司出具给托运人的货物收据，第三是货物所有权的证明，提单的法定拥有者，即货物的拥有者。按照提单是否可转让，提单可分为三种：记名提单、指示提单和不记名提单。记名提单是指在提单的收货人栏内具体填明了收货人的名称，该收货人是由托运人指定，只能由该收货人提货，不能由第三方拥有该提单，这种提单不能背书转让给第三方，当然，记名提单照样具备作为海运提单的上述三种的功能，尤其是作为货物所有权证明的功能，根据汉堡规则及国际货物运输惯例，交付正本海运提单方可从船公司处提取货物，如该记名海运提单是根据汉堡规则签发，托运人可依据规则和惯例向船公司据理力争要求赔偿。

另外，中国出口商还可考虑改变货款的支付方式，由托收改为信用证，将商业信用转变为银行信用，降低收款风险，尤其是在外国进口商资信状况不佳或者中国出口商对外国进口商的资信状况不十分了解的情况下，这种改变，更有意义。

Section 7 Cases on Insurance

第7节 货物运输保险案例

Case 1 Insurance on CFR basis
案例1 CFR条件下的保险

Description of the case:

A deal of international business is concluded on CFR basis. The exporter loads the cargo on board and sents shipping advice by cable to importer without delay, reminding importer to effect insurance for the cargo, Import gets shipping advice on the weekend, insurance company does not work, on the first working day after the weekend, importer covers the cargo against risk with the insurance company and finishes all of insurance formalities. In the morning of the second working day, importer receives a cable from exporter and agent of shipping company telling the cargo was damaged because of fire of vessel on the weekend. Importer immediately files claim with the cable against insurance company. Could insurance company decline the claim by arguing that the loss of the cargo happens before insurance applying?

案例描述：

有一笔CFR条件出口交易，出口商装船后及时以电报向进口商发出装船通知并提请保险，进口商收到装船电报的时间恰逢周末，保险公司不上班，周末刚过，第1个工作日进口商向保险公司投保，当天办妥保险手续，第2天早上又收到出口商以及船公司代理的电报，告知货轮周末发生了火灾，货物被焚毁，进口商马上持电报向保险公司索赔，保险公司可否以被保货物损失发生在投保之前为由拒绝理赔？

Analysis of the case:

According to ICC INCOTERMS, under CFR The seller should send the buyer shipping advice without delay, otherwise, the seller should be responsible for the failure of insurance on the other side, In this case, the seller sents out shipping advice by cable without delay and the buyer covers the cargo promptly, at the time of applying for insurance with insurance company, the buyer does not know the damage to the cargo by fire of vessel, and the insurance company has accepted to cover, Insurance contract is concluded, when the loss of the cargo happens, the insurance company should settle the claim to compensate the insured, this is the basic principle of international cargo transport insurance" If the applicant is really ignorant, insurance contract keeps valid", anyway the insured should prove for his ignorance.

案例解析：

根据国际商会《国际贸易术语解释通则》规定在 CFR 条件下，卖方应无迟延地向买方发出装船通知，否则造成买方漏保，一切责任应由卖方负责，本案例中卖方及时发出了装船电报，买方也及时投保，买方在投保时并不知道货物已被焚毁，保险公司又已承保，即构成了保险合约。因发生保险责任内的损失，保险公司应当承担义务接受索赔，这就是国际保险业务中的"在投保人确实不知情的情况下，保险人承保的保险合约仍然有效"的原则精神，但是被保险人必须对"不知情"举证。

Case 2 Which party files claim against the insurer on CIF basis?

案例 2 CIF 条件下，谁向保险公司索赔？

Description of the case:

A deal is concluded on CIF basis, the seller is responsible for effecting insurance for the cargo and pays insurance premium, when the loss of the goods in insurance coverage occurs, should just only the seller file claim against insurance company on the strength of insurance policy or certificate together with other necessary files?

案例描述：

按照 CIF 条件成交，由卖方负责办理保险并支付保险费，因此当被保险货物发生保险责任范围内的损失时，是否应仅由卖方持保险单或保险凭证随同有关证明文件向保险公司索赔？

Analysis of the case:

The applicant for insurance, the insurer and the insured are involved in international cargo transport insurance. The applicant submits application for insurance, the insurer is the insurance company accepting insurance application and charges insurance premium and issues insurance policy or certificate, in case loss of the goods in the insurance coverage occurs, the insurer should assume the responsibility for the compensation. The insured is the beneficiary of insurance contract, having the right of filing claim against the insurer for covered goods. Generally the applicant is the insured. Insurance policy or insurance certificate stands for insurance interest, it is transferable through endorsement, actually the insurance interest is the right of filing claim for the covered loss.

In this case, under CIF the seller contracts for insurance with insurance company, the seller is the applicant for insurance. Referring to L/C, the insured could be the seller, the buyer or other party, If the seller is nominated by L/C as the insured, he could transfer through endorsement the insurance interest to the buyer or other party(bank as an example). After the buyer pays opening bank in exchange for documents including insurance policy or certificate, he becomes the holder of insurance policy or certificate and it is the beneficiary, in case loss of the goods in the insurance coverage occurs, the buyer has the right of filing claim against insurance company on the strength of insurance policy or certificate together with other necessary files.

案例解析：

国际贸易货物运输保险的当事人有投保人、保险人、被保险人。投保人向保险公司提交保险申请；保险人指接受保险的保险公司，保险人接受投保人的投保后，向投保人收取保险费，签发保险单或保险凭证，一旦保险标的物遇难受损，如属承保责任范围就应负责赔偿损失；被保险人指保险合同的受益人，当保险标的物遭受损失而属保险人承保责任范围，被保险人有权向保险人索赔并接受赔偿，一般情况下投保人是被保险人。保险单或保险凭证代表保险权益是一种可以转让的单证，即保险单上的被保险人通过背书可以将其保险权益转让给其他人，实际上这种保险权益就是指受损的被保险货物的索赔权。

本例，CIF 条件下，由卖方投保，保险单上的被保险人依据信用证的规定，可以是卖方、买方或者其他方，如果被保险人是卖方，则卖方可通过背书将保险权益转让给买方或者其他方(比如银行)，买方向开证行赎单之后，即为保险单或保险凭证的持有人和受益人，货物抵达目的港，买方如果发现有由于责任范围内的货物受损，买方即可持保险单或保险凭证及有关证明文件向保险公司索赔。

Section 8　Cases on Payment

第8节　支付案例

Case 1　Collection under L/C?

案例1　证下托收？

Description of the case:

Chinese exporter concludes a deal of canned beef with Dutch importer on CIF Rotterdam, quantity 10,000 cartons, amount USD400,000.00. Payment stipulated in the contract: 50% of the total amount is paid by sight L/C, the remaining 50% is paid by D/A 30 days after sight.

Dutch importer opens an L/C covering USD200,000.00, L/C stipulates credit available not more than the total amount prescribed herein against beneficiary's sight draft and full set of shipping documents of 10,000 cartons of canned beef, and states that we are informed that the remaining 50% of the invoice value will be paid on collection basis.

According to L/C, Chinese exporter makes delivery, presents a sight draft and full set of shipping documents for negotiation, at the same time draws a clean usance draft to collect payment for the remainning USD 200,000.00. Chinese exporter gets payment of the first USD 200,000.00 duly, however 1 month later, he is informed by bank that Dutch importer has gone bankruptcy, the clean usance draft is returned, the remaining USD 200,000.00 is unpaid. It is collected according to statement in L/C, it should be "collection under L/C", should opening bank pay for it?

案例描述：

我与一荷兰商人按 CIF 鹿特丹条件成交牛肉罐头 1 万箱，总金额为 400,000 美元。合同规定总金额的 50%，以即期信用证方式付款，其余 50%以 D/A 见票后 30 天付款。对方按合同规定开来金额为 200,000 美元的信用证，规定："凭受益人开立的不超过本信用证规定金额的即期汇票与 1 万箱牛肉罐头的全套单据付款"，并在证内声明："We are informed that the remaining 50% of the invoice value will be paid on collection basis"。

我凭信用证装运出口交单，如期结回信用证项下的 200,000 美元，合同余额也按照来证声明，制作汇票通过银行光票托收，然而一个月后，接到银行通知，进口商倒闭，光票退回。由于这项托收是根据信用证声明办理，是为"证下托收"，开证行是否应保证付款？

Analysis of the case:

Opening bank shouldn't be responsible for undertaking of guarantee of payment for the amount of collection.

L/C and collection are different modes of payment, althrough in this case both of them are handled by bank, the former is bank credit, If only the documents presented by beneficiary are strictly in conformity with the stipulation in L/C and opening bank accepts, opening bank should pay whatever applicant does, the later belongs to commercial credit, neither remitting bank nor collecting bank is irresponsible for guarantee of payment to be made by payer. According to condition of documents transfer, collection falls into 2 kinds, D/P and D/A, under D/P documents are transferred from exporter to importer on the condition that payment is effected, D/A calls for delivery of documents against acceptance made by importer. In terms of safety of getting payment, collection is riskier than L/C, D/A is riskier than D/P.

In international business, use of 2 modes of payment in 1 deal is common, key point is safety of payment. In this case, L/C and collection are used at the same time, amount of L/C is just 1/2 of total amount of the contract, only 1/2 of total amount of the contract is guaranteed by opening bank, while full set of shipping documents for total quantity of the contract should be under L/C to be presented, obviously it is unfavorable for exporter, although L/C states the remaining 1/2 of total amount of the contract to be collected, it seems in accordance with the contract on surface, it's not guarantee of the opening bank for payment, exporter himself has to undertake the risk of unpayment by importer, so called collection under L/C is unrealistic misunderstanding.

In connection with this case, when L/C and collection are used in 1 deal, exporter should notice:

(1) D/P is prior to D/A to be considered to be used for amount of collection.

(2) Full set of shipping documents would be better be attatched to draft under collection, amount of credit is available against clean draft.

(3) Both contract and L/C stipulate shipping documents transfer after payment for total value of invoice.

案例解析：

开证行不承担托收部分的保证付款责任。

信用证与托收是两种不同的支付方式，本案例虽然都是通过银行办理，但前者属于银行信用，只要受益人提供的单据符合信用证规定并被开证行接受，无论开证申请人付款与否，开证行保证付款，而后者属商业信用，无论托收行或代收行均不保证付款人必须付款的责任。托收按交单条件的不同分为 D/P 与 D/A，前者以付款人付款为交单条件，后者以付款人承兑为交单条件。就出口商安全收汇而言，托收比信用证风险大，D/A 比 D/P 风险大。

国际贸易中，一笔交易使用两种不同的支付方式并不少见，如何保证安全收汇是问题的关键。本案例采用信用证与托收相结合的做法，信用证金额只有合同总金额的 50%，而须提交总金额 100% 的全套单据，出口商必须按合同交足 1 万箱罐头，而货款只有 50% 的银行信用保证，显然对出口商不利，尽管信用证对其余 50% 货款作了将按托收付款的声明，似乎与合同规定相符，但并非开证行的一项付款保证，对托收部分而言，出口商仍得承担付款人不付款的风险，所谓"证下托收"属不切实际的错误理解。

结合本案例，在具体业务实践中，如果采用信用证与托收相结合的支付方式，出口商应注意：

(1) 托收部分优先考虑采用 D/P，而非 D/A；

(2) 全套单据最好随附于托收项下的汇票，信用证部分凭光票付款；

(3) 合同和信用证内，订明"发票金额全部付清后方可交单"。

Case 2　Does confirming bank have recourse to beneficiary?

案例 2　保兑银行有追索权吗？

Description of the case:

Notifying bank is requested by opening bank to confirm a credit, but it is not prepared to do so, accordingly, it informs opening bank without any delay, and at the same time delivers beneficiary the credit without confirmation. This credit is freely negotiation credit, after beneficiary performs contract and does as requested in credit, beneficiary presents documents for negotiation with this notifying bank, this bank pays in exchange for documents, then asks opening bank for reimbursement, but opening bank refuses reimbursement, could this notifying bank recourse beneficiary? If this notifying bank accepts to confirm the credit, does it have recourse to the beneficiary?

案例描述：

某信用证的开证行要求通知行保兑付款，通知行不准备照办，并毫不迟延地通知开证行，同时向受益人未加具保兑通知此信用证。该信用证为自由议付信用证，受益人履行合同信用证各项规定后，向该通知行交单议付，该行付款买单，然后向开证行要求偿付，遭开证行拒付，该行可否向受益人追索？如果该通知行接受保兑，又可否向受益人追索？

Analysis of the case:

If this notifying bank does not confirm the credit, it has recourse to beneficiary as a common negotiating bank.

If this notifying bank confirms the credit, it has no recourse to beneficiary as a conforming bank.

Confirmation means a definite undertaking of the confirming bank in addition to that of the opening bank to honor or negotiate a complying presentation. Confirmation is usually made by adding confirmation words to credit by confirming bank, for examples, "This credit is confirmed by us", " We hereby add confirmation to this credit and we undertake that documents presented for payment in conformity with the terms of this credit will be duly paid on presentation", and so on. The security provided by an irrevocable credit is further enhanced if a bank is requested by opening bank to add it's confirmation, thus making it a confirmed credit, the exporter then has a confirmed irrevocable credit and he is then double guaranteed against payment by both confirming and opening banks.

Confirming bank means the bank that adds its confirmation to a credit upon the opening bank's authorization or request. It is usually notifying bank. According to UCP600, if the credit is available by negotiation with the confirming bank, negotiate without recourse.

Negotiation means the purchase by the nominated bank of draft and/or documents under a complying presentation by advancing or agreeing to advance funds to the beneficiary on or before the banking day on which reimbursement is due to the nominated bank. This is to say, under a complying presentation negotiating bank pays for openning bank to beneficiary in exchang for beneficiary's documents, and claims on openning bank to be repaid later.

Negotiating bank means the bank which undertakes negotiation. If reimbursement is refused by reimbursing bank or opening bank, negotiating bank has the right of recourse to the beneficiary.

In this case, notifying bank does not accept the request from opening bank for adding confirmation to credit and informs opening bank without delay according to UCP600, at the same time delivers credit to beneficiary, when beneficiary presents documents for negotiation with this bank, it plays the role of a common negotiating bank other than a confirming bank, if reimbursement is refused by opening bank, no doubt this bank has the right to recourse beneficiary, on the contrary, if this bank accepts the request from opening bank to add confirmation to credit, when beneficiary presents document for negotiation, it is a confirming bank, if reimbursement is refused by opening bank, this bank has no recourse to beneficiary.

案例解析：

如果该通知行没有保兑信用证，作为普通议付行，它对受益人有追索权。

如果该通知行保兑了信用证，作为保兑行，它对受益人没有追索权。

保兑，指保兑行在开证行承诺之外做出的承付或议付相符交单的确定承诺。保兑的手续一般是由保兑行在信用证上加列保兑文句，例如："此证已经由我行保兑"，"兹对此证加保兑并保证于提示符合此证条款的单据时履行付款"等。一份不可撤销信用证，在加具保兑之后，成为保兑的不可撤销的信用证，既有开证行的付款保证，又有保兑行的兑付保证，双重保证对出口商最为有利。

保兑行，指根据开证行的授权或要求对信用证加具保兑的银行，保兑行通常是通知行。根据UCP600，如果信用证规定由保兑行议付，保兑行无追索权地议付。

议付，指指定银行在相符交单下，在其应获偿付的银行工作日当天或之前向受益人预付或者同意预付款项，从而购买汇票及/或单据的行为。即，在相符交单下，议付行为开证行先垫付给受益人取得受益人的单据，然后向开证行索偿。

议付行，指承担议付的银行。如果议付行向偿付行或开证行索偿被拒，议付行有权向受益人追索已预付的款项。

本案例中，通知行没有应开证行的要求加保兑，且按UCP600规定的及时告知了开证行，并对受益人通知信用证，在受益人向该行交单时，该行是普通的议付行而非保兑行，该行索偿如遭开证行拒付，当然可以向受益人追索。相反，如果通知行应开证行要求加具了保兑，则受益人向该行交单时，该行的身份是保兑行，如遭开证行拒付，不可再向受益人追索。

Section 9　Cases on Disputes Settlement

第9节　纠纷解决案例

Case 1　What are extraordinary circumstances?

案例1　什么是异常情况？

Description of the case:

The buyer receives a letter as follows, what could he do?

"We have received your letter of 15th July, informing us that the sewing machines we shipped to you arrived damaged on account of imperfectness of our packing.

Upon receipt of your letter, we have given this matter our immediate attention. We have studied your surveyor's report very carefully. We are convinced that the present damage was due to extraordinary circumstances under which they are transported to you, we are therefore not responsible for the damage, but as we do not think that it would be fair to have you bear the loss alone, we suggest that the loss be divided between both of us, to which we hope you will agree."

案例描述：

买方收到卖方的下述信函，他该怎么办？

"我们收到了贵方7月15号的信函，告知，我们所装运给贵方的缝纫机，货到了，但因包装不良受损。已收到该信函，我们立即给予关注，并你细研究贵方的调查报告。我们确信，货损损是由于运输途中异常情况所致，因此不该由我方负责。但我方认为，由贵方单独承担损失，并不公平，因而我方建议由贵我双方来分担，望贵方同意。"

Analysis of the case:

"Extraordinary Circumstances" mentioned in above letter, in a sense, refers to force majeure, the key to this problem lies in that so called "Extraordinary Circumstances" is stipulated exactly in the contract or not, if so, the writer of above letter is not responsible for the loss because of the contracted clause of force majeure, otherwise, it may caused disputes between two parties.

There are different interpretations to the term of force majeure among countries in the world, but in most cases it refers to those accidents caused by natural phenomenon or social factors such as earthquake, flood, tempest, war and governmental prohibition of import and export of certain commodities in order to clarify what the term of force majeure covers under a particular contract, different ways have been adopted. In order to clarify what the term of force majeure covers under a particular contract, different ways have been adopted.

(1) Stipulate the Force Majeure Clause in a General Way

If the shipment of the contract goods is prevented or delayed in whole or in part due to force majeure, the seller shall not be liable for non-shipment or late shipment of the goods of this contract. However, the seller shall notify the buyer by cable or telex and furnish the latter within 15 days by registered airmail with a certificate issued by the China Council for the promotion of International trade attesting such event or events.

(2) Stipulate the Force Majeure Clause in a Way to List the Contents

If the shipment of the contract goods is prevented or delayed in whole or in part by reason of war, earthquake, flood, fire, storm, heavy snow, the seller shall not be liable for non-shipment or late shipment of the goods of this contract……

(3) Stipulate the Force Majeure Clause in a Way to Colligation

The seller shall not be held responsible for failure or delay to perform all or any part of this contract due to war, earthquake, flood, fire, storm, heavy snow or other cause of force majeure……

Among these three ways, the last one is the best, because it is of some flexibility. If the contingency not stipulated in the contract occur, the way will be useful and helpful for the parties in question to solve the problems. It is better use the way in the contract.

案例解析：

上述信函中提到的"异常情况"，某种意义上指不可抗力，解决此问题的关键在于所谓"异常情况"是否准确地在合同中规定，如果确有规定，上述信件的发信人可以因合同的不可抗力条款而免责，否则可能引发双方之间的争议。

不同国家对于不可抗力这个术语的解释不同，虽然在大多数情况下它指自然现象或者社会因素所引起的事故，如地震、洪水、暴风、战争以及政府禁令等，但是为了明确界定不可抗力术语在某一特定合同中的范围，通常采取以下几种方式，订立合同的不可抗力条款。

(1) 概括式

若因不可抗力，致使卖方不能全部或部分装运或延迟装运合同货物，卖方对于这种不能装运或延迟装运本合同货物不负有责任，但卖方须用电报或电传通知买方，并须在15日内以航空挂号信件向买方提交由中国国际贸易促进委员会出具的证明此类事故的证明书。

(2) 列举式

若因战争、地震、洪水、火灾、台风、雪灾原因，致使卖方不能全部或部分装运或延迟装运合同货物，卖方对于这种不能装运或延迟装运本合同货物不负有责任……

(3) 综合式

若因战争、地震、洪水、火灾、台风、雪灾或者其他不可抗力的原因，致使卖方不能全部或部分装运或延迟装运合同货物，卖方可不负责任……

在这三种方法中，最后一种方法既明确又有一定的灵活性，若发生合同未列明的意外事故，有利于双方当事人协商处理，合同中的不可抗力条款最好采用这种方法规定。

Case 2　Translations of Agent and General Agent

案例2　一般代理和总代理怎么翻译

Description of the case:

A foreign business person signs an agency agreement with a Chinese foreign trade company, while General Agent Agreement is printed clearly on the English vertion of the agreement. Later on the foreign business person makes many advertisements for himself stating that we are general agent of…

Should the Chinese company contact foreign business person to correct the error with reasonable cause?

案例描述：

某外商与一中国公司签订一般代理协议，在英文文本上载明 general agent agreement，事后该外商在外大登广告称 We are the general agent of…

对此中国公司是否应该立即与对方联系，说明理由予以纠正。

Analysis of the case:

The Chinese company should immediately contact the foreign business person, and correct wrong translation about agent.

Agency is one of modes of international business, the Chinese may sign an agreement with the foreign customer, appointing foreign customer to act as his agent to sell stipulated commodities in a territory and a period of time on behalf of and in the name of him, they are the principal (owner of the goods) and agent, the agent acts within the scope of authorization, pushes the sale of the goods and enjoys commission. According to the extent of authorization, agent could be classified into general agent, sole/exclusive agent, agent/commission agent, and so on, general agent is fully authorized, sole/exclusive agent enjoys the exclusive right of agency in authorized area and period of time, agent/commission agent has just only the smallest right of agency, in prescribed area and period of time there are probably more than one agent/commission agent.

In this case, an Agency Agreement is actually signed by both parties, but it is incorrectly translated and printed as General Agent Agreement in the English version, foreign business person makes use of the error to advertise for himself. As above mentioned authorrization to general agent, the foreign business person may be fully authorized to represent the Chinese company, if it is not stopped and corrected, Chinese company has to bear the whole of consequence brought by the foreign business person.

案例解析：

中国公司应该立即联系外商，纠正代理协议英文文本中关于一般代理的错误翻译。

代理是国际贸易中的一种贸易方式。中国外贸公司可跟国外客户通过协议的形式，给予该客户在特定的地区和一定的时间内，享有代销指定商品的权利，双方为委托代销的关系，中国公司是委托人、货主，国外客户是代理商，在授权范围内有积极推销商品的义务，并享有收取佣金的权利。根据代理商代表货主的权限，代理可分为：总代理(general agent)、独家代理(sole agent/ exclusive agent)、一般代理/佣金代理(agent/commission agent)等。总代理可全权代表委托人，独家代理在获授权的地域和时间内具有排他性的代理权，一般代理权限最小，在同一代理地区、时间范内内，可同时有几个一般代理。

本案例中中国外贸公司与外商签订的是一般代理协议，英文应该是 Agency Agreement，而我方翻译为 General Agent Agreement，明显有错误，正是由于这一漏洞，外商趁机在外大打广告：We are the general agent of… 如按上述总代理的权限，该外商在外有全权代表中国公司的资格，如不及时制止、纠正，将来该外商在外造成的一切后果将由中国公司承担责任。

参 考 文 献

[1] 黄锡光，吴宝康. 国际贸易实务(第三版 英文)[M]. 上海：复旦大学出版社，2018.
[2] 卢立伟，王芬. 国际贸易实务(第二版 英文)[M]. 北京：清华大学出版社，2018.
[3] 李为，叶允清，季祖强. 国际贸易实务(双语)[M]. 北京：清华大学出版社，2018.
[4] 傅龙海，从晓明. 国际贸易实务双语教程[M]. 3 版. 北京：对外经济贸易大学出版社，2018.
[5] 易露露，陈新华，尤彧聪. 国际贸易实务双语教程[M]. 4 版. 北京：清华大学出版社，2016.
[6] 吴百福，徐小薇，聂清. 进出口贸易实务教程[M]. 7 版. 上海：格致出版社，上海人民出版社 2015.
[7] 尤宏兵. 国际贸易实务[M]. 北京：人民邮电出版社，2016.
[8] 联合国国际贸易法委员会. 联合国国际货物销售合同公约. (United Nations Convention on Contracts for the International Sale of Goods)(1980)
[9] 马俊，郑汉金. 实用外贸英语[M]. 北京：清华大学出版社，2015.
[10] 李振琦. 进出口业务 100 例[M]. 北京：对外贸易教育出版社，1988.
[11] 易露露，方玲玲，尤彧聪. 国际贸易实务案例教程[M]. 2 版. 北京：清华大学出版社，2016.
[12] 博斌，袁晓娜. 国际贸易实务与案例[M]. 北京：清华大学出版社，2007.
[13] 余庆瑜. 国际贸易实务原理与案例[M]. 北京：中国人民大学出版社，2014.
[14] 邓旭，陈晶莹. 国际贸易术语解释与国际货物买卖合同[M]. 北京：经济管理出版社，2012.
[15] 杨海芳，李哲. 国际货物运输与保险[M]. 3 版. 北京：北京交通大学出版社，2018.